THE MOVIES:
AN AMERICAN IDIOM

THE MOVIES:
AN AMERICAN IDIOM

Readings in the Social History
of the American Motion Picture

Edited by
Arthur F. McClure

Rutherford • Madison • Teaneck
FAIRLEIGH DICKINSON UNIVERSITY PRESS

Library of Congress Catalogue Card Number: 72-146164

Associated University Presses, Inc.
Cranbury, New Jersey 08512

ISBN: 0-8386-7824-2
Printed in the United States of America

To
Dad, H. L., Auntie, and Pete—
For their loving contributions.

Contents

Part III. Whither, Hollywood?

Preface

This volume is an attempt to describe the historical relationship between the American motion picture and the environment in which it operates as well as the functions and problems of the movies as a mass medium with a vast potential for human betterment. The following readings dealing with the American movies are drawn from journalists, critics, historians, sociologists, humorists, novelists, and other writers who simply admire the movies' contribution to American life.

The selections appear in roughly chronological order, ranging from Foster Rhea Dulles's overview of the American film to Arthur Knight's discussion of Hollywood problems and aspirations today. Several of the concluding selections offer assessments of the present state of the American motion picture. The publication of monographs and articles concerning the movies has increased steadily in number in recent years as their serious historical study has become more extensive. In varying ways, each essay represents an exploration into American social history. It cannot be claimed, of course, that the only significant articles in this area have been reprinted. The editor is confident, however, that the articles decided upon will prove to be of considerable value to students of American cultural history.

It is the hope of the editor that these essays reflect his boundless enthusiasm for the history of the American film. The brief title, *The Movies: An American Idiom,* is intended to suggest that movies are the most distinctive and the most clearly indigenous portion of our culture and heritage in the twentieth century.

If this book has any merit, it has to be the honesty, the clarity, and the conviction of the individual essays. Thanks must go to many people. My friend and colleague, William E. Foley, provided constructive assistance and wise counsel. My thanks also go to Martha W. T. Foley, who wields a savage blue pencil, for her suggestions about the manuscript. As always, my excellent secretaries, Judy B. Bond, Debbie Hibdon and Mary Helen McCoy, were patient and meticulous in their efforts. Betty Van Blair of the Central Missouri State College Library was extremely helpful. My wife and constant moviegoing companion, Judy, provided me with her inspirational qualities, for which I am grateful.

It is the final hope that this volume will afford the reader not only a broad outlook concerning the history of American motion pictures, but a real sense of the vitality of its study today.

ARTHUR F. McCLURE

Warrensburg, Missouri

Introduction

The so-called "moving spotlight" theory of film history holds that different countries become prominent in film production at different times. Between 1895 and 1914 most countries proceeded at approximately the same rate of technical and creative discovery. After that, the spotlight shifted more rapidly, as many countries developed significant films simultaneously. Such is true today, but most film historians agree that the motion picture has had its most profound impact on American society. Since its beginnings in international birth and childhood, Americans have displayed the most intense interest in movies. Movies have thus become native to Americans because they are closely related to American life in the twentieth century, and they are idiomatic because they are distinctly a part of our way of communicating with each other.

Another widely held theory about movies is that Hollywood has been stunted or maybe even destroyed by television and the influx of outstanding, foreign films. Some recent observers have implied that movies coming from Europe are universally good, while those produced in America are superficial and lacking in substance. In the 1960s, however, *Time* probably struck closer to the truth when the magazine observed that the "movies have suddenly and powerfully emerged as an international art, indeed as perhaps the central and characteristic art of the age. . . ." America continues as an important influence in movie making. Such American films as *To Kill a Mockingbird, A Patch of Blue, Bonnie and Clyde, The Graduate, The Heart Is a Lonely Hunter,* and *Goodbye, Columbus* demonstrate the high quality of American movies.

Social historians have long been aware of the important distinction between work and leisure, and have emphasized the increasing significance of leisure in American life. In particular, historians have been interested in cultural pursuits during leisure time. Since movies are both an art and a mass medium, serious scholars have reacted ambiguously to them. Because movies are a relatively young art, originating as light entertainment, the realization that they represent one of the principal cultural forces in American society is sometimes overlooked. The academic world only recently has recognized their intellectual respectability. Evidence of Hollywood's impact on American culture and history becomes apparent when the Organization of American Historians conducts sessions on "The Popular Film and the Mass Mind." In 1968 the American Historical Association announced the launching of the Feature Films Project. American producers made virtually all of their feature films available for study to present historical problems and issues of interpretation. In recent years the commercial film industry in Hollywood, long attacked as The Establishment, has begun a number of programs aimed at not only preserving a salable product but in addition a portion of America's history. The American Film Institute is one example. Cooperation between the film industry and the federal government organized and funded it.

Donald R. McCoy, a noted American historian, has written of what he calls "the underdeveloped sources" of American history which are the "omnipresent molders of life." He includes motion pictures among them and maintains that American historians need to know more of their influence.

There are ballets, operas, and plays for which more than 100,000 Americans are willing to buy tickets of admission. But a run-of-the-mill motion picture usually plays to at least one million people, and most of the large productions aim at and get a minimum international audience of five million. With revivals and television showings, the figures can become astronomical. Who knows how many tens of millions of people over the years have seen *All Quiet on the Western Front, Gunga Din,* and H. B. Warner's portrayal of *The King of Kings?*

However, the startling swiftness of the movies' development has added to the problem of looking at the importance of movies as a part of our history. Andrew Sarris, a respected film historian, once suggested that only "in film history is half a century treated as a millenium." On the other hand, the motion picture historian has an advantage. Because movie history is brief, barely over sixty years, and because most films have been preserved, we can study the works in their original form.

Every decade has seen developments in the American motion picture and their influence upon audiences that should be of interest to social historians. In the 1920s, for example, movies stimulated the senses of the American moviegoer. The public tolerated almost any subject shown on the screen and welcomed fads and sensations with the ensuing escape into a dream world. American silent films reflect this era of romantic make-believe, and though the gestures and situations may seem exaggerated and ludicrous today, these films dazzled audiences in their day. Unquestionably by 1929, the motion picture had achieved an impact on American life of greater power and influence than any other medium or agency in our culture. Since Al Jolson first spoke and sang to his mother in 1927 in *The Jazz Singer,* the motion picture has developed as an entertainment, as a social force, and as an art form—all the elements of social history.

In a variety of ways the American people have shown a commitment to films over the years. During the lacrymal days of social isolation in the 1930s the movies proved a source of comfort for one's fantasies. The historian Arthur Schlesinger Jr. argues that the greatest impact of the motion picture on American life was in the Depression years when "the movies were near the operative center of the nation's consciousness. They played an indispensable role in sustaining and stimulating the national imagination. . . ." In recent years they have become documents of cultural history and vehicles for sociological comments for many who feel the alienation of modern society. Furthermore, the continuing interest in the medium remains firm in the American mentality.

In the 1930s many Americans preferred movies to books. The greatest social novel of the Depression, *The Grapes of Wrath,* also became one of its greatest motion pictures. The movie carried with it a visual impact that at once deepened the viewer's comprehension of the world of the 1930s and provided a better understanding among men.

For Americans, movies have helped to lend insight into their own interpersonal problems from moral, social, psychological and historical viewpoints. People are sometimes unaware of what is happening around them. Movies are one of the chief means of depicting life situations and revealing human relationships for Americans. Movies allow the audience to see life as it unravels someplace else, and to someone else. Although the motion picture was not entirely an American phenomenon, it was this country that gave it its impetus and established it as not only entertainment but as an art form with a nearly universal appeal.

In recent years numerous changes have occurred in the once near monopolistic position of the American film. Some observers see these changes as the signs of decline. Predictions have been made that the American film, as represented by Hollywood, is dead. It is certainly a different Hollywood, but hardly dead. American films continue to display a stunning degree of vitality. They are still artistic and are a major source of social commentary on the issues of the day. If one asks the question of whether or not the American film makes valid statements about the human situation, then certainly the affirmative answer assures its existence in the future. Much is written about the decline of movie attendance in America. One report shows that the decline starts after the age of 29, but that sharp drop is more than offset by increased attendance on the part of younger people to a point where it is estimated that one-half of the movie-going audience is under 25 years of age. What this means then is that young people today are still very much involved in watching movies, just as were the young in the 1930s and 1940s, although for entirely different reasons. Today's young people find movies fascinating as did previous generations during the Depression or World War II, but the reason is television. The generation growing up now is one which was born to the moving image on television. The showing of the great movie classics on television has created an enormous interest among the young and acquainted them with both current and past films.

The movies in America have provided a form of culture whereby people of divergent backgrounds can share the same cultural experience. Because of movies, members of different social classes can be quickly and deeply influenced in their behavior and taste. Although movies have erected artificial taboos and mistaken impressions about the realities of life, they have also increased the potential of mass entertainment by improving, enriching and expanding American culture. The American motion picture has allowed people all over the world to indulge their fantasies and enjoy themselves. Today Americans are probably the most disturbed and yet the most ingratiating people in the world. American motion pictures also reflect this interesting contrast: At times unsettled and neglectful of meaning, collectively movies have been one of the revitalizing contributions to creative art in the twentieth century. This is a laudable achievement for what is certainly an American idiom.

THE MOVIES:
AN AMERICAN IDIOM

Part 1
Admission and Ascendancy
1900-1949

The Role of Moving Pictures

Foster Rhea Dulles

The following careful, detailed analysis is the work of Foster Rhea
Dulles, Emeritus Professor of History at Ohio State University. This
essay provides an overview of the importance of the motion picture in
*the history of American popular recreation.**

The twentieth century was to be marked by changes quite as revolutionary and far-reaching in the patterns of popular recreation as in any
other phase of American life. The growth of industry and further scientific and technological advance, new trends in urban and suburban
living, the remarkable increase in leisure time for the great masses of
the people—all had their pervasive effect on the popular pursuit of
pleasure. The amusement scene of the new century soon came to bear
little resemblance to that of the 1890's, whether in the realm of fashion
or in the countryside, in metropolis or on Main Street.

Three inconspicuous events in 1895 foreshadowed what were to become the major innovations in a still unperceived future. Two young
men who had been closely following an invention of Thomas Edison
called the kinetoscope, succeeded in producing a jerky, flickering moving
picture on a small screen at a public performance at the Cotton States
Exposition in Atlanta. A pioneer race for the new horseless carriages was
held at Chicago on Thanksgiving Day, two of the six entries (gasoline-
driven) actually completing the fifty-two-mile course in a little over ten
and one-half hours. And, on the other side of the Atlantic, Guglielmo
Marconi publicly demonstrated (although the continuing skepticism of
the Italian Government sent him the next year to England) the prac-
ticality of the wireless telegraphy that was to lead first to radio broadcasting and then in time to television.[1]

---

* By permission from Foster Rhea Dulles, *A History of Recreation: America*
Learns to Play, Appleton-Century-Crofts, Division of Meredith Publishing Company, New York. © 1965.

There were to be many other developments in the field of recreation, most notably a great expansion in both spectator and participant sports, but these products of the new technology were ultimately to provide the predominant ways in which Americans sought out entertainment. An industrial age that crowded people into great cities and deprived them of so many of their traditional diversions, that was constantly increasing the leisure time of the country's great mass of workers, had finally brought into being new and compensating forms of amusement.

Moreover for all the remaining vestiges of the old puritan attitude toward play, the twentieth century was to see general acceptance of the principle that it was the natural right of the American people, whatever their social status, to use their new-found leisure for recreation as they saw fit. The movies were to become the equivalent of the popular theatre for everyone, no matter how poor; the automobile was in time to be made available for all elements in society; and radio-television would bring entertainment directly into the homes of virtually every family the length and breadth of the land. The concept of democracy coalesced with the profitable economy of mass production to make the movies, automobiles, radio and television so widely available. It was not by accident that in no other country of the world did any comparable diffusion of these new means of amusement take place among the masses of the people.

Moving pictures were the first of these inventions in point of time and also the first to reach any great number of people. They were originally displayed as a curious novelty in phonograph parlors, billiard-rooms, and penny arcades in the early 1890's. One put a nickel in the slot of one of the new-fangled kinetoscopes, looked eagerly through a peep-hole, and saw the magic of tiny figures actually moving against a dim and blurred background. It might be a man sneezing, a girl dancing, or a baby being given its bath. It was a very brief entertainment, but the wonder of moving figures brought a steady flow of nickels to the pockets of enterprising showmen.[2]

When the experiments of several other inventors (Mr. Edison soon lost interest in what he regarded as a rather childish toy) succeeded in transferring these moving pictures to a screen where a large number of people could see them at the same time, they were taken up by the variety houses. The year following the showing at the Cotton States Exposition, a first New York performance took place at Koster and Bial's Music Hall on Broadway and "living pictures" soon thereafter became one of the popular features on vaudeville programs everywhere.[3] They still had little more than their novelty to commend them. The flickering figures on the screen could hardly compete with live acrobatic dances and popular song hits. Gradually losing their appeal for patrons at the better variety shows, the movies consequently retreated again to the penny arcades. Their proprietors set up their machines in darkened rooms ("pickpockets could go through you as easy as an eel through water") and drew in masses of the city's workers, often immigrants, who could not afford any better entertainment.[4]

In 1905 an important forward step was taken in the presentation of these pictures. A few years earlier an Electric Theatre had been established in Los Angeles solely for their exhibition, but it was the Nickelodeon that John P. Harris opened in McKeesport, Pennsylvania, just a decade after the movies had first been shown, that started the real boom.[5] The nickelodeons were soon numbered in the thousands. A writer on the "Nickel Madness" in *Harper's Weekly* stated in 1907 that nearly a quarter million people—men, women, and children—were flocking daily "through the gaudy, blatant entrances."[6]

"In almost every case," reads a contemporary description of these theatres, "a long, narrow room, formerly used for more legitimate purposes, has been made over into what is popularly known as a 'nickelodeon.' At the rear a stage is raised. Across it is swung a white curtain. Before the curtain is placed a piano, which does service for an orchestra. Packed into the room as closely as they can be are chairs for the spectators, who number from one hundred to four hundred and fifty. Directly above the entrance is placed the moving picture, which flashes its lights and shadows upon the white curtain dropped in front of the stage. Many of the machines are operated by means of a tank filled with gasoline or some similarly inflammable material."[7]

The same story was being repeated not only in every city in the country but in every town and hamlet. A vast public that had never attended the theatre, even the popular "ten, twent, thirt" melodrama, found in these brief twenty-minute shows entertainment which had never before been within its reach.[8]

The moving picture inevitably had caustic critics. The nickelodeons were called silly and time-wasting, if not actually pernicious. Anthony Comstock found in the darkened theatres intimations of immorality which sent anticipatory shivers up his puritanic spine. Censorship was threatened from the day when social reformers in Atlantic City protested the "hypogastric rhythm" of a peep-show depiction of Dolorita's Passion Dance. "The authorities request us not to show the Houchi Kouchi," the exhibitioner sadly wrote the producer, "so please cancel order for new Dolorita. . . ."[9] The kinetoscope's first kiss created a sensation and it was perhaps the editor of a small Chicago magazine, *The Chap Book*, who most forthrightly expressed a widespread disapproval. "In a recent play called The Widow Jones," he wrote, "you may remember a famous kiss, which Miss May Irwin bestowed on a certain John C. Rice, and *vice versa*. Neither participant is physically attractive, and the spectacle of their prolonged pasturing on each other's lips was hard to bear. When only life size it was pronounced beastly. Magnified to Gargantuan

proportions and repeated three times over it is absolutely disgusting.
. . . Such things call for police interference."[10]

A decade later the Chicago *Tribune* attacked the nickelodeons, declaring that in a majority of cases no voice was raised to defend them
"because they cannot be defended. They are hopelessly bad."[11] On
Christmas Eve of 1908 Mayor McClellan of New York revoked five
hundred and fifty licenses because of objections by the city's pastors.
He announced that future permits would be granted only on agreement
not to operate on Sundays and not to show pictures tending "to degrade
the morals of the community."[12] More generally, however, these show-
places were treated with casual condescension, being dismissed as "a
harmless diversion of the poor" and "an innocent amusement and a
rather wholesome delirium."[13]

In the past popular amusements had generally evolved from diversions that were originally available only to the wealthy. In America
this had been true to a great extent of the theatre itself, for the audiences
in colonial days were the rich and the fashionable. It was a long time
before the popular theatre developed. The first appeal of the movies,
however, was to the masses rather than the classes. They were cheap
and popular from the very beginning. The support which in time enabled them to raise their standards came entirely from their nickel-
paying customers.

This had not happened by chance. The early promoters in the moving
picture industry were often New York garment-workers or fur-traders
who had bought up the penny arcades, and then the nickelodeons, to
merchandise films as they would try to sell any other commodity. And
their dependence on a mass market led to their continuing to place
emphasis on quantity rather than quality. They were not troubled by an
artistic conscience or concerned with culture in promoting this profitable
new business. They wanted only to please the greatest possible number
of nickel-paying customers. Combined with the democratic idea that
popular entertainment should be made available for everyone, this
brought about a development of the moving picture in the United States
which was not paralleled in any other country.

In European nations, notably France, where pioneer work in moving
pictures was actually more advanced than in the United States, the
evolution of the new amusement followed a quite different course.
Instead of appealing to a mass market, the movies essayed the role of
sophisticated entertainment. Foreign producers made far better films
in these days (which is sometimes said to be the case a half century
later), but in seeking to uphold high artistic standards they did not gain
the broad, popular market that American producers won with everyday subjects that had a more universal appeal.[14] Moving pictures became
a leading feature of American recreation because they were geared to
popular taste and because they represented the culmination of the

democratizing influences in the field of urban entertainment that had been at work for over a century.

The films shown in the nickelodeon era represented a striking advance over the flickering glimpses of dancing girls first seen in the penny arcade kinetoscopes. With the production of longer pictures in the late 1890's, incidents (man sneezing) had first been elaborated into brief scenes (employer flirting with stenographer). As the films then stretched out to perhaps a thousand feet, endless variations were developed on the chase motive. The cowboy hero began to track down the western bad man, the city sleuth to pursue bank-robbers and hold-up men. In the simplest form of the latter, the thief was chased through streets crowded with city traffic until the inevitable collision with a fat woman, who felled him with her umbrella and sat on him until the police arrived. Other pictures exploited even more blatantly the opportunities for comic relief. The subtle uses of a banana peel, of a small boy with a hose, and of a precariously balanced can of paint were developed with highly successful consequences. The custard pie was discovered.

Prize-fights and religious pictures also made their debut, two outstanding events in motion-picture progress being the filming of the Corbett-Fitzsimmons fight and the Oberammergau Passion Play. News and travel had a wide appeal. For presentations of Hale's Tours of the World, the theatre was darkened, a whistle blew to announce the start of the trip, the seats began to sway through an ingenious system of rockers and brakes, and on the screen were flashed scenes of some distant part of the world taken from the window or rear platform of a speeding train.[15]

In 1903 an entirely new departure was *The Great Train Robbery*. Here for the first time the moving picture attempted to tell a story, and the success of the experiment was so immediate that every producer turned to one-reel thrillers.[16] The old melodramas, especially those of the West, were taken over from the popular theatres. By 1908 one magazine writer reported that the magnates of the nickelodeon world were paying from $15 to $30 for a good plot—"or even more"—and that the actors performing in these pictures received "all the way from $15 to $40 a week."[17]

In most of these films the modern movie-goer would still have felt something strangely lacking. There was no romance, no sex interest. It took time to adapt the formula of boy-meets-girl to the screen, but when the motion pictures had once discovered love, they clung to it. All its various aspects were promptly developed with unflagging zeal— love as sentiment and love as biological instinct. If the latter interpretation was to await fuller exploitation in later periods, romance had won a place for itself well before the nickelodeon days were over. Among the pictures being shown in Chicago in 1907 were *Cupid's Barometer*,

A Seaside Flirtation, The Course of True Love, and *The Gaieties of Divorce.*[18]

Culture was not entirely ignored in the popularity of humor, thrills, and love. Shakespeare duly appeared on the silver screen. The patrons of one theatre were advised that, without any change in the five-cent admission charge, they could see "the superb, soul stirring, heart rendering tragedy, Romeo and Juliet . . . accompanied with an intensely tragic lecture by Dr. Lamberger."[19]

For some time there were no stars. The best known of the early screen actresses, Florence Lawrence, was known only as "The Biograph Girl."[20] Not until the closing years of the nickelodeon era did feature films and feature players emblazon their starry path across the cinematic skies. "Little Mary" films, first shown in 1909, pointed the way. They enshrined Miss Pickford as America's Sweetheart and fastened the star system upon moving pictures even more firmly than it had been fastened upon the theatre. Every audience, Keokuk or New York, was convulsed by the antics of John Bunny; held its breath in fear and trembling as Bronco Billy or Tom Mix thundered across the western plains, and became easy prey (at least its male components) to the charms of Norma Talmadge and Lillian Gish.[21] The nickelodeons had become something far more than "flimsy amusement for the mob." With ten thousand theatres playing to a nationwide audience of ten million weekly, they were doing a greater volume of business by 1910 than all the legitimate theatres, variety halls, dime museums, lecture bureaus, concert-halls, circuses and street carnivals combined.[22]

Before the outbreak of the First World War, the movies had graduated from the nickelodeon era. Improvements in the techniques of photography, transforming the flickering films of the early days to increasingly clear-cut, distinct pictures; the introduction of multireel films; the appearance of a host of new movie stars, and more comfortable, higher-priced theatres were together responsible for a new day. One of the films pointing the way was a comedy Mack Sennett produced in 1914 in which Marie Dressler had the star role—*Tillie's Punctured Romance.* With Miss Dressler played a newcomer to the movies—an odd little man with a postage stamp mustache who wore baggy pants, carried a cane, and walked with a queer waddling gait.[23] Charlie Chaplin was an immediate success. Within two years, so rapidly were the movies now forging ahead, in no small part owing to his own inimitable, universal appeal, he received a fabulous offer of $670,000 for a year's work.[24]

Incidental to a circulation war among Chicago newspapers, the year 1914 also saw an epidemic of moving-picture serials which proved to be a greater drawing-card than almost anything so far produced. A nationwide public breathlessly followed weekly installments, released both in the newspapers and on the screen, portraying the thrilling adventures of Dolly of the Dailies, Lucile Love, or the mysterious Florence Gray. The most famous of all the serials was *The Perils of Pauline,* with Pearl White:

> Poor Pauline, I pity poor Pauline
> First they tie her to a tree
> Then they send her out to sea. . . .[25]

Still more important, marking as definite an advance in moving-picture production as had *The Great Train Robbery,* was D. W. Griffith's filming of *The Birth of a Nation.* This famous picture (it was to earn in all more than $18,000,000) had harsh overtones of racism that unhappily reflected the prevailing attitudes of that day, but from a technical point of view, it proved once and for all that American movies could provide entertainment which neither the fashionable nor the sophisticated could scorn. It broke away from the limitations of the stage and utilized the improved motion-picture techniques as had no previous film. Its distant scenes, switchbacks, fade-outs, and close-ups revealed what imagination and intelligent direction could really do with this new medium. The producers were able to give a first-run showing of the picture at a legitimate theatre, with legitimate-theatre prices. Here was a far departure from nickelodeon days. While the moving picture remained primarily entertainment for the masses, it now began to reach as well a more discerning and exacting public.[26]

The growth of more luxurious and higher-priced theatres, slowly driving out the nickelodeons, both reflected and furthered this new development. It was again in 1914 that Samuel L. Rothafel, who six years earlier had been exhibiting films in the unused dance hall above the saloon where he worked as a barkeep in Forest City, Pennsylvania, opened the Strand on New York's Broadway. It was the prototype of the new-styled moving picture palaces—large, elaborate, and expensive, with pipe-organs and full scale orchestras replacing the jangling pianos of an earlier day. A decade later this famous showman opened another theatre—Roxy's—which awed even New York with its gaudy magnificence. This Cathedral of Motion Pictures could seat six thousand people in its auditorium, and its squads of uniformed ushers were often required to maintain order among another two thousand waiting in the lobbies for admission.[27] With its musical numbers and ballet-dancing, the show built about the feature moving picture almost rivaled grand opera. As other cities struggled to keep up with New York through bigger and better theatres, the movies had come of age.

The 1920's found this most popular entertainment scaling new heights with a reckless abandon which reflected the pervasive extravagance of that exciting decade. Production costs skyrocketed. A million, two million, three million, four million (*The Birth of a Nation* had cost $100,000) were spent on a single spectacle.[28] The ballyhoo about the stars, drawing their ten and twenty thousand dollars a week, would have filled even P. T. Barnum with envy. And the public loved these stars all the more because they were such expensive luxuries. A society in which money played such an important role basked in reflected glory.[29]

Hollywood had now become the great center of the movie industry. Jesse Lasky pointed the way when in 1911 he rented a barn, for $200 a week, to film *The Squaw Man* against a western background.[30] The advantages of California sunshine soon became apparent, and the rising film magnates flocked to the Coast. Here the movie world worked and played, and a host of inspired press agents described with intoxicating detail the fabulous life that centered about Hollywood's burgeoning studios. Movie magazines carried to every fan the fascinating, and sometimes lurid, details of the community's loves, marriages and divorces. The stars became the arbiters of fashion and the molders of form. Shopgirls, stenographers, and high school students were dutiful worshippers at the Hollywood shrine. When Rudolph Valentino, the passionate sheik of millions of love-lorn maidens' dreams, died in 1926, the crowd that waited to see him lying in state in a New York funeral parlor stretched for eleven blocks.[31]

There were good performers and good films in these years. Charlie Chaplin remained the screen's greatest actor bar none, and Mary Pickford was still America's sweetheart. Constance Talmadge and Lilian Gish continued to be favorites; Gloria Swanson worked havoc with her glamorous charm; Harold Lloyd won tremendous popularity with his comedy roles; the muscular Douglas Fairbanks was a certain drawing card. . . . And among the pictures were *Ben Hur, The Covered Wagon, The Thief of Bagdad, Gold Rush, Beau Geste,* and *The Three Musketeers.* But for every such film there were also scores of second-rate movies that exploited the more blatant features of the postwar letdown in manners and morals. Their titles were revealing. As reported in the sociological survey *Middletown,* the citizens of one small city could in a single week choose among four such alluring pictures as *The Daring Years, Sinners in Silk, Women Who Give,* and *The Price She Paid,* and when the programs then changed, the offerings for another week were *Rouged Lips, The Queen of Sin,* and *Name the Man—A Story of Betrayed Womanhood.*

"Brilliant men, beautiful jazz babies, champagne baths, midnight revels, petting parties in the purple dawn," advertised the producer of *Alimony,* "all ending in one terrific, smashing climax that makes you gasp." The features of *Flaming Youth* were graphically described: "neckers, petters, white kisses, red kisses, pleasure-mad daughters, sensation-craving mothers, by an author who didn't dare sign his name; the truth, bold, naked, sensational."[32] Even though continued progress was being made in turning out pictures of far higher standards, the sex dramas and ultrasophisticated comedies, with their exaggerated emphasis on the supposed fast life of high society, often appeared to dominate the scene.

There was no question that the public liked these pictures. As ever greater crowds nightly packed what had now become the country's twenty thousand theatres, people from every walk of life found in them the vicarious excitement, the thrills, and the heart interest that for a time enabled them to escape the troubles and disappointments of their own lives. The man working all day on the assembly line in an automobile factory, the tired housewife leaving the children with a neighbor for her weekly night at the pictures, did not want entertainment on any higher plane:

> Please don't uplift me when I go
> To see a moving picture show.

"The movie," an English observer wrote in the *Adelphi,* "is the art of millions of American citizens, who are picturesquely called Hicks— the mighty stream of standardized humanity that flows through Main Street. . . . The cinema is, through and through, a democratic art; the only one."[33]

So the movies in the 1920's. But even greater triumphs awaited this popular entertainment which had so marvelously evolved from the kinetoscope of only three short decades earlier. In 1928 Warner Brothers released a new film—Al Jolson in *The Jazz Singer.*[34] Science had brought together sight and sound: here was the talkie. There had been a few earlier talking pictures, but it was the great success of *The Jazz Singer* that marked the real turning point in the movies' evolution. Within a year the conquest of the silent film was complete. Sound effects were hurriedly inserted in such films as could not be entirely made over, vocal numbers were added whenever possible, and all-dialogue pictures were produced as quickly as the necessary equipment could be obtained. As theatres throughout the nation were wired for sound, the movies boomed as never before. The industry's annual receipts rose by 1929 to the tremendous total of $1 billion and weekly attendance jumped to an estimated 110,000,000—the equivalent of four-fifths of the entire population going to a show once a week throughout the entire year.[35]

The depression brought about a drastic decline in these figures as forced economies curtailed all private spending. The theatre managers had to watch dwindling audiences and declining receipts. Moreover the industry was almost overwhelmed by an immense superstructure of wildly extravagant production costs and fabulous salaries for the stars. In a frantic attempt to attract greater patronage, everything possible was done to make the movies more enticing. The practice of offering double features was inaugurated, and many houses also resorted to bank nights and money games—screeno, lucky numbers, and bingo. These novel lures eventually combined with improving economic conditions to reverse the downward trend in admissions, and before the end of the 1930's, the industry was once again back on its feet.[36]

The revolution wrought by sound had in the meantime given rise to a new galaxy of stars and introduced new types of pictures. Many of the familiar figures of the movie world continued in the talkies after their success in silent films; a few staged remarkable comebacks after a period of eclipse while they adapted themselves to an unfamiliar technique. Actors and actresses of the legitimate stage, who had often scorned the pantomime of the silent film, made their hopeful way to California in droves, and a good many remained. Singers and dancers, for whom the talkies represented an entirely new opportunity, were suddenly in great demand. In a whirl of expanding energy, Hollywood was willing to give almost anyone a chance to demonstrate what could be done in this new form of entertainment.

The diversity of the pictures was perhaps the most characteristic feature of the movies in the 1930's. In filling the democratic role that the popular theatre itself had once played, their nightly programs often showed a marked resemblance to those of the nineteenth-century playhouses. The movies not only offered straight theatre, but modern equivalents for the old equestrian melodramas, burlesque performances, variety shows. At first-run houses there might be seen in quick succession a classical play filmed with all the artistry the producers could now command, an extravagant girl-and-music show, a blood-and-thunder western melodrama, a detective thriller, a sophisticated comedy, and a slap-stick farce. A single performance, again like the theatre a century earlier, invariably included one of these feature films as a major attraction; a specialty act which might be dancing or singing; a news reel (an innovation for which the popular theatre had had no parallel), and a comedy short which took the place of the nineteenth-century afterpiece.

The feature films derived from the plays of the legitimate stage ranged from *Camille* to *Petticoat Fever,* from *Pygmalion* to *Idiot's Delight.* Historical romances were elaborately produced: *Disraeli* was a favorite picture one year, and in another *Cimarron,* a story of Oklahoma pioneering. *Gone With the Wind* was a sensation in 1939. Well known classics were adapted to the screen, with such notable successes in these years as *Captains Courageous* and *David Copperfield.* With the use of sound tracks new possibilities opened up with animated cartoons. The "Silly Symphonies" had a great success, but far more important—then and for the future—was Walt Disney's inauguration of cartoon fairytales with *Snow White and the Seven Dwarfs.*

The reigning stars during the 1930's also revealed how diverse moving-picture entertainment had become. Mickey Mouse rivaled Greta Garbo, and the Dionne quintuplets competed with Clark Gable. Lawrence Tibbett and Zazu Pitts, Will Rogers and Jean Harlow, Adolph Menjou and Shirley Temple, Bette Davis and James Cagney, Mickey Rooney and Vivien Leigh, each had an enthusiastic following.[37]

Throughout these years in which the movies were reaching an even broader segment of the public, with children constituting something like a third of the nationwide audience, the inevitable question again arose of their effect on manners and morals. The reformers who had protested the "hypogastric rhythm" of Dolorita's Passion Dance in nickelodeon days became more than ever aroused with the lurid tone of so many of the movies of the 1920's. They could not close their eyes to advertisements that invited the youth of the land to learn through the movies "what love really means, its exquisite torture, its overwhelming raptures. . . ." Surveys which showed that the love theme led all others, followed closely by crime and sex; that the heroes of the films, if not "great lovers" were usually gangsters and criminals, led to widespread agitation for official censorship.[38]

When these threats from reform quarters were reenforced by a storm of popular disapproval aroused by the revelation of a number of scandals in Hollywood, the motion-picture industry decided it would have to take action. In some trepidation it summoned to the rescue Will H. Hays, a politician high in the councils of the Republican party, and appointed him czar of the Motion Picture Producers and Exhibitors of America. Taking over his responsibilities in 1923, Hays issued an ultimatum. "We must have toward the mind of a child, toward that clean and virgin unmarked slate," he announced, ". . . the same sense of responsibility, the same care about the impressions made upon it, that the best teacher or the best clergyman, the most inspired teacher of youth would have." Having thus sternly admonished the movie producers, he sought also to reassure the public that in spite of some temporary overemphasis on jazz babies and red-hot kisses, the industry still held Service as its Supreme Purpose.[39]

Some progress was made in the exercise of a reasonable restraint over the content of films under the auspices of the Hays organization and except in six states (Pennsylvania, Ohio, Kansas, Maryland, New York and Virginia), the movie industry succeeded in averting the threat of censorship. There continued to be a profusion of movies playing up the supposed fast life of society and the exploits of gangsterism, but the clean-up campaign did at least something to restore the movies' prestige.

A decade later, however, the old problem arose even more seriously. Producers and exhibitors had let down their self-imposed bans in desperate efforts to combat the effects of the Depression. Everything went. A worried public became deeply concerned, and the mounting protests of the Legion of Decency and other citizens' groups finally convinced the moguls of Hollywood that unless they moved more strenuously to put their house in order, it would this time be done for them. Galvanized into action, the Hays organization undertook to cooperate with the reform agencies and establish a Production Code which it was prepared to enforce throughout the industry.

This code set up certain standards governing the portrayal of crime, love-making, exposure of the human body, and profanity. There were to be no more scenes of seduction—"the treatment of bedrooms must be governed by good taste." More specifically, as revealed in the correspondence of the code's administrator, film characters were not to kiss savagely, get too drunk, lie around in their underwear, or use such words as "louse" and "floozy." One producer was advised to delete the business of "spraying perfume behind the ears," and another was told to cut out a character's stepping on a cockroach since "such action is always offensive to motion picture patrons." Robin Hood was not allowed, in the film of that name, to kick the Sheriff of Nottingham in the stomach; in *Dead End* there was a ban on "the action of Spit [one of the Dead End kids] actually expectorating."[40]

The code led to marked improvement after its adoption in 1934 but many critics now turned about to agree that the controls being exercised were much too strict. They found the movies at the mercy of every pressure group in the country and unable to deal realistically with any serious theme or important social problem. One commentator caustically declared that he "would rather take a chance on sullying the great American public rather than stultifying it."[41] While censorship whether from within the industry or without remained a constant and insoluble problem, the changing mores of another generation were soon to leave the moralities of the Hays code far behind.

The movies in any event continued to maintain and build up their tremendous popularity as the theatres that had successfully weathered the storm of the depression drew ever increasing crowds. It was estimated in 1935 that weekly attendance had dropped to some 77,000,000, but two years later it had risen by some fifteen per cent. Before the decade ended, it was passing the 100,000,000 mark and approaching the record figures of 1929.[42]

Never again would the movies play quite such a prominent role in the recreational life of the American people as they were playing on the eve of America's entry into World War II. Attendance naturally fell off sharply during the period of hostilities and then enjoyed a brief spurt of popularity comparable to pre-war days in 1946–47. But apart from other problems in a new age, there was a shadow over the future of the moving picture industry in the form of the countless television aerials that now began to pierce the sky over all the land. Americans by no means gave up going to the movies, but a good many of them were to prefer to stay at home and watch television—often seeing re-runs of the old movies that the booming new entertainment industry was bringing to the more convenient screen in the corner of the living room. An increasing number of motion picture theatres found themselves forced to close as patronage fell off, and in the mid-1950's attendance was averaging little more than half what it had been in the golden days of the movies' greatest popularity.[43]

Hollywood—although it had lost its position as the almost monopolistic center of the moving picture industry—fought valiantly against this trend. Its slogan was that "Movies Are Better Than Ever" and it did everything possible to justify such a claim. Whether or not there was any improvement remained, as in the case of everything about the movies, subject to continuing controversy. Some critics nostalgically asked what had happened to the pictures of the good old days; others found the movies more realistically attempting to depict the modern scene, and, going beyond mere entertainment, dealing honestly with the problems of the human condition.

The general run of films nevertheless conformed very much to pre-war patterns with a shifting emphasis from year to year on musical extravaganzas, science fiction, war stories, horror films, and the time-proved westerns. There was nothing quite like *Gone With the Wind* (which was re-issued and by 1962 had grossed in its nearly quarter century $75 million), but a number of spectaculars were both immensely expensive and highly successful. *Ben Hur* and *Quo Vadis* fell into such a category and also *Cleopatra,* which was to be quite as renowned for the tangled affairs of Richard Burton and Elizabeth Taylor as for its great crowd-filled scenes. Among other much less ambitious but notable pictures were *The Best Years of Our Lives, High Noon, Marty, A Street Car Named Desire, The Diary of Anne Frank,* and *Hud.* Once again novels were often adapted to the screen. A new *David Copperfield* was one very successful film, and even more critically acclaimed as well as popularly received was *Tom Jones.* A number of documentaries won high favor, the *March of Time* continued, and there was always Walt Disney.

Some of the stars survived the war; many new ones glittered brightly in the movie firmament. Spencer Tracy, Humphrey Bogart, Gary Cooper and Cary Grant were among the more popular, and also Ava Gardner, Marilyn Monroe, Susan Hayward and Audrey Hepburn. Occasionally the immense vogue for some teen-agers' idol—James Dean or Elvis Presley—recalled the hysteria of the days of Rudolph Valentino. In the early 1960's a new generation of young stars—sometimes teen-agers playing for teen-agers—made their appearance.

As for new technical developments, there was nothing quite so dramatic as the introduction of talking pictures had been. However, there was increasing use of Technicolor (especially in the spectaculars), and the advent of the wide screen and three-dimensional pictures marked an exciting new advance in photography. Cinescope was a pioneer, *This is Cinerama* was first shown in 1952, and four years later *Around the World in 80 Days* was produced by the Todd-AO process.[44]

A more general development of particular importance was the change-over, which proceeded very rapidly during the 1950's, from the large moving picture palaces of the years between wars to small neighborhood houses in the cities, "twin movies" in suburban shopping-centers, and drive-ins everywhere else.

Among the small urban movie houses, the rising number of art theatres was a postwar phenomenon which did not necessarily encourage the American movie industry. They generally imported foreign pictures: Italian films, which first won recognition with *Open City* and *Shoeshine;* Swedish films, as conspicuously represented by Ingmar Bergmann's *Wild Strawberries;* French films, which introduced Brigitte Bardot; and even Japanese films, beginning with *Rashomon.* Going back to the earliest traditions of foreign film-making, these pictures often had a beauty and sensitivity that still seemed to elude Hollywood, and in many cases their directors handled sex with an even greater disregard for convention than the most uninhibited of American producers.

The drive-ins were not greatly concerned with the artistic excellence of the movies they exhibited. Found on the outskirts of towns and cities, and sometimes along highways seemingly far from any population center, they were family entertainment ("Remember the Kar and Kiddies are Free") and a haven for teen-agers. They invariably presented double features—such combinations perhaps as *The Gun Hawk* and *Bikini Beach,* or *Red Lips* and *The Horror of It All*—but given a balmy, moonlight night in July or August, the quality of the film hardly mattered for a good part of the audience. The drive-ins were also long on refreshments: popcorn, candy bars and hot dogs were very much a part of the evening's entertainment.[45]

By the 1960's these drive-ins accounted for more than a third of the country's moving picture theatres. Their popularity was further attested by the telling statistic that in comparison with an annual weekly movie attendance of 50,000,000, they brought the average summer attendance up to 80,000,000 weekly.[46]

What had been the effect of the movies on other forms of popular entertainment during these years of their rapid growth and later comparative decline? They had begun, even in nickelodeon days, to draw away the patrons of popular melodrama and the devotees of variety and burlesque. In the 1920's, the onetime people's theatres were either closed or made over into movie palaces, the variety shows were so completely eclipsed that the old two-a-day vaudeville circuit disappeared altogether, and the doors of the local opera houses (unless they were wired for sound) were everywhere boarded up. So, too, the movies overshadowed the circus and the country fair; the traveling carnival and the amusement park. Such simple small-town diversions as lodge night, the Grange meeting, and the church social could hardly match their strident appeal. None of these traditional forms of recreation disappeared. But farm families no longer looked forward to circus or fair with the eager anticipation of the day when they provided the only semblance of urban entertainment, and people in small towns lost some of their taste for older, simpler diversions with the movies' easy accessibility.

As time went on, the changes the movies had brought about in the recreational scene were still further emphasized as other factors also served to turn people away from the popular amusements of the nineteenth century. The role of the automobile in breaking down the isolation of rural life and the advent of the radio and then television were indeed even more important than the movies. The latter only initiated that process of change, bound up with scores of other new developments—technological, economic and social—that has in this century created new patterns of recreation throughout the country.

The movies also had a significant effect on the legitimate theatre which was to prove somewhat paradoxical in its long-term consequences. They brought about the rapid decline of the traveling companies which had once carried Broadway shows to small towns, and led to the consequent concentration in a few cities, primarily New York, of almost all major theatrical productions—classical drama, the modern comedy, the problem play, and musical revues. At the same time, by so substantially limiting the legitimate theatre to the more sophisticated audiences of metropolitan centers, the movies indirectly encouraged theatrical producers to present more serious plays and to foster the drama as a cultural force as well as entertainment. Without attempting to intrude into the field of dramatic criticism, it may at least be said that beginning with the 1920's, the legitimate theatre increasingly offered plays which were of a different caliber than those designed to appeal to the largest possible nationwide audience. It was able to give more scope to such dramatists as Eugene O'Neill, Tennessee Williams, and Arthur Miller.

If the legitimate theatre was unable to recover the universally popular position it had held while hundreds of traveling companies were constantly on the road, it nonetheless continued to play a highly important role in the entertainment world. There was something of a revival of stock companies, especially summer stock, in the 1930's; other cities were to follow the lead of New York with its Theatre Guild and Group Theatre, and during the depression years, the Federal Theatre Project became for a time an active force in promoting new plays.

Under such stimulating influences there was also a mushroom growth of community theatres with some 500,000 amateurs playing before an estimated annual audience of fifteen million.[47]

There were impressive indications in these developments of a new growth of popular interest in the legitimate theatre. But it was still true that the audience it reached, even when stock companies and community theatres were taken into account, remained a relatively limited one. In numbers it could in no way compare with the many millions who were still streaming into moving-picture houses in every city, town and hamlet throughout the land.

A very restricted role but also a fresh vitality characterized the theatre in the years following World War II. Broadway annually produced—with varying success and sometimes complete failure—from fifty to a hundred plays attended not only by New Yorkers but by visitors from all over the country. Also, a new departure in the 1950's which greatly stimulated all kinds of theatrical experimentation was the increasing production of "off-Broadway" shows. However, from the point of view of popular interest, which is the major concern of this narrative, New York's greatest contribution to the entertainment of the country as a whole was the musical. Beginning with *Show Boat* and *Oklahoma,* and then continuing (among many others) with *South Pacific, The King and I,* and *My Fair Lady,* a series of such plays had record runs on Broadway itself, toured all major cities, and were then made into equally successful moving pictures.

Away from New York, summer stock—"the straw-hat circuit"—expanded far beyond its prewar scope with hundreds of resident companies, often strengthened by visiting stars, playing in tents and made-over barns. This phase of theatrical activity, reaching far more people than the ten million or so who annually bought tickets for New York shows, soon led to the formation of professional summer stock companies (there were about 150 as early as 1952) and to what were called "package companies," in which a star with a complete supporting cast made the summer theatre circuit. They staged both old and new plays, participated in the Shakespearian revivals, and especially in New England became a permanent fixture of the summer scene. Still another innovation was the growth of "musical tents" which put the Broadway shows under canvas. It was reported in 1964 that thirty-two such theatres were in operation and staged their performances (including most notably *My Fair Lady*) for several hundred thousand people.[48]

Again nothing could bring back the good old days of the 1890s when as many as 500 traveling companies might be on the road throughout the entire year, but neither the movies nor any other kind of entertainment could wholly kill off the age-old appeal of the live theatre.

The place of moving picture theatres in American life at the opening of the 1960's may not have been as impressive as it had been
between the wars. Wholly apart from any revival on the legitimate
stage, they had been forced into a very secondary role by the universal
appeal of television. Nevertheless, admissions at moving picture theatres
which at the opening of the 1960's averaged 2.5 billion a year (account-
ing for receipts of $1.2 billion) could hardly be ignored.[49] The movies
still held a very important position in the entertainment world.

They remained for the most part adapted to that level of popular
taste which would bring in the largest number of cash-paying customers.
With some notable exceptions, the great majority of the several hundred films produced annually (about half the number produced in the
1930's), made no pretence of aspiring to any higher goals.

Critics were as always in a state of constant alarm, and many of them
felt that the postwar movies were exerting an unhappy influence not
only—as in the 1920's—by exaggerating the violence in American life,
but by producing "sick" films in which the heroes or heroines might
be alcoholics, homosexuals or other neurotic characters. A great deal too
much attention, it was said, was being given to "symbolism, sadism
and sex." But while most of these pictures were obviously designed to
titillate the taste of a mass public, some were honestly seeking to explore
the basic social and personal issues of the day. There was less sentimentality and more realism than ever before in the best of these pictures, and in their treatment of modern life they were portraying on
the screen something of the troubles, uncertainties and psychological
frustrations of an age of anxiety. Their very strength sometimes carried
them beyond what many people considered the bounds of good taste,
but they could hardly have expressed the message they were seeking
to convey if their preoccupation was always good taste rather than
reality.

"So long as true filmmakers continue to probe the many complexities
of man, to analyze his strange behavior under all stresses and strains,"
wrote Bosley Crowther, the film critic of the *New York Times,* "there
is reason to respect the medium. It is when they fail to do so that it's
time to scream."

It was still true, however, that both the movies which dealt with sex
and violence for their own sake, and those in which such themes were
seriously treated as inescapable aspects of the condition of man, were
generally overshadowed by films that were wholly innocuous—"formula
films"—in their handling of romance, adventure and high comedy. The
producers were constrained by the very nature of their business, as it
had developed in this country from the days of the penny arcade and
the nickelodeon, to try to give the great masses of the American people
what it was believed they wanted. The movies were originally projected

as a democratic amusement, and they were as much so in the 1960's as in the early 1900's.

The Growth of the Movies

1. Ben J. Lubschez, *The Story of the Motion Picture* (New York, 1920), 43; *Outing*, LXIV (July, 1914), 499–505; Paul Schubert, *The Electric Word* (New York, 1928), 3ff.
2. Benjamin B. Hampton, *A History of the Movies* (New York, 1931), 7.
3. *Ibid.*, 11; Terry Ramsaye, *A Million and One Nights* (New York, 1926), 233; "The Motion Picture in Its Economic and Social Aspects," *Annals of the American Academy of Political and Social Science*, CXXVIII (1926), 7.
4. Hampton, *A History of the Movies*, 12.
5. *Ibid.*, 44–45; Ramsaye, *A Million and One Nights*, 429–30.
6. Barton W. Currie, "The Nickel Madness," *Harper's Weekly*, LI (1907), 1246–47; George E. Walsh, "Moving Picture Drama for the Multitude," *Independent*, LXIV (February 6, 1908).
7. Quoted in Mark Sullivan, *Our Times* (New York, 1925–35), III, 552–53.
8. Hampton, *A History of the Movies*, 57; Walsh, *loc. cit.*, 306.
9. Ramsaye, *A Million and One Nights*, 256.
10. *Ibid.*, 259.
11. *Ibid.*, 473ff.
12. Sullivan, *Our Times*, III, 551–52.
13. Currie, *loc. cit.*, 1247; *Review of Reviews*, XXXVIII (December, 1908), 744.
14. Hampton, *A History of the Movies*, 29–39.
15. Walsh, *loc. cit.*, 307; Lubschez, *Story of the Motion Picture*, 58; *Annals of American Academy of Political and Social Science*, CXXVIII (1926), 10; Ramsaye, *A Million and One Nights*, 281–89, 363–78, 429.
16. Hampton, *A History of the Movies*, 31; Ramsaye, *A Million and One Nights*, 416ff.
17. Walsh, *loc. cit.*, 307–08.
18. Ramsaye, *A Million and One Nights*, 474.
19. Sullivan, *Our Times*, III, 553.
20. *Annals of the American Academy of Political and Social Science*, CXXVIII (1926), 11.
21. Hampton, *A History of the Movies*, 86ff; Ramsaye, *A Million and One Nights*, 544–45, 547–49, 605.
22. Hampton, *A History of the Movies*, 57, 92.
23. Ramsaye, *A Million and One Nights*, 645ff; Marie Dressler, *My Own Story* (Boston, 1934), 168–69.
24. Ramsaye, *A Million and One Nights*, 734.
25. *Ibid.*, 661; Pearl White, *Just Me* (New York, 1919).
26. Hampton, *A History of the Movies*, 130; Ramsaye, *A Million and One Nights*, 635ff.
27. Ramsaye, *A Million and One Nights*, 675–77; Hampton, *A History of the Movies*, 333.
28. Hampton, *A History of the Movies*, 342.
29. Ramsaye, *A Million and One Nights*, 748.
30. *Ibid.*, 625.
31. Frederick Lewis Allen, *Only Yesterday* (New York, 1931), 101.
32. Robert S. and Helen Merrell Lynd, *Middletown* (New York, 1929), 266.
33. Quoted in Hampton, *A History of the Movies*, 362.
34. *Ibid.*, 387ff.
35. Julius Weinberger, "Economic Aspects of Recreation," reprint from *Harvard Business Review*, Summer, 1937, 450.

36. Preston W. Slosson, *The Great Crusade and After* (New York, 1931), 394; Hampton, *A History of the Movies*, 362.
37. *Film Daily Yearbook*, 1939.
38. Edgar Dale, *The Content of Motion Pictures* (New York, 1935), 17, 227.
39. Allen, *Only Yesterday*, 102; Will H. Hays, "The Motion Picture Industry," *Review of Reviews*, LXVII (1923), 65–80.
40. "The Hays Office," *Fortune*, XVIII (December, 1938), 3; J. C. McEvoy, "The Back of Me Hand to You," *Saturday Evening Post*, CCXI (December 24, 1938), 8ff.
41. *Current History*, L (March, 1939), 47.
42. Weinberger, "Economic Aspects of Recreation," 454.
43. *Encyclopedia Americana*, "Motion Pictures"; "The Good Life," *Life*, XLVII (December 28, 1959), 73.
44. Contemporary moving picture articles and reviews.
45. "Movie Theatres Stage Comeback," *New York Times*, Section 3, July 5, 1964.
46. *Encyclopedia Americana Annual*, 1964.
47. Albert McCleery and Carl Glick, *Curtains Going Up* (New York, 1939), 332.
48. Emily Coleman, "From Red Barn to Package and Tent," *New York Times Magazine*, July 19, 1964.
49. "The Good Life," 73.

The Rise and Place of
the Motion Picture

Terry Ramsaye

*Terry Ramsaye was born in Tonganoxie, Kansas, and educated at the
University of Kansas. He was a newspaper writer and editor from 1906
to 1915. He joined the Mutual Film Corporation in 1915 as a publicity
man and while there he produced some Charlie Chaplin comedies. He
authored* A Million and One Nights—The History of the Motion Picture
*in 1926. In 1931 he joined the Quigley Publishing Company as editor
of the* Motion Picture Herald, *a post he held for ten years. He continued
his association with the* Herald *as consulting editor until his death in
1954.**

The screen has arrived at the middle of the twentieth century, with a
swift fifty years of evolving experience behind it, as a dominant form of
expression. Among the masses it shares with the printed word and the
radio, somewhat remotely related instruments of communication, and
exceeds them both in effective penetration, especially in the great
illiterate and semiliterate strata where words falter, fail, and miss.

Being a basic, primitive implement, the film reaches low and deep,
with an order of authority to the senses enjoyed by no other form of
expression.

It is estimated that there are between seventy-five and eighty thousand
motion picture theaters functioning around the world. The weekly attendance is calculated to be in the vicinity of 235,000,000. Statistics
of the motion picture industry, especially world statistics, are not to be
viewed as records of extreme precision.

* By permission from James C. Charlesworth, editor *Annals* . . . , "The Rise
and Place of the Motion Picture," *The Motion Picture Industry,* ed. Gordon S.
Watkins, *Annals of the American Academy of Political and Social Science.* CCIV
(November 1947) , pp. 1–11. © 1947.

Somewhat indirect evidence of the effective penetration and high competence among the media is afforded by the rising and long continuing pother about the screen from politicians of all lands and the fierce nationalistic film movements to be observed around the world.

RELATION TO OLDER ARTS

The motion picture is anomalously anachronic. While it is the newest of the major media, it is in fact a belated arrival at the primary purpose of man seeking to communicate and to re-create events of interesting, exciting, and enjoyable impact. It may be contended that man became intricately articulate, and with alphabets, because of his inadequate capacity to make pictures as facile instruments of narration. So it has come that the ancient quest, after the centuries, has been empowered by involved technologies of optics, kinetics, photochemistry, and materials. The simple function is, and must be, completely performed.

Both artists and scholars have come to confusion about the motion picture by seductively automatic endeavors to relate it to the older arts. The picture is in very truth at once the belated predecessor and the successor to the older media of pageant, dance, drama, and such relatively minor devices of communication as sculpture, painting, and opera.

Those older media down the centuries have developed their special sophistications and elaborations of culture, fenced about with conventions and orthodoxies maintained and protected by their priestly zealots of the rituals of art. The motion picture, by reason of unique opportunity, has come to strike its roots into and take its nurture directly from the fundamental soil of the human wish, largely escaping the confusions of derived and interdependent older forms of record and narration.

THE KINETOSCOPE

The history of the motion picture, unlike that of any of the other arts, having covered so short a span of years, is so immediately available for examination that the processes can be seen with clarity. After more than a century of conscious striving toward the motion picture, it was achieved in October of 1889. The machine was the peep-show Kinetoscope, invented by Thomas A. Edison, building on the endeavors of the prior workers, and empowered especially by George Eastman's film for "roller photography," made available in September of that year.

The world was not consciously waiting for the motion picture. Mr. Edison was not much concerned about it, either. He had supervised it into being with desultory attention across two years, apparently mostly because of an assignment to himself to make a machine to do for the eye what his phonograph did for the ear. He was of the pioneer culture of the Middle West, concerned with work—not play, not entertainment. The phonograph had been evolved to be a robot stenographer, and was developing as an entertainment device, with problems and commercial headaches. He let the kinetoscope stand in a corner of his laboratory at West Orange, gathering dust. He did not trouble to patent it in Europe.

By the enterprise of promoters impelled by showmanship, the kineto-scope presented the first film pictures to the public the night of April 14, 1894, after five years, at the Kinetoscope Parlor, 1155 Broadway, New York, with a battery of machines. The pictures were brief snatches and shards of vaudeville acts, boxers in fractional rounds, trivia which had challenged the interest of the shop mechanics who had custody of the new mechanism. One customer at a time could peek into each machine. The little show in Broadway was a moderate success. The invention drew a ripple of Sunday supplement attention. Meanwhile, the machine went into export sales and carried the seeds of film technology to the capitals of the Old World.

THE SCREEN

Within months the pressures of showmanship demanded a union of the kinetoscope's moving pictures with the magic lantern, so that a screen could entertain a whole audience at once. In less than two years that was achieved, and by the spring of 1896 the career of the film in the theater had begun. The pictures immediately and automatically found their place as a component of the variety shows, just then begin-ning to reach for the pretentious name of "vaudeville." Also black tent theaters became attractions with traveling carnivals and at the amuse-ment parks with which electric traction companies were creating car-ride traffic. The screen was certainly starting at the bottom of the ladder.

The production function continued in the hands of the tinkerers and mechanics and the flotsam of the backwaters of showmanship. The screen was not finding anything to say beyond the level of the dime museum interest.

The screen sensation of 1898 in London was a subject in Charles Urban's endeavor at a scientific series in which he presented some microscopic studies of life in a Stilton cheese, thereby bestirring the British cheese industry into a demand for censorship. Indicative of the cultural status of the art, the American Mutoscope and Biograph Company of New York, competing with the Edison enterprise, made a brave step by interesting the famed Joseph Jefferson and presenting some excerpts from his Rip van Winkle performances. That classic material aroused no interest, but the Biograph subject entitled *Girl Climbing Apple Tree* became a hit and keynoted a policy.

The industry was beset by patent wars, infringements, piracies, and all the devices of chicane the pitchmen vendors of movies could invent. The business was at low tide. In the vaudeville theaters the pictures had been moved to the end of the bill, to tell the audience the show was over and to clear the house. The films had come to be called "chasers." The Battle of Santiago was pictured with models in a Brooklyn bathtub, and the Boer War was fought for the screen in Flatbush with glimpses of the metropolis in the background.

Here and there appeared some timid steps toward giving the screen a story to tell. For instance, Edwin S. Porter, Edison cameraman, experimented with a bit of a tale to give excuse for that perennial picture of the fire engine making a run. It was a race for life in which the fire chief saved his own child, and then fell from his chair and found it was a dream. The title was *The Life of an American Fireman.* Enough interest and print sales resulted to encourage the production of *The Great Train Robbery,* that now historic classic known as "the first story picture." It was made in 1903. Moving through the tedious, unorganized distribution of the time, this primitive drama of bandits, bravery, fast riding, and excitement was two years becoming a hit. It also incidentally highlighted the program of the Nickelodeon, a little house casually opened to a film program for the lack of other entertainment, by John P. Harris in Pittsburgh about Thanksgiving time in 1905. With a five-cent admission the theater played to standing room for weeks on end.

THE EARLY AUDIENCE

The five-cent theater of the movies had arrived. In a wildfire wave, imitative nickelodeons rose across the land, all of them in centers, like Pittsburgh, with a high content of foreign-born polyglottic population. Immigration was at high tide. American industry was bringing in labor for mines and mills. Steamship and labor agents were plastering the ports of the Mediterranean with posters of the United States as a land of golden promise, with life made gay with buffaloes, Indians, excitement, and natural wonders.

The workers came over, high of hope, poor in pocket, and finding workaday life dull and demanding. They brought none of their native arts, and they were not literate enough to enjoy their feeble foreign-language press. As for American amusements, there was the language barrier, besides the price. The motion picture's new theater, with a five-cent admission and the silent films of the big open places and excitement, romance, thrills, and success on the spot, made good in a fashion on the promises they had read in Trieste.

Meanwhile, the petty tradesmen of the foreign-labor quarters, shrewd, nimble, anxious, behind the counters of their candy shops, soda fountains, banana stands, and pawnshops, saw the new interest of their customers. They became vendors of the new entertainment. Within a year of that opening in Pittsburgh, there were nearly five thousand of the little five-cent shows.

Demand took production off the roofs and out of the back yards of Manhattan into studios on Long Island, in the Bronx, at Fort Lee over in New Jersey, in the suburbs of Chicago and Philadelphia. Cameramen and some of Broadway's idle actors became directors of the "story pictures." Also, the demand for "story suggestions" rose to the point that $15 was a standard price for "a suggestion." A typical story sale was a plot summary of *Enoch Arden* which one author sold repeatedly. That went on until the Kalem company was required by court order to pay $25,000 for making *Ben Hur* without consulting either the estate of General Lew Wallace or Harper's, the publishers.

In that period the budding industry had everything to learn. It had no recognizable precedents, and its accidentally acquired personnel brought little knowledge of any other businesses. Procedure was on the general assumption that anything could be done until forbidden, specifically, positively by law—and thereafter only in the cover of the Jersey highlands.

Somewhat marginally, as the pictures reached up into middle-class levels of consciousness, some eyebrows were raised at the Mediterranean tastes manifest on the screen. The protest began with the peep show *Dolorita in the Passion Dance* in Atlantic City in 1894, and got really articulate in the New York papers about 1906 when the Children's Society went to court about exhibition of pictures on the Thaw case. Regulations of sorts, including censorships by various cities, resulted.

EVOLVING ORDER

A new order of discipline was brought into the industry with the arrival of an iron-handed businessman. Jeremiah J. Kennedy, retired engineering expert, was sent uptown by the Empire Trust Company to see what was to be done for the bondholders of the fading American Mutoscope and Biograph Company. He was expected to order liquidation. Instead, he decided to reorganize the whole industry. Out of that decision came the Motion Picture Patents Company, licensing as partners all reputable producers and ending the patent wars, also seeking to end all manner of competitive abuses, such as making "duped" versions of competitive product.

The while, a socially minded organization known as The People's Institute was engaged in trying to be a friend to the struggling art of the common people in its ordeals with the law and the political forces mustered by the jealous New York stage. The Patents Company substantially underwrote the resultant National Board of Censorship, in recent years known as the National Board of Review. It began as a friendly advisory body, and with its internal support, functioned with an authority and power now long since departed. Its authority could not long outlive the Patents Company, soon to be swept into history by evolutions in the industry.

Prosperity came with order. Profits improved swiftly; the product improved slowly.

The Kennedy-Patents Company control movement went into the next phase, the organization of the distribution arm, the General Film Company, with a national system of film exchanges. More order came into film rentals to theaters, and more profits to the membership of the big combine.

DEVELOPING AUDIENCE AND ART

It began to be apparent that the audience was developing selectivity. Each of the major contributors to the General Film program had for awhile a designated day. When the little one-sheet poster out in front said "Biograph Day," the attendance was better. That was presently traced to story and picture quality, and that in turn traced to the work of one "Larry" Griffith, ex-actor, who had left the stage in 1906 in a "resting" period to essay a job in the humble art of the films. He was due presently to come to fame as D. W. Griffith, later David Wark Griffith. Some of those rather able but anonymous persons in his little Biograph dramas had names like Walthall, Lawrence, Pickford, and Gish.

The audience was expanding. The screen was seeping up into the middle class with neighborhood houses of considerably more comfort and pretense than the little nickelodeons of the labor districts. A ten-cent admission price became a commonplace. "Nickelodeons" began to give way to fancies like "Bijou Dream" and such invitations as "The Family" and "The Cozy."

The old stage institution of the road show, with its "direct from Broadway" melodramas—remember Sag Harbor, Way Down East, East Lynne, Under Southern Skies, Cameo Kirby—was feeling competition. Also the town opera house was venturing a try at movies. The motion picture was bringing drama within walking distance of most of urban America; and the stage was trying to live from the carriage trade. At the peak of this development, in the period 1913–16, there were probably twenty-eight thousand motion picture theaters of all sorts in the United States.

Meanwhile, the art of story telling on the screen was acquiring skill, quality, and fluidity. The principal influence was Griffith, who with his cameraman extraordinary, William Bitzer, was first to explore the narrative uses of the close-up, the cutback, and the development of parallel lines of action—invaluable to the Griffith suspense technique of "relief on the way." The dramas were still in single reels.

Also, the audience was growing up with its art. The original immigrant audience was acquiring an improving buying power, and by experience was evolving an order of taste. Its exhibitors who started with it were keeping pace, and keeping a step ahead, learning the melting-pot populace as it was simmering into the new America.

Over in Europe the film had come upon no such fertile opportunity of a land and an economic era in the making. The motion picture planted there by the Edison Kinetoscope fell mostly into scientific hands and tended to become an ineffective medium for pursuit of the patterns of the older arts. Its address was at no time so focused on the masses of the community as in the United States. The European screen's ambition was addressed to spectacles and ancient classics. And yet that too was to have an influence in America, homeland of the screen.

LONGER PICTURES INTRODUCED

By 1912 the American motion picture was close to a ceiling. Its horizontal development across the land and its audiences had neared a saturation. The next move had to be a break-through. Again, as ever, the situation found its instrument—in this instance Adolph Zukor, born in Hungary, educated in the American industrial scene, beginning as a furrier's apprentice, and becoming incidentally an investor in a penny arcade enterprise which he had to take over to save the investment. So he came to the amusement world with evolving interests in exhibition. By 1912 he had come to a parting of the ways in his associations. He found inspiration and opportunity in the availability of the American rights to a foreign-made four-reel picture entitled *Queen Elizabeth* with Sarah Bernhardt in the title role. The time had come, considered Mr. Zukor, for the screen to take its place along with the stage in offering a whole evening's entertainment. He also arrived at the line "famous players in famous plays" to keynote a policy. Thereby the "feature" era was born, meaning the rise of the hour-long picture taking over against the established program of short pictures.

The public gave encouragement by patronage of the longer pictures and responding to the promotion which presented them. A signal success was had from road-show type presentations of *Quo Vadis,* a long spectacle production made in Rome and vastly more successful in America than in Europe. D. W. Griffith, irked by Biograph's reactionary adherence to the short-picture policy with which it had risen, went off into an independent project which delivered *The Birth of a Nation* which by its success gave powerful impetus to the feature movement in 1915.

A new and ever growing public was becoming aware of the screen. There were growing pains and problems. The exhibition plant was not adequate for the delivery of the expanding pictures. A new order of more pretentious screen theater was initiated in 1914 with the opening of the Strand Theater on Broadway, soon to be followed by others equally ambitious in the larger centers.

PRESS PUBLICITY

Concurrently, manifestations of the increasing impress of the screen on a larger public came from the field of publication. Scatteringly magazines began to discover the new art of the people. Out in Chicago *The Tribune* pioneered recognition of the motion picture with participation in the promotion of serials, parallel on screen and printed page, as a device to encourage circulation, and succeeded. Joseph Medill Patterson, a *Tribune* editor, became a daily patron of the movie houses, the more lowly the better. That was some years before he became the dominant factor in the founding and operation of *The Daily News,* New York picture newspaper, with the greatest circulation in the Nation. Out in Buffalo, Norman E. Mack, publisher, eyed the *Tribune*'s serials with interest and became the producer of one entitled *The Perils of Our Girl Reporters.* In New York, Robert McAlarney, city editor of the old *Tribune,* summed up the situation in a notice to the staff, which he tacked on the bulletin board in that venerable office down in Nassau Street, saying: "Remember you are in competition with the movies now." He demanded graphic writing. William Randolph Hearst went into serial picture production and newsreel enterprises.

The public was hearing about the screen as it never had heard before. The printed word was carrying the interest up from the proletariat into the reading classes.

THE INDEPENDENTS

Along with that, the feature development was rapidly improving the quality of the product, lifting it to the tastes of new audiences. An amazing order of new competition arose among the new sort of picture makers, the oncoming "independents."

The decisive turn had come for a complex of reasons back in 1912–13, when Adolph Zukor had brought over *Queen Elizabeth.* It had been produced in Europe outside the pale of patent protection. Jeremiah J. Kennedy of the Patents Company, supported by Henry Norton Marvin of Biograph, took authority in his hands and issued a license for its exhibition in license-controlled theaters, customers of General Film. The success of the picture and the unfolding picture movement aroused jealous protests among the contributors to the General Film program, and unhappily encountered more than whispered racial bias. Sigmund Lubin of Philadelphia, a first-wave pioneer, was the only Jewish member of the Patents group.

The majority of the General Film producers, prosperous beyond any anticipation, sat in haughty assurance condemning "the feature craze." They had some interior alarms about the costs and the labors of the new order of production. It was uncomfortable, disturbing. "We have the know how," they told themselves and all else who would listen.

Frank N. Dyer, president of General Film and attorney for Thomas A. Edison, observing the vast display of diamonds and emeralds worn by the members of his board, one day whimsically appeared to preside wearing smoked glasses.

When Mr. Zukor appeared seeking a license for his second picture, an American production, he sat waiting for hours on end at the office of the Patents Company in New York, and was refused. He went out entirely on his own. As a lone man he could have been defeated. As the exponent of a development rooted in the service of the great American majority, he was armed with an unrecognized but real authority. Quickly other independents took courage and went into production. They too had all to gain and little to lose, and knew the customers better than their complacent predecessors. There was litigation, of course, but as it threaded through the courts the racing development of the art defeated the Patents Company control by sheer force of product long before final adjudication was had. The Patents group fell apart with dissensions and scattered while issues were pending.

GROWTH OF THE INDUSTRY

The very American process of swift obsolescence with expanding replacement, under the same order of pressures and laws of development all across the industrial scene, was in demonstration as the motion picture, becoming somewhat more of an art, also became very much more of an industry. It was on the final authority of the consumers.

A minor statistical indication of the swiftness of the upturn was afforded in the case of Charles Chaplin. In 1913 he left a vaudeville act to take employment in Keystone's slapstick comedies at $150 a week. In the autumn of 1915 he signed a contract to appear in twelve two-reel comedies in one year at a salary of $10,000 a week, plus a bonus of

$150,000. In turn The Lone Star concern sold the British Empire rights to the comedies for the total of Chaplin's salary, $670,000. The deals all made money. By 1916 the patrons of the lowly cinema were willing to pay real millions at the box office for one comedian.

The motion picture made its own order of fame. When Adolph Zukor had launched his Famous Players company, he presented a schedule of attractions in three classes—A, B, and C. Class C was to present famous *picture* players in famous plays. Bernhardt was typical of Class A. Mary Pickford was Class C. Brief experience showed that the public which the screen had assembled knew nothing about and cared nothing for the great ones of stage and opera, and cared very much for their own people, the stars of the movies. The older arts obviously were without status in melting-pot America.

As the films grew up and their theater with them, the number of houses tended to diminish while seating capacities increased. In part this represented improved and wider drawing power for better theaters, but very considerably it was connected with the new mobility of the customers brought about by the coming of the inexpensive automobile. That encouraged shopping for entertainment and it removed the limitation of walking-distance locations. In 1914–15 the neighborhood theaters played continuously to the same audiences week after week, as reflected by the extraordinary success of serial pictures, requiring repeating attendance. In 1918 the most ambitious serial of them all came to abysmal failure. There was irony in the fact that its first conspicuous fall was in Detroit, the motor center.

Imposing and luxurious theaters of large seating capacities began to rise in outlying residential districts of high buying power and at suburban centers. Downtown districts were left to the houses of the dying art of the stage and its fading gilt and dusty plush.

INFLUENCE OF WORLD WAR I

Starting with and continuing across this period the American motion picture became a special beneficiary of the First World War. The war shut down the studios of Europe and England in 1914, just as the feature era came to flower, and delivered the screens of the world to the American product. That product was almost automatically attuned to a diverse world market by reason of the foreign heritages from many lands of both the initial film audiences and the producers which their patronage encouraged. The American motion picture born to serve a vast polyglottic patronage was born international in its own home market. It took the world's screens without opposition and with few problems of adjustment. The American motion picture came to occupy something like 80 per cent of the world's screen time.

The prosperity of the pictures in World War I, as through World War II, was lavishly supported by the eager buying of the free-spending workers temporarily rich on war wages. The box-office-admissions curve inevitably follows the pay-roll graphs. And sometimes the doles, too. The only exception in history was the onsweep of the nickelodeon wave through the "stringency" of 1907, when the industry was too small to figure in national reactions. The people's art lives out of the people's pocket.

The American industry continued to fortify its world position by the acquisition of the outstanding talent of production abroad as rapidly as it appeared, adding continually to the great talent pool of Hollywood. This enhanced and enriched the product for the markets both at home and abroad, and incidentally reduced competitive developments. Britain contributed able players, and from Germany and France came notably skilled technicians and directors.

ENTER THE TALKING PICTURES

In 1926 the art of the motion picture came to revolutionary change with the arrival of electronic sound recording and reproduction, a by-product of telephone and radio. The personal instrument was the late Sam Warner, one of the four sons of Benjamin Warner who had come to these shores and the land of opportunity nearly a generation before. Contemporaries in the industry of the screen looked askance and doubtingly on the talking picture, but demonstration by Warner Brothers prevailed. The silent esperanto of pantomime of nickelodeon days was no longer an asset. By 1926 the audiences all spoke American. So in the next three years the industry was made over with pictures laced with words and music. Importantly, the American talking picture was still to be dominant on the screens of the great market of the English-speaking lands. In fact, the English understood American perfectly, despite the fact that there has been found to be a lot of English that most Americans cannot understand.

When the screen acquired its voice, a new order of material was required. The silent picture had become a hybrid art of mingled pantomime and printed word presented in the subtitles. Some pictures, incidentally, required a capacity for swift reading. They did not do so well.

Seeking talking picture play material, the screen turned to the stage and its playwrights, and thereby reaped a reaction in direct retribution for what it had done to the stage when it swept the road shows out of the hinterlands. The stage, driven back from that contact with the larger public, had taken refuge in the service of sophisticated metropolitan minorities. In direct consequence came sometimes painfully sophisticated drama and dialogue of candor that would never be tolerated by Dubuque, Bad Axe, or Abeline. Translated to the screen and taken out to the provinces, and even a few squares from Broadway, this material gave rise to protests, threats and acts of censorship, and movements toward Federal regulative legislation.

Back in 1922 the industry, confronted with a wave of public disapproval pertaining mostly to conduct of players and other more official figures in the public eye, had organized the Motion Picture Producers and Distributors of America, Inc., and installed Will H. Hays as president and titular "czar of the movies." He became in effect a super public relations counsel. By 1928–29 it was not personnel but product that was out of hand.

REGULATION

Now to the rescue came Martin Quigley, publisher of journals of the industry since 1915, a Catholic layman of prominence, with the device of self-regulation entitled the Production Code, a document of guidance to picture makers calculated to help keep the pictures in line with common decency and American mores. It began and continues essentially as a formula intended to apply the principles of the rather nonsectarian and accepted Ten Commandments to picture production. It is convenient, and accurate enough for the moment, to say that the code requires that a picture, while portraying sin for dramatic purposes, shall not become the Devil's advocate. It was formally adopted by the organized industry in March 1930—forty-six years after *Dolorita in the Passion Dance* got the pictures into trouble on the Boardwalk in Atlantic City.

The public has apparently accepted the product made under the code with equanimity, and probable unawareness, with few further threats of censorship. In 1946, 98 per cent of the product on the American screen bore the Seal of code approval. Objections to the code continued to dot the published discussion of the screen, emanating mainly from professionally articulate persons in the Hollywood production community inclined to ask for the American family theater the viewpoints of the art museum and the medical clinic.

Regulative pressures of sorts from government, taking their origins mainly from minority complaints in the field of exhibition, against the trade practices arising from acquisition of theaters by distributor-producer interests, began early in the history of the Federal Trade Commission. They came to flower for apparently special reasons of political design early in the New Deal administration. There was a program, under long and careful consideration at the White House, which looked to profound control of both the screen and the radio. In sequel came the National Recovery Administration and the setting up of an elaborate, and allegedly co-operative, control of the trade practices of the industry under the wings of the NRA Blue Eagle.

After the famed "Chicken Case" decision ended the NRA there was a pause until the filing of the now venerable but continuing—at midyear 1947—antitrust case, the *U. S. v. Paramount et al*, filed July 20, 1938. The original bill professed to be concerned with the whole public interest and promised to seek control of everything from the Hollywood talent pool to the price of film fourth run at Bad Axe. As the case moved into the final phase on appeals to the Supreme Court it had narrowed chiefly to film sales issues between distributor and exhibitor. The public at no time appeared interested. It probably had nothing important at stake.

NATIONALISTIC BARRIERS

While the United States was New-Dealing at home, the new world war was in the making in Europe. Along with that, the walls of nationalism were rising, and in the lands of the Left those walls were raised to varying heights against the American film. Russia would have none of the pictures of this land of luxury, showing a happy and exciting life of capitalism. Germany let in, under assorted and varying restrictions, enough pictures to take a share of screen time. Italy put up dollar barriers by which the American pictures could play but not pay. In Japan the American product was interlarded with government-controlled exhibition to draw in the people for Japan's propaganda injections. England established trade quotas, only partly enforceable by reason of the inadequacy of domestic production and the preference of exhibitors and patrons for the American product.

When World War II swept across the global scene the American industry sustained important invasions of foreign revenue and there were piercing cries. However, the war-enriched masses at home so besieged the box office that it entered into a period of unprecedented prosperity.

In sequel to the end of the shooting aspects of World War II, sometimes called the peace, the walls of nationalism and the issues of nationalism became even more sharply defined. Additionally the fringes of the Russian iron curtain were extending over the screen in lands of Soviet influence. Every nation, great and small, strove for a motion picture industry of its own, mainly for propaganda reasons of its own.

Most important of all came the manifestations from Britain, foremost of America's allies in the war, determined and ambitious as never before to establish a world-wide British film industry. The reasons were obvious. The Empire was *in extremis*. The motion picture was at long last recognized as an instrument of trade, a medium which had quite unconsciously and unpurposefully sold American products and gadgets around the world. Trade for manufactures the tight little isle of Britain must have, or else.

The chosen instrument became, and is, Mr. J. Arthur Rank, British industrialist with his investments, interest, and connection spread over the whole pattern of British enterprise. As an incident of his concern over social well-being he turned his attention, some years ago, to pictures for Sunday school classes. That led to his becoming an important investor in British production and exhibition. That activity has expanded until in this 1947 he has some millions of pounds of his and stockholders' money invested in the new medium of service to the Empire, or maybe Commonwealth, with interests in American production, distribution, and exhibition.

After a succession of American visits and soft approaches, Mr. Rank by midyear of 1947 was in substance demanding for British product a decided share in the playing time of the American screen. He was exerting the not too subtle pressure of the picture buying power of his theaters in Britain, the largest consumers there of American productions. There was also the fact that the British Government had empowered the Chancellor of the Exchequer to assess against all imported pictures duty charges to be scaled according to the success of the picture —a tariff device without precedent.

Significant of the continued appeal of the Hollywood product, with its roots in melting-pot America and basic universal applicability, British exhibitors were resisting endeavors to tax American pictures off their screens.

The motion picture has thus become a stuff of empire, a concern of statesmen and national economies. The film takes a place in history along with amber, salt, spices, gold, steel, and oil—also uranium.

MASS SUPPORT NECESSARY

Clearly, the motion picture, in coming of full estate, seeks to serve all peoples and all classes. That is a wide straddle. Its costs are such that it can be generally supported only by the massed buying power of majorities. Inevitably, many minorities cannot be served as they are by the less expensive stage or the relatively inexpensive printed word. Some of those minorities include the most erudite, critical, and articulate persons. From that condition of limitation arises much of the impatient, often militant, criticism of the screen. Some censorship requirements and many projected movements actually represent only areas of unsatisfied demand. Few indeed of the militants who would influence the course of screen development are aware of anything beyond superficial aspects and casual observation. The screen has done little and continues to do little to tell its own story. Few are interested. The people who pay for the pictures want to see them as emotional experience, not as subjects of study.

Almost Purely Emotional

Richard Schickel

A life-long student of the motion picture, Richard Schickel has had numerous articles published in such periodicals as Life, Look, Show, Esquire, Commentary, *and* The Nation. *In the following essay he discusses the innovative years of the American motion picture before and after World War I.**

D. W. Griffith may have been the most important creative force in the movies during the pre-World War I era, but his contributions to the emerging financial and manufacturing structure of a modern, million-dollar industry were negligible. Indeed, his lack of talent for finance and organization were major factors in contributing to his ultimate downfall. While he was making his masterpieces, the real power in the American motion picture industry was being consolidated in the hands of others.

Among them, none was more important than a man now almost forgotten except by the most devoted film historians. His name was Thomas Ince. His time at the top was relatively brief, but in less than a decade he became a major factor in establishing the pattern of studio production which prevailed in Hollywood until the early 1950's and which, for better or worse, set the terms under which American films were produced during the decades when our industry dominated the film world.

Ince's background, like that of Griffith, was the theater in which he, too, had had an indifferent acting career. He began directing for Biograph shortly after Griffith and like The Master he was schooled the hard way—making one film a week, frequently editing it at home in his kitchen at night. He moved quickly to another studio, then another. In 1914 he was head of his own operation, Inceville, in Hollywood. In

* Chapter 4 of *Movies: The History of an Art and an Institution.* © 1964 by Richard Schickel, Basic Books, Inc., Publishers, New York. Used by permission of Basic Books, Inc. and the author.

turn it became the nucleus of Triangle Productions, with Griffith and Mack Sennett as partners. As this empire grew, Ince directed less and less himself, gradually assuming command of a staff of directors well-schooled in his methods. It was only in the processes of preparing a project for the camera and in the final editing that he was likely to intercede personally.

It was said that Ince never finished reading a property when he bought it for translation to the screen and had to be briefed by assistants so that he could talk intelligently to authors. Nevertheless, he was instrumental in setting the great American screen style, which is direct in its methods of story-telling and emphasizes fast, concrete action, tight dramatic construction, economy of statement, and a minimum of reflection and subtlety. He would work on a script until it was perfect, then stamp it "produce as written" and wait for the first "rough cut" of the finished film. These he worked on intensively, constantly trying to sharpen and simplify his films. His most devastating criticism was "it wanders" and when this judgment was passed, out would come the shears. In the trade he was known as the greatest film editor of his time; even in retrospect it is hard to name anyone who surpassed him, at least in the creation of a viable, commercial style.

He should have had a long career, steadily gaining in power and prestige. But somehow Ince seemed to tire very rapidly. By the middle of the twenties, having lost his top stars, William S. Hart and Douglas Fairbanks, having seen other studios adopt his system of supervision and use it even more profitably than he had, he was through. His studio collapsed, and he died in 1924 after suffering a heart attack while cruising on the yacht of William Randolph Hearst, whose Cosmopolitan Productions Company he was then heading.

Mack Sennett, the third in the Triangle triumvirate, credited Griffith as being "my day school, my adult education program, my university." Like his Triangle partners he began as an indifferent actor working in that capacity for Griffith at Biograph, graduating to scenario writing, and then to supervision of "rube" (i.e., country) comedy. But Sennett's heart was really in the world of steel and concrete, of gadgets and man gone amuck. It is said that he borrowed capital for his Keystone studio from a pair of bookies (to whom he was already in debt) and his trademark from a passing car of the Pennsylvania railroad. His idea of what would seem funny on a movie screen he borrowed from no one. As James Agee noted, Sennett's clowns "zipped and caromed about the pristine world of the screen as jazzily as a convention of water bugs." Speed was the essence of Sennett's comic theory. He thought a gag should be planted, developed, and capped within a hundred feet of film; ideally, the payoff for one joke should lay the groundwork for the next. Sennett, at his own studio and later at Triangle, was principally a supervisor, with his production units organized along the same line as Ince's.

He, too, approved scripts, stayed away from their shooting, but supervised every inch of the cutting process. In the screening room he habitually sat in a rocker, and his associates claimed they could tell how he liked the product by the rhythm of the chair's squeakings. They say he always called for more speed.

But speed was not the whole story with Sennett. He also had a taste for the grotesque, and it was probably safe to say that no movie company, before or since, has ever had so many odd-looking people under contract at the same time. Almost every comedian of note, including the great Chaplin, worked for Sennett at one time or another. But at Keystone the real star was Sennett himself, personally recruiting his ensemble of zanies, then supervising the molding of their talents into the closely meshed repertory company, the sum of which was somehow greater than its parts. Strong personalities—like Chaplin, Harry Langdon, or Fatty Arbuckle—would appear from time to time with the group, learn a good deal about their craft, then strike off on their own, unwilling to submerge their unique gifts to the demands of the Sennett style.

These demands were extraordinary, to say the least. "You know," the late Snub Pollard, one of the original Keystone Kops, said, "I guess I've been bathed in no less than ten tons of very wet cement. I figured up once I'd caught about 14 thousand pies in my puss and had been hit by 600 automobiles and two trains. Once I was even kicked by a giraffe." Beyond these natural hazards there were the implacable demands of the production schedule. Sennett was committed to making at least one of his little comedies every week. Salaries were by no means exorbitant and the casts were kept on the run as Sennett sought out public events—like *The Kid Auto Races at Venice* (California) in which Chaplin first donned his tramp costume—to use as cheap background for the little films.

Sennett's supreme creation was that magnificently inept constabulary, the Keystone Kops. All his life Sennett regarded the policeman as one of God's more absurd creations, believing that his pitiful attempts at dignity in the face of man's obvious irrationality were a sure sign of the world's essential idiocy. Sennett longed to record the fools cops made of themselves. When he succeeded at last in doing so, he discovered that his pictures seemed to focus a grand old American habit of thought, one shared and savored by millions of his countrymen. If there is one symbol of the art of Sennett, it is of the Kops, mounted on a decrepit flivver, their blue-clad arms and legs protruding in wild tangles, their faces set in masks of stolid dignity, pursuing a miscreant through the wastelands of southern California, on which the outlines of the megapolis to come were barely sketched in. A wild swerve around a trolley car, a near miss of a wandering mongrel, a brush of the bumper with a speeding train, the sudden disembarkation as the car crashes against tree or hydrant (how was it that the Kops always missed the moving hazards and hit the stationary ones?). Then the chase on foot, through the alleys and backyards, in which all the sprinklers were unaccountably turned on, finally the quarry coming to ground, naturally, in a pastry shop or restaurant, offering its tempting array of missiles to be hurled by one and all.

What did it all mean? The chase offered a dozen possibilities of interpretation: it was a comment on all who pursue goals with too much zeal and not enough sense, it was a dramatization of the individual's struggle against society or organization, it was a grand thumb in the eye of authority. But most of all it was good, clean fun. And it is one of the things for which our movie-makers have lost the knack, one of the things about which nostalgia plays us no tricks. The chases (and comedies in general) were better and funnier in the old days than they are now. And Mack Sennett was one of the very, very few who made genuine folk art while working in a mass medium.

Alas, his day was short. As the trend toward feature-length films gained momentum his little films came to seem unimportant, and his attempts to make longer ones were not totally successful. As the twenties wore on, his inventiveness waned and his best clowns left him for grander enterprises. The sound film finished him completely. But in the directness, energy, and wild humor of his best work he set a style and a standard for American films of all types that have great historic importance.

Griffith, Ince, Sennett—these are the great creative names of the American motion picture in the days of its lusty adolescence in the period 1912–1918. But they were by no means the only ones bending the twig which would become the mighty papier-mâché oak the industry was at its height.

There was, for instance, the matter of sex. Despite the outcry of the reformers, the early one-reel films were, for the most part, remarkably free of this dangerous element. But it is doubtful that any product designed for mass consumption by the American public can long remain in a state of total innocence. In 1913, the industry, again against the better judgment of its proprietors, finally reached out and firmly grasped the forbidden fruit. The instrumentalities of fate were a director for Carl Laemmle's IMP concern and a film cutter. It was the studio's frugal policy to let its directors think they were shooting one-reel films but, in various devious ways, encourage them to shoot enough extra material so that a clever film editor could stretch the product to two reels. The fear, of course, was that if the directors knew they were filming longer, more important films, they would demand higher salaries. It is, incidentally, an excellent measure of the contempt in which even those most intimately connected with the movies held the medium, that the directors apparently never checked the final product closely enough to observe that it had magically been lengthened.

Anyway, in the course of encouraging director George Loane Tucker to shoot extra film, editor Jack Cohn became friendly with him and, in time, his collaborator on a mighty project kept secret from their IMP employers. They were attracted by the possibilities of a screen play based on the widely publicized investigations of white slavery which had occupied the minds of the popular press and the reformers for at least twenty years around the turn of the century. On the sly, Tucker, Cohn, and three other collaborators shot the film, using IMP equipment and actors. All pledged to underwrite the production should their employers refuse to accept it when it was finished. Laemmle hesitated before agreeing to release *Traffic in Souls*. It was, despite its highly moral ending, a very racy item for its time, and it was also six reels in length—dangerously long for an industry still trying to make up its mind about the wisdom of feature-length films.

Pictures of that length had been mainly foreign imports and, since they dealt with more exalted subjects, were shown at advanced prices in legitimate theaters. Although Laemmle, on second thought, believed the $5,700 production might have some exploitation value, he did not quite know what to do with the film. Opposition on the board of directors was accusing him of running a very slack ship. Imagine a picture being produced in his own shop and Laemmle not knowing about it until it was finished! In an effort to find theaters to show the feature— the nickelodeons could not handle it—he sold a one-third interest to the Schubert chain for $33,000. Universal now had an almost 700 per cent profit and the picture had not been shown yet. By the time it completed its sensational run it grossed $450,000.

Sex had reached the screen to stay. Competitors rushed to the screens with other versions of the "Vice Trust" story; there were studies of abortion, unwed motherhood, even the perils of contraception. All were profitable, but all surrounded their subjects with a great deal of moral uplift. It remained for William Fox, Laemmle's greatest competitor in the publicity sweepstakes, to allow the American screen to pursue sex just because it was—and is—there.

The instrument of Fox's grand design was one Theodosia Goodman, the "circumspect and demure" daughter of a Cincinnati tailor. For her, Fox and his associate genies concocted a new name—Theda Bara—and a legend. She was, they said, born in the Sahara, the love child of a French artist and his Arabian paramour. Her name was an anagram for "Arab death." They cloaked her in black, accenting the deathly pallor of her flesh, surrounded her with the symbols of death—mummy cases, ravens, skulls. To love her, they implied, was to die, or at the very least to be unmanned. Her first film, *A Fool There Was*, demonstrated this innuendo graphically. The name for her sort of girl, a "vamp" (short for vampire), became a part of the language. Alas, Miss Bara's career was considerably shorter than that of the word she introduced. Her first film was made in 1914. Within four years her fad had waned, and by 1925 she had made her last abortive attempt at a comeback. The trouble was that the screen personality concocted for her was just too rich. To audiences beginning to awaken from Victorian prudery she may have seemed the very incarnation of their long-repressed fantasies. But to audiences just a few years later, after World War I had succeeded in overturning the old morality, she must have seemed a ludicrous figure indeed. She was quite simply too *fatale* a *femme* to be believed—particularly in an age just learning that sex could be fun.

Her historic importance is, perhaps, as the first example of a star personality created entirely by the boys in the back rooms of the movie business; the first of those pathetic creatures who, trying to live up to their publicity, are finally overwhelmed by it; whose public, first bemused by the grotesque exaggeration of the manufactured personality, suddenly finds its fascination turning to amusement. Such creatures become self-created parodies almost without knowing it. Their only hope is to join in the fun being created at their expense, and every movie age has had its sex symbol who has attempted to rescue her career by playing her role for laughs—Harlow, Monroe, even Garbo just before her retirement. Unfortunately, Miss Bara paid the price of pioneering. She discovered the new country but did not know how to get home again.

Others did. They reached the heights in those early days, and they were heights as towering as any have since scaled; some of them even made it back to civilization again with psyches and bankbooks intact. None were to do better than the first three superstars of the screen— Mary Pickford, Charles Chaplin, and Douglas Fairbanks—who would, with D. W. Griffith, climax the emergence of the actor as the most important component of the movies as a commercial package when they formed United Artists, the first major production company controlled by stars, in 1919.

Until they joined forces, Pickford and Chaplin were rivals, in the sense that each attempted to gain contracts which would top the other's latest deal. "Little Mary" preceded Chaplin to the screen by some four years, but her background, like that of so many of the early stars, was similar to his—full of small parts and long tours, theatrical boarding-houses, and high hopes.

Mary Pickford was born Gladys Smith in Toronto and inherited from an ambitious mother the tenacity and shrewdness which marked her quick climb to the top. She played her first role in a Toronto stock company at age five (allegedly having been forced to the stage when the family business, a candy store, failed); at twelve she was playing leads;

in her early teens she was touring; and when she was either sixteen or seventeen (historians disagree on the point) she got her first Broadway job in *The Warrens of Virginia,* whose producer, David Belasco, also gave her the Pickford name.

When the play closed, she headed downtown to 11 East Fourteenth Street, to look for a summer job at Biograph. D. W. Griffith was then in charge of production and he immediately gave her a part in a one-reeler called *The Lonely Villa.* It was about a mother and her children besieged by bandits in, of course, a lonely villa. Liking her performance, he gave her the feminine lead in Biograph production number 3575, publicly known as *The Violin Maker of Cremona.* Within the next three years "the girl every man wanted—for his sister" (as Alistair Cooke put it) was lured from studio to studio by ever higher offers—from Biograph to IMP to Majestic and back to Biograph. Her sojourn there was short, just long enough to introduce a couple of friends from her touring days—the Gish sisters—to Griffith. She returned to the stage to appear in Belasco's *The Good Little Devil,* and it proved to be the best of her many moves.

At the time Adolph Zukor was launching his Famous Players company. This was the first of many attempts to add "class" to the movies and was, as we have noted, the outgrowth of Zukor's success with the importation of a Sarah Bernhardt film from France. Famous Players had two classifications for its picture (A and B). The A films featured famous stage actors in cinematic reconstructions of legitimate successes. The B's were routine program movies similar to those the other studios were grinding out. It was decided that Little Mary had enough of a stage reputation to qualify as a "Famous Player" in the little B pictures and, indeed, enough of a screen reputation to help them at the box office.

Of course, the A pictures, with the Broadway hams strutting and fretting in their parts, turned out to be the least successful of the Famous Players releases. The mass public did not have enough "culture" to appreciate the art of these films. All they saw were stilted, photographed stage plays, lamentably lacking in the action and narrative drive they had come to expect of the movies. What the public liked were the B's, which moved along at a merry clip. And what they liked best of all was the golden, innocent Mary Pickford, plucky and resourceful as she defended all the virtues—and most importantly, her own—from the manifold perils her inventive scenarists endlessly devised. By 1914, with movies growing longer and longer and with each of them therefore representing a bigger gamble, Adolph Zukor realized that his youthful star was the strongest source of his prosperity. The promise of being able to show the newest Pickford when it came along was enough to make exhibitors swallow a quantity of indifferent pills. The Pickford movies themselves were wildly successful; Zukor was paying his star $1,000 a week.

An offer from a Chicago company to make a serial—that year's rage in the movie business—for $208,000 forced Zukor to give Little Mary a raise. It was to an amount exactly half that offered by Chicago, but Zukor could promise her much more prestige than the serial men could offer. A year later Miss Pickford was half-owner (with Zukor) of a production company releasing her films through Famous Players, with a drawing account of $2,000 a week. By the spring of 1916 Zukor was prepared to raise the drawing account to $4,000, but Little Mary had other ideas. In that spring at least a half-dozen production concerns were briefly under the impression that the "Glad Girl" (who was also earning pin money by lending her name to soap endorsements, a music publisher, and a manufacturer of automobile radiator caps) had agreed to come to work for them. It was part of an elaborate campaign to raise Zukor's ante. It worked. On June 24 Mary Pickford received the screen's first million-dollar contract, guaranteeing her $1,040,000 for two years of work for Famous Players. "She never stopped listening and learning," D. W. Griffith, who could have used some of her business acumen, commented mildly. "She was determined to learn everything she could about the business." How very well she learned! An early film historian, Benjamin Hampton, was to note that by 1917–1918 movie theaters, studios, and exchanges represented investments of several million dollars and employed 100,000 people but that "Mary Pickford remained the industry's most valuable asset. . . . Mary Pickford is the only member of her sex who ever became the focal point of an entire industry. Her position was unique; probably no man or woman will ever again win so extensive a following." Samuel Goldwyn however, and as usual, had the last word. "It often took longer to make one of Mary's contracts than it did to make one of Mary's pictures," he sighed.

It took Charles Chaplin less time to reach the financial pinnacle he was to share with Pickford, though it required just as much hard bargaining to bring him to contractual terms. After a poverty-plagued London childhood he came to this country as one of the players in the Karno Pantomime Company, presenting such English music-hall routines as "A Night in a London Club" on the American vaudeville circuits in 1913. Mack Sennett caught the act in Los Angeles and decided that Chaplin might be a useful addition to his stock company—perhaps even a replacement for Ford Sterling, his leading comic, who was about to leave for a more lucrative job. His East Coast partners caught up with Chaplin in Philadelphia and signed him. He spent some time idling about the Keystone lot before he was put to work—wearing a handlebar moustache and a top hat—in a one-reeler, *Making a Living*. He donned his famous tramp costume for the first time when Sennett saw him standing around watching another film being made and asked him to contribute some gags to it. Chaplin claims that by the time he had scrounged the elements of his attire from the wardrobe department, the entire nature of the character who was to become the most famous in screen history had become clear to him. Amidst the frantic activity of the Keystone gang, the little fellow quickly attracted attention through the quiet subtlety of his performances, the almost balletlike precision of his comic inventiveness. By the spring of 1914, Chaplin had begun to be noticed, and the posters of him in his inimitable make-up and costume had a decidedly good effect on a theater's business. Whereupon Mack Sennett decided that it was time for him to embrace the feature craze. Since 1914 was also the year Griffith started to make *The Birth of a Nation,* it was logical for his comic counterpart to attempt to wedge himself back into the limelight now focused on the European features as well as on the gradually lengthening American product. Sennett's first feature was a six reeler, still frequently shown on American screens today—*Tillie's Punctured Romance.* His star insurance was not Chaplin, but rather a popular vaudevillian, Marie Dressler. It was Chaplin, however, who stole the picture and whose career benefited most from the picture's success. By January 1915, Chaplin was working for a rival firm, Broncho Billy Anderson's Essanay, directing and starring simultaneously. His salary was $1,250 a week, which the studio guaranteed with a publicity blast that fixed Chaplin firmly in everyone's mind forever. A year later Chaplin went on to yet another studio, this time for $670,000 a year. Two years after that he signed with First National for $1,075,000 to produce a dozen two reelers. By 1919 he was a partner in United Artists, producing his own films.

Unlike Mary Pickford, who was but the first of the many virginal types to become the embodiment of the American dream of perfect femininity, Chaplin was a screen artist of genuine distinction. There have been a thousand Pickfords through the years. There has been but one Charlie Chaplin. The simplest interpretation of his tramp character—the "little fellow," as he called him—is probably the best. He was eternally the average man at his best: hopeful, inventive, constantly at war with his environment, constantly acting out the dream so many of us share—the dream of being able to escape simply by setting off down the road to find a new life when things get too tough.

The character maintained its viability through the years of World War I, through the gaudy twenties, even late into the thirties when Chaplin kept his silence despite the revolution caused by talking pictures in Hollywood. But his production slowed, and after the coming of sound he made only two films that revolved exclusively around the character of the "little fellow." These pictures, *City Lights* and *Modern Times,* were, in their comic sequences, as inventive as any others he had done. But both contained heavy doses of sentimentality, while the later movies, *The Great Dictator* and *Limelight,* were more self-consciously arty than Chaplin's admirers enjoyed admitting. Only the ill-received *Monsieur Verdoux,* shocking in the bitter absurdity of its humor, had an artistic integrity to match the early films. The trouble was that the tramp character had lost some of its validity as a comment on the human condition. As Robert Warshow shrewdly pointed out, the relationship between the tramp and the rest of society had been, until the cataclysmic thirties, an essentially innocent one. Neither understood the other when they came into accidental conflict, but these conflicts, however hilarious, contained no anger. If there was any message in them it was "live and let live." But as fascism rose in Europe and depression spread in America, the retention of innocence in the relation between the individual and the great world became increasingly difficult. The society through which the "little fellow" moves in *Modern Times* and *The Great Dictator* is actively malevolent. It refuses to allow the individual to escape. No longer can the little tramp shrug, adjust his pitiful raiment, and set off down the open road in search of a better place. The open road is itself a superhighway, out of human scale and no place for a man alone on foot. No wonder Chaplin seemed to grope in the late years of his career. No wonder his one clear, successful artistic statement of the last two decades has been a remarkably bitter one, reflecting, perhaps, his own mood, as publicity about marital troubles, tax problems, and political beliefs turned the know-nothing public against him. He has lived in exile in Switzerland for years, generally refusing to allow his films to be shown in America.

Other early stars also had to face the problem of adjusting to changing times and tastes. Douglas Fairbanks, a high-spirited stage actor, was brought to Hollywood by Triangle. D. W. Griffith, during his sojourn as production chief of that studio, could not abide him. Fairbanks was entirely too bouncy, too ever-smiling for his taste. He therefore assigned a team to produce Fairbanks epics and stayed away himself. The result was considerable freedom for Fairbanks to develop his screen acrobatics to great heights, and the concoction of a screen character, chiefly by screen writer Anita Loos (later author of *Gentlemen Prefer Blondes*), of Fairbanks as a quick, breezy, optimistic, shallowly bright young man. He represented the best characteristics of the new urbanized (or urbanizing) male; his scripts generally imposed upon him the task of bringing this new wisdom, generally in wisecrack form, to various nations less privileged than the United States. "At a difficult time in history [around World War I] Douglas Fairbanks appeared to know all the answers and knew them without pretending to be anything more than an 'all around chap, just a regular American,'" Alistair Cooke wrote. He quickly became enormously popular, but once the war ended, and a new mood came to America, Fairbanks changed his screen vehicles, producing at United Artists the huge, swashbuckling, romantic adventures for which he is now best remembered. His gymnastics became more elaborate than ever, but so did his plots, settings, and basic characterization. His critics missed the lightness of his older films, a lightness which was the equivalent of his character's lightness of mind and foot. But Fairbanks, like his wife, Mary Pickford, was a shrewd businessman; he sensed the changing mood of the times and willingly sacrificed some of his old art to retain his eminence.

Fairbanks summed up his aesthetic of the film in an article for *Vanity Fair* in this fashion: "The art of the screen is almost purely emotional—as a painting, an opera, or a church service is emotional. Without sacrificing this most important value, it cannot teach, philosophize too much, or, in short, attempt to address itself, as words do, to the thought process." It is a very sensible film-making philosophy, and though it may have been simply an easy explanation for the ease with which Fairbanks shifted his film goals as the emotional climate changed, it is well for the modern reader to bear it in mind in this period when the intellectual appreciation of cinema has reached a height and emotional values are at a critical discount.

Adaptation to changing tastes did not appeal to the other great star of the prewar days, William S. Hart. He had spent most of his boyhood in the West and had conserved a great passion for it—though he had spent a great deal more time as an actor in stage melodramas. When he drifted into the movies in 1914 it was thought that westerns were a vanishing vogue at the box office. Thomas Ince paid Hart just $75 a week to make his first film, in which he played a villain. Ince then starred him in two heroic roles, in *The Bargain* and *On the Night Stage*, after which he sent Hart back East, thinking he had got all the use he could out of him. He was very wrong. *The Bargain* turned out to be a box office hit. Hart was hastily summoned back to the Coast, before he could find out just how valuable he was, and given a $125 a week contract—very low even for 1914. Hart began directing, and frequently writing, his own pictures. Compared to the nonsensicality of Broncho Billy's earlier westerns and the romantic unreality of the films turned out by his only serious rival, Tom Mix, Hart's westerns were models of form. They had a stark reality, combined with a sensitive appreciation of the symbolic values of western scenery, that was quite remarkable, particularly at this moment of screen history. But Hart's major creation was his screen character—the good-bad man who rides out of nowhere, sets things to rights, and moves on toward an unknown future. Where has he come from? What does he want? Why does he appear on the side of law and order when it seems that he could as easily enlist on the enemy's side? This ambiguous character, the staple of westerns (and of other action dramas as well), has had a limitless appeal for American audiences, representing as he does a sureness about his individuality, his masculinity, that needs no explanation, no external motivation. He acts not so much to defend abstract concepts of justice and morality as to defend his self-image against the intrusive world.

So, at least, goes the most persuasive explanation of Hart's personality and the hundreds of screen characters that extend in an unbroken chain from it to our own time. Hart took a simpler view of his activities. As his success grew greater and greater he developed a mystical attachment to the American West. "These hills were mine, and had been mine since my birth," he wrote in one of his books. He hated the Hollywood high life, was ill-used financially, first by Ince, then by Zukor's Famous Players Company, and finally by United Artists, where he sought to improve his fortunes. He was really only happy on his ranch or on location making a film where he "was surrounded by no greedy grafters, no . . . slimy creatures—just dogs, horses, sheep, goats, bulls, mules, burros, and . . . men."

His own inventiveness declined (or at least became erratic) in the twenties and popular favor attached itself firmly to his more glamorous contemporary, Tom Mix. Ten years after his screen debut Hart retired for good to his ranch and devoted himself to writing ornate, oddly old-fashioned books about "his" West. He never married, and he emerged from the ranch only occasionally, to make cameo appearances in a handful of shorts and features, to act as technical advisor on westerns, to sell an original story to some producer. He turned down the comeback opportunity of a lifetime when he rejected a part in the twenties' greatest western success, *The Covered Wagon*. He thought the script lacked his kind of realism. He also refused to develop the valuable oil deposits which lay beneath his land because he did not want derricks cluttering up his horizons.

Thus, the rise of the star system and the careers of the four greatest stars of the movies in what has been called "the age of innocence." There were literally hundreds of others who, like them, helped Hollywood stabilize itself through the simple process of repeatedly lending their names—and, occasionally, talent—to exploitation. All of them, then and now, have faced the crises of shifting public favor, of new styles replacing the ones they developed. Some have survived, like Fairbanks and Pickford; some gave up, like Hart; some found themselves lost and groping, like Chaplin, for new modes in which to express themselves. The importance of the stars of the period 1913–1920, however, transcends any single screen personality. The success of this early group proved an economic theory—that personalities could give a studio a kind of continuity of sales which could not be achieved by ideas, exploitation, or even art. With production and distribution apparatus already in place (and working well), with a technique of cinematic story-telling rapidly developing, thanks to Griffith, Ince, Sennett, and the director-stars, Chaplin and Hart, the perfection of the star system was the final touch needed to assure an infant industry that it would grow into healthy economic (if not aesthetic) adulthood. The production system that developed in the teens of this century is that system that prevailed, with very few changes, through all the years of Hollywood's greatness. It is a system that is only now coming full cycle, returning to the proportions (and to the opportunities for some freedom of artistic action) which prevailed in the years before, during, and just after the World War I.

Films of the Postwar Decade

Lewis Jacobs

*Lewis Jacobs is one of the ablest historians of the American motion
picture. The following selection is a part of his monumental work,* The
Rise of the American Film.*

The movies produced between 1919 and 1929 are eloquent social
documents on a lively era in American life. So thoroughly does the
spirit of the decade saturate the films that they are distinguished perhaps more for their innocent reflection of contemporary life than for
their technical advances, remarkable though these were. This is true
even in the case of such important directors as Erich von Stroheim,
Fred Murnau, and Ernst Lubitsch. While valuable innovations in the
motion picture craft were coming into being in Europe, Hollywood
was content almost exclusively with titillating the senses of the increasingly prosperous American movie-goer.

The addition of the middle class and well-to-do to the movie audience,
already apparent on America's entrance into the World War, was now
complete. After 1919 motion pictures with rare exceptions—notably
Charlie Chaplin's comedies—were made to please the middle class. The
working man as a subject for films disappeared after the war, reappearing only when the depression reawakened interest in his milieu. It was
the leisure class that now became the focus of the cinema: their life
was mirrored on the celluloid slickly and ingratiatingly.

Recovering from the excitement of the Armistice, the public soon
became aware that the so-called victory was an empty honor; the war,
a business maneuver. The shattering of principles, the loss of confidence
in leaders, the liberals' lack of resolution at the crucial time all induced a contempt for political progressivism. Prohibition became a
federal law; the "Red scare" reached unprecedented extremes in the
Palmer Raids; intolerance was rampant.

* By permission of Lewis Jacobs, *The Rise of the American Film: A Critical
History.* Harcourt, Brace & World, Inc., New York. © 1939.

Assailing the objectives of the war, denouncing the atrocity stories as myths, salving an embittered and tired populace with the slogan "back to normalcy," Warren G. Harding—staunch Rotarian and dark horse, of whom Alice Longworth once said, "Harding was not a bad man. He was just a slob"—replaced Woodrow Wilson, the broken idealist, as President of the United States in 1920. The government was now in the hands of the business men. Extreme conservatism replaced progressivism as the cynical nation eschewed political embroilments of any kind and began to ride high on prosperity.

The end of the war saw violent reverses in manners and morals. "The license of war time, trench coarseness and materialism, the sex life of great masses of young males held long without feminine companionships Fred Lewis Pattee,[1] now bore their fruits. Changes in morals already of the better kind, the atheism and pessimism bred in camps," to quote begun as a result of the new scientific discoveries and attitudes were speeded by the popularity of Freudian psychology and the growing economic independence of women. The lust for thrills, excitement, and power, the recklessness and defiance of authority condoned by governmental policy, and a general social callousness due to the war, all combined to produce a moral uncertainty and laxity unprecedented in American history.

Two social currents therefore ran parallel at this time: reactionism in political and economic life and revolutionary attitudes in ethics. Belief in the old order of things having been undermined, idealism fell back before materialism; respectability and gentility became old-fashioned. Most of the post-war generation, impatient and bitter, wanted above all to be free of the old dogmas. Disdainful of anything that smacked of the past, they constantly rebelled against tradition and convention.

Restrained as life had been during the war days, it was now unbridled. Sexual promiscuity, faithlessness in marriage, divorce, bad manners, the hip flask, and general cynicism became popular as millions of people attempted to escape from responsibilities of all kinds. Americans surrendered themselves to fads and sensations: Emile Coué's "every-day-in-every-way" philosophy, the tabloids, the radio, Mah Jong, the Leopold and Loeb "thrill murder," Freud and the Libido, crossword puzzles, the Dayton trial, Florida and the building boom, golf, Eskimo pies, speakeasies, night clubs, roadhouses, bathing-beauty parades, Lindbergh, Ford's new Model A automobile, the stock market, Al Capone and gang rule in Chicago. All the while King Jazz titillated the nerves of the nation and gave the era its name.

Movies, like the Supreme Court, followed the election returns. They took up the cause of business, grew cynical, and participated in the repudiation of pre-war conventionality. Like the tabloids of the day, hundreds of films specialized in speed, spice, and spectacle. "Jazz films" by the middle of the period had superseded the last of the pictures in the pre-war tradition, substituting materialism and freedom for the old idealism. Popular directors of the previous era, such as Porter, Blackton, and even Griffith, could no longer satisfy the national appetite, just as popular novelists of the past—Hall Caine, Marie Corelli, Laura Jean Libby—were now "old stuff." These producers and writers were all moralists, and the public was tired of morality. People wanted to shock and be shocked.

Films attacked the genteel tradition with ever-increasing boldness, mirroring a nation that was recklessly experimenting, experiencing, asserting its right to live its own life regardless of age, class, or tradition. Hollywood movies pivoted almost exclusively on sex and sensation. Toward the close of the period the critical realism that had been evident in the works of literary rebels began to be manifested on the screen and to portend a change. The main traits of these ten years as reflected in films, however, were indifference to social responsibility and absorption in the "individual."

The reaction from progressivism was sharply revealed in film attacks on labor, liberalism, and Bolshevism. In the fright over the recent successful revolution in Russia, intolerance was running high. The business man's government unofficially enlisted the motion pictures, now that their war duties were ended, to do their bit in upholding capitalism. The government condoned Red scares, Palmer raids, race riots, and the expulsion of Socialist assemblymen in New York State, and sought to end the post-war tide of strikes in the building trades, shipping, stockyards and shipyards, subways, the shoe industry, communications, mines, and railroads. At the same time it had the task of pacifying the men returning from France. A "gentlemen's agreement" was soon concluded between the national administration and the motion picture industry. It was reported in *The New York Times* for January 12, 1920:

> The movies will be used to combat Bolshevik propaganda as the result of the conference held yesterday. . . . Mr. Lane [Secretary of the Interior] emphasized in his address the necessity of showing films depicting the great opportunities which industrious immigrants may find in this country, and of stories of poor men who have risen high. He suggested that the industry organize immediately to spread throughout the country the story of America as exemplified in the story of Lincoln.

Movie makers earnestly set about to do their duty. Pictures painted Bolshevism in the blackest terms and declared that Americans would not for long ". . . tolerate or be misled by such foreign ideas." *Bolshevism on Trial,* based on Thomas Dixon's *Comrades* and advertised as an impartial representation of all sides of the question, was in reality a violent denunciation of the "impracticability of idealism, the eternal selfishness of human nature," and "the lunacy of free love." *The New Moon* caricatured the Bolshevik as indolent, lustful, cruel, vile. *Dangerous Hours* demonstrated how Bolshevism victimized everybody—the dreamer, siren, fanatic, coward, good-natured dupe, misguided student, bully, street woman, sneak, and old lady. *The Uplifters*, a film based on Wallace Irwin's book, satirized parlor Bolshevism. *The Undercurrent*, a variation on a favorite theme, told of the returned soldier who, "misled," becomes embroiled in "Red plots," only to perceive the danger at the last moment and turn on "the destroyers."

A steady and emphatic stream of movies pointed out the need for the laborer and employer to get together and co-operate against their mutual foe, Bolshevism. *The Right to Happiness* posed the question, "Which would you rather have in this country—destruction under the Red flag or construction and co-operation under the American flag?" *Democracy, The Vision Restored* urged capital and labor "to kiss and make up." *The Other Half* showed that the man from the "classes" as well as the man from the "masses" has his problems. *A Child for Sale* suggested that striking laborers and profiteering capitalists were both responsible for the prevalent industrial unrest. *Paid in Full* told the tale of a clerk who "thought the world owed him a living" and of "the wife who saved him from his own folly." *The Little Church Around the Corner* depicted angry coal miners striking for better safety conditions. (The minister, performing the miracle of curing a deaf-mute before their eyes, convinces the workers to return to their mines and arbitrate their differences with the employer, who has also been chastened by the miracle.) *The Dwelling Place of Light*, boldly advising wealthy mill owners not to pursue working girls, was one of the few films to indicate that strikes may be caused by injustices.

These pictures clearly indicate the post-war antagonism between capital and labor, but as the years advanced, the issue lost some of its urgency. With a rising bull market, with prosperity seeping through the nation, labor was placated, industrial unrest diminished, and confidence in business rule became entrenched. The "gentleman's agreement" between the government and Hollywood no longer demanded action. Hollywood was learning, in fact, that the populace was more interested in sensations than in politics or economics, and desired above all to escape social controversy. The screen therefore devoted itself to meeting these new demands.

At this time the pre-war type of movie, with its emphasis on religion, parental love, self-sacrifice, duty, devotion to home and family, and contentment with one's lot, was making its last stand in such pictures as *Humoresque, Madame X, The Little Shepherd of Kingdom Come,*

Way Down East, Broken Blossoms, Over the Hill, and *Eyes of Youth.* These films were holdovers of pre-war sentimentality. Their values were based upon virtues soon to be mocked and openly defied, upon a code of loyalty soon to be completely broken up.

The new materialistic standard and the rebellion against outmoded dogmas were first manifested on the screen in two signal "hits" of the blundering post-war year of 1919: *The Miracle Man* and *Male and Female. The Miracle Man* frankly and shockingly depicted the hero (Thomas Meighan) as a racketeer and crass materialist who seeks only easy graft. It openly acknowledged sex magnetism and the "sheer brute instinct which holds Rose to Burke." Such outspokenness and emphasis on sex were indicative of the new frame of mind, which dealt in "essentials." The exposure of racketeering, a new phenomenon in American life, with its exploitation of honest people for selfish ends, was in itself a significant disclosure of popular interests. Despite the spiritual note on which the film closed, *The Miracle Man* was a portent of the new, hard order of things in which principles were being discarded for material things.

Even more suggestive of the new era was the significantly titled *Male and Female.* A modernization of James Barrie's *The Admirable Crichton,* it related the intimate adventures of a lady (Gloria Swanson) and a butler (Thomas Meighan) on a desert isle, emphasizing the supremacy of sex over class barriers and condoning marital infidelity, "spice," and sensation for their own sake. More daring in its subject matter than any other picture Hollywood had produced, bolder in its attack on the genteel tradition, this film ushered in the new movie showmanship. Throughout it played on the audience's senses with luxurious settings, cave-man love scenes, sensual display. As DeMille, the director, pointed out,[2] "The ruined woman is as out of style as the Victorian who used to faint."

DeMille's quip found ample support in fact during the following years. Hundreds of films, like *The Miracle Man* and *Male and Female,* attacked the genteel tradition, flaunted sex, advocated new morals, condoned illicit and illegal relationships, set up new ideals, established a new tempo in living, and broke down pre-war class distinctions with the new emphasis on money, luxuries, material success. Refinement went out as aggressiveness came in. Films set the pace for the nation as cynicism and disillusionment marked the gradual decline of an old order and the upsurge of a new.

The breakdown of the old order on the screen was signalized first and most markedly by the pictures of Cecil B. DeMille, condoning the loosening of marriage bonds and questioning responsibilities until now conceded to be necessary in home life. The promiscuity and new attitude toward marriage presented in *Male and Female* were carried further in his series of domestic dramas that reversed the previous moral order. *Don't Change Your Husband* (1919) told how a young and beautiful wife (Gloria Swanson) goes to the seashore to arouse her neglectful business-engrossed husband (Elliot Dexter) to remember her. There she meets a "home wrecker" (Lew Cody) and divorces her husband to marry him, only to discover he nags at her continually. Five years pass and they are in bad financial circumstances. Her former husband, on the other hand, has gained greater success. On meeting, they become reconciled and remarry. Ostensibly an argument against divorce, the film predicated the new notions that a woman had a right to break her marriage bonds as she saw fit.

For Better, For Worse (1919), *Something to Think About* (1920), *Why Change Your Wife* (1920), *Forbidden Fruit* (1921), *The Affairs of Anatol* (1921), *Fool's Paradise* (1922), *Saturday Night* (1922), *Manslaughter* (1922), *Adam's Rib* (1923), formed a glittering array of DeMille problem plays of sex intrigues among the wealthy. They disregarded the sanctity of the home and of woman's duty, at all costs, to be a loyal wife and mother, and subordinated all problems to the new major interest of the post-war age, Sex.

Reinforcing these DeMille films were the hundreds of domestic dramas by others that stemmed from these. All emphasized the importance of love in marriage and woman's rights to independence. Wives became the heroines in all sorts of situations. Movies taught them to keep up their appearance and "style" after marriage, convinced them that they had a right to love and attention after marriage, and finally began to suggest that legal bonds should not prevent wives from having an independent life of their own—a prerogative heretofore looked upon as exclusively the property of husbands. *The Amateur Wife, The Misfit Wife, Poor Men's Wives, Behold My Wife,* and *Old Wives for New* all eloquently lectured on "the frump who learns it is important to remain stylish and good-looking after marriage." *Blind Husbands, The Devil's Passkey, Don't Neglect Your Wife, Foolish Wives,* and *The Merry Widow* pointed out that wives and mature women have a right to love after marriage and that business-engrossed husbands cannot expect to hold their "love-starved" wives. *Virtuous Wives, Flapper Wives, Bluebeard's Eighth Wife, Other Men's Wives, Scrambled Wives, The Married Flapper, Week-End Wives,* and *Miss Bluebeard* all mirrored the increasing daring and independence of the woman who engaged in flirtations and was growing ever more astute in using "her chastity as a fence between her and men."

As we already know, a new note in Continental sophistication and marital laxity was brought to the screen in the films of von Stroheim. These were sly thrusts at traditions and sentiments, and their gleeful acceptance by the public indicated how rightly attuned they were to the national state of mind—despite *Photoplay*'s prim remark,[3] regarding *Foolish Wives,* that it was "an insult to every American." Von Stroheim did not treat sex so frivolously as other directors; the underlying tone of even his lightest works was earnest. His insistence upon sex as a serious matter to be openly acknowledged rather than mockingly and teasingly exhibited was one of the reasons for the vast amount of antagonism—and praise—that his films inspired.

As the importance of love in marriage grew and sex became ever more predominant, pictures began to emphasize that disappointment and repression in marital relations (here Freud's influence was plain) were valid reasons for a married woman to have a fling at love and romance. Marriage became an open sesame to freedom rather than a responsibility. Elinor Glyn became the popular author of the day, and her novels were transposed regularly to the screen. *Three Weeks,* perhaps the most renowned of the movies based on her work, told the story of a queen who, bitterly disappointed in marriage, allows herself one romantic interlude. Hundreds of similar tales swamped the screen, thumbing their noses at "Victorian" codes as they justified adventures outside the bounds of marriage.

In the prevalent post-war disillusionment most people sought "escape." The movies obligingly offered substitutes for life in the form of exotic and erotic costume dramas, all affording vicarious satisfactions and extravagant visual magnificence. The phenomenal success of *The Sheik* (1921) climaxed the series of exotic "red-hot romances" begun toward the close of the war and started a cycle of dramas of the "great, throbbing desert": *Arabian Love, Burning Sands, One Stolen Night, When the Desert Calls, Tents of Allah, Sons of the Desert.* The men in all these films were passionate and aggressive lovers who, casting aside all prudence, swept the women off their feet. Films of this sort waned toward the middle of the period as dramas in the jazz spirit became ever more daring.

Serving the same yearning for escape into dream worlds in the early twenties were the excessively sentimental and nostalgic adventure tales of by-gone days. Douglas Fairbanks reached the high peak in his career as a swashbuckling hero in *The Thief of Bagdad, Robin Hood, The Mark of Zorro,* and *The Three Musketeers,* being rivaled by the dashing Ramon Novarro of *The Prisoner of Zenda,* the heroic Milton Sills of *The Sea Hawk,* and the chivalrous John Barrymore of *Beau Brummel.* Sentimentally expressing the "back to normalcy" nostalgia were the sweet Norma Talmadge of *Smilin' Through,* the old-fashioned Marion Davies of *When Knighthood Was in Flower* and *Little Old New York,* and the endless series of films about imaginary kingdoms with imaginary kings winning imaginary queens: *The Bohemian Girl, Young April, Bardelys the Magnificent, If I Were Queen, Valencia*—Graustarkian fables all. These pictures catered to the public desire to forget the brusque, hard world of the moment in a make-believe world of grand romance.

Such story-book films grew fewer in number as the years of prosperity wore on and America grew more hardened and reckless. The farcical treatment of situations that would have been tragedies in pre-war days no longer appeared shocking, and movies had to become ever more daring if they were to titillate their audiences. Marital fidelity was now even ridiculed; adultery and philandering among mature married people were not only frankly condoned but made fashionable and attractive.

Lubitsch's films in particular were attuned to this attitude. In risqué and teasing terms his films all dealt with the flirtations and playfulness of the rich and carefree. His characters were always mature men and women of the world who engaged in their little games with full knowledge of what they were doing: sinfulness was now a spicy social sport rather than the road to a dire fate. *The Marriage Circle, Forbidden Paradise, Kiss Me Again,* and *Lady Windermere's Fan* were high-water marks of this movie fad. *The Marriage Circle* with its humor and its sophistication, portraying the promiscuity in high society between other men's wives and other wives' husbands, all engaging freely in the interplay, became a model for other movie makers and even for the national way of living.

Hollywood offered advice liberally in such films as *Don't Tell Everything, Secrets, Should a Wife Tell?* (the answer was *No*), and recommended philandering in *Honeymoon Flat, Husbands for Rent, Breakfast at Sunrise.* One film bluntly called *Sex* moralized, "Don't do anything to another woman's husband that you would not have done to your own," and included the usual scenes of "wild" dinner parties, amorous adventures, and—despite prohibition—drinking orgies.

In such films marriage as an institution broke down utterly. Desires for family life and its responsibilities were looked upon as old-fashioned. The woman in the home became a whimsicality, and wide-eyed Mary Pickford an emblem of the past. People on the screen lived in apartments, ate out, gave up the home life their elders knew. Childbearing was disapproved, as in *The Very Idea* and *Children Not Wanted,* and the new vogue of adoption was discussed, as in *Married People.* "Companionate marriage," "modern marriage," "free love," terms that rang through the nation, filled the screens: *Affinities, Man and Wife, Modern Marriage, Is Matrimony a Failure?*

Marriage being regarded as a license for escapades, divorce was viewed as the path to even greater freedom. Divorcees and widows, like wives, were considered far more fascinating than young girls. The new pictures time and again showed divorcees victorious in their lives despite their unconventional position in society, as in *The Impossible Mrs. Bellew* and *Divorce Coupons*. Divorce was offered as an excuse for frivolity and excitement in such films as *On to Reno, Reno Divorce, The Merry Widow,* and *Beware of Widows*.

Once marriage and the home had broken down on the screen, there was a breakdown in morals all along the line. Impropriety, promiscuity, illicit sex relations, and bad manners generally were shown as prevailing among married and unmarried alike. Movies reflected the vogue of hip flasks, cocktail parties, speakeasies, petting parties, necking, and recklessness and defiance of all laws, written or unwritten. Morality having been proved to be a useless asset, lovemaking and golddigging and excitement for its own sake became the chief pursuits of the nation —at least in the nation represented by films.

Thus began that remarkable series of jazz-age pictures exemplified in DeMille's works, which, speaking for the hedonism of a nation on the wave of prosperity, helped to set new styles in social behavior and reflected the new standards of living. The old order now crumbled away entirely. The screen world became crowded with dancing mothers, flaming youth, jazz babies, cake eaters, flappers. Revolutions in etiquette, culture, and conduct generally broke out in this new film domain of electrified apartments, Bagdadian bathtubs, seductive boudoirs, hilarious speakeasies, night clubs, and petting parties. Movies, like the tabloids and the confession and sex magazines, now booming, gave their all to the task of giving America sensations.

The screen was invaded by hordes of "hot mammas," bathing beauties, and Volstead violators, as each movie tried to outdo its predecessor in daring licentiousness. Modesty and virginity became absurd as lovemaking took on the appearance of a wrestling match. The movie woman was now thrown around, carried off, flung on the couch by her man in the holocaust of primitive passion. Bedroom farces and other teasers were multitudinous: *The Gilded Lily, Lying Lips, Mad Love, Temptation, Passion Flame, More Deadly than the Male, Love Is an Awful Thing, One Week of Love; Parlor, Bedroom and Bath; La, La, Lucille; Twin Beds*. Movies glorified the smart set (*The Smart Set*), the Long Island set (*Upstairs and Down*), the country-club set (*Darling of the Rich*), and the "very rich, moral and very human humans of the Rolls Royce set" (*The Fighting Chance*). They depicted the *Wildness of Youth, Madness of Youth, Risky Business;* asked *Has the World Gone Mad? Why Be Good?;* and captured the hysteria of *The Jazz Age, The Plastic Age, Flaming Youth, Reckless Youth, Our Dancing Daughters, Children of Divorce, Children of the Ritz,* and *Modern Maidens*. The sermonizing with which such films ended was mocked by the attractiveness with which they portrayed sin. When F. Scott Fitzgerald's *The Beautiful and Damned* was filmed, it was said that

If he depicts life as a series of petting parties, cocktails, mad dancing and liquor on the hip, it is because he sees our youthful generation in these terms . . . it is our youthful fascisti possessing its measure of money and knowledge, fighting against the swing of the pendulum which has brought us the you-must-not era.[4]

Married men and women were shown keeping up with the wild parties and recklessness of their children: *Dancing Mothers, Paid to Love, Love Mart, Man and the Moment, Gigolo, The Mad Whirl* (1925), adapted from Richard Washburn Child's "Here's How," depicted the new family life:

11 A.M. is Bromo-Seltzer hour, when three servants march to the rooms of father, mother and son, who have been out carousing the night before, as well as every other night. The mother "does at 40 what she was not allowed to do at 20." The father has [the] "Jazz microbe at 60." And the subtitle calls him an "expert at squeezing the hand that feeds him." At breakfast table mother dates up with another man and father with another woman, and the servants take advantage of the situation by asking for afternoons off; otherwise they might divulge the secrets. They drink till daylight. Lying around [on the] floor in each other's arms. Girl so drunk the son carries her home, and so the fun goes on.[5]

Middle-aged men and women were advised "to make hay while the sun shines." *Only 38* told the tale of a widow's quest for lost youth. *The Dangerous Age* was a society drama of a husband who runs wild at forty. *The Young Diana* proved that even an old maid can become young if she has the right spirit.

Films featured the lust for youth (beauty packs, bobbed hair, and short skirts were essential in pictures), flattered the masses' new taste for finery and culture (films were notable for interior decoration, travel, sophistication), fed the romantic desire for "freedom" (speakeasy gods and goddesses gamboled in and out of parties), and stumped for the mercenary business psychology of the day by demonstrating the great American dogma that any man can achieve success by high-pressure salesmanship, aggressive scientific business methods, and football-conference huddles.

The mockery of ethics, of the old "inner goodness" of the film heroes and heroines, was paralleled by the new regard for material things. A burning ambition to be identified with the rich, a deep reverence for material goods, characterized American attitudes. Silk stockings, silk underwear, furs, automobiles, phonographs, elaborate furniture, servants, apartment houses, electrically equipped kitchens, hotels, night clubs, country clubs, resorts, sports, colleges—these were paraded across the screen in exaggerated splendor. *Brown of Harvard, The Quarter-*

back, The Flirt, were typical of dozens of films of the "higher learning" variety, all featuring raccoon coats, roadsters, and swank fraternity parties. Money alone talked; clothes were an index of position in life; aggressiveness and ruthlessness were the real virtues; material success alone mattered.

A Slave of Fashion, Ladies Must Dress, Pretty Clothes, Fashion Madness, Let's Be Fashionable, and the equally blatant *Charge It, Madame Peacock, Gimme, Extravagance, The Thirteenth Commandment,* reflected the contemporary passion for clothes and fineries.

Forbidden Fruit (1922), one of DeMille's biggest successes, dramatized the current goals to reach society and to be identified with the rich. A seamstress wife (Agnes Ayres) of a "worthless" husband, poses for a rich woman as one of her dinner guests in order to "vamp" a rich man to delay his departure. At the dinner party, the scene of her hesitation as to which fork to use for the different dinner courses, is said to have amazed Ernst Lubitsch. The importance given such a detail—which had little to do with the plot itself—no doubt served to give him an insight into American psychology. Such an incident mirrored a common predicament of the day, for every shopgirl longed to be accepted as the heroine of the film, into the social circles of the rich, and sought a knowledge of table etiquette, how to dress, how to be introduced, how to order, and how to conduct oneself in general.

Eloquent of the new materialistic credo were such titles as *Look Your Best, It Pays to Advertise, Go and Get It, Do and Dare, The Go-Getter, If You Believe It, It's So, Putting It Over, Success, Get-Rich-Quick-Wallingford, The Three-Must-Get-Theirs, The Miracle of Money,* and *Money, Money, Money.*

Such films encouraged respect for, and even envy of, the expensively "kept" woman, the high-class prostitute. The motto *Ladies Must Live* was proved by silks and satins. The "sisterhood of those that toil not, neither do they spin" were objects of admiration in such films as *Outcast, Rouged Lips, Trifling Women, Pretty Ladies, Lilies of the Field, Ladies of Ease, Bought and Paid For, The Joy Girl, Silk Legs, The Rag Doll.* The harlot and the adventuress were no longer hussies but women to esteem and emulate (*Lady of the Night, A Woman of Paris, A Woman of Affairs*). Money and luxury were presented as major goals in life to be gained at all costs.

The worship of money, hard-boiled materialism, irresponsibility, living for the moment, callousness toward human life, and violent lust for excitement formed a background for the large-scale racketeering and other criminal activity that broke out after the war. The Volstead Act itself made lawbreaking fashionable. The bootlegger, the highjacker, the gangster, and the racketeer flourished as drinking became "smart," as speakeasies and gambling rooms replaced the old saloons, as bars were set up in glamorous surroundings. Colorful entertainment in these establishments where men and women drank freely covered the cheapness of the underworld, investing it with an air of splendor, wealth, and luxury, and above all a spirit of adventure. The illegal liquor and drug traffic thus built a new underworld that was patronized by the respectable; it created a new stratum of life for American society.

At first movies featured racketeering and crooks for their dramatic possibilities, blaming crime on personal afflictions, animosities, and the desire for thrilling adventure. *The Penalty* displayed Lon Chaney as "the legless wonder" who has sworn revenge on society because both of his legs were amputated by a careless doctor after an accident. Bitter and violent, he becomes ruler of the underworld. The removal of a blood clot from his brain by a surgical operation finally restores him to decency. Ridiculous though such a solution appears to us today, in the light of more recent realism regarding crime, it was accepted as plausible then.

In a stream of films Lon Chaney became famous for his characterizations of the underworld ruler: *Partners of the Night, Black Shadows, The Girl in the Rain, Kick In, One Million in Jewels, Dollar Devils, Boston Blackie, Outside the Law,* and the celebrated *The Unholy Three.*

The sinister, ruthless criminal of these films gradually was transformed in succeeding pictures. The underworld became inhabited by the smart set, "the right people"; the gangster was revealed as an enviable hero, quick and intelligent, refined, influential politically and powerful financially. Movies like the tabloids glorified his life, showing it full of exciting adventure, beautiful women, and plenty of money. Although gangsterism was becoming a national scandal, gangsters were not yet popularly regarded as a vicious group of public enemies.

By 1925 Chicago, considered the world center of crime and the Mecca of gangsterdom, had become the cynosure of the nation's attention, and movies were following the tabloids and the stage in reflecting the racketeering and gangster rule prevalent in that metropolis. One of the most popular and revelatory of the films was *Chicago,* adapted from the play of that name. It drew an uncompromising picture of the jazz-mad wife of a simple worker who is unable to supply the luxuries she demands. Failing to get those luxuries, she goes out with a playboy who, by her dispassionate order, is subsequently "bumped off." The ensuing publicity is far from distasteful to her; she revels in the newfound excitement and importance. The outraged husband comes to her defense in court. Sympathy, however, is not with him, but with the luxury-loving wife.

As gangsterism became a more critical national problem toward the close of the twenties, an increasing number of gangster films reached the screen. They were now more realistic. *The Big City, Tenderloin,* and *Chicago After Midnight* emphasized the fact that the complexities of city life make racketeering possible. *The Street of Forgotten Men*, in a tale described as "sordid," exposed the street beggars' racket. Josef von Sternberg's series—*Underworld, The Drag Net, The Docks of New York, Thunderbolt*—and Roland West's *Alibi* acidly depicted the underworld as aggressive and ruthless, as a plague in society. Lewis Milestone's *The Racket* attempted to expose the perfunctory activities of the police against the big city rackets with frankness and seriousness—an attitude soon to become pronounced. It is notable that the hardness and realism introduced in these films were to become the dominating tone in the next period.

The revolution in morality and manners that was taking place had introduced new ideals of personality. The modern girl evolved from flirt to flapper, to jazz baby, to baby vamp, to salamander, and finally to the sophisticated, colorful woman of the world. Wanda Hawley, Julia Faye, and Constance Talmadge were typical of "the young rascals whose bite was more dangerous because it was hidden behind innocent eyes" (*A Virtuous Vamp, Dangerous Business, The Love Expert, In Search of Sinners*). Colleen Moore, Clara Bow, Sue Carol, Madge Bellamy, Louise Brooks, and Joan Crawford typified the "frivolous, promiscuous, mocking type" with "a hard body and long, exposed legs, bobbed hair, bold eyes" (*The Perfect Flapper, Flaming Youth, It, Daughters of Pleasure, Get Your Man*). Gloria Swanson, Pola Negri, Norma Shearer, and Greta Garbo were the prototypes for the ultra-civilized, sleek and slender, knowing and disillusioned, restless, over-sexed and neurotic woman who "leads her own life" (*Flesh and the Devil, A Woman of the World, The Single Standard, Lady of Chance*).

Short skirts, boyish figures, silk stockings, step-ins, cigarettes, and drinking not only emancipated the modern girl from "woman's passive role" but freed her for masculine pursuits as well. The new girl was shown in airplanes, roadsters, and petting parties, with rolled stockings, hip flasks, bobbed hair, and bold aggressiveness. The advertisement for DeMille's *Adam's Rib* prated:[6]

> The modern girl in a new light. . . . With all the luxury of beautiful gowns and magnificent sets that are an integral part of C. B. DeMille's art, *Adam's Rib* reveals the modern girl in her true color, and in a story crammed with action, interprets her impulsive heart to all who wish to appreciate her for what she is.

Provocative, tantalizing, beautiful, the modern girl was further imbued with a fascination that lay in her frank flaunting of sex. Sex appeal became the ultimate criterion of personality. Elinor Glyn's "It" was now an idiom of the American language.

Independent, level-headed, ambitious, the new movie girl used her femininity to obtain a good living, ease, pleasure. In *Soft Living* the stenographer finds it easier to get alimony than to work for a living. *The Taxi Dancer* and *Love 'Em and Leave 'Em* were two of dozens of films showing the emancipated working girl who was out to get what was coming to her. When *Gentlemen Prefer Blondes* reached the screen, *Photoplay*'s editor declared, "If you don't want to see this film version . . . something is wrong with you." *The Golddiggers, The Exciters, The Flapper,* were stories of money hunters, thrill hunters, and sensation mongers.

Typical of contemporary films was *Manhandled,* the story of Tessie McGuire, a little shopgirl whose sweetheart, a shop mechanic, has an invention for a new carburetor. Tessie is invited by the boss to a wild party, where she "plays with fire." Finally she tires of the men she encounters on the boss's level and returns to her old love—now, happily, a millionaire. This story, endorsing the woman's right to sow her wild oats, gave the word "manhandled" to the American vernacular.

The Cinderella tradition of feminine modesty, in which woman is a vassal-in-waiting, was thus supplanted by the post-Ibsen concept of a "devastating," aggressive creature, attractive, smart, seductive, independent, daring, fast. Prince Charming, for his part, was transformed into a dynamic, pursuing, commanding Atlas, crammed with sex appeal, lasciviously bouncing into every parlor, bedroom, and bath of female America. The gods of the screen were no longer spoken of as matinee idols but as great lovers. At first the vogue for the exotic, passionate, Latin man of the world brought to the forefront such personalities as Antonio Moreno, John Gilbert, Ricardo Cortez, Ramon Novarro, Gilbert Roland, and most sensational of all, Rudolph Valentino. Later the American ideal became the energetic, clean-cut, high-pressure go-getter, the apostle of post-war speed and pep—the wise-cracking William Haines (*Brown of Harvard*), the hard-drinking, cynical Richard Arlen (*Rolled Stockings*), the bouncing Douglas MacLean (*A Man of Action*), the self-assured William Boyd (*Two Arabian Knights*), the dynamic George Walsh (*Dynamite Allen*), and the "natural-born world-beater" who summed up all the qualities of this type, Harold Lloyd.

Lloyd, whom Gilbert Seldes[7] called ". . . a man of no tenderness, of no philosophy, the embodiment of American cheek and indefatigable energy," was the particular ideal of the younger generation. The titles of his pictures summed up admirably the philosophy of his apostles: *Never Weaken, Now or Never, Why Worry? Speedy, Get Out and Get Under, Welcome Danger.*

Screen villains were streamlined into "gigolos." They were attractive, nonchalant, sophisticated, witty, "humanly wicked." Lew Cody, Adolphe Menjou, Earle Fox, Roy D'Arcy, Rod La Rocque, Stuart Holmes, Nils

Asther, Lowell Sherman, William Powell, and most strikingly Erich von Stroheim, were the fascinating menaces, the hated, envied men of the world.

Although DeMille's films held the limelight in this period and set the pace, tone, and temper of the movie medium during these gay twenties, a reaction against middle-class materialism began slowly to appear. The first indication of a critical attitude appeared in the work of literary rebels. With the publication of Sinclair Lewis' book *Main Street*, the dominance of the business man's values was challenged. *Main Street* was soon reinforced by other blasts against American civilization, notable among which were H. L. Mencken's book *The American Credo*, Theodore Dreiser's *An American Tragedy*, and John Dos Passos' *Manhattan Transfer*. A bevy of radical magazines such as *Gargoyle, Broom, The Little Review*, and *transition* provided further ammunition for the attack. The flight of intellectuals and artists to Europe to work in an atmosphere "free from Puritan inhibitions," and the publication of that collective cannonade *Civilization in the United States: An Inquiry by Thirty Americans*, called attention to a growing if still localized dissatisfaction with contemporary American life.

The critical realism of the literary vanguard was taken up by various film makers sporadically. Stroheim's brutally realistic *Greed*, Cruze's domestic satires, Vidor's *The Crowd*, Seastrom's sensitive *The Wind*, King's and Robertson's attempts at naturalism, and Chaplin's social satire were all significant. These signs of a serious concern with reality suggested that the broad social outlook that had been coming into being before the war had not been entirely lost.

Auspicious was the popular welcome given to the "documentary" films—factual records of man's struggle with his environment. The first of the "documentaries," Flaherty's *Nanook of the North*, appeared in 1922 in the midst of the deluge of "jazz" films. Its popularity was remarkable in view of the fact that the interest of the nation was at that time in escape, thrills, and personal sensations. *Nanook of the North* initiated a style for motion pictures which has only recently been revived with new vigor. Within the eight years that followed Flaherty's hit a dozen and more such efforts appeared in whole or partly fictionized treatments, notably *Grass, White Shadows in the South Seas, Moana, Tabu*, and *Trader Horn*.

Allied in spirit to the semi-documentary films were the realistic regional dramas, appearing concurrently, that dealt fictionally with contemporary life in various regions and of many classes. These were intended to portray actual social conditions realistically. Some of the stories centered on personal conflicts (*Stark Love, White Gold, Sunrise*), some on social struggles (*The Barker, The Crowd, The Vanishing American*), others on the battle with nature's forces (*Down to the Sea in*

Ships and *The Wind*) and still others with man's own nature as conditioned by himself (*Greed* and *The Tower of Lies*) . A few were accurate appraisals of regional life (*Driven* and *Tol'able David*) .

Other films openly began to mock the false standards of materialism. *Beggar on Horseback* ingeniously travestied the *nouveau riche*, while *The King on Main Street* lightly jeered at the smug small-town life and popular secret societies that had rooted themselves in America. The latter picture shocked one reviewer into exclaiming, "Imagine that two years ago!" Other films such as *Babbitt, Proud Flesh,* and *The Goose Hangs High* derided the inanities and vanities of the social standards people were trying to live up to. A number of films exposed the peculiar twists and idiosyncrasies of people who were concerned only with making money, using it as a yardstick in all their judgments. *The Four-Flusher, The Show-Off, The Nervous Wreck, The Snob, The Idle Rich,* are self-descriptive.

Will Rogers' film *Don't Park There* satirized modern progress and the big city. He finds horses so out of date that he acquires a Ford, but he has to travel over the country trying to find a parking space and, in doing so, gets into the toils of the police. *A Poor Relation* was the story of an empty stomach and the high hopes of poverty. Raymond Griffith, the sophisticated humorist, ridiculed sophistication itself in such parodies as *Paths to Paradise, Hands Up, Wet Paint, You'd Be Surprised, Waiter for the Ritz.* Buster Keaton's satires (*The General, The Navigator*) poked fun at conventions and pomposity, Buster being the weakling lost in a world of gigantic he-men. All such travesties pointed out the weaknesses in contemporary living and, like the gangster films, were to become increasingly common in the next period.

Toward the end of the twenties, the country was riding along merrily on a rising bull market. At no time had wealth appeared so abundant nor was the stampede for a share of it more pronounced. Misgivings and criticisms of the business men's rule were left largely to the literary vanguard and the "ex-patriates." Movies, acquiring sound, burst forth in lavish musicals and when the stock market catapulted in 1929, were out-dazzling each other with ever more spectacular effects.

The national craving for thrills, excitement, escape, and experience during the twenties was manifested by the tremendous patronage movies enjoyed. By 1926 the United States had 20,000 theatres, attended by 100,000,000 Americans weekly. The effect of motion pictures upon the very people whose desires it was attempting to satisfy had increased enormously in thirty years. When Willard Huntington Wright, the noted art critic, observed in 1919[8] that "The motion picture industry's staggering and far-reaching effect on American life has not yet been given proper recognition by historians and scientists," he hardly imagined what vast social territory the American film would yet encompass. In hundreds of towns the moving picture theatre had become the outstanding building—according to Charles Pettijohn,[9] "a civic monument pointed out with pride by citizens, a place of culture where good music and good taste were being cultivated and reading encouraged."

Films during Porter's day, in reflecting reality, had made audiences more receptive and more reflective. Now films were helping people to forget, helping them to avoid reflection. Knowledge and awareness of the real world were rarely dispensed by the screen. Movies were framed to assist people to escape their personal problems, their frustrations, their unhappiness. The Lynds reported in their book *Middletown,* the classic record of the post-war decade, that movies quickened life for the

> youngsters who bulk large in the audiences, for the working man, for the wife and for the business class families who habitually attend. . . . At the comedies Middletown lives for an hour in a happy sophisticated make-believe world that leaves it, according to the advertisement of one film, "Happily convinced that Life is very well worth living."

The American film had thus become by 1929 a more powerful social agency than ever. Reflecting current states of mind, it also deeply influenced them. Its persuasiveness won not only natives of America but Europeans, Asiatics, South Americans, and even Africans. Hollywood, nationally and internationally supreme, was very nearly Americanizing the world. What Maurice Maeterlinck[10] had said at the beginning of the period was, at its end, generally recognized to be true:

> . . . at no time in history has there been such a means of influencing the spirit of men and particularly of women and children. . . . All ideas of duty, justice, love, right, wrong, happiness, honor, luxury, beauty, all ideas regarding the goal of life . . . are ideas implanted by movies.

NOTES

1. *The New American Literature,* p. 461.
2. *Photoplay,* December 1919.
3. March 1922.
4. *Photoplay,* February 1923.
5. *The Educational Screen,* May 1925.
6. *Photoplay,* February 1923.
7. In *The Seven Lively Arts,* p. 15.
8. *Photoplay,* December 1919.
9. *The Motion Picture* (pamphlet).
10. *Photoplay,* 1921.

The Celluloid Safety Valve

Louise Tanner

*Louise Tanner is a perceptive student of the decade of the 1930s. With a particular relevance for the student of the American motion picture, the following essay defines the meaning of movies in that age of sometimes comical and cruel contrasts.** *

"When my father was out of a job during the Depression he would often go to the movies and sit through the feature three times."

This simple statement, more than any other, accounts for the curious fact that the movies of the Thirties were such a flop as a source of Communist propaganda. Some studios—notably Warner Brothers—tried to bring Father to grips with social reality. But most of the cinemoguls agreed with Louis B. Mayer that Dad got all the social significance he needed at home. The script writers of Hollywood might take the Spanish Civil War to heart but they were more concerned with a public that preferred Carole Lombard doing secretarial work in a penthouse with a white telephone. Father sitting there in the dark forgot his own plight as he watched the gods and goddesses of the screen sweeping down marble staircases into dining rooms with a footman behind every chair.

Depression movies portrayed an America devoid of economic conflict. It was—after 1934—also an America devoid of sex. In the pre-Code days Miss Mae West strutted brazenly through *Night After Night* (1932), *She Done Him Wrong* and *I'm No Angel* (1933), sinning without the slightest hint of suffering and adding such classic injunctions to the language as "Beulah, peel me a grape."

Not that pre-Code heroines never suffered. Irene Dunne had a rough time of being John Boles' mistress in *Back Street* in 1932. The wages of sin were visited—in the form of a healthy baby—upon Marlene Dietrich

* From *All the Things We Were* by Louise Tanner. Copyright © 1968 by Louise Tanner. Reprinted by permission of Doubleday & Company, Inc.

in *Blonde Venus,* and Clara Bow in *Call Her Savage.* Constance Bennett suffered the same fate in *Common Clay* (1930), *Born to Love* (1931), and *Rockabye* (1932) —a record which might have discouraged a lesser girl from illicit dalliance. Before the arrival of the little stranger in such pictures the camera focused long and lovingly on the heroine's preparations for bed.

Before 1930 and 1932 there had been a spate of blood-ridden gangster pictures: *The Big House, Little Caesar, The Public Enemy, The Secret Six, Quick Millions,* and *Scarface.* Prominent among the bad boys were Paul Muni, Edward G. Robinson, George Raft. Wallace Beery, Humphrey Bogart, and James Cagney. In *The Public Enemy,* Cagney achieved eminence among male and female audiences by smashing a grapefruit in one girl's face and clipping another on the jaw. In *Vice Squad* in 1931, Paul Lukas immortalized the infamous stool pigeon, "Chile Acuna, the human spittoona."

There were some who claimed that such high jinks had led to the prosecution of Al Capone and other notorious gangsters. A more strait-laced section of the public cried that something must be done.

In 1933 the bishops of the Roman Catholic Church banded together to form the National Legion of Decency. Jewish and Protestant organizations joined with the Legion in a mass boycott of sex and sensation. The old Production Code of 1927–30 was exhumed and rewritten, and the Breen Office—a branch of the old Hays Office—was set up to enforce the code. Penalties were stiff—a $25,000 fine for transgressors. The bishops were able to make the Code stick because at that time the Motion Picture Association held the movie theater circuits in a death grip.

After 1934, sexual overtures were made principally in sign language and desperadoes had it borne in that crime doesn't pay. In *G-Men,* James Cagney switched over to the side of law and order. The *Literary Digest* in 1935 commended Edward Paley and Barton MacLane in a review of that picture for what was termed their "clean cut portrayals of two vicious killers."

Having opened the gates of larger censorship, they were open to smaller censors, too. Movies after 1934 were subject to secular as well as ecumenical wrath. Glass blowers protested the showing of canned beer. Beer can manufacturers resented bottled drinks. Insurance companies wanted to delete all references to accidents. The National Billiard Association protested low-grade poolrooms. The State Department worried over America's reputation as projected by *The Grapes of Wrath* and *Tobacco Road.* When *Beau Geste* was refilmed in 1939, the villains were given Russian names because the export market to Russia was small. When *Idiot's Delight* was filmed by Hollywood, to avoid offending any ethnic group it was set in a mythical country whose inhabitants spoke Esperanto. Movies were accused by a Senate Investigating Committee of fomenting war. Filming of Sinclair Lewis' *It Can't Happen Here* was scrapped out of deference to the delicate sensibilities of Hitler and Mussolini.

Every serious play or book underwent a metamorphosis when it crossed the Mississippi. It was fumigated to meet Code requirements, peopled with a reliable stable of character actors. The result was often barely recognizable to the author. Sometimes a jarring happy ending was tacked onto a fine picture as with James Hilton's *Lost Horizon* or onto the screen version of the grim Broadway play *Little Man What Now*. Sometimes a gamey rustic was physically and morally deloused . . . the Okies in *The Grapes of Wrath,* the hillbillies of *Tobacco Road.* Grandpa Joad and Jeeter Lester were both played by Charley Grapewin. Of the two, Grandpa traveled better. Enough of the tragedy of the Dust Bowl survived in *The Grapes of Wrath* to win for the picture the New York Film Critics Award for 1940. Jeeter Lester, shorn of his sexual and physical itches, was a straw man. As the harelipped Ellie May—sans harelip—Gene Tierney was cornpone Junior League.

The Primrose Path, which on Broadway had shown a dynasty of loose women having a whale of a lot of fun, was presented by Hollywood as a problem drama. Joel McCrea saved Ginger Rogers from a fate which the Broadway heroine was all too ready to embrace. Miss Rogers did not quite make it as a "pigtailed slum Diana." "As a vehicle for the waxing dramatic talents of Ginger Rogers," *Time* magazine commented wryly, "*The Primrose Path* is something of a tumbril."

Sidney Howard's *Dead End* came to Hollywood almost intact with the good guys and the bad guys split—as their creator had intended— strictly along class lines. In the movie version of *Winterset* a gangster got his Production Code deserts when he was killed by his henchmen. He had gone scot free on the stage. *The Children's Hour,* a Broadway drama of boarding-school Lesbianism, was played strictly hetero on the coast. Arthur Kober's *Having Wonderful Time*—once a Rosetta Stone of Jewish dialects—was played by a cast who had undergone mass Aryanization.

Only the cute Sunday School cherubim and seraphim of *Green Pastures* made no attempt to "pass." In 1936 Marc Connolly preserved every Uncle Tomism intact: the dusky angels fishing for catfish from fleecy clouds; Noah laying in a keg of whiskey as a precaution against snakebite. Custard which needed more "firmament" was whipped up by a new Lawd (fresh from a triumph as the cannibal chief in *Tarzan of the Apes*).

A man from Mars seeing *Black Legion, Fury, Dead End, I Was a Fugitive from a Chain Gang, The Grapes of Wrath, Of Mice and Men,* or Warner Brothers' *Wild Boys of the Road* might have gotten the impression that Depression America was something less than the land of milk and honey. Yet few realistic pictures presented the free enterprise system in the merciless light of that social satirist Charlie Chaplin.

City Lights in 1931 opened ironically upon the unveiling of a monument to "Peace and Prosperity" where the homeless little tramp had fallen asleep.

His fortunes throughout the film were dependent on a millionaire inebriate who elevated him to untold heights of prosperity during periodic alcoholic reunions, but who had no recollection of the Little Tramp when cold sober.

Modern Times in 1936 was a savage satire on machine age mores. One had to look to Chaplin to see the Little Tramp turned into an automaton by an assembly line speedup, to see Hoovervilles and luxurious department stores, "free" men jobless on the streets—while criminals in jail at least had the guarantee of a square meal. Chaplin the social philosopher had lost much of his following by the late Thirties, when he made his first talking picture, *The Great Dictator*. The public preferred noncontroversial "screwballs" to Charlie as Adolf Hynkel, "Der Phooey," lasciviously eyeing a globe.

Walt Disney to millions of children was simply the creator of Mickey Mouse, Donald Duck, and Snow White. He had, to be sure, won an impressive number of Oscars: for *Three Little Pigs* in 1933, for *Three Orphan Kittens* in 1934, for *Ferdinand the Bull* in 1938. He also produced *Pinocchio*, invented "Fantasound," and made the chase between a bemused cat and a crafty mouse as much a comic cliché as the custard pie.

Like Chaplin, Disney was often accused of profundity. Author Lloyd Morris in *Not So Long Ago* saw significance in the timing of the hit tune from *Three Little Pigs*. Coming on top of Roosevelt's statement that "We have nothing to fear but fear itself," "Who's Afraid of the Big Bad Wolf?" was for Mr. Morris "an anthem of hope for the whole nation."

When Disney peopled his cartoons with talking steam shovels and garrulous rocking chairs, "was he not depicting a world in which scientists would speculate about the analogies between electronic 'thinking machines' and the human brain?" It was the comedians of the Thirties who inspired the thoughtful search for anthill- and machine-age-type parables.

The moviemakers of the Thirties had a Depression tolerance for what Alistair Cooke has called "the vast progressive school on the steppes." As the earnest Communist of *Ninotchka*, Garbo was converted to capitalist fripperies by Melvyn Douglas. The process could work in reverse. In *Tovarich*, Charles Boyer and Claudette Colbert played down-and-out White Russians forced to hire out as a couple. They ended by coughing up the forty million francs left them as a legacy by the Tsar to the commissar who was messing about with oil rights in Baku and Petrovolsk. Basil Rathbone promised to show the gratitude of the Soviet people by removing the mustache from Claudette Colbert's portrait in the Imperial Palace.

Director Frank Capra occasionally injected a nebulous message into such vehicles as *Mr. Smith Goes to Washington*. But many delightful Capra hits, like *It Happened One Night* (1934), *Mr. Deeds Goes to Town* (1936), and *You Can't Take It With You* (1938) were totally devoid of "preach."

Comedy was the forte of the Thirties. There are few Tab Hunters or Tuesday Welds who can match Myrna Loy and William Powell in the Thin Man series, Jean Arthur and Gary Cooper feeding doughnuts to a horse in *Mr. Deeds Goes to Town,* or Hepburn and Cary Grant in *Bringing Up Baby, Holiday,* or *The Philadelphia Story.* The felines of *The Women* were by-products of the Depression. Will Rogers, a wit of a homelier order, has yet to find an opposite number today. Marx Brothers' revivals still pack them in. Delighted audiences to this day flock to see W. C. Fields in bed with a goat in *My Little Chickadee* or as *The Bank Dick* luring the epicene Franklin Pangborn to his downfall in the Black Pussycat Café.

The drawing room comedies of the Thirties dared but never defied the Production Code. The suspected adulteries of the heroine always turned out to be the result of some hilarious misunderstanding. In *It Happened One Night* Claudette Colbert and Clark Gable find themselves, by a hilarious misunderstanding, sharing a room. They bed down on either side of the tremulous Walls of Jericho in a typical bit of Production Code naughty-naughty-naughty, but damn it all, nice.

In *Theodora Goes Wild,* Irene Dunne became the archetype of the screwball heroine. *The Awful Truth* established her in a league with Claudette Colbert and Jean Arthur. *The Awful Truth* promised more to the prurient than it delivered. Cary Grant suspected Irene Dunne of carrying on with her music teacher. In the ensuing divorce Miss Dunne got custody of Mr. Smith (a fox terrier who already pulled down a fat paycheck as the Thin Man's Asta). Mr. Smith involved Miss Dunne in an embarrassing interlude when he played "go find" with what *Time* called "two shriekingly circumstantial" derby hats in her apartment.

In *My Favorite Wife* (1940) she once again had some explaining to do about an interlude she spent as a shipwrecked lady anthropologist on a desert island with Randolph Scott. Gail Patrick, the Society Menace, had meantime married Cary Grant—with lots of Enoch Arden complications—in front of a comically confused judge.

Miss Dunne hired a balding shoe clerk to impersonate the companion of her island odyssey (provocatively nicknamed "Adam"). When the real Adam stood up on the diving board at the local bath club, she had a *quart d'heure* with Cary Grant almost as *mauvais* as the one with the derby hat.

An art form which was dominated by sweetness and light was the musical. The immense popularity of Deanna Durbin and Judy Garland was attributable to their girl-next-door quality. Both had been launched in the mid-Thirties in the MGM short *Every Sunday Afternoon.* Judy remained with MGM. Deanna was driven into the arms of Universal when MGM failed to pick up her option. Twentieth Century-Fox borrowed Judy for *Pigskin Parade* and she made an immediate hit as the leather-lunged hillbilly singing "It's Love I'm After." She went on to triumph as the beloved Dorothy in *The Wizard of Oz;* to career and marital difficulties with David Rose, Vincente Minnelli, Sid Luft, and Mark Herron; and to return trips to the Palace Theatre where middle-aged spectacles fogged up in a Pavlovian reaction to "Over the Rainbow."

Miss Durbin made her first big hit in *Three Smart Girls.* Later cast as a perennially burgeoning adolescent, in *One Hundred Men and a Girl, Mad About Music, That Certain Age, Three Smart Girls Grow Up, It's a Date, Spring Parade,* and *Nice Girl,* she sweetened for the public an unpalatable dose of classical music. When she attempted to act her age (her first marriage was in the offing about the time of her picture *First Love*) the music went sour. She went on to marital difficulties (Vaughan Paul and Felix Jackson), to career difficulties (*It Started With Eve, The Amazing Mrs. Holliday*), to a third marriage, retirement from the screen, and a weight problem.

The talents of Fred Astaire and Ginger Rogers were more durable. Mr. Astaire was an elegant streak of lightning whose sparse hair, nimble feet, Pinocchio profile, and twirling coattails added up to a strange kind of magic. Like Rex Harrison he was a past master at the art of putting a song across without a voice. A whole generation remembers with delight when he and Miss Rogers went *Flying Down to Rio* in 1933, Mr. Astaire doing "I Won't Dance" in *Roberta* (1935), tapping over Venetian bridges in *Top Hat.* He was assisted by a gallery of minor character actors—Eric Blore, Victor Moore, and Edward Everett Horton, and by writers of *dernier cri* dialogue, as from *Swingtime* (1936): "I often talk to myself. I'm my own grandmother and I have to keep the old girl interested."

The cycle of Dick Powell musicals began when he played opposite Ruby Keeler in *Forty-Second Street* in 1933. In *Gold Diggers of 1935* he danced amid Busby Berkeley settings, introduced the "Lullaby of Broadway," surrounded himself with one hundred beauties playing one hundred pianos and with a predictable cast of minor characters: Gloria Stuart, Alice Brady, Glenda Farrell, and Hugh Herbert as a dimwitted millionaire with a passion for snuff boxes. The same personnel was on hand for *Gold Diggers of 1937*—Dick Powell, Glenda Farrell—titillating the sensibilities of Victor Moore who had taken over Hugh Herbert's role of the tycoon—in this case an amusing hypochondriac. In successive *Gold Diggers* and *Broadway Melodies* Busby Berkeley dressed girls in geometric and floral patterns and photographed them from above. His greatest triumph was in *Flying Down to Rio* where a whole chorus did the Carioca on the wing of a plane.

Stars of the Met—like Broadway playwrights—joined the gold rush. Grace Moore went to Hollywood in *One Night of Love* in 1934, Lily Pons in *I Dream Too Much* in 1935, Gladys Swarthout in *Rose of the Rancho,* even Kirsten Flagstad, who emerged from a miasma of fog, complete with spear and horned helmet, in *The Big Broadcast of 1938*—proof that nobody was above making a bargain with Old Nick.

When Jeanette MacDonald breathed her last "I love you" in 1965 her parting words were right in character. She had appeared with Maurice Chevalier as a somewhat lantern-jawed Merry Widow, in an MGM version in 1934. Like all musicals of the day, it had its amiable eccentric, Edward Everett Horton playing a distraught ambassador, George Barbier as a Balkan monarch and Una Merkel—a figure whose diction established her irrevocably as a child of the twentieth century—as Barbier's coquettish consort.

In 1935 Miss MacDonald was paired with Nelson Eddy in *Naughty Marietta.* The team went on to a succession of hits: *Rose Marie, Maytime, Girl of the Golden West, Sweethearts,* and *Bittersweet.* In *Maytime* she was a singer who fled from loveless marriage into the arms of Nelson Eddy. The Code decreed that the star-crossed pair should not meet till ten years later on the stage of the Met when consummation was well nigh impossible. The whole thing ended with a shooting and was graced with an extraordinarily mixed bag of songs: "Carry Me Back to Old Virginny," "Les Filles de Cadiz," and excerpts from Tchaikovsky's *Fifth Symphony.*

Like Fred Astaire, Mr. Eddy occasionally strayed from the straight and narrow to make a picture with Eleanor Powell. Such was *Rosalie,* in 1937. Eddy studied for five weeks with Lieutenant Frederick M. Thompson of West Point to give credibility to scenes where he led a flying wedge of chorus boys in "The Caissons Go Rolling Along." It is not recorded what Lieutenant Thompson thought when Mr. Eddy stood under Eleanor Powell's window and announced, "I'm your dream soldier reporting for duty."

Rosalie pulled a switch on the Balkan prince wandering among his people incognito. Miss Powell was a Balkan princess disguised as a Vassar girl. Eddy hopped a plane for the spring festival in Romanza, knowing only that Rosalie would be wearing a Pierrette costume. The dream soldier was confronted by an entire troupe of Pierrettes, but Miss

Powell stood out in any crowd. She danced down a graded pyramid of drums on legs described by *Time* magazine as "animated by a baleful intelligence of their own."

History provided Cecil B. DeMille with material for a number of super-spectacles: *The Sign of the Cross, Cleopatra, The Crusades.* Also in costume but far higher in quality was the output of Irving Thalberg: *The Barretts of Wimpole Street, Mutiny on the Bounty, The Good Earth,* and *Romeo and Juliet.* Studios sought inspiration in the works of Shakespeare, Dumas, Kipling, Victor Hugo, Charles Dickens, Elizabeth Barrett Browning, and Louisa May Alcott. Charles Laughton drifted through history, throwing bones into the rushes in *The Private Life of King Henry VIII,* dogging the footsteps of Fredric March in *Les Misérables,* screaming "Mr. Christian . . ." at Clark Gable in *Mutiny on the Bounty,* and turning a slightly mellower face toward the public in 1936 in *Rembrandt*—always a fine, if unphotogenic performer.

Other character actors perennially lost in the past were George Arliss and Paul Muni. As Richard Griffith and Arthur Mayer pointed out in *The Movies,* Arliss played Disraeli, Voltaire, Richelieu, and Alexander Hamilton as identical "crafty but benevolent old gentlemen who spent most of their time uniting unhappy young lovers." In *The House of Rothschild,* a typical Arliss vehicle, the only accurate date was that of the Battle of Waterloo.

Paul Muni, in *The Life of Emile Zola* (1937) and *Juarez* (1939), played costumed reformers. (Reformers in modern dress carried the suggestion that society might be in need of reform.) Twenty years later the McCarthy era would brand Muni's *Juarez* and *Zola* as Communist propaganda. It was doubtful if they had much influence on the generation which saw history as Bette Davis praying for fertility and who thought that Arliss engineered the purchase of the Suez Canal.

Paul Muni played Louis Pasteur. Gangland's Edward G. Robinson went legit as the discoverer of *Dr. Ehrlich's Magic Bullet* in 1940 with the usual quota of trials which beset the patient researcher. With the assistance of Donald Crisp, Ruth Gordon, and Otto Kruger he pursued truth, despite a racking cough, and kept bursting in with news of ground-breaking discoveries: "The horses have thrown off the effects of the toxin." On glancing at a wiggling spirochete he remarked, "Hardly more than a motion. That motion is a dance of death."

Irving Thalberg produced *Romeo and Juliet* in 1936. Warner Brothers was indebted to the Bard in 1935 for *A Midsummer Night's Dream.* Warner Brothers imported Max Reinhardt to direct an array of somewhat un-Shakespearean types: James Cagney in picturesque Robin Hood costume as Bottom, Joe E. Brown as Flute, Hugh Herbert as Snout, Verree Teasdale as Hippolyta, Dick Powell as Lysander, Mickey Rooney as Puck. . . .

There were certain fixed stars in the firmament: Johnny Weissmuller in the Tarzan series, Warner Oland as Charlie Chan, the Bulldog Drummond pictures, Bela Lugosi as Dracula, and Boris Karloff as Frankenstein. There was King Kong chasing Fay Wray up the Empire State Building—which a later generation would classify as "high camp."

There were the Fu Manchu pictures, where Myrna Loy got her start as an Oriental Menace.

The College of Physicians and Surgeons, contemporary division, numbered in its ranks Herbert Marshall, dragging Garbo off to China to cure cholera in *The Painted Veil;* Robert Donat losing his integrity and splitting fees in *The Citadel;* Lionel Barrymore, the brilliant diagnostician Dr. Gillespie, and Lew Ayres as Dr. Kildare; Jean Hersholt as the fanatical surgeon in *Men in White.* Then there were those reporters to whom the Newspaper Guild once took exception: the cast of *The Front Page;* Paul Muni donning contemporary dress for once as the Lonely Hearts editor in *Hi, Nellie!* No roundup of the 1930s cinema would be complete without mention of Rosalind Russell, the career girl. Her employers, like Cary Grant in *His Girl Friday,* liked her for trying to throw things at them. Because of her a whole generation of secretaries got their walking papers for talking tough to the boss when they wanted a raise. Beginning with *Bring 'Em Back Alive,* Frank Buck performed intrepidly in the jungle, surrounded by torpid tigers and superannuated snakes.

Between the Crash and Pearl Harbor there were a dozen or so truly memorable pictures: *Cavalcade* in 1933; three great Selznick offerings: *Gone With the Wind, A Star Is Born,* and *Rebecca.* Claude Rains, Robert Donat, and Robert Montgomery gave marvelous performances; Claude Rains in *The Invisible Man,* Donat in *The Ghost Goes West,* Montgomery in *Night Must Fall.* Luise Rainier will always be remembered for the telephone scene in *The Great Ziegfeld.* Rosalind Russell was unforgettable in *Craig's Wife* ("I still hate her," was a common tribute to her acting). Also in the Memorable Performances Division: Victor McLaglen in *The Informer,* Wendy Hiller and Leslie Howard in *Pygmalion,* Orson Welles as *Citizen Kane,* Laurence Olivier and Merle Oberon in *Wuthering Heights.*

Most amusing to look back on was the avant-garde. Ben Hecht and Charles MacArthur's *Crime Without Passion* was an "experimental" drama about a psychiatrist bent on committing, in the spirit of research, the perfect crime. Characters' thoughts were superimposed by double exposure so that one could watch Claude Rains wrestling with his conscience. Other affectations included stream-of-consciousness dialogue and an opening shot of the Eumenides plunging down the side of a skyscraper.

The Scoundrel, another Hecht-MacArthur offering, presented Noel

Coward as the merciless publisher Horace Liveright trading quips with Edith Wharton and rejecting manuscripts with cruel and witty epigrams. Mr. Coward got his comeuppance when he drowned and was doomed to walk the earth forever until someone could be found who would shed a tear for him. Who would do that? Certainly not the victims of those cruel and witty epigrams. At last Julie Haydon shed a tear for him, putting his troubled shade to rest. Audiences who can still catch an occasional art house revival of *The Scoundrel* are somewhat taken aback by the spectacle of Mr. Coward, a distraught revenant, walking into a room clutching a handful of seaweed.

Margo—an actress who had appeared in *Crime Without Passion*—also appeared in Maxwell Anderson's *Winterset*. Mr. Anderson was incapable of saying anything in prose. His *Mary of Scotland* with Katherine Hepburn and Fredric March was cast in blank verse.

Many of Eugene O'Neill's works were transplanted to the screen: *Anna Christie* in 1930, *The Emperor Jones* in 1933, *The Long Voyage Home* in 1940. Most experimental and daring of all was *Strange Interlude* in 1932. Characters relayed their inmost thoughts about incest ("my heart pounding at the thought of seeing her again"), hereditary insanity ("You don't mean Nina's going to have a . . ." sound of maniacal laughter . . . "That's my husband's sister—hasn't been out of her room for years."), nymphomania ("lips on my lips . . . strong arms around me, spooning, necking with the patients . . . I've been bad, Charlie.").

Clark Gable seemed somewhat ill at ease with Norma Shearer as his partner in a therapeutic mating experiment.

If the actors and actresses of the Thirties seem slightly more than lifesize, it was because the starring system with its seven-year contracts made gods and goddesses of Gary Cooper, Tyrone Power, Clark Gable, Fredric March, Errol Flynn, Cary Grant, Bette Davis, Marlene Dietrich, Joan Crawford, Claudette Colbert, Rosalind Russell, Norma Shearer, and Katharine Hepburn. Sometimes a star transcended the limitations of human clay and became a legend. There were three ways that this could happen: the star could a) die young, b) refuse to give out interviews and retire from the screen, or c) have the more intimate details of her sex life described posthumously to an audience numbered in millions. Ingrid Bergman later on was to take a fourth route, by having a son out of wedlock. In the Thirties she made her first bow to a fiercely loyal public in *Intermezzo*. Jean Harlow, who qualified under categories *a* and *c*, has had the best publicized legend of them all. Harlow made her first big hit as the tough blonde of *Hell's Angels* in 1930. Subsequently a certain sameness about her screen roles seemed to set in: daughter of the underworld in *The Secret Six*, a gangster's moll in *Public Enemy*, the temperamental movie star of *Bombshell*, the tough chick of *Dinner at Eight.* She was Lew Ayres' albatross in *Iron Man,* Spencer Tracy's wife in *Riffraff* and China Doll in *China Seas.* One of her most entertaining films was *Red Dust* with Clark Gable. Her casting problems could be summed up in the anguished question: "What kind of a whore am I now?"

In *Suzy* and *Personal Property,* she took a crack at the let's-take-off-our-shoes-and-jump-into-the-fountain-cute-girl-in-boy's-pajamas type of comedy. Her only musical, *Reckless,* brought forth the comment that singing was best left to Jeanette MacDonald. Jean Harlow died in 1937 at the age of twenty-six. The details of Miss Harlow's boudoir life have already been raked over the coals by Irving Shulman, and in two movies, one starring Miss Carroll Baker. Suffice it to say that it was a hell of a life and a hell of a legend, and that the amiable and much maligned girl, who late in her career was found to have an engaging comic gift, was indeed a *Bombshell.* It is interesting to note that for all her emotional difficulties there was no Harlow picture whose filming took more than three months.

Greta Garbo's allure was more subtle. Richard Griffith and Arthur Mayer, the authors of *The Movies,* summarize it thus: "For the old, bold movie vamp, Miss Garbo substituted the more complicated and credible charmer—doomed neurotic, torn by inner conflicts. She was poison to men and to herself, yet held in her eyes the promise of Cleopatra. Her eyes had held a direct invitation throughout various silent films of the Twenties. When Maurice Stiller, her Svengali, went back to Sweden Miss Garbo refused to speak to interviewers and became to her detractors "a sphinx without a secret."

The silence was broken in 1930. "Garbo talks!" the ads proclaimed. Nearly everyone of the right age remembers the ad; few remember what she said to start off. Her first words in *Anna Christie:* "Gif me a viskey, ginger ale on the side—and don't be stingy, baby." She appeared in *Grand Hotel* and *Queen Christina* in 1933, *Anna Karenina* in 1935.

By 1936, as Griffith and Mayer say, "the legendary face had both hardened and softened into a mask of tragedy." Garbo, according to an MGM executive, was "the only one we could kill off." All those unhappy endings, however, were giving her stature. In *Camille,* in 1936, she was transformed by director George Cukor into what he describes as "a sorrowing statue" and gave a performance that swelled the membership of the Garbo cult. In 1939 it came as a delightful surprise in *Ninotchka* to discover that the Tragedy Queen could be a laugh riot.

Garbo the movie queen died with her retirement in the early Forties. Garbo the Legend still lives on. New Yorkers are sometimes lucky enough outside of Schrafft's or over a counter at Bloomingdale's to get a glimpse of the fabulous face.

Carole Lombard, like Harlow, died young. She was, quite simply, everybody's darling. She could play a dizzy society girl, as in *We're Not Dressing* with Bing Crosby in 1934. She played thankless roles, as for example in *Fools for Scandal* in 1938 opposite Fernand Gravet. (Gravet got his job because of a superficial resemblance to the Duke of Windsor.) She took a crack at tragedy as the female half of a Depression-ridden couple with Jimmie Stewart in *Made for Each Other* (1939). But it is as a comedienne that she will be remembered: in *Twentieth Century* with John Barrymore in 1934; in *Nothing Sacred* (1937), as a girl who, through a series of mishaps, attends her own funeral; above all, as bored and beautiful Irene Bullock in *My Man Godfrey* (1936).

Irene Bullock wins William Powell in a scavenger hunt. The ground rules for this favorite 1930s sport are laid down by Miss Lombard as follows: "A scavenger hunt is just like a treasure hunt, except in a treasure hunt you find something you want and in a scavenger hunt you find things you don't want, and the one who wins gets a prize, only there really isn't any prize, it's just the honor of winning because all the money goes to charity if there's any money left over but then there never is."

Among the other idle rich in the picture was Mischa Auer, a sad-faced Slav who could imitate a gorilla. Miss Lombard, Mr. Powell, and Mr. Auer point up once more the great Hollywood paradox of the Depression—that the pictures which have stood up best from the decade of Social Significance deal mainly with high jinks in the high surtax brackets.

The popularity of many an adult star, unlike that of Miss Lombard, waned before the end of a seven-year contract. There was one class of performer whose talents were even more ephemeral—the child actors and actresses who stormed the gates of Hollywood doing everything from soft shoe shuffles to bird imitations. It had all begun with that cosmic moment in the early Thirties when Shirley Temple was taken from a series called Baby Burlesks and sent for an audition in the Fox Studio. She won a part in *Stand Up and Cheer* (1934), and the rest is history. She was loaned to Paramount for *Little Miss Marker* and later featured in *Baby Take a Bow* and *Now and Forever*. *Bright Eyes* got her star billing and an Oscar as the outstanding personality of 1934. Between 1934 and 1939 some of the films she made were *The Little Colonel, Curly Top, The Littlest Rebel, Poor Little Rich Girl, Heidi,* and *Rebecca of Sunnybrook Farm*. She was No. 1 at the box office and at the age of ten was making more money than FDR.

She was an accomplished little dancer. Each picture contained some cute song and dance routines: "You Gotta Eat Your Spinach, Baby" and "But Definitely" in *The Poor Little Rich Girl* (it was particularly cute that she pronounced it "definally"). There was a Dutch dance in wooden shoes in *Heidi*. In *Captain January* she tap-danced down a forty-five-foot lighthouse stairway delivering a line at every turn.

She spread good wherever she went. In *Stand Up and Cheer* she was involved in a never-never land where a Secretary of Amusement was pitted against a bunch of crooks bent for some abstruse reason on prolonging the Depression. In *Little Miss Marker* she was left as payment on an IOU and had a mellowing effect on a bunch of Damon Runyon gangsters. In *Now and Forever* she was teamed with Carole Lombard and Gary Cooper and acted once more as a force for good upon a group of international swindlers. The sex of Kipling's *Wee Willie Winkie* was changed out of deference to Shirley. She brought peace between her crusty old uncle, Old Boots (played by C. Aubrey Smith), and Cesar Romero, a Latin character actor somewhat miscast as Tribal Chief Kohda Khan.

Every studio began auditioning child stars in the hope that lightning would strike twice.

Shirley's co-thespians were legion. Some, like Jackie Cooper, who had made his first big hit in *Skippy* in 1931, had guardians who wisely stashed their money away. Jackie Coogan, already a has-been in the Thirties, was worth five million dollars before he could balance a two-wheeler and had bought his own Rolls-Royce at the age of ten. His adult life was spent selling airplane parts, playing summer stock and night clubs, burlesquing his great role in *The Kid* (1920), playing monster parts on TV, and renting out the Rolls-Royce for period scenes.

Among others, Jane Preston, Scotty Beckett, Richard Ralston Arlen, Virginia Weidler, Carmencita Johnson, Ronnie Cosby, Buster Phelps, Edith Fellows, Billy Lee, Dickie Moore, Bobby Breen, Gloria Jean, Baby Le Roy, and Jimmy Fay are all candidates for the Where Are They Now Sweepstakes.

Jane Withers, like Shirley Temple once a hot Fox property, has dropped her screen career for the more profitable business of making TV commercials. Freddie Bartholomew, a talented little English actor, followed his triumph in *David Copperfield* by appearing with little Cora Sue Collins in Garbo's *Anna Karenina*, and in *Little Lord Fauntleroy* in 1936. In Kipling's *Captains Courageous* he played the brat who was fished out of the ocean by Spencer Tracy, who later made a man of him. For a time Freddie's fan mail exceeded that of Clark Gable. Freddie is a Vice-President of Benton and Bowles. Like Shirley Temple Black, he is one of the few to land on his feet.

It was nevertheless a bad time for grown-up players. "The nervous director," wrote June Hampton in a 1934 *Photoplay*, "once furious at the least delay, is now off in some corner with The Child (they speak of him with reverence) perched on his knee. Together they are going over the scene. If it takes an hour or days even, what of it? The Child must understand. Let the adult actors stand around and get corns if they want to. The child is the one who will draw in the shekels."

One could sympathize with W. C. Fields, who was alleged to have spiked Baby Le Roy's orange juice, when one read of the plight of Helen Mack in *You Belong to Me*. She approached the director to inquire how she had made out in the seventeenth take, only to be informed that he had been so busy watching *wunderkind* David Holt that he had forgotten that she was in the picture.

Dolly Dimple and Bobby Bounce often gave out gratuitous advice on acting. In *Imitation of Life* little Baby Jane Quigley looked up strangely at Claudette Colbert at the end of a scene. "It's wrong. It's wrong," she cried. "She said it wrong." Claudette admitted that she had changed a word and promised Baby Jane to be a better girl in the future.

One of the greatest hams of all time was Mickey Rooney. In *Orchids and Ermine* he played a cigar-smoking midget. He appeared in the Mickey McGuire series and somehow seemed to turn up in practically everything from *Riffraff* to *Ah! Wilderness,* from *Manhattan Melodrama* to *A Midsummer Night's Dream.* In 1937, in *A Family Affair,* he played his first role as Andy Hardy with Lionel Barrymore as his father, the Judge. Judge Hardy's role was abdicated to Lewis Stone, who played it until 1946, when, with *Love Laughs at Andy Hardy,* the series was finally laid to rest. In 1939, 1940, and 1941 Mickey had replaced Shirley Temple as Peewee Box Office Champ.

As Andy Hardy's colleague, Judy Garland often gave him a dose of his own medicine when it came to upstaging. Singing "Alone" and "Nobody's Baby" in *Andy Hardy Meets Debutante,* she avenged Lewis Stone, Wallace Beery, and Lionel Barrymore, to mention only a few who had suffered from Mickey's determination to walk away with anything up to a death scene. Another footnote to the longest adolescence in history: Well after Mickey was embarked on one of many real-life marital disasters, he was still going to Lewis Stone for information about the birds and bees, introduced inevitably by a blushing request for a man-to-man talk. The offshoots of the star system were legion. They ranged from Shirley Temple dolls to movie palaces, from Hedda Hopper to tours of the Homes of the Stars. There was Pickfair and San Simeon, and Norma Shearer's "Provincial French cottage." There was the Fifth Avenue Theatre in Seattle, where a monstrous golden dragon grasped for a white globe below, "symbolic of the Pearl of Perfection." Movie theater architecture came in a variety of exotic styles: Egyptian (Grauman's Egyptian), Hindu (Loew's State in Syracuse), Chinese (Grauman's Chinese in Los Angeles, the Oriental in Chicago), Hispano-Persian (the Missouri Theatre in St. Joseph), French baroque (the San Francisco Fox), Siamese-Byzantine (the Fox Theatre in Detroit).

But nothing could compare with the magnificence of New York's Roxy. Gazing at the Roxy rotunda with its huge green marble columns, its twenty-foot chandelier, its gilded catafalque, its 2½-ton rug (the largest oval rug in the world), a Hokinson child in a *New Yorker* cartoon was depicted as asking, "Does God live here?" Buckingham Palace had nothing on the Roxy when it came to ritual. The changing of the guard ceremony at the palace was matched at the Roxy by the daily Changing of the Ushers.

It was the fan sitting at the Roxy—thirsty for details of life in Screenland—who imparted such formidable power to two commonplace ladies on the coast: Louella O. Parsons and Hedda Hopper. Louella Parsons as a writer was dreariness incarnate. She could misquote the most common cliché ("Oh to be in England now that it's May"). She had gotten her start at the Essenay Studios when Gloria Swanson was chasing Wally Beery, when Mary Pickford's mother was trying to get her daughter's salary upped to fifty-five dollars a week, and when Ben Turpin was a cross-eyed office boy who was said to bring the company luck. William Randolph Hearst offered her a job on the New York *American*. At the height of her career Lolly was syndicated in twelve hundred papers. Her nose for news led her devoted followers to overlook her style.

A case in point involved her biggest scoop—the news of the Fairbanks-Pickford split-up in 1935. It was announced over lunch to Lolly by Miss Pickford, who later claimed she had no notion that she was speaking for the record. Louella's version had been a bit different. Mary had said, "Douglas and I are separating." She had insisted that Lolly write the story forthwith. Miss Parsons claimed to have been too shocked to speak but had finally acceded to "brave little Mary's orders."

In 1934 Louella O. Parsons became emcee of a radio program—*Hollywood Hotel*. The stars who appeared on it were recompensed by a free case of Campbell's Soup, and after their second stint they were allowed to specify the variety. Only Greta Garbo demanded additional financial remuneration. The program established Louella as a force, though it was dropped after four years when James Cagney and the Screen Actors Guild put down their collective foot and announced that man did not live by Campbell's Soup alone.

Such was the power of Miss Parsons that she almost managed to scuttle Orson Welles' *Citizen Kane,* which presented an extremely unflattering picture of Miss Parsons' employer.

Hedda Hopper became a pundit in 1938. Her hats also became a Hopper trademark; her accuracy was somewhat suspect. Indeed, at a Hollywood party, Miss Hopper once suggested that Hearst's San Simeon be turned into a national shrine. She waxed eloquent on what a bonanza the castle of Mad Ludwig of Bavaria had been to Austria.

Lesser literary lights were engaged in the business of reporting on the doings of the stars. Who were the Box Office Darlings of 1937? . . . Who was the greatest screen lover of 1933? . . . These were the cosmic questions that occupied the readers of *Photoplay* and *Modern Screen,* along with those ideal Hollywood marriages which had generally ended up in the divorce court by the time the magazine went to press. Sometimes the public might be titillated by the tale of what Shirley Temple ate for breakfast or by a confession of weakness—like the one indulged in by Hedy Lamarr in "Hedy Wine."

Miss Lamarr, like Luise Rainer, was one of Hollywood's exotic imports. She had come out in the Austrian import *Ecstasy* in 1937, and with much heaving of bosom she had looked with distaste upon her aging husband, and longingly upon symbolic matings which took place between flies on the window pane. A nude swimming scene was such a flagrant violation of the Production Code that one had to journey to a different city to see it. Managers of movie houses often advertised scenes from *Ecstasy* (with adhesive tape covering Miss Lamarr's shame) , scenes which were excised from the cut version—a fact which the patron did not realize until safely ensconced in the theater. *Photoplay* in 1938 told how Hedy was just plain folks and hated being an "Ecstasy girl," attempting with little success ("She's just about as much an Ecstasy girl as I am.") to present the star as a product as American as corn pone and apple pie.

By 1938 fans had something really important on their minds: the search for Scarlett O'Hara. David O. Selznick had announced that the role would be played by an unknown from the South, and had even devoted two years to going through the motions of looking for her. Every actress in Hollywood saw herself as Scarlett. Might it be Tallulah Bankhead, smoldering Miriam Hopkins, red-headed Erin O'Brien Moore, flashing Paulette Goddard? Selznick was reported to have considered Margaret Tallichet, Arlene Whalen, Liz Whitney, and Katharine Hepburn. The role was offered to Norma Shearer, who did not consider herself worthy of it.

Rival studios thought they might beat Selznick to the punch. Bette Davis, who had built up quite a reputation as a mean girl since her performance as Mildred in *Of Human Bondage,* all but spit tacks in *Jezebel,* kicking aside the code of Southern chivalry, biting her lips to make them red, giving amiable aristocrat George Brent the air. It did not win her the role of Scarlett, though it was suggested that the only person who could play Scarlett after Bette Davis' performance was Paul Muni.

Warner Brothers, which had produced *Jezebel,* had another string to their bow. Rachel Field's *All This and Heaven Too* was scheduled for production in 1940, with Bette Davis as a love-crossed governess and Charles Boyer as the Duke de Preslin. *Gone With the Wind* was sometimes referred to as GWTW and Warners alluded to ATAHT—as it turned out, a trifle optimistically.

Photoplay interviewed some of the aspiring Scarletts, including Paulette Goddard, whose desire to play the part had her on the brink of hysteria. Of the group, *Photoplay* put its money on Miss Hepburn. Vivien Leigh, an Englishwoman, furnished a surprise ending to the search by unexpectedly walking off with the most coveted role in cinema history. Disappointed xenophobes saw her as a spurious daughter of Dixie.

If the search for Scarlett made the fur fly, the child stars made the treacle flow. In September 1938, Sara Hamilton visited a few of the kiddies in their native habitat and recounted their doings. Little Billy Lee informed *Photoplay*'s reporter that the red button on top of his skullcap was his "tail light." "Fred MacMurray," *Photoplay* said cryptically, "can't get over him."

Then over to "hazel-eyed, honest-souled, straight-from-the-shoulder" Virginia Weidler. "Make it ten," said Virginia when asked her age. "Studio reasons. Always chopping off a year." Besides her hazel eyes and honest soul, she boasted "two chicken pox marks above her right eyebrow, sixty-two freckles across her perfect little nose and six owls in her attic," and the fact that she thought Queen Victoria was a figure from American history.

George Ernest of the *Jones Family* was interviewed in the company of his best friend Marvin Stephens. *Photoplay* solemnly reported the following epic interchange:

> "Well, good night Marvin," he'll say at the end of day's work on the set.
> "See you tomorrow" and for a moment the two friends will stand in the center of a huge movie set, hands raised in salute, and then go.
> Two American lads off for home.

In *What Makes Sammy Run*, Sammy Glick gives a musical tribute to the "little people" who, he feels, abetted his greatness. In the long run they were the ones who had the last laugh. The character actors of Hollywood were grouped in a 1934 edition of *Photoplay* by studio.

Basil Rathbone, Roland Young, Elsa Lanchester, Una O'Connor, C. Aubrey Smith, and Cedric Hardwicke might be said to furnish the personnel for the English Division of Minor Players. There was also a Latin Division who peopled the gambling hells, ran the night clubs and peddled an occasional tomato. Prominent among them were Henry Armetta, Cesar Romero, Joseph Calleia and Eduardo Cianelli. The Latin Division had a way of turning ugly. In *Riffraff* Joseph Calleia portrayed a sinister purveyor of cheap labor. Eduardo Cianelli could be egghead ugly as the gangster in *Winterset* or just plain ugly roughing up the girls as the proprietor of a clip joint in *Marked Woman*.

The Negro Division furnished such hewers of wood and drawers of water as Hattie McDaniel, Rochester, Stepin Fetchit; such song-and-dance men as Paul Robeson and Bill Robinson.

There were the eccentric millionaires described above, without which no musical would have been complete. In addition there was Lionel Atwill, the corrupt captain of industry, Walter Connolly who took up the cudgels for free enterprise in Hecht and MacArthur's *Soak the Rich.* Eugene Pallette in *My Man Godfrey* was an amiable tycoon who wanted to go to jail so that he could get up and do an honest day's work without worrying about who was going to pay the bills.

The women—God bless 'em—came in all sizes and shapes: good old shoes, like May Robson and Alison Skipworth; Maria Ouspenskaya, who could travel at the drop of a hat to India when *The Rains Came,* or who could act broadminded for Dr. Ehrlich when he announced what he'd been up to with that magic bullet. Dame May Whitty was a good old shoe who always found herself mixed up in something sinister, as in *The Lady Vanishes* and *Night Must Fall.* Beginning with *Dead End,* Marjorie Main was a poor old shoe who never had sufficient upward mobility to make it out of the slums.

There were fluttery women like Billie Burke and Alice Brady, who portrayed Carole Lombard's flighty mother in *My Man Godfrey.* Mary Boland was one of the screen's leading birdbrains. Spring Byington fluttered but had moments of depth as Marmee in *Little Women.* It was Fay Bainter who first gave Jezebel a name.

The worldly women included Helen Vinson and Binnie Barnes (who was one of the wives of King Henry VIII, but who was more at home in modern dress.) The archetypal worldly woman was society bitch Gail Patrick—in real life an amiable performer—who sneered obligingly while Shirley Temple broke up her love affairs, or as Irene Dunne popped up coyly at her husband's side on her honeymoon.

Paramount had its stable for the De Mille spectacles, *The Sign of the Cross, Cleopatra,* and *The Crusades.* These included Warren William, Henry Wilcoxon, and C. Aubrey Smith, Dean of the English Division—who also carried the banners of Empire in *Lives of a Bengal Lancer* and was generally to be found when the dawn came up like thunder out of China 'cross the bay.

United Artists' *Stagecoach* brought together Claire Trevor, whose disreputable trade was disclosed to John Wayne when he found a bunch of fancy women whooping it up on the site of the old homestead. Also among the passengers was John Carradine, prominent also in *The Grapes of Wrath* and as Rizzio in *Mary of Scotland*—in short, wherever the script called for someone sinister with the features of a razorback hog. Donald Meek was aboard the *Stagecoach,* as was Andy Devine. Devine was so devoid of period sense that it mattered little whether he was in a Stetson or in more contemporary dress in *Hold 'Em Yale*. He was always to be found when the script called for a comic who had lost his voice.

The same could be said for Thomas Mitchell, who won an Academy Award for his performance in *Stagecoach*. That time he happened to be a doctor. In *Lost Horizon* he had been a stock manipulator. In *Gone With the Wind* he was Scarlett O'Hara's father. He was called to the colors whenever the script demanded someone grizzled.

It was all but impossible for a character actor to break out of the mold. Frank Morgan for years played someone who giggled. He amazed critics with his excellent acting as a non-Aryan professor in Phyllis Bottome's *The Mortal Storm*.

If his was a rare departure from a rigid orbit, there were compensations. The character actor was spared the publicity build-up of an Anna Sten, a Rochelle Hudson, a Fernand Gravet, a Miliza Korjus, or a Sigrid Gurie. But any of the latter would have traded their eyeteeth for the steady income of a Charles Bickford, a Henry Daniell, a Jessie Ralph, an Allen Jenkins, a Raymond Walburn, a Cora Witherspoon, or a Helen Westley. More durable than many stars were Thelma Todd and Patsy Kelly, queens of the selected short subject. Minor players were mixed, matched, loaned, put into doublet and hose, and they became part of the landscape for many who were never sure whether they were watching Donald Meek, Donald Woods, or Donald Crisp. They were better off than many whose names rated larger letters. They outlasted children whose careers started out so promisingly—giving the interviewer a big yawn or kicking Clark Gable in the shins.

What of father who came in from the cold to forget his troubles? Did he really believe that Bette Davis had given up "everything" in *Dark Victory* to live in a cottage that cost $12,000 a year to run? Did he seriously think that Loretta Young and Clark Gable would be off in the frozen north in *The Call of the Wild* without anyone ending up in the wrong sleeping bag? Did he believe that Irene Dunne and Randolph Scott were off on that desert island with "nothing happening"? Did he believe in MacDonald and Eddy as they did the Wiener-schnitzel Waltz through the kingdom of Graustark? Did he think that child stars were really unspoiled, or that Shirley Temple had come up with the cure for the Depression? Decency's double standard was shown up when Joseph Mankiewicz's *All About Eve* implied at last that two people were living together. No one was shocked that they were doing it. All were surpised that they were doing it in a *movie*.

Hollywood in the Thirties operated under an alien set of assumptions. The ninth beatitude in this Shangri-la was an unwritten one. "Blessed are the meek who serve the star—for they shall always work." Today the Roxy is only a nostalgic line in a bright revue ("There was a lobby!"). The marquees of old movie palaces advertise bargains in celery and lamb chops. With their passing so went those chaste Production Code heroes and heroines. Racier talent is recruited from foreign capitals. It is hard to remember the days when all moral problems were simplified—for ninety minutes—till one left the theater and went out into the world.

Movies in the Thirties were not long out of the days when moviemakers went West to find sunlight, wrote scripts as they went while slapsticking up and down the concrete runways that were to become Hollywood and Sunset Boulevards. D. W. Griffith and the first close-ups were not far behind us in the Thirties. And yet here we were, all of a sudden, with scripts and money and scenery and turntables and crowd scenes of extras, building to a technical virtuosity as yet unsurpassed—and to an impact upon the public not always fully appreciated by the very people who were turning the pictures out.

One famous director—long since gone on to bigger and better things—has been enshrined by film historians for movies whose endings he barely remembers today. Nostalgia for the Thirties? He dismisses it with a wave of the hand.

"The gangsters in fact were so sweet and everybody was so well behaved. Even the villains . . . there was something likeable about them. It's a dear dead world. It doesn't touch any raw nerves."

Ça va.

But those of us who were part of the dear dead world did go to Saturday matinees and sit through two or three full showings, on occasion bringing a meal along with us. We did know practically every line of dialogue by heart. It was not unsual to find a teen-ager who could—God save us—go word for word through the book and lyrics of Naughty Marietta. Some of us changed the signs at the local movie theater to earn free passes to the Saturday night show. Teenagers of those dear dead days listened endlessly to apocalyptic rumblings from their parents. "You'll never amount to anything if you spend all your time reading Silver Screen." There was the breathless anticipation as we listened for "Louella's first exclusive" on the radio, or as we licked the neapolitan ice cream off the top of the Dixie cup to get to the picture of Greta Garbo.

Echoes from that dear dead world could be heard in unexpected corners of the earth. Ann Frank's room was embellished with pictures of Hollywood movie stars. A snapshot of Shirley Temple was found by a GI on the body of a Japanese sniper. Long after John Wayne made his first halting declarations to Claire Trevor in Stagecoach, Yves Montand is making a fortune singing about what goes on "dans les plaines du Far West."

A Decade of Coming Attractions

John Clellon Holmes

*John Clellon Holmes is one of the leading writers of the Beat Genera-
tion. The following is a discussion of the movie idols of his generation in
what he calls a "valentine to the vanished-phantoms of the Saturday
afternoons of long ago" during his boyhood in the 1930s and 1940s.**

It has been said that if you would understand the mind of my generation you must start with World War Two, on the theory that a
widespread attitude is shaped by a common experience. The war seems
a likely enough starting place, and yet in a subtler sense everyone who
is now between the ages of thirty-odd and forty-odd had already shared
a common experience by the time they entered the armed services. It
was an experience that was vastly more formative than the bad circumstances of the Depression or the anxieties of the post-Munich years,
because it happened to us on the inside, down in the psyche where the
adolescent is most receptive and most vulnerable. It was the experience
of moviegoing in the thirties and early forties, and it gave us all a
fantasy life in common, from which we are still dragging up the images
that obsess us.

When comedian Lenny Bruce snarls, "Don't give me any of those
Barton Maclaine takes!" it is more than a face or a role that is evoked
in Harvardmen and hipsters alike. It is a whole big-shouldered, thick-
faced attitude toward life—the attitude of the spoiler, the strikebreaker,
the sadistic warden, the lumberjack bruiser, the smasher of things. The
name itself summons up a promise of violence (heavy and unimagina-
tive) that is as different from the psychotic violence of Peter Lorre as
Sammy Glick's machinations are from Iago's. When we think of
Barton Maclaine, we immediately think of a blunt object about to
run amok.

* From the book *Nothing More to Declare* by John Clellon Holmes. Copyright
© 1967 by John Clellon Holmes. Reprinted by permission of E. P. Dutton & Co., Inc.

Equally, when poet Frank O'Hara writes an elegy to Margaret Dumont, everyone recalls the grudging respect you had to accord her lofty gentility, besieged as it was by the maniacal Dada of the Marx Brothers. Impregnable in bosom and coiffure she survived their inspired vulgarity with a touch of dignified good humor—rather as you imagined your very proper grandmother might survive a burlesque show; and who can say how much she taught us about a world of social niceties that we would never really know? The point is that at the simple mention of a name we all re-experience the nostalgia, vividness and perception of the same childhood dream, no matter what has happened to us since.

Whether the theater was the smalltown two-hundred-seater (down near the railroad tracks) that seemed eternally drifted in O. Henry wrappers or sticky with Juicy Fruit, the sooty brick building with the fading black and yellow billboard advertising *Photoplays,* where, on Saturday afternoons, an unruly army in corduroys stomped their feet, raced up and down the aisles or pelted disapproving girls with ice cream; or whether the theater was one of those huge, Moorish big-city picture palaces, with arched Scheherazade balconies, stars that twinkled, fountains that played and platoons of uniformed ushers, the images that flickered on the silver screen and the dreams and visions they aroused were identical. The veteran of Iwo Jima may feel a resentful superiority to the veteran of Normandy (the resentful superiority the proletariat sometimes feels for the bourgeoisie), and find himself wondering if they are talking about the same war, but if *Gone With the Wind* comes up both are securely in the same army fleeing Atlanta. One's boyhood experience of the Depression may center around a Hooverville or a house in the suburbs, but one's fantasies of those years are likely to inhabit that carefree world, as shiny and as shallow as patent leather, where Fred Astaire and Ginger Rogers denied all shabbiness and anxiety for a few hypnotic hours. When I think of the midthirties, for instance, an odd image always comes to my mind: the image of a dismal milltown in New Hampshire, complete with shuttered brick factory, rotting bandstand on the green, and NRA stickers in the windows of Woolworth's, over which the outline of a mythical RKO Venice, made of plastic and cellophane, and piped to antic joy by the fleet Astaire, hovers like a double exposure. The quick dream and the dead reality remain so wedded in my memory to this day that it is impossible for me to know how much my particular vision of the world was formed by them.

The power of the film as a molder of mass emotions was recognized within little more than a decade after *The Great Train Robbery,* but it was probably not until the advent of sound, together with the death of vaudeville and the insecurities of the Depression, that moviegoing became as universal a part of puberty as acne and masturbation. If sound produced a lowering of artistic standards, it also made possible a heightening of psychological involvement so persuasive that the gulf between the audience and the image was all but obliterated. In a sense, sound transformed the film from a ritual to an hallucination, and the movies have been more Freudian than Aristotelian ever since. Vaudeville's death multiplied by many thousands the number of darkened theaters in which the flicks could flicker, until there was hardly a town in America that did not have its Orpheum, Bijou or Rex, dispensing the same fable in Bangor and Butte. The idleness and bewilderment of the Depression awakened a hunger for fantasies that would compensate for the impoverishment of reality, and by deceit or cajolery, with permission or without it, most of an entire generation went to the movies two or three times a week, and accumulated, in common, a surrogate reality.

It should be admitted right off that we were indiscriminate. We went to good films and bad films alike, to M-G-M super-spectacles that cost more than the historical events they depicted, and 20th-Century-Fox musicals about as nutritious as Kool-Aid, and Universal horror films that used the same bit of fabricated Transylvania in picture after picture. We would go to see anything that moved, and we probably learned as much from the B-films as we did from the A's. We revelled in their sleazy sets, indifferent acting and skeletal plots; for every Saturday we spent with Gable or Shearer, we probably spent four with Richard Arlen or Arline Judge, and they taught a lot of us to relish the back-of-town, wrong-side-of-the-tracks America where motives were simple and the action was brisk. We still have our favorites—what a friend of mine calls Great Bad Films—and our affection for them is undiminished by the fact that they grow worse with every viewing. I still drop everything whenever *A Message to Garcia* comes around on television, if only to watch Wallace Beery's superbly awful hamming with his torn straw hat.

It would be difficult to calculate the number of hours that people of my age spend simply talking about the movies of those years. The talk is carried on in the sort of shorthand that is all but unintelligible to outsiders, and a snatch of it might go like this: "Name the Lane Sisters, and you're out of the game if you include Gale Page. . . . Remember Henry Armetta with his head askew? Porter Hall the Eternal Conniver? George Zucco's Grey Eminence? Jane Darwell the Earth Mother of Arkansas? . . . Who played opposite Loretta Young in *Zoo in Budapest?* What about O. P. Heggie in *The Count of Monte Cristo?* . . . That wasn't C. Aubrey Smith, it was Sir Guy Standing. . . . Remember the Three Musketeers of Warner Brothers: Allen Jenkins, Frank McHugh, and Edward Brophy? . . . Who can cast *all* the secondary roles in *King's Row?* . . . You're only eligible for the Movie

Team if you can name at least three Isabel Jewell films, or Henry Fonda's last line in *Blockade,* or the picture that had a shot of Ann Sheridan without a brassiere. . . ."

Everyone has his favorite William Powell scene (mine is the drunk scene in *My Man Godfrey*), his essential Marx Brothers sequence (I have been torn for years between the end of *Duck Soup* and the stateroom routine in *A Night at the Opera*); and that special film, mostly obscure, often undistinguished, something about which opened the consciousness (that was all ready to flower) to a new perception about life or the world that remains as vivid and evocative as the madeleine in Proust. For reasons which defy description, my awareness of the existential character of modern history was first evoked by a brief scene in a wine cellar from an unimportant 1937 film, *Last Train from Madrid.*

Equally, everyone carries in his head the memory of a special girl, with a special fleeting beauty, that is as graphic and moving today as it was in those years when they pursued that face through film after film until it vanished into death, obscurity or character roles. I know a man who has never really gotten over the death of Thelma Todd, and she exists in his mind, not as the object of Groucho's lechery or as the dumb steno of countless low-budget comedies with Patsy Kelly, but as a fragile ash-blonde wraith, fine-boned and petal-lipped, with that vaguely solemn aura in which some girls, cursed with startling beauty, seem to move. I myself am an Elissa Landi man. I remember her face with the poignance and awe that are reserved for one's first crush on an older woman, and even when I was only ten her beauty seemed to me to be too rarefied, too breathtaking, for this world. I remember watching her as you watch an exotic flower in full blossom, knowing that ahead of such perfection lies only a withering. There are Myrna Loy men (reporters and wits), and Jean Harlow men (sportsmen and boozers), and Marlene Dietrich men (intellectuals and homosexuals); and I suppose we are all Garbo men—at least a little.

Everyone, as well, has a particular star who embodies for him the first full awareness of the rousing eroticism of adolescence, a fantasy love image that initiated him into manhood. Kerouac writes: "My dream has in it a wife beautiful beyond belief, some gorgeous new blonde gold sexpot of starry perfection with lovely lace neck, soft long skin, inturned mouth top—I pictured the gorgeous Gene Tierney—a young beautiful American girl getting excited in your arms." To people of my age, the reference is as precise as the mention of Helen or Hecuba was to classical times, and serves the same purpose. Whether Tierney is your meat or not, you know her, you have considered her, and the leap is made.

For myself, I recall the soft, white, trembling curve of Jean Harlow's breast momentarily revealed (I saw the film three times to be certain) in the seduction scene in *Hell's Angels*. There it was, unmoored beneath her robe, that object of ceaseless, exhausting midnight speculations. And Ben Lyon was sitting not two feet from her, and it! Not to mention the dozen-odd technicians who were assisting, and whose presence I felt just as strongly, just as thrillingly. I remember her moistly hesitant half smile, which at first I simply refused to believe indicated her acquiescence to *that*. I remember the embrace that followed which, of course, silenced all doubts. And I remember, as well, that I left the theater with my first awareness that women could be more than just reluctant mannequins in the sexual encounter. There are men of my age who have been more or less searching, since those days, for Luise Rainer's gamin smile, or Madeleine Carroll's deep-breasted elegance, or June Lang's indescribably delicate neck, or the buttocks of Frances Farmer, or Ruby Keeler's thighs. In some cases, they have even gone so far as to marry reasonable facsimiles.

The movies were also a continuation of our schooling by other means, and the degree to which they affected our appreciation of literature, for instance, is difficult to overestimate. In almost every case, however, we saw the movie, and only *then* read the book. Though I have been with Tolstoi's *Anna* many more times than I have watched Garbo's, whenever I read the book it is the film star who moves so darkly toward the accelerating railway wheels in my mind's eye, giving the chapters an uncanny third dimension. And is there any way to imagine Mr. Micawber except in the carrot-nosed, garrulous, shabby-genteel figure of W. C. Fields? Is it possible that Sidney Carton did not have the quenched, whimsical eyes and resolute mouth of Ronald Colman? Or that Kipling didn't have Spencer Tracy in mind when he created Manuel in *Captains Courageous?* Not to me. And when I finally plunged into the great English novels of the nineteenth century, I found all of them richly peopled by the likes of Edna May Oliver, Roland Young, Freddie Bartholomew, Basil Rathbone, Montague Love, Herbert Mundin, Elizabeth Allan, Miles Mander, Una O'Connor—indeed, the entire Metro-Goldwyn-Mayer stock company of the thirties, those marvelous Cruikshank-like faces that popped up in film after film, like so many utility outfielders. My first direct exposure to Shakespeare was the Pickford-Fairbanks version of *The Taming of the Shrew* (it was also my first film), and after seeing *The Blue Angel* I struggled through the novel, only to be disappointed. Gary Cooper sent me to Hemingway, and Paul Muni to Zola; and certainly my vision of war was almost exclusively the result of *All Quiet on the Western Front*, which I never would have read at such an impressionable age had it not been for an opportune (?) exposure to the movie at eleven.

The war is a good example of how subtly we were shaped by those far off Saturday afternoons. Unlike our fathers, we went off to our war with no illusions about "glory and patriotism." Though it was far more worth the fighting than theirs, most of us viewed it (in advance) as an unpleasant, monotonous, dispiriting task that had somehow been shoved on us by the follies of our elders. A large part of the explanation for this lies in the simple fact that we had been exposed to almost a decade of antiwar movies, and the abrupt shift to antifascist films in the early forties could never quite make us forget the image of Lew Ayres, as the young German, begging the bayoneted Poilu to forgive him there in the shellhole, or the obvious meaning of the doughboy-turned-gangster in *They Gave Him a Gun,* or the smashed hopes behind James Stewart's smashed eyes in *Seventh Heaven.* These pictures filled our heads with memories of trench fighting, gas attacks and hopeless years of mud and agony that were no less bitter for being secondhand, and we knew that the only enemy worth struggling against was War Itself. By the time that Hollywood retooled to prove that all Germans and all Japanese were nonhumans, we were incapable of any real enthusiasm for the idea. The war was a fact, a dirty job that had to be done, but very few of us could view it as a crusade or a war to end wars. Could we so easily forget John Gilbert howling like an animal in no-man's land in *The Big Parade?* Or Eric Von Stroheim's sympathetic prison camp officer in *Grand Illusion?*

I remember, for instance, when they reissued *All Quiet* sometime in 1941, with a commentary that attempted to turn it into an antifascist tract. Though I was perfectly willing to be convinced, the images were too stark, too appalling, and no injection of ideology could harness them to the war effort. The futility and simple horror of modern warfare overcame all the sloganizing, and the movie was quickly withdrawn, to be replaced by those numberless films about Nazi atrocities, in which Conrad Veidt, Martin Kosleck and Fritz Kortner made such a good living after Pearl Harbor. But it has always astonished me that almost no one has perceived that one reason that we fought a war (against very real evils) so laconically, with so little rhetoric, and with our eye out mainly for personal survival (not only against the enemy, but against the military system itself) was because we knew that all wars were basically frauds, even just wars. After all, hadn't we learned precisely that in our local movie theater?

The films of the thirties and forties reflected the zenith of the star system, and above all they were vehicles for great personalities, always somehow bigger than the roles they played, their power commensurate to how completely they embodied an archetype. To my generation, for instance, Humphrey Bogart is not merely Sam Spade in *The Maltese Falcon,* or the cabaret owner in *Casablanca,* or the down-and-out prospector in *Treasure of Sierra Madre.* Sometimes a hero, sometimes a villain, he is always pre-eminently the Existential Knight, suspicious of sentiment, verbosity and cheap idealism, alike capable of that fatalistic violence which sometimes seems the only way to survive if you have the cruelty of modern cities in your eyes, and that reticent toughness of spirit (which Bogart's famous wince of the upper lip has incarnated forever) that indicates awareness of how slim the odds really are, and a besieged personal code. He was Bogey to us, we knew his style and attitudes as well as we knew our own, he taught us something about the world we would inherit that was no less contagious than what Hemingway taught us, and will probably last as long.

I remember, as well, when Carole Lombard died in a wartime plane crash. I was genuinely saddened. It was not that she had ever been an object of romantic reverie to me, or even that I knew (or cared) anything very much about her personally. It was that something witty, madcap, tough, earnest, and even noble had gone out of life, something I would always associate with the thirties: the zany rich girl with the good heart; the honey-blonde broad, with the prominent hipbones, who could drink with the boys; everyone's hip older sister who brought a whiff of the Big World with her when she visited home. She was funny and she was fun; she had something more substantial than glamor; her very name evoked a point of view that I still encounter (and fancy I understand down to its minutest detail) in the women of my generation that you meet at cocktail parties, or on the afterdecks of motor-cruisers, or in the executive offices of publishing houses or TV networks.

Since it appeared after the war, everyone has been intimidated (perhaps justly) by James Agee's brilliant piece on silent film comedy, but I'm sure there are many of my generation who, like me, feel that the laughmakers of our era have been sadly neglected as a result. As evidence that great comedy did not die after *The Jazz Singer,* we would offer just three examples, to each of which sound itself was essential.

The Marx Brothers, for instance, are unthinkable without the verbal insanity of Groucho and Chico. Their shameless punning, their deliciously infantile literalness, their eruptions of outright gibberish, drove a decade of Douglas Dumbrilles, Sig Rumans and Herman Bings to the very brink of epilepsy. And can anyone seriously imagine even mute Harpo without his piercing two-handed whistle or the lewd honk of his automobile horn? The adult world of sense, and gravity, and dullness, which the Marx Brothers invaded like a gang of surrealist kids on a perpetual 4th of July, was exactly the pompous, problem-filled world to which we had to return when the film was over, and we went back to it renewed by the knowledge that the Bores could be foiled by the cagey irrationality of Groucho, and the Girls would succumb to Harpo's mysterious and angelic smile when, out of the horrendous ruins of a grand piano, he resurrected a moment of fleeting melody that was like a hint of eternity in a world demented by time. It you looked at it from the vantage of energy and joy, life was absurd, but the absurdity itself was endearing, and the fact that this message was not lost on us can be found in the work of such diverse people as Terry Southern, Gregory Corso and Robert Rauschenburg.

Though they began in the Silent Era, we feel that Laurel and Hardy belong to us, and we cannot imagine Laurel—whey-faced, looking either like a weeping sheep or a grinning horse—without his unmatchable whimper that built so slowly into pathetic sobs, or his droll and somehow tender English accent. Hardy's tiny mouth, and tiny moustache, and tiny eyes in that great runny pudding of a face would always be incomplete to us without his exasperated *"Stanley!"* delivered with all the prissy impatience of a boy scout master from Georgia, coping with a gang of juveniles in Brownsville. Laurel and Hardy were Outsiders, always broke, somehow innocent, certainly ill-equipped to handle a world of hard facts and solid objects (as much by Hardy's fastidiousness as Laurel's incompetence), and yet they were always optimistic, no defeat was final, their pretensions were as sweetly naive as their confusions, and the sequence which reoccurred most often in their films found them sitting on the curbstone (having been summarily ejected from the warmth of Life Within), trying to decide what to do next. We often felt exactly the same.

With W. C. Fields, we are on higher ground. Indeed, we are in the realm where mythic figures reside, and Fields probably comes closer to being the secret Dutch Uncle of my generation than any other single artist. To this day, we lapse into the musing, rhetorical, nasal rasp by means of which he sought to evade the hostile world of Una Merkel, Franklin Pangborn and Baby Leroy. I have heard television producers and five-times-busted junkies imitate it with the same uncanny perfection. It is our connection with an older America of frontier gamblers, carnie barkers, talltale tellers; an America now on the con, on the bum, on the sauce; an America heading inexorably for the Grampian Hills, pursued by the Four Horsemen of the Apostasy—moderation, conformity, affluence and humorlessness. In it, we hear train whistles, the click of poker chips, saloon-talk, whorehouse pianos, cars gunning insanely for a light, the shrewd lies that outwit cops and wives, the monologues that can be heard at midnight under the trestle where men, for whom this world is not enough, gather around a can.

We were in immediate rapport with the profounder aspects of Fields' character: the besieged Fields forever menaced by inanimate objects, the impatient Fields trying to get a scoop of ice cream to his mouth by means of two limp soda straws, the outraged Fields finding himself in bed with a goat, the insatiable Fields vaulting out of an airplane after his flask, the fatalistic Fields making for the Black Pussy Café like a wounded elephant lumbering off into the bush. His mouth full of windy jargon, his mordant eye a-scheme, his bulbous nose hinting at thirsts and joys he had managed to thieve from under the very eyes of convention—all this had a lasting influence on us, and what Fields taught us was invaluable, for he was neither merely crazy nor innocent, but a flawed, eccentric man, making out in a reality geared to the silly abstractions of the middle class. One has only to think of such people as Nelson Algren and William Burroughs, their works *and* their personalities, to see the extent of that influence on the generation just before mine. Burroughs, in particular, reflects the Fieldsian accent and point of view, and *Naked Lunch* is probably the way Fields would have rewritten *1984* had he lived. For the rest of us, it is enough to mention the New Old Lompoc House, or Mahatma Kane Jeeves, to start us trading stories back and forth about the same rank-breathed, lying, reprobate old uncle, who passed through all our lives despite the alarums of our parents, leaving a delicious and unsettling aroma of bay rum, whiskey and musty railway depots.

Off the streets where these giants roamed, there was a luxurious room, soundproofed and deodorized, where William Powell, Franchot Tone and Robert Montgomery traded glittering bon mots with Myrna Loy, Jean Arthur and Margaret Sullavan, for sound also brought to our ears (whether they were cocked in Montana or Manhattan) nuances of irony and wit as sibilant as so many cocktail pianos. In this room, Eric Blore spluttered and buttled like a paranoid chipmunk, Eugene Pallette huffed and paid the bills, Billie Burke arrived in a flutter of chiffon, Mischa Auer preened in a rented tuxedo and a bogus title, Edward Everett Horton gabbled like a huge absent-minded rabbit, and Helen Broderick cast a cold, satiric eye on the whole proceedings. Irene Dunne consoled herself with Ralph Bellamy after her misunderstanding with Cary Grant over Gail Patrick, but the orchestra was always ready just out of camera range to supply the lush accompaniment for the reconciliation. People got pixilated, but never drunk. No one worked for a living, and everyone always carried enough cash on their persons to pay first-class passage to Europe when they over-stayed the bon voyage party. If the hilarity was irresponsible, the hangover was mostly imaginary. But so was the film, and it was as essential a part of the fantasy life of the thirties as the musicals that made us wonder (as Kerouac has written) "about the world that spoke of beautiful piney islands and Indian love calls and Jeanette MacDonald yet had nothing to show for it but jailhouses, arrested fathers, [and] distant moanings." Who is to say that our sense of the ambiguity of life—a distinctive trait of this generation—

did not begin when we watched Nelson Eddy singing "Ah, Sweet Mystery of Life" and then walked home through the bitter hardtime streets of 1935?

We learned so much from the movies, and the lessons were so painless, that I, for one, still associate certain films with the dawning of certain ideas. The social idealism of Frank Capra, for instance, probably reached its apogee in *Meet John Doe,* but it wasn't the betrayed utopianism of the film which impressed me so much as the dangerous heat and dire manipulations of mass politics that it crystallized in three faultless images. Edward Arnold's reptilian eyes behind his pince-nez will always signify for me the desperate lust for power out of which the powerlessness of modern life produces totalitarians. Barbara Stanwyck's gradual involvement in her own Frankenstein still seems to me one of the most succinct examples of how the liberal professional (or vice versa) can be tripped up by trying to walk both sides of the street. And James Gleason, magnificently drunk, attempting to light that memorably bent cigarette, and muttering, "Chalk up another one for the Pontius Pilates," expresses for all time the bitterness and disgust a decent man feels at the debauching of hope by one of Orwell's "smelly little orthodoxies." In the years that followed, when I became attracted to, and then involved with, and finally disaffected from, party politics, the memory of this film (and others like it) had an influence on my decisions and aversions that is incalculable.

But most of what we learned was not this specific. There was the horror film, for instance—a venerable and once-dignified genre which, like the detective novel, has degenerated in these latter days into a moronic comic book of meaningless gore. The thirties were the great years of the horror film—the age of *The Mummy* as well as *Frankenstein, The Old Dark House* as well as *Dracula,* and *Freaks* as well as *The Wolf Man*—but far from merely titillating tastes so jaded by newsreels of Belsen and Dachau that nothing but gouged-out eyeballs in lustful technicolor will serve to jog them, the great classics of our day were specifically films of moral complexity. We sympathized with Dr. Frankenstein's Monster, for his tragedy was the inability to love; we pitied King Kong, for after all wasn't he the visual embodiment of our own overgrown, inarticulate desires for Fay Wray? We knew even Dracula's loneliness before the empty mirror, and his daytime vulnerability there in the coffin. One reason why we became so absorbed in these grisly films was probably the crudity of the photography (the special effects were not as badly apparent as they are these days), but the deeper explanation certainly lies in the fact that they were fantasies erected on a solid foundation of psychological truth, and not mere *Grand Guignols* to raise the hackles.

We even learned to recognize such esoterica as the difference between the production values of one studio and another, and mine is the last generation for whom the name Cedric Gibbons, for instance, summons up that creamy, middle-tone elegance, that vast spectrum of subtle grays, with which he invested a thousand M-G-M films; a "look" that was as different from the work of his counterparts at other studios as a Cadillac is from an Oldsmobile. Warner Brothers films had the grainy, emphatic alternation between lights and darks that has typified social realism since Goya's day, and 20th-Century-Fox movies were as shiny, confidently vulgar and eye-catching as an electric toaster that will be out of date by next year.

Mine may have been the first generation which produced fans of directors, as well as stars, and I know half a dozen men, none of whom are connected with films today, whose boyhood ambition it was to wield a megaphone. I am one of them. For we knew a great deal about pictures and picturemaking, and I have seen our shot-by-shot re-creations of the movies of the thirties baffle a room full of our elders and our juniors. One night, for instance, I watched the face of a world-famous lady philosopher as two college professors, a poet and a novelist (myself) talked for two solid hours about Bela Lugosi. For the first half hour, she assumed he must be an obscure Hungarian writer, and when she learned the truth, her perplexity at the sight of four intellectuals lavishing on a film actor the sort of enthusiastic analysis that is usually reserved for a Poem or an Idea, brought home to us all, in a flash, how different moviegoing in the thirties was from moviegoing before or since.

We were a generation that no longer waited for the Great American Novel, but that spoke of the Great Hollywood Novel with the same spurious certainty that it would inevitably appear. Hollywood embodied for us the crucial dilemma of American society (the integrity of the individual vision in conflict with the pleasure- and profit-seeking materialism of an industrialized democracy) and the theme, plus its setting, has never lost its fascination for us, though the Hollywood of Scott Fitzgerald and Louis B. Mayer has all but vanished to the four corners of the earth.

But perhaps it was the experience of moviegoing itself that left the deepest impression on us. For moviegoing was sitting in the Plaza Theater in Englewood, New Jersey, with your imagination so heated by images of London or Paris that years later, when you found yourself there, your keenest response was a kind of *déjà vu* that made you round every corner fully expecting to come upon Nigel Bruce or Simone Simon. It was recognizing in yourself, even at thirteen, the anchorless, half bitter, half lyrical, unkempt, rebellious figure of John Garfield in *Four Daughters*—a romantic image of the disaffiliated hobo-artist that has been as difficult for some of us to shake off as the Hemingway sportsman-artist has been for others. It was seeing *Gunga Din* thirteen times with guilty, gluttonous pleasure that was tinged with the wistful knowledge that our world would never be as gallant, rollicking and simple as the one in which Sam Jaffe climbed that golden dome and saved British India from Eduardo Ciannelli. It was coming out of the theater at night, by yourself, and walking home under the summer-heavy trees, the drama continuing to spin on inside your head, so that years later you would realize that it was on those nights that you first learned that the dark is made for fantasies, freedoms and aspirations—unlike the Saturday afternoons of earlier years when the harsh light of day, somehow more graphic and revealing after the hours of darkness, returned you with a jolt to the same old street, the same old houses, with nowhere to take your aroused imagination but home to supper. It was fifteen-cent ticket stubs come upon weeks later in the tiny pockets of trousers rolled up at the cuffs; and counting off the minutes until the lights went out with all the impatience of a lover; and knowing the "Coming Attractions" announcement, different in each theater, as well as you knew your own saddle-shoes from those of your best friend.

But it was also the sharing of an initiation rite with your contemporaries (like suffering the same trauma and being supplied with the same clues to its cure), for the movies of the thirties constitute, for my generation, nothing less than a kind of Jungian collective unconscious, a decade of coming attractions out of which some of the truths of our maturity have been formed.

Censor the Movies!
Early Attempts to Regulate the Content of Motion Pictures in America, 1907-1936

Arthur F. McClure

The movement to censor the subject matter of the American motion picture began very early in its history. It has persisted since that time with varying degrees of intensity. The following is an investigation of the attempts to regulate movie content both inside and outside of the film industry during the first three decades of the American movie.

I. GROWING PAINS OF AN INDUSTRY

In the early part of the twentieth century, motion pictures were still largely a curiosity: they were inexpensive to make; individuals sometimes produced only one picture, which was then rented to exhibitors; a number of the stories had "daring" scenes which were often popular with audiences. Such considerations as moral content, or even good taste, were absent from many of them.

These crude pictures gave rise to criticism on the part of reform-minded people, which in turn led to attempts at both self-regulation by the industry and to legal censorship. In 1907, Chicago was the first city to pass a municipal law establishing censorship of motion pictures. From 1909 to 1922, seven states passed censorship laws, as did a number of cities. Federal censorship of the motion picture industry was advocated by various groups. There were some attempts to clean up motion pictures from within the industry. A few early producers tried to improve their pictures by an avoidance of the kinds of scenes that had been deleted from other pictures by censor boards.

Lewis Jacobs, in his *Rise of the American Film,* states that it was

117

in the period from 1903 to 1908 that the foundations of the motion picture industry were established. The industry rapidly grew from a novelty into a large, permanent business. Production, distribution, and exhibition of the motion picture expanded to a national level. As the industry grew, it suffered a number of censorship difficulties.

In 1903, Edwin S. Porter produced the "first picture story" with a full length theme, *The Great Train Robbery,* which took two years to become a national hit due to the unorganized distribution methods of the time. This picture brought about the popularity of the "nickelodeon." The first one of these movie houses was opened in Pittsburgh on Thanksgiving Day in 1905 by John P. Harris.[1] The five-cent admissions were so popular that there were soon eight to ten thousand exhibitors in the United States.[2]

The industry was beset by patent wars, infringements, and piracy. The keen competition produced petty jealousies, cutthroat practices, law violations, and lawsuits. During this time of dissension the industry was frequently attacked by outside agencies. In March 1907, an editorial entitled "The Five Cent Theatre" appeared in the *Chicago Tribune* describing the nickelodeon in scathing phrases:

> without a redeeming feature to warrant their existence . . . ministering to the lowest passions of childhood . . . proper to suppress them at once . . . should be a law absolutely forbidding entrance of boy or girl under eighteen . . . influence is wholly vicious . . . There is no voice raised to defend the majority of five cent theatres, because they cannot be defended. They are hopelessly bad.[3]

Movie-baiting became common throughout the United States. The attacks came from ministers, theater critics, and social reformers. Jacobs states that the chief motive for this flood of protest was economic; the movies had become a competitor of the church, vaudeville, and the saloon.[4]

In 1907, in New York City, the Children's Society instituted a regulative movement against an exhibitor for showing pictures of "The Great Thaw Trial" to minors. On December 24, 1908, Mayor George B. McClellan closed all the movie houses in New York City pending an investigation which led ultimately to the formation of the National Board of Censorship. This extra-legal group that viewed and passed pictures on to the public satisfied some of the agitation for cleaner films.[5] Since the board had the approval and backing of the Motion Picture Patents Company, formed by the ten leading producers in the industry, the name of the board was changed in 1916 to the National Board of Review. The word "censorship" was distasteful to producers. The attack by censorship advocates during 1907–1908 caused the movie producers to adopt fiction and plays with an approved literary standing because it was felt that material taken from these works would not provide critics with an excuse for further attacks.[6]

By 1908, thousands of people were attending the nickelodeons regularly. Movies were recognized by this time as not just a curiosity but a powerful means of social expression. Films were said to be the chief sources for "new ideas, points of view, attitudes toward government and society, habits of mind, standards of taste, conduct, morals, canons of convention, culture"[7] for children and the uneducated.

Nationally, the leadership in the censorship movement belonged to the Reverend Wilbur Fisk Crafts (Presbyterian), superintendent of the International Reform Bureau, who advocated a national censorship law and was instrumental in Congressional committee hearings as early as 1915. The Reverend William Sheafe Chase, Canon of Christ Church (Episcopal), in Brooklyn, was also one of the leaders. He wrote much censorship literature during the 1920s and served as Secretary of the Federal Motion Picture Council, an organization devoted to the passage of federal censorship.[8]

From 1908 to 1914 the motion picture business was in the midst of a bitter fight for economic control. There was a constant squabble over patent rights. By means of the Motion Picture Patents Company, the ten leading manufacturers of cameras and projectors monopolized the rental of films and its viewing equipment. Exhibitors were charged two dollars per week for use of the companies' projectors. The only films that exhibitors could show on this equipment were those produced by licensed members of the trust. If exhibitors violated this agreement, they were fined or deprived of film service.[9] Following a long series of litigations, the power of the company was broken by 1914 and outlawed in 1917 as the result of an antitrust suit.[10] This competition improved the quality of films, and the themes became more sophisticated before the questioning attitudes and more educated thinking of the middle class audiences who were now becoming aware of the art of the motion picture.[11]

During World War I, the American film industry became the world's leading producer of motion pictures. Because of the strain of the war, the film industries of France, England, Germany, and other European countries collapsed. There was rapid expansion in the industry in the United States due to the war boom. The world's "capital" of movie-making became Hollywood, a small community near Los Angeles. It was during the war that the producers created the "star" system and publicity campaigns reached phenomenal proportions.

Stars were deliberately created, and established ones were strengthened by the publicity. They were the means by which producers stabilized production. Nothing was too outlandish in an effort to try to build up a following for the stars. Their salaries, and other production costs, made competition keen. By 1929, the studios were spending an aggregate of $20 million annually for salaries and another $12 million for raw materials.[12]

Hollywood became the glamor center of an industry that grew too fast; too many individuals were made rich overnight. Some of the stars "began to react like children in a room full of bright new toys—only, their toys included high-powered cars, bootleg whiskey, expensive women, and drugs. They believed their own publicity."[13]

After the war, the motion picture industry was caught in two conflicting social attitudes. One was the belief in the old dogmas with their moralistic idealism; the other was the desire of the new postwar generation to be free from all tradition and convention of the past. Sex began to be exploited by the producers in their films and advertising. Cecil B. DeMille became the most famous director of this period with his films of the "modern" generation. Such pictures as *Adam's Rib, For Better or Worse,* and *Forbidden Fruit* were a few of the many such pictures he made of this variety. He commented:

> The 1920's were the era of, among other phenomena, the flapper. With her bobbed hair, her short skirts and rolled stockings, her preference for the athletic Charleston over the sedate waltz, she became as much an obsession to the pointers-with-alarm as Hollywood itself. . . . I did feel that the flapper was a maligned and plucky little person. Youth always revolts; it would not be worth its salt if it didn't.[14]

DeMille's films depicted the revolt of youth vividly.

The advertising of the films of this type was even more sensational. One advertisement read:

> HER HUSBAND DREW THE GIRL TO HIM AND—
> A long, long kiss, a kiss of youth and love and beauty, all concentrating like rays into one focus, kindled from above; such kisses as belong to early dawn. Where heart, and soul, and sense in concert move, and the blood is lava, and the pulse is ablaze!![15]

Another was worded:

> Does it pay to love without question? If you are in doubt, love without question. Stop, look, love without question. All women love without question. It haunts you to love without question. It is passion that makes one love without question.[16]

Benjamin Hampton, one of the best of movie historians and president of four production companies, remarked that "it makes you anxious to rush the kiddies to the show, doesn't it?"[17]

Newspapers and censorship advocates showed to the public the sordid side of Hollywood life. Many young girls had come to Hollywood to become stars and had been put in spurious "talent schools" or had gone on to worse fates. Stories circulated over the country telling of the amount "of prostitution, of studio 'call girls,' casting couches, and orgiastic parties."[18] The public believed that these were common things rather than the exception, as was the fact.

Beginning in 1920 there occurred a series of unfortunate scandals involving movie people that further put Hollywood in a bad light. In March of 1920, Mary Pickford, "America's Sweetheart," quietly left California and traveled to Nevada and obtained a divorce from her actor husband, Owen Moore.[19] A few days later she announced that she would never marry again. Before the month was over she was married to Douglas Fairbanks, the star of adventure films.[20] The day following the wedding, the Attorney-General of Nevada opened an investigation to determine whether the divorce was valid.[21] After a year in the Nevada court system, the Nevada Supreme Court upheld the divorce.[22] The whole affair put the motion picture industry in a bad light.

Late in the summer of 1921, Roscoe "Fatty" Arbuckle, a comedy star who had become famous as one of the "Keystone Kops," had a party in his San Francisco hotel room. Virginia Rappe, a young actress, died three days after the party.[23] Arbuckle was arrested on a manslaughter charge.[24] The story made headlines all over the country. The press hinted that Arbuckle had committed a sex crime.[25] Arbuckle pleaded that he was innocent of all charges.[26] A friend of Miss Rappe's, Mrs. Bambina Maude Delmont, testified that Arbuckle had dragged Miss Rappe into a room and raped her.[27] Arbuckle's films were withdrawn from the screen by his producers. After three trials, with much sordid testimony, Arbuckle was acquitted.[28]

There were other incidents in which famous motion picture people were involved. William Desmond Taylor, an English movie director working in the Lasky studios, was mysteriously murdered. Several female stars' careers were permanently damaged by the bad publicity they received in the affair. The story was said to have sold more newspapers than the entry of the United States into World War I.[29] Wallace Reid, a matinee idol of the day, died suddenly from the effects of narcotics.

These and lesser incidents created the impression over the country that Hollywood life was all bad. Many public groups condemned the industry, and a demand for federal censorship gained strength. The producers were still fighting among themselves, and this increased the bad publicity. For the first time in the industry's brief history, the box office began to waver. Many smaller producing companies were forced out of business. It was of great importance to the producers to get the business and moral questions settled and at the same time to stop the censorship movement.

Some of the troubles of the industry were remedied by the formation of the Motion Picture Producers and Distributors Association on March 11, 1922. Will H. Hays, Postmaster-General in the Harding Administration, accepted the position as president.[30] The choice of Hays was wise in that his prominence acted as a buffer against groups condemning the industry.

The censorship movement reached its peak in 1921. Nearly 100 bills in 37 state legislatures were presented in 1921 for state censorship of motion pictures. Federal censorship was advocated in Congress. Many suggestions for ways to censor the movies were discussed. Hays pointed to the situation of the industry in 1922 when he said:

> The industry had grown like a mushroom, more in scope and dollars than in self-control. Tougher or more ruthless competition would have been hard to find, or greater rewards for courage and resourcefulness. It was that kind of business. And too often there was an apparent conflict between making fine pictures and making more money. . . . Motion pictures were suffering from the rashness of youth and a bad case of growing pains. . . . As I went about the country talking with editors and others who knew what was going on, it was evident that the motion picture situation was bad. It was more than a question of mild censorship. *It was a case of self-regulation or prohibition.*[31]

II. CONTROLS WITHIN THE INDUSTRY

The National Board of Censorship of Motion Pictures was organized in March 1909, by the People's Institute of New York City. Charles Sprague Smith was founder and director of the People's Instiute, an organization for adult education and social research.[1] The Board was formed because of the showing of sensational pictures in New York City, principally *The Great Thaw Trial,* which included such scenes as a man being drugged and the portrayal of a murder on the roof of Madison Square Garden. There was much public protest because there were children present at the showings.[2] As has been seen, Mayor McClellan ordered that all of the nickelodeons in the city be closed. The Board was organized with the cooperation of the theater owners in New York City. In June of 1909, at the request of the motion picture producers and various communities across the country, the Board began to view pictures made by producers in other parts of the country. The Motion Picture Patents Company was one of the Board's backers, and this later caused a complaint from reformers that the Board was actually a tool of the motion picture producers. The Board was self-governing. It elected its own officers and executive staff and controlled its own finances. No member of the Board was engaged in any branch of the motion picture industry, and no member received a salary for his work on the

Board. The principal authority of the Board rested in a General Committee of twenty members, chosen from civic and educational organizations. The chairman of this committee was Dr. Frederick C. Howe, who later became the Commissioner of Immigration at New York City.[3]

The actual work of censoring was done by several subcommittees chosen by the General Committee. The Review Committee was a large group of 250 members that was divided into subcommittees which met daily in the various motion pictures studios provided by the producers.[4] The large size of the Review Committee was to insure fairness of judgment and represent the general public opinion.

The Review Committee viewed the films and made criticisms of them. The films were changed when it was thought necessary, or completely approved or rejected for public viewing. The Committee determined its action by a majority vote. The film producer could appeal any decision by the Board. The original censoring committee stated its reasons for changes, and a notification of the final action of the Board was sent to the producer. If the Board found that a producer ignored its findings, then all relations with that producer were severed.[5]

The Board had no legal authority. Its power was in the acquiescence of the member producers to that form of censorship. The Board set up eight standards upon which it based its judgments. They were as follows:

1. The Board prohibits obscenity in all forms.
2. The Board prohibits vulgarity when it offends or when it verges toward indecency, unless an adequate moral purpose is served.
3. The Board prohibits the representation of crime in such a detailed way as may teach the methods of committing crime except as a warning to the whole public.
4. The Board prohibits morbid scenes of crime, where the only value of the scene is its morbidity or criminal appeal. Nevertheless, the Board cannot judge films exclusively from the standpoint of children, or delicate women, of the emotionally morbid, or of any one class of audience. But the Board does take into consideration, as one of the controlling motives governing it, the fact that possibly twenty-five per cent of the total motion-picture audience is made up of children under sixteen.
5. The Board prohibits the unnecessary elaboration or prolongation of scenes of suffering, brutality, vulgarity, violence, or crime.
6. The Board prohibits blasphemy, by which is understood the careless or wanton or unnecessary offence against religious susceptibilities of any large number of people in the country.
7. The Board prohibits anything obviously or wantonly libelous in films, anything calculated to cause injury to persons or interests from an obviously malicious or libelous motive, and films dealing with questions of fact which relate to criminal cases pending in the courts.

But the Board does not censor motion pictures from the standpoint of protecting the exhibitor or manufacturer from the consequences of producing a film which may alienate some powerful element in the community. To illustrate: the Board would permit the production of a film containing a non-libelous attack on a great political party, even though the circulation of this film would result in making enemies for the producer of the films, or for the whole motion-picture business.

The Board does not, in judging films, allow itself to be influenced by the moral character of persons who may be concerned in the production or acting of films. But the Board does retain the right to forbid, at its discretion, the exploitation of unworthy reputations, such as the morbid representation of persons who may have been associated with famous criminal cases.

8. In addition to the above specifications, the Board feels in general that it is right in forbidding scenes or films which, because of elements frequently very subtle which they contain, have a deteriorating tendency on the basic moralities or necessary social standards.[6]

By 1914, it was estimated that the Board inspected 98 percent of all films exhibited in the United States.[7] This seems to be a large estimate because the percentage of uninspected films provided enough bad films to keep the censorship advocates clamoring for censorship laws. The chief criticism of the Board was that it was too voluntary and that some producers paid no attention to the requests of the Board.

In 1916 the Board changed its name to the National Board of Review, and the slogan of the organization became "Selection Not Censorship."[8] The stamp "Passed by the Board of Review" was used to promote the betterment of the content of motion pictures, but the Board was opposed to legal censorship as the means for that end. There is no doubt that the Board was influenced by the producers of motion pictures. Its financial support came mainly from the fees that it imposed for the viewing of films. Just how much this dependence on previewing fees affected its decisions would be difficult to determine exactly, but its findings were so liberal that censorship advocates were very critical of the Board. When the censorship question arose through the years, the Board always opposed it by printing many pamphlets and by having its members make numerous public speeches. It worked very closely with the industry in its fight against deletions by the various state censor boards.

On July 6, 1916, the National Association of Motion Picture Industries was formed by a majority of the producers and distributors in an effort to avert federal censorship. This organization was a cooperative effort by leading producers and distributors much like the "Hays Office" that was formed in 1922. The members announced a self-censorship program aimed at stopping the censorship movement.[9] They were in favor of having the First Amendment cover the motion pictures. This idea failed. They were also in favor of including motion pictures in the penal laws of the United States so as to forbid the transportation by any common carrier of indecent pictures in interstate commerce. This attempt to control obscenity of films at the federal level was passed by Congress on June 5, 1920, as a revision of section 245 of the *United States Penal Code.*

There was no immediate improvement because of slowness in executing the law, and the demand for federal censorship remained strong. The Association's plans for self-regulation were embodied in the "Thirteen Points" which it announced on March 7, 1921. The president of the Association, William A. Brady, did much to push these reforms, but the industry did not support the organization either financially or morally.[10] The "Thirteen Points" were resolutions condemning pictures:

1. Which emphasize and exaggerate sex appeal or depict scenes therein exploiting interest in sex in an improper or suggestive form or manner.
2. Based upon white slavery or commercialized vice or scenes showing the procurement of women or any of the activities attendant upon this traffic.
3. Thematically making prominent an illicit love affair which tends to make virtue odious and vice attractive.
4. With scenes which exhibit nakedness or persons scantily dressed, particularly suggestive bedroom and bathroom scenes and scenes of inciting dancing.
5. With scenes which unnecessarily prolong expressions or demonstrations of passionate love.
6. Predominantly concerned with the underworld or vice and crime, and like scenes, unless the scenes are part of an essential conflict between good and evil.
7. Of stories which make gambling and drunkenness attractive, or of scenes which show the use of narcotics and other unnatural practices dangerous to social morality.
8. Of stories and scenes which may instruct the morally feeble in methods of committing crimes, or, by cumulative processes, emphasize crime and the commission of crime.
9. Of stories or scenes which ridicule or deprecate public officials, officers of the law, the United States Army, the United States Navy, or other governmental authority, or which tend to weaken the authority of the law.
10. Of stories or scenes or incidents which offend religious belief or any person, creed or sect, or ridicule ministers, priests, rabbis, or recognized leaders of any religious sect, and also which are disrespectful to objects or symbols used in connection with any religion.
11. Of stories or with scenes which unduly emphasize bloodshed and violence without justification in the structure of the story.

12. Of stories or with scenes which are vulgar and portray improper gestures, posturing, and attitudes.
13. With salacious titles and subtitles in connection with their presentation or exhibitions, and the use of salacious advertising matter, photographs, and lithographs in connection therewith.[11]

These "Thirteen Points" were the first written set of standards by the industry. They might have sufficed if the members of the Association had not been so distrustful of each other and had done more than pay lip service to them.

From 1915, the year that the first censorship bill was introduced, the criticism of the motion picture grew steadily. The press recognized that some motion pictures were not clean enough for public use, but no periodical or newspaper was a defender of censorship laws. Many articles appeared with titles such as "Movie Abuses a National Calamity,"[12] "Time to Clean Up Movie Morals,"[13] "Where the Blame Lies for Movie Sex Stuff,"[14] and "How Motion Pictures Promote Crime."[15] Many editorials and articles against censorship appeared in such magazines as the *Independent,* the *New Republic,* and *The Nation.* The *Literary Digest* tried to give both sides of the controversy. *The New York Times* also reported the question quite objectively. In 1916, in an editorial, the paper said that "censors are not good because in their attempt to obtain their purpose they go too far into the field of taste and opinion. They tend to magnify their authority, and to become ruthless and despotic."[16] This attitude toward censorship laws persisted in its editorials and in 1921 it noted:

When it comes to deciding what is and what is not "immoral, inhuman, sacrilegious or of such character that their exhibition would tend to corrupt morals or incite crime," the controversies will be simply innumerable, and the censors will find themselves the constant objects of denunciation or ridicule—for the most part well deserved. To put on the movies any restrictions from which books, the speaking stage, painting, and sculpture are exempt will be logically indefensible and practically impossible.[17]

At the time of the passage of the censorship law for New York, *The Times* commented that "It can do no more for the suppression of the rather limited amount of indecency now existent in the movies than other agencies already at work."[18] The publishers of *The Times* and other periodicals no doubt were reluctant to place any restrictions on any form of communications medium. They realized the advantages of freedom of the press and were not anxious to see any curtailment of this freedom.

There were many suggestions for cleansing the content of motion pictures short of censorship laws. It was suggested that, to avoid the evil influences sometimes exerted on children by pictures of violence and vice, special theaters for children be established or programs be presented at special hours of the day that were suitable for children.[19]

One critic wanted a broad public opinion formed by having the members of organizations such as the General Federation of Women's Clubs see a picture each week and write letters to theater-managers expressing an opinion. This, he said, would create "a sound, broad public opinion."[20]

The Better Films Committee of the National Congress of Mothers and Parent-Teacher Associations suggested that there be a mother-teacher censorship of the motion pictures. They conducted a study of movies that they considered suitable for children. It was the hope of the committee that with the help of the teachers, the taste of the children could be so improved that in time they would not care for trash in motion pictures.[21]

Most critics felt that the National Board of Review was too voluntary and realized that many "pirate" films were not being reviewed. It was suggested that perhaps the motion pictures might be supervised by the Department of Education in Washington, D.C.[22] By 1921 it was evident that regulatory measures were needed as a means to clean up the movies. Enemies of censorship felt that sooner or later the decisions of the censor boards would turn their own opinions into terms of popular ideology. The producers feared censorship laws in any form, but they recognized that drastic action was needed to combat them.

In December of 1921, there appeared rumors of an offer having been made to Will H. Hays, Postmaster-General, to head a new motion picture cooperative trade association.[23] There is no evidence to show that the producers were interested in forming the new association because of their sense of responsibility to the public.

On January 15, 1922, Hays announced that he was leaving the Harding cabinet to become the president of the new trade association.[24] On January 18, Hays signed a contract to head the new organization at an annual salary of $100,000.[25] He officially took office on March 4, 1922.[26] He had shown ability in his direction of the postal department and was a shrewd politician with a good businesslike touch. He was an elder in the Presbyterian church, and this gave him a respectability before the public that the motion picture industry was lacking at the time. He became the spokesman for the industry to the public. Hays said in New York:

> The potentialities of the moving picture for moral influence and education are limitless, therefore its integrity should be protected as we protect the integrity of our churches, and its quality developed as we develop the quality of our schools.[27]

The Motion Picture Producers and Distributors of America, Incorporated, as the new trade association was called, was incorporated in New York state on March 11, 1922.[28] (Hereafter it will be referred to as the MPPDA.) When it was formed it had nine member companies. Eight were producers and one was a distributor. Approximately 60 percent of all American films were made by these companies.[29] By 1930 the membership numbered 21 producers,[30] and the percentage of films produced was estimated to be more than 90 percent. Hays was president and chairman of the board of directors. The bylaws gave the president the power of veto over decisions by the board of directors, with two-thirds vote by the board required to override the veto. In the certificate of incorporation the purpose of the organization was said to be:

> to foster the common interests of those engaged in the motion picture industry in the United States by establishing and maintaining the highest possible moral and artistic standards in motion picture production, by developing the educational as well as the entertainment value and the general usefulness of the motion picture, by diffusing accurate and reliable information with reference to the industry, by reforming abuses relative to the industry, by securing freedom from unjust and unlawful exactions, and by other lawful and proper means.[31]

The home office was to be in New York City. A sister organization was the Association of Motion Picture Producers, Incorporated, with its offices in Hollywood. The Hollywood office was actually only a branch offices of the MPPDA. Under the bylaws of the MPPDA there were five classes of members:

Class A: Producers of motion pictures
Class B: Distributors of motion pictures
Class C: Individuals appointed by members of Class A
Class D: Individuals appointed by members of Class B
Class E: Other Individuals[32]

The MPPDA was financed by the dues of company members. The dues were based upon the amount of business done by each member and computed upon the annual gross earnings of each of the producers and distributors in their domestic business.[33] There is no evidence that Hays ever practiced the tactics of a "czar." He was sincere in his efforts to clean up the content of motion pictures and very cooperative with his attackers. The connotation of "czar" probably came from the "czar" position of Judge Kenesaw Mountain Landis as baseball commissioner. Hays was the spokesman for the organization, and as far as the matter of censorship was concerned, it was recognized as speaking for the entire industry.[34] It performed most of the functions of a trade association in its handling of trade practices, public relations, and legal matters. The "Hays Office" was the nickname given to the MPPDA because of Hays's utterances in behalf of the industry until his retirement in 1945.

The formation of the MPPDA did not solve all of the problems of the industry. The accent on sensational themes in motion pictures continued through the nineteen twenties and thirties. Attacks from censorship groups were still common. The Federal Motion Picture Council, W.C.T.U., Protestant Episcopal Church, Methodist Episcopal Church, National Grange, and more than thirty other religious and educational groups advocated the adoption of censorship laws by distributing leaflets, giving public addresses, and passing resolutions in annual conventions.

The MPPDA was an organization formed for self-regulation within an industry. Its standards varied from what some thought to be proper content for motion pictures. Public and civic groups were shocked at various pictures that were made. Hays always stressed cooperation with civic, welfare, and educational agencies in an effort to develop a demand for better pictures and to encourage producers to make them.[35] He felt that this was the way to combat any legal censorship. A few months after the formation of the MPPDA, Hays arranged a conference with outside organizations interested in the motion picture problem. The more than two hundred persons who attended represented numerous organizations.[36] A majority of the representatives were from women's societies. For the most part the women were interested in cleaning up motion pictures because of their effects on children.

Some of the organizations, with nation-wide memberships, that cooperated with the MPPDA by distribution of printed material, speeches, and conferences, throughout the country were the General Federation of Women's Clubs; Daughters of the American Revolution; Y.M.C.A.; International Federation of Catholic Alumni; and the National Congress of Parents and Teachers.[37]

Catholic organizations supported the MPPDA until the formation of the Legion of Decency in the 1930s. These organizations and the Roman Catholic Church grew tired of what they referred to as the "promises of the 'Hays Office'" to clean up films, but at no time did the Roman Catholics advocate legal censorship. They felt that it would run counter to their fight for religious freedoms.

Hays made several trips to Hollywood in 1922 and advised the producers to play down flamboyant publicity such as the fabulous salaries of the stars. He suggested that the better aspects of Hollywood life be emphasized, and he wrote numerous articles and made many speeches on this subject. He tried to win the public's favor for the industry. He concluded that "nothing is wrong with motion pictures . . . except youth."[38] No one was quite sure what he meant by that statement, but neither did anyone question it.

In the fall of 1922, the MPPDA formed a Committee on Public Relations. Its duties were to promote to the public the organization's approved pictures and to report to the MPPDA objections to pictures that it had disapproved.[39] This committee lasted for two and one-half years and acted as a channel for criticism to the various civic groups cooperating with the MPPDA. In 1924, the National Congress of Parents and Teachers and the General Federation of Women's Clubs withdrew their support of the Committee and publicly condemned the MPPDA when Hays refused to stop "Fatty" Arbuckle from trying to return to the screen.[40] Hays maintained that he only meant to allow Arbuckle to become a director of films.[41]

The first test of strength for the MPPDA came in November of 1922, when it threw its strength against a referendum in Massachusetts calling for state censorship. When the motion was defeated by a three to one vote, the MPPDA was encouraged. Although the opposition was not well organized during the campaign, Hays felt that a great victory had been won.[42]

In March of 1925, the Department of Public Relations was formed to take the place of the Committee on Public Relations.[43] Hays then inaugurated his famous "open door" policy. He announced that:

> Here in our Department of Public Relations is the Open Door of the industry. The public individually or through organization is invited to come in, bring complaints, suggestions, plans and ideas. Inside the open door is a table. On the table are motion picture problems. The solution of the problems challenges the help of every well-wisher for better things. . . . The organized industry sits in one chair. There is another chair right here for the organized moral forces of the country to occupy. Together, we can continue the solution of the problems. Every one is invited who has a constructive suggestion. The door will always be open.[44]

The director of the Department was Jason S. Joy. The "open door" policy proved to be a successful one. There was a marked increase in the number of organizations cooperating with the MPPDA from approximately 75 to more than 200 in three years.[45] The Committee on Public Relations had limited itself to organizations with national memberships. By 1930, the new department cooperated with three to four hundred organizations, on the national, state, and local levels.

A number of speeches were made by Hays, Joy, and Carl E. Milliken. Milliken had been Governor of Maine and in 1926 became Secretary of the MPPDA. On January of 1927, he took over from Joy in the Public Relations Department.[46] Letters were written to groups and individuals specifying the functions of the MPPDA to the public. These letters were not stereotyped but were individual answers to various criticisms and suggestions. Hays was grateful that leading newspapers, including *The New York Times,* viewed the MPPDA in a favorable light.[47] His "open door" policy was the first significant success for the MPPDA. The second was to be the twin "codes" of 1930.

Attacks on the MPPDA continued. Hays was often powerless because a large percentage of the pictures were produced by non-member producers who were looking for quick profits. But member producers also would go as far toward borderline themes as they felt the MPPDA would accept for distribution.

A number of organizations and individuals were offended by these "modern" themes in motion pictures. The American Cinema Association said that movies should be cleaned up for the public.[48] Reverend Chase, the perennial censorship leader, said that the movies that showed gangsters in a favorable light instigated crime.[49] The motion picture committee of the General Federation of Women's Clubs conducted a study and decided that gangster pictures and pictures that emphasize sex were bad for children. The committee called upon the MPPDA to act.[50]

There were also attacks from minority groups. For example, the American-Irish Vigilance Committee protested against anti-Irish pictures at their annual meeting in New York City in 1927.[51]

Hays was criticized for using his position as elder in the Presbyterian Church to influence its decisions toward censorship. Before the inception of the MPPDA, the Presbyterian Church had, at various annual meetings, proposed that rigid censorship laws be enacted. In 1922, the General Assembly of the Presbyterian Church met in New York City. The Assembly instructed the Board of Temperance and Moral Welfare to begin a movement which would seek "to unite all the moral agencies of America in a concerted request to Congress that such legislation be enacted" that would make mandatory the production of pictures "in accordance with certain well-defined moral standards, this legislation to be applied at the point of production; that is, before the picture is made."[52]

Later it was charged that Hays had used his position in the Church to bring about this softening of regulatory proposals by the Presbyterians. Hays denied using any influence to bring about the change. The charge was never proven, but there was a possibility that the new measures advocated by the Presbyterians were a partial compromise to the position held by their famous elder.

In 1924, Hays promoted the first step toward self-regulation by the MPPDA with what was called the "Formula." The Formula was strictly a voluntary acquiescence by producers not to produce pictures that were suggestive in their theme, titles, or advertising.[53] Formal notices were sent to all of the members of the MPPDA stating when a proposed picture had been rejected by a producing company. No other company was supposed to produce a rejected story. The names of the plays or books were published but not the names of the companies that had proposed to make the picture. The cooperation in respecting the decision of the rejecting company was not legally binding to the members, and there was only an unwritten understanding among the members to respect the rejections.[54] The voluntary nature of the Formula was because of the fear of coming into conflict with the Sherman Anti-trust Act.

Some difficulties arose. Before the notice could be sent out to the members telling of the rejection, another company would buy the picture rights. The first company would often reject a title simply because they had no star to fit the leading role, but a rival company would have such a star. Constant squabbles arose from such a voluntary effort. The only means of enforcement was Hays's persuasive powers, and that was not enough to stop companies when they were looking for good profits.

In spring, 1927, the MPPDA set up a committee to make a study of the eliminations made by official censor boards in the various cities and states. In June of 1927 the California branch of the "Hays Office" adopted the committee's report. A resolution was signed that listed eleven things which "shall not appear in pictures produced by the members of this association, irrespective of the manner in which they are treated," and twenty-five other subjects with respect to which the producers agreed to exercise special care "to the end that vulgarity and suggestiveness may be eliminated and that good taste may be emphasized."[55] This resolution was labeled the "Don'ts and Be Carefuls." They were adopted unanimously as Rule 21 of the trade practices code at a conference conducted by the Federal Trade Commission in New York City in October of 1927.[56]

The "Don'ts" were:

> 1. Pointed profanity—by either title or lip—this includes the words "God," "Lord," "Jesus," "Christ," (unless they be used reverently in connection with proper religious ceremonies), "hell," "damn," "Gawd," and every other profane and vulgar expression however it may be spelled;
> 2. Any licentious or suggestive nudity—in fact or in silhouette; and any lecherous or licentious notice thereof by other characters in the picture;
> 3. The illegal traffic in drugs;
> 4. Any inference of sex perversion;
> 5. White slavery;

    6. Miscegenation (sex relationships between the white and black races) ;

    7. Sex hygiene and venereal diseases;

    8. Scenes of actual childbirth—in fact or in silhouette;

    9. Children's sex organs;

    10. Ridicule of the clergy;

    11. Willful offense to any nation, race or creed.[57]

The "Be Carefuls" included warnings concerning the treatment of such things as the use of the flag, international relations, arson, firearms, theft, robbery, brutality, murder techniques, smuggling methods, hangings or electrocutions, sympathy for criminals, sedition, cruelty to children and animals, branding of people or animals, the sale of a woman's virtue, rape or attempted rape, first-night scenes, man and woman in bed together, deliberate seduction of girls, surgical operations, drugs, and excessive or lustful kissing particularly when one character or the other was a "heavy."[58]

The subject of the entire resolution was very similar to the "13 Points" of the defunct National Association of the Motion Picture Industry. The content of pictures was still being filled with cheap topics that the producers thought would hold an audience. There was a growing tendency for members to take lightly admonitions from the MPPDA and to make pictures on the borderline of art and simple bad taste. The cautions might have been retitled "Do" and "Be Careless."[59]

The introduction of sound in the late nineteen twenties made the job of the Hays organization even more difficult. The uses of double-meanings and profanities in the talking pictures brought more protests down upon it from various groups.[60]

On March 31, 1930, the MPPDA adopted the Motion Picture Production Code. This Code was conceived by Hays, Martin J. Quigley, and Father Daniel A. Lord, S. J. The need for a Code had been evident since the unsuccessful attempts made at administering the "Don'ts and Be Carefuls" of 1927.

In the summer of 1929, Hays looked at a rough draft of a set of rules that Quigley had drawn up.[61] These rules closely paralleled the "Don'ts and Be Carefuls." Quigley had consulted Father Lord during the writing of this draft. The three men were in constant communication for the remainder of the summer. Hays did little or no writing of the Code, but many of his own ideas went into the writing of it.[62] Hays dismissed as absurd the accusation that the Code was only an instrument of the Catholic Church.[63] Quigley, the publisher of the *Motion Picture Herald*, was a devout Catholic, and Father Lord was a drama professor at St. Louis University, but Hays said that the charge was ridiculous and that anyone reading the Code would note no specific Catholic influence in it. Father Lord denied the accusation and stated that he had participated in writing it as an individual and not a Catholic priest.[64] The Code was formally adopted by the Hollywood branch of the MPPDA on February 17, 1930.[65] On March 31, 1930, the MPPDA in New York also adopted it.[66]

The New Code included all of the "Don'ts" and a majority of the "Be Carefuls" of 1927. The Code began with the statement of the three "general principles" which were followed by rules relating to particular application, divided into twelve headings. The new Code, besides containing new items, expanded and clarified the meaning of the "Be Carefuls" at several points. The new material included the rules regarding brutal killings, revenge, uses of liquor, adultery, scenes of passion, obscenity, costume, dances, and titles.

The enforcement of the Code was faulty. Producers again were placed in too much of a voluntary position, and the MPPDA did not rigidly enforce the Code. Producers would go as far as they could in interpreting the provisions of the Code. Some producers felt that several of the things that the Code forbade and restricted were the very things that audiences wanted. At the same time the full effects of the depression hit the industry. The years immediately following the adoption of the Code were financially bad for the industry. Deviations from the Code, in numerous instances, came out of desperation.

The Advertising Code was adopted in June of 1930, to provide "truth, honesty, and integrity" in motion picture advertising. It too was well-meaning, but was very loosely enforced.

The adoption of the two codes decreased the amount of agitation by reformers and censorship advocates for more than a year. There were not many magazine or newspaper articles that appeared during this quiet period. Dissatisfaction began to appear by July of 1931 concerning the way the Codes were being enforced. One of the first of these criticisms came from the Catholics. At a convention of the Catholic Daughters of America in Atlantic City, New Jersey, on July 9, 1931, a resolution was formulated stating that motion picture laws and self-regulation attempts were not being enforced properly.[68]

Protestant groups also were not satisfied with the work of the MPPDA. The *Christian Century* was especially outspoken in its criticism.[69] The Northern Baptists,[70] W. C. T. U.,[71] Protestant Episcopal Church,[72] Methodist Episcopal Church,[73] and the United Lutheran Church of America[74] were a few of the groups that advocated federal censorship of the movies and the strengthening of the state laws to stop the flow of the cheap stories.

The pressure from groups like these, and the Legion of Decency campaign by the Catholics in 1933–1934, finally caused the MPPDA to set up a more efficient means of enforcing the Codes. The Production Code Administration was established in July of 1934.[75] Joseph I. Breen, a former newspaperman, was put in charge of the P. C. A. No producer in the MPPDA could release or distribute a picture without a certificate of approval from the P. G. A. There was also a resolution that established a $25,000 fine for releasing any picture without the certificate of approval.[76] The producers agreed to be bound to this resolution as if it were a contract. The P. C. A. put more power in the hands of the MPPDA with the result that motion picture content was cleaned up in the middle part of the 1930s.

III. CENSORSHIP LAWS

In 1895 the first known instance of motion picture censorship by a legal means occurred in Atlantic City, New Jersey, when some unknown spectator protested to the police about the showing of a film depicting Dolorita's "Passion Dance" in a peep-show on the Boardwalk.[1] In 1896 objections arose over the famous May Irwin–John C. Rice "kiss," the first love scene in the history of the motion picture.[2]

A movement for government control of the content of motion pictures persisted throughout the period of 1907–1936. Attempts were made on the federal, state, and city levels to clean up the content of pictures. No federal law providing for general censorship of motion pictures was ever passed, but several laws were enacted that affected pictures. The state and city laws were more precise and they comprised the most successful and powerful attempts at censorship legislation.

Federal regulation of motion pictures was exercised in various ways. In 1920, a statute of the criminal code forbade the interstate transportation of "any obscene, lewd, or lascivious, or any filthy"[3] motion picture, under a penalty of a fine not to exceed $5000 or imprisonment not to exceed five years, or both. An earlier statute in 1913 had made unlawful the importation or interstate transportation of "any film or other pictorial representation of any prize fight or encounter of pugilists, under whatever name, which is designed to be used for purposes of public exhibition."[4] This act was passed as a result of strong racial feeling that accompanied the victory of Jack Johnson, a Negro, over Jim Jeffries, a white man, in a heavyweight championship boxing match in 1912. The law was not repealed until 1940.[5]

In 1916, a law was passed that made it unlawful to wear the uniform of the Army, Navy, Marines, or similar uniforms, in such ways that could bring discredit or reproach upon those branches of the armed forces of the United States.[6] The Tariff Act of 1909 provided that all films imported from other countries were to be subject to censorship by the Secretary of the Treasury.[7] The authority to censor pictures was never exercised by the Secretary of the Treasury mainly because the number of films imported into the United States was very small during the period of 1907–1936. The Tariff Act of 1930 forbade the importation of any picture which was obscene or immoral or which advocated treason or insurrection.[8]

The above federal censorship was seldom enforced stringently, as the prosecution of violators was a slow and cumbersome process. Most of the attempts at regulation by the federal government were rendered useless by their vagueness and ineffectual methods of enforcement.

Various bills were introduced in Congress providing for federal censorship of motion pictures. Generally these bills fell into two categories. Some advocated the prohibition of the interstate transportation of films portraying criminal activities. Others were designed to set up a federal motion picture commission empowered to establish standards for the motion picture industry and to license films as a prerequisite to their entering into interstate or foreign commerce.[9]

The first important federal censorship bill was known as the Hughes Bill. In May of 1916, Congressman Dudley M. Hughes of Georgia, Chairman of the House Education Committee, introduced a bill that provided for the creation of a Federal Motion Picture Commission.[10] The Commission was to be composed of five commissioners appointed for a term of six years by the President, and approved by the Senate. The license section of the bill provided that:

> The commission shall promptly license for interstate and foreign commerce every motion picture film presented to it as required herein, unless such film or a part thereof is obscene, a reproduction of an actual bullfight and prizefight, or is of such a character that its exhibition would tend to corrupt morals or incite to crime.[11]

The cost of the commission was to be borne by the industry. The bill provided for an initial appropriation by Congress, but after its organization the commission was to collect two dollars per thousand feet of film licensed and fifty cents for each additional copy of films. For violations of the license there was to be a thousand dollar fine or imprisonment not to exceed one year. The commission was empowered to establish as many branch offices throughout the country that it thought necessary.

A large amount of publicity surrounded this bill, but the bill was defeated after hearings held by the House Committee on Education. Chairman Hughes submitted a report that contained a letter that had been signed by representatives of the Paramount Pictures Corporation, Famous Players Films Company, Jesse L. Lasky Feature Play Company, and the Equitable Motion Picture Corporation stating a favorable attitude toward the proposed commission.[12] These larger producing companies maintained that they recognized the evils of cheap productions, and they, as "permanent companies," wanted no filth in pictures and therefore desired the establishment of the commission in order to stop any such practice.[13] Whether or not the larger companies were sincere in favoring the commission, the letter is unique because of the fact that it is the only expression favoring government control by any producers that the author has seen.

A bill was introduced by Congressman Theodore F. Appleby of New Jersey in February of 1922.[14] The Appleby Bill was similar to the Hughes Bill because it would have created a Federal Motion Picture Commission as a new division under the Bureau of Education. Appleby stated that his bill not only provided for censorship of motion pictures, but also for inquiry and research into the recreational and educational possibilities of motion pictures and for distribution of such information to the public. He felt that no two state censor boards thought alike; therefore, federal censorship would be better. He said that censorship was important in the relation of the motion picture to children and illiterates and the lasting impressions left on their minds.[15]

The most stringent bill ever introduced in Congress for federal censorship was the Upshaw Bill.[16] In December of 1925, Congressman William D. Upshaw of Georgia presented a bill that also provided for the creation of a Federal Motion Picture Commission as a division of the Department of Interior. The commission was to have seven members, composed of the Commissioner of Education and six commissioners, selected by the Secretary of the Interior. Two of the seven members were to be women. There were to be a minimum of two lawyers, two teachers, and one person who had been on a city or state censor board. The proposed bill would have given the commission the power to preview and license all motion pictures and to supervise the production of all motion pictures at the studios.[17] No film was to be accepted for interstate commerce until it had a license from the commission. The bill would have banned all films that showed illicit love, vice, white slavery, scenes of exaggerated sex, and nudity. Films showing current events were not to be subject to censorship. The commission was to have the power to fix the rentals for films and the admission rates of theaters. The commission could have taken over all of the distribution of films in the United States as a government function if, at any time, it ever felt it would be wise to do so.[18] The bill was never passed. The Roman Catholic Church and the American Federation of Labor were both opposed to the Upshaw Bill because of what they felt to be encroachments on basic American freedoms.[19]

Approximately sixty bills were introduced in Congress from 1915 until 1940 that provided some governmental control of the motion picture industry. Forty-four of these bills were introduced in the period of 1924–1940. New bills were introduced almost every year.

The Swoope Bill, introduced by Congressman William I. Swoope, was similar to the Upshaw Bill and was defeated in 1925. Senator Smith W. Brookhart of Iowa introduced several bills in the Senate in the early nineteen thirties that called for some sort of federal motion picture commission. In 1934, Congressman Raymond J. Cannon of Wisconsin introduced a bill which would have prohibited the interstate transportation of films that employed in their casts any persons convicted of moral turpitude. The bill also provided a ban on pictures which were "Suggestive and morally objectionable."[20] This bill was aimed at gangster films and films that emphasized sex. Congressman William C. Lankford of Georgia introduced a bill in 1931 that provided for the creation of a Department of General Welfare to censor both radio and motion pictures.[21] The Patman Bill of 1934, introduced by Congressman Wright Patman of Texas, and the Culkin Bill of 1937, introduced by Congressman Francis D. Culkin of New York, both attempted to establish federal regulation of motion picture content at the production point in the studios.

The only official censorship of motion pictures in the United States was through the passage of various state and municipal laws. Seven states passed laws that created state boards of censorship, and three states accomplished state censorship by indirect means.

The Pennsylvania State Board of Censors was formed on June 19, 1911, and was composed of three members and appointed by the governor for terms of three years. No motion picture could be exhibited until it had been submitted and approved by the Board of Censors. A certification that read "Approved by the Pennsylvania State Board of Censors" was put on every approved film. The board established rules and regulations and formulated standards of censorship in accordance with the films which were reviewed. Films for educational, charitable, fraternal or religious purposes were not subject to review.[22] The Pennsylvania law served as a pattern for the other state boards that were formed, and the provisions of several of the other state censorship laws were similar to the Pennsylvania law.

The second state to adopt a state board was Ohio in 1913. The Ohio Board of Censors was created and put under the authority of the Ohio Industrial Commission. The three members on the board were appointed by the Industrial Commission for terms of three years and were subject to the approval of the governor.

In 1921, the Board of Censors was abolished and censorship authority was given to the Division of Censorship in the Department of Education. In this instance, the censorship was done by an Advisory Board of Film Censorship in the Department of Education. This board consisted of three members who served without pay. The board worked closely with women's clubs and community organizations in its eliminations and rejections.[23] The protection of children was one of the primary purposes for the board's authority being shifted to the Department of Education.

The first censorship law in Kansas was introduced in the Kansas Senate on January 29, 1913. Senate Bill 367 provided for the prior censorship of all films exhibited in the state.[24] The act became law on April 1, 1913.[25] The law gave the Superintendent of Public Instruction the power to review and pass the films.

On January 23, 1917, House Bill 335 was introduced to alter the censorship process by the transfer of censorship responsibility from the Superintendent of Public Instruction to an independent board with three members.[26] The law was passed on March 31, 1917.[27] The provisions of the law were basically the same as the Pennsylvania censorship law. The name of the board became the Kansas Board of Review. This board had the power to censor advertising as well as motion pictures.

In 1915 the censorship of films by previous restraint was placed on a firm legal basis by the unanimous decision of the United States Supreme Court in the case of *Mutual Film Corporation v. Industrial Commission*.[28] It was contended that the Ohio censorship statute violated the state and federal constitution, interfered with interstate commerce, violated the freedom of speech, and placed legislative power in the hands of the Ohio censors. The Supreme Court ruled that the statute was a reasonable exercise of state police power.

The first Kansas censorship law was also contested in the case of *Mutual Film Corporation v. Hodges*,[29] on the grounds that it abridged freedom of opinion. The United States Supreme Court reasoned the same as in the Ohio case and said that the law was a valid exercise of the state police power.

Maryland passed a law in 1916 that created a Board of Censors with three members. One of the three had to be a member of the political party which had polled the second highest vote at the last general election prior to their appointment by the governor.[30] This law was also similar to the Pennsylvania statute.

New York passed an act in 1921 that provided for a Motion Picture Commission. On March 16, 1927, the Motion Picture Commission was put under the State Education Department. An amendment of the state education laws set up the duties and powers of the Commission. The statute provided that films be licensed unless they were found to be wholly or partly "obscene, indecent, immoral, inhuman, sacrilegious, or is of such a character that its exhibition would tend to corrupt morals or to incite to crime."[31]

A censorship law was passed in the General Assembly of Virginia on March 17, 1922. The law was passed after being one of the most "bitterly contested in the legislative annals of Virginia."[32] During public hearings that accompanied the bill, the Reverend Wilbur Crafts supported its passage. The law set up a State Board of Censors with power to censor films that were obscene or would incite to crime.[33]

On July 8, 1935, Louisiana passed a law providing for a censor board. This board was established by Governor Huey P. Long for use as a political bargaining weapon, but because of his death it never functioned actively.[34]

The state of Florida had an unusual method of censoring films. In 1921, a law was passed that gave the governor the right to appoint three persons from the state to be members of the National Board of Review. The law also stipulated that it was unlawful for any film to be exhibited in the state that had not been approved by either the National Board of Review or the state censorship board of New York.[35] This law was held unconstitutional in 1937 as an unwarranted delegation of legislative power to a foreign board.[36]

Connecticut achieved motion picture regulation under a revenue act that was passed in 1925. This was a taxation law that indirectly regulated the films that could be shown in the state by their examination before the issuance of the tax certificate necessary for public showings.[37] This act was repealed in 1927.

In Massachusetts, a general censorship law was never passed, but censorship was achieved in 1932 by a statute that provided for all public entertainments held upon the Lord's Day to be approved by the Commissioner of Public Safety.[38] This form of "Sunday Censorship" was never very strictly enforced by the state.

Between 1922 and 1927, 48 bills that sought to impose censorship were filed in various state legislatures.[39] Bills for censorship were defeated in states such as Iowa, Maine, South Dakota, Wisconsin, and Nebraska. The Nebraska state legislature passed a censorship law in 1921 only to have it vetoed by the governor.

The idea of state boards in every state made the industry suffer. The possibility of these boards, each with varying procedure and standards, and varying interpretations of those standards, was a constant fear of motion picture producers. At every opportunity the motion picture industry fought the passage of any type of prior restraint on its productions.

Cities throughout the country had licensing policies for motion pictures. Much of this licensing was in the hands of the local mayor or the police commissioner. In some cities the police department viewed and passed the films on to the public. In other cities the censoring was done by established censor boards.

In a great number of instances censorship in cities was lethargic. Many cities did not use the censorship measures that they had until some sensational film came to their city. This made any estimate of the number of cities that used censorship difficult to determine. Estimates ran as high as several hundred for the number of cities that used some form of censorship. A reasonable estimate of the number of censor boards in 1939 was 79.[40]

The earliest municipal censor board was established in Chicago in 1907. At first the board consisted of ten policemen appointed by the mayor. The board was later changed to five men and five women citizens appointed by the mayor to pass on the films shown in the city.[41] Other boards were established in Kansas City, Missouri; Seattle; Houston; Spokane; Green Bay, Wisconsin; Portland, Oregon; Detroit; Atlanta; Memphis; Milwaukee; Springfield, Missouri; and Palo Alto, California.

The variance of opinions by the censor boards was a factor that made them less effective than they might have been. In some instances one board would not delete the same portions of an identical film as another board. This was a real weakness in the system of censorship by states. Another weakness was that it was difficult to establish standards for the different parts of the country and even more difficult to get qualified personnel to administer judgments concerning the moral content of motion pictures.

A good side of the state and city boards was that they protected children from pictures that were not fit for them to see. In spite of the good efforts of the MPPDA and other attempts by the industry to clean up the content of films, some producers thought of profit more than artistic achievement. The censor boards were successful in a limited way, therefore, when they stopped the presentation of filthy films in their respective areas.

The censorship movement never died out in the period of 1907–1936. In general, the advocates of censorship in the controversy were not as organized as the motion picture industry. Outcries for censorship came from individuals with varying ideas as to the method and degree that censorship should be enacted upon the content of films.

One of the strongest advocates of federal censorship was the Reverend William Chase, who, in 1914, before the House Education Committee in Washington, urged legislation to create a Federal Board of Censorship. He estimated that 900,000 children atttended motion pictures every day in the United States and declared that if one child was injured by the exhibition of an immoral picture it should be a matter of concern to the federal government.[42]

Another censorship leader was Dr. Wilbur Crafts, Superintendent of the International Reform Bureau. Dr. Crafts wrote the Hughes Bill of 1915 for the establishment of an official National Motion Picture Commission.[43] During the hearings that accompanied the Hughes Bill, a report was made to the House Education Committee which contended that state and municipal censorship laws were not adequate. The report recommended the passage of the Hughes Bill and also stated that 95 percent of films were viewed by the National Board of Review at New York, but "still there would remain five percent which could be immoral and unfit to be shown."[44]

In October of 1916, the House of Bishops of the Protestant Episcopal Church passed a resolution that favored the Hughes Bill.[45] The General Federation of Women's Clubs urged legislation for better films in 1920.[46]

The censors themselves argued for stronger laws on an artistic basis. Dr. E. P. Oberholtzer, the well-known American historian, who was a member of the Pennsylvania board, stated:

> I shall, three times out of four, leave the film nearer the author's original form than I found it. I, as a censor, have never taken Clyde Fitch's play *The Bachelor,* and called it *The Virtuous Vamp;* Barrie's *The Admirable Crichton,* and called it *Male and Female; La Tosca* and called it *Sin; La Gioconda* and called it *The Devil's Daughter.* The celluloid people have done these things.[47]

An article in the *Literary Digest* likened the state boards of censorship "to a State Board of Health to protect us from the moral pestilence which lurks in the attractive, seductive motion pictures."[48] Dr. A. T. Poffenberger of Columbia University was among those that felt that motion pictures promoted crime. He stated that "a survey of any group of posters advertising motion pictures will show a surprisingly large portion suggesting burglary, violence, or crime of some sort. Considering the almost unlimited audiences which the advertising posters command, their careful control would seem a greater necessity than that of the play itself."[49]

In the referendum in Massachusetts on the question of censorship in 1921, the motion picture industry spent large amounts of money to stop the proposed regulatory legislation. The industry, with Hays as its spokesman, boasted of the large vote cast against censorship in that referendum, but it failed to mention the vast organization it affected and the large amount of money it spent. The advocates of censorship had no money, no newspaper support, and were unorganized, and yet they secured 210,000 votes, nearly 30 percent of the total vote cast on the question.[50]

The chief expression of the censorship movement on a national level was the Federal Motion Picture Council. This organization was formed in 1925 as a result of three annual conferences held in Washington, D.C., that began in 1923.[51] Dr. Charles Scanlon, Secretary of the Moral Welfare Department of the Presbyterian Board of Christian Education, called these conferences that had been attended by representatives of several Protestant denominations and other social welfare organizations.[52]

Dr. Scanlon was elected the first president of the Federal Motion Picture Council. Other leaders of the organization included Dr. William Chase; Miss Maude M. Aldrich, national motion picture chairman of the W. C. T. U.; Mrs. Robbins Gilman, general secretary of the Women's Cooperative Alliance of Minneapolis; and Reverend Clifford B. Twombly, rector of St. James' Church, Lancaster, Pennsylvania.[53]

The organization advocated the enactment of federal legislation to establish a permanent commission to regulate the industry's trade practices and the content of its films. The council sought to arouse public sentiment to support the creation of a government commission through the distribution of leaflets, public addresses, and national conferences, usually held in Washington.

The council did no previewing, but the Reverend Twombly and the Reverend Chase saw many pictures and published articles containing their comments. The Council had no local chapters, but members of the board of directors and the advisory committee carried on local activities through other organizations that supported its program.[54]

Nearly forty national religious and educational groups adopted resolutions that called for some form of federal regulation of the industry.[55] The Protestant Episcopal Church, at its annual convention which met in Denver in 1930, adopted a resolution stating that "only such a centralized authority as the U. S. government can wisely and effectively regulate the centralized motion picture industry."[56]

The Northern Baptists,[57] W. C. T. U.,[58] North American Home Mission Congress,[59] and the Methodist Episcopal Church[60] all favored some form of federal legislation for motion pictures in their annual meetings in the early nineteen thirties. The National Grange favored "federal regulation"[61] at its convention in Rochester, New York, in 1930.

IV. THE LEGION OF DECENCY CAMPAIGN

For several years after its adoption by the MPPDA the Catholics had accepted Hays's promises that the Production Code would be more rigorously enforced. When the promises were not fulfilled, the Catholic hierarchy angrily spoke out in the *Commonweal*:

Constantly and assiduously, Catholic committees, and individuals, and societies, have labored to bring about some change for the better. They have accepted at their face value the many professions of a willingness to do better, made by the industry. They have collaborated in drawing up codes which were intended to improve the situation. They have given Mr. Will Hays all the time . . . that any man required to make such an improvement, provided he had any real will to effect improvement; or, granting the good-will, any real power to do more than act as a dummy of respectability for the unscrupulous real masters of the Hollywood machine for the mass production of filth. Nothing ever came of all such efforts save more and more filth.[1]

The first public announcement of a Catholic reform movement came in October 1933 when Archbishop A. G. Cicognani, apostolic delegate to the United States, addressed the National Conference of Catholic Charities at the Metropolitan Opera House in New York. He stated:

An example of the forces of evil in our day is the moving picture, with its incalculable influence for evil. . . . Catholics are called by God, the Pope, the Bishops, and the priests to a united and vigorous campaign for the purification of the cinema, which has become a deadly menace to morals.[2]

In November the Catholic bishops of the United States met at Washington, D.C., and decided to organize the National Legion of Decency. An Episcopal Committee on Motion Pictures was appointed to run the campaign. The committee was composed of the Most Reverend John T. McNicholas, O. P., archbishop of Cincinnati, Ohio, who was chosen as chairman; the Most Reverend John J. Cantwell, archbishop of Los Angeles, California; the Most Reverend John F. Noll, bishop of Fort Wayne, Indiana; the Most Reverend Hugh C. Boyle, bishop of Pittsburgh, Pennsylvania; and the Most Reverend Stephen J. Donaghue, auxiliary to the archbishop of New York.[3] These men organized and ran the Legion of Decency movement.

Bishop Cantwell spoke of the Code and expressed a typical Catholic viewpoint of censorship laws when he stated:

Steadily during the past two or three years the regulations of the Code have been honored more in the breach than in the observance, with the result that a new and complete overhauling is imperative if the motion picture industry is to survive unhampered by additional state censorship bodies or a federal censorship law.[4]

The Catholic Church never endorsed any type of censorship law in the United States.

On April 28, 1934, in Washington, D.C., the formation of the Legion of Decency was officially announced by the Bishop's Committee.[5] The plan was to enroll in the Legion all of the 103 Catholic dioceses of the United States. Non-Catholic groups also were invited to join the campaign.

The Bishop's Committee sent copies of a pledge to all of the bishops throughout the country, and Catholics were asked to sign or repeat it.[6] The pledge read:

I wish to join the Legion of Decency, which condemns vile and unwholesome moving pictures. I unite with all who protest against them as a grave menace to youth, to home life, to country and to religion.

I shall do all that I can to arouse public opinion against the portrayal of vice as a normal condition of affairs, and against depicting criminals of any class as heroes and heroines, presenting their filthy philosophy of life as something acceptable to men and women.

I unite with all who condemn the display of suggestive advertisements on bill boards, at theatre entrances and the favorable notices given immoral motion pictures.

Considering these evils, I hereby promise to remain away from all motion pictures except those which do not offend decency and Christian morality. I promise further to secure as many members as possible for the Legion of Decency.

I further promise never to buy or read indecent books or magazines.[7]

There was no national organization with branch offices or dues, but a New York headquarters was established. The method of getting Catholics to join the campaign was left up to each diocese. There is no accurate record of the actual number of enlistments in the Legion, but estimates range between seven and eleven million Catholic pledges during the first two years of the movement.

The Catholic press, especially the weekly newspapers, carried on a vigorous campaign.[8] Catholic newspapers and periodicals in the United States numbered 310 and their combined circulations exceeded seven million copies.

The Legion movement was, for the most part, an economic boycott against pictures that violated the Code. The Catholic hierarchy maintained that they simply wanted filthy pictures and gangster pictures cleaned up.

Father Lord, who had been one of the writers of the Code, was disappointed in the failure of the Code's enforcement. He wrote a booklet entitled *The Movies Betray America* condemning the producers for continuing the production of objectionable pictures.

In addition, Bishop McNicholas said:

The tragic thing about the producers is that they seem to have set aside the permanent code of the Ten Comandments which binds every human being. They seem to have no fixed moral standards; they do not seem to be able to distinguish between what is moral and immoral.[9]

The Catholics carried on an intense campaign throughout the country. Protestant and Jewish leaders praised the drive for its effort to raise the moral level of motion pictures. The Chicago Legion enrolled a half million women. The Brooklyn Legion enrolled the same number of members. Detroit Catholics put "We Demand Clean Movies" stickers on their outomobiles.[10] In Chicago, fifty thousand school children paraded downtown, many carrying banners that said such things as "Films we must see, but clean they must be."[11] Speeches were made at Catholic group meetings, and in a number of cities theaters that showed indecent pictures were picketed.

Many non-Catholic groups endorsed the Legion's drive. The Federal Council of Churches of Christ in America,[12] United Lutheran Church of America,[13] National Conference of Christians and Jews,[14] Inter-faith Conference of New York,[15] National Conference of Jewish Women,[16] National Education Association,[17] Emergency Council of Fraternal Organizations,[18] organized by the Odd Fellows, and the Women's Christian Temperance Union,[19] are a few of the organizations and societies that joined the crusade. On the other hand, the American Civil Liberties Union opposed the drive, declaring that "we believe any form of religious censorship would be subversive to the religious liberty clauses in our basic law, which guarantees the separation of church and state."[20]

In June of 1934, Hays sent Martin Quigley and Joseph Breen to Cincinnati as representatives of the MPPDA to try to make peace with the Legion.[21] The Bishop's Committee told them that they did not have to fear any boycott of theaters as long as clean pictures were shown.

Hays commented that "The films had to be decent. The yardstick was nothing new—just the Code that we had had for four years. All they asked was that the industry live up to it."[22] He maintained that he was glad that the Catholics had started the Legion rather than advocated federal censorship like some Protestant groups.[23] He evaluated the Legion by saying:

> Our whole open-door policy had always sought honest reaction and advice from high-minded organizations. Humanly speaking, it was the moral force of the Catholic Church that gave the *coup de grace* to Code breakers. And it was the concrete program of the Legion of Decency, quickly taken up by other groups, that spearheaded the public demand for Code enforcement.
>
> Far from considering the Legion an enemy, I welcomed its cooperation with open arms. Here was one of the most striking examples of "Let's get together" I ever experienced . . . the majority of people probably consider the Legion's work an "attack." I saw it as a defense pact that finally made the Code a working reality. Letters that passed between the bishops and myself give ample evidence of that fact.[24]

According to Raymond Moley in his book *The Hays Office,* the producers were advised as early as the summer of 1933 that the Catholics were going to organize opposition to objectionable pictures.[25] Hollywood first thought the Legion's boycott was like other censorship groups in the past and that it would be inactive in a few months. As the Legion campaign gained momentum, the criticism left Hollywood "scared, and silent, and pure."[26] Production stopped, and the producers were bewildered. It was said that the crisis caused by the Legion drive was the most serious for the industry since the financial and artistic readjustment that accompanied the advent of the talking picture.[27]

The Legion campaign had an important effect on the Hays Office. The Production Code Administration was established. The $25,000 fine for violating the Code put teeth into the machinery of the MPPDA. Hays announced this move toward more strict self-regulation on June 22, 1934, just a few months after the sensational beginning of the Legion's drive.[28]

By the fall of 1935, the effects of the Legion's boxoffice pressure became evident when a procession of pictures appeared with such titles as *Mrs. Wiggs of the Cabbage Patch, Anne of Green Gables, Bright Eyes,* and *The Little Minister.* Shirley Temple's career and success at the boxoffice was at least partly a result of the pressure by the Legion as Hollywood attempted to deify personalities.[29] Better and more intelligent films were produced and were supported by the Catholics. Profits of the industry went up. By 1936, the improvement of the industry caused the *New York Times* to comment:

> True, films of low intellectual quality predominate. But they are demanded by those known as fans. And even those pictures are better than the same class of product of 1934. . . . A definite movement toward mature entertainment has been one result of the crusade.[20]

Beginning in February 1936, the Legion reviewed and classified motion pictures. The review work was done by the Motion Pictures Department of the International Federation of Catholic Alumnae, which was selected by the Bishop's Committee as the official reviewing group for the Legion. The reviewers, in cooperation with the producers, viewed the films before they were released to the public. Reports on the moral content of the picture were made on a printed ballot which was processed by the executive staff of the Legion.[31] The classification of films was then made in accordance with the ballots and the following categories.

A-I—Morally Unobjectionable for General Patronage. These films are considered to contain no material which would be morally dangerous to the average picture audience, adults and children alike.

A-II—Morally Unobjectionable for Adults. These are films which in themselves are morally harmless but which, because of subject matter or treatment, require maturity and experience if one is to witness them without danger of moral harm. While no definite age limit can be established for this group, the judgment of parents, pastors and teachers would be helpful in determining the decision in individual cases.

B—Morally Objectionable in Part for All. Films in this category are considered to contain elements dangerous to Christian morals or moral standards.

C—Condemned. Condemned films are considered to be those which because of theme or treatment are what has been described by the Holy Father as "positively bad."[32]

Between February, 1936, and November, 1950, more than 7400 films were reviewed and classified by the Legion.[33]

In July of 1936, Pope Pius XI issued an Encyclical, the *Vigilanti Cura*, to "the archbishops and bishops to the United States of America, and to other ordinaries enjoying peace and communion with the Apostolic See, on motion pictures."[34] The Pope praised the results of the Legion's campaign. He approved the classification of pictures by the Legion and favored such reviewing groups for every country.[35] He stressed the need for proper personnel for these groups when he said:

> The office force must be composed of persons who are familiar with the technique of the motion picture and who at the same time are well-grounded in the principles of Catholic morality and doctrines. They must, in addition, be under the guidance and direct supervision of a priest chosen by the Bishop.[36]

The Legion campaign was a success for several reasons. While the estimates of the number of pledges seem large, and the number of practicing pledges impossible to estimate, the timing of the movement was nearly perfect. The pressure exerted by the Legion was the action needed to make the industry bolster its self-regulation machinery. The fact that the Legion's objectives were endorsed by non-Catholics made the movement a force national in scope, and one which the producers could hardly ignore.

NOTES

i

1. Terry Ramsaye, "The Rise and Place of the Motion Picture," *The Annals of the American Academy of Political and Social Science*, CXXVIII (November, 1926), 3.
2. Ruth A. Inglis, *Freedom of the Movies* (Chicago: University of Chicago Press, 1947), p. 26.
3. Quoted in Terry Ramsaye, *A Million and One Nights* (New York: Simon and Schuster, 1926), p. 473.

4. Lewis Jacobs, *The Rise of the American Film* (New York: Harcourt, Brace and Company, 1939) , p. 63.
5. Ramsaye, *loc. cit.*, p. 12.
6. Jacobs, *op. cit.*, p. 76.
7. *Ibid.*, p. 77.
8. Ramsaye, *loc. cit.*, pp. 14–15.
9. Jacobs, *op. cit.*, pp. 81–84.
10. Inglis, *op. cit.*, p. 28.
11. Jacobs, *op. cit.*, pp. 156–158.
12. Arthur Knight, *The Liveliest Art* (New York: MacMillan Company, 1957) , p. 110.
13. *Ibid.*, pp. 110–111.
14. *The Autobiography of Cecil B. DeMille*, Donald Hayne (Englewood Cliffs, New Jersey: Prentice-Hall, Incorporated, 1959) , p. 248.
15. Quoted in "Overdoing the Sex Motive in Moving Pictures," *Current Opinion*, LXX (March, 1921) , 362.
16. *Ibid.*, p. 363.
17. *Ibid.*, p. 362.
18. Knight, *op. cit.*, pp. 110–111.
19. *New York Times*, March 4, 1920, p. 9.
20. *Ibid.*, March 31, 1920, p. 1.
21. "Schoolteachers as Film Censors," *The World's Work*, XLVIII, Number 3
22. "The Motion Pictures—The Good and the Bad of It," *Outlook*, July 13, 1912,
23. *Ibid.*, September 11, 1921, p. 1.
24. *Ibid.*, September 12, 1921, p. 1.
25. *Ibid.*, September 11, 1921, p. 1.
26. *Ibid.*, September 13, 1921, p. 1.
27. *Ibid.*, September 13, 1921, p. 2.
28. *Ibid.*, April 13, 1922, p. 1.
29. Inglis, *op. cit.*, p. 67.
30. *The Memoirs of Will H. Hays* (Garden City, New York: Doubleday and Company, Incorporated, 1955) , p. 328.
31. *Ibid.*, pp. 330–331.

ii

1. "Passed by the National Board of Censorship," *Review of Reviews*, L, Number 6 (1914) , 730.
2. Department of Research and Education, Federal Council of Churches of Christ in America, *The Public Relations of the Motion Picture Industry* (1931) , p. 54.
3. "National Board of Censorship. . .," *loc. cit.*
4. W. A. Barret, "The Work of the National Board of Review," *The Annals of the American Academy of Political and Social Science*, CXXVIII (November, 1926) , 180–181.
5. Frederick C. Howe, "What to do with the Motion Picture Show: Shall it be Censored?" *Outlook* (June 20, 1914) , p. 414.
6. *Ibid.*, pp. 414–415.
7. *Ibid.*, p. 414.
8. Barret, *loc. cit.*, p. 179.
9. *New York Times*, April 28, 1919, p. 13.
10. Inglis, *op. cit.*, pp. 83–86.
11. *Ibid.*, pp. 83–84.
12. "Movie Abuses a National Calamity," *Literary Digest*, March 12, 1921, p. 32.
13. "Time to Clean Up Movie Morals," *Literary Digest*, October 15, 1921, pp. 29–30.
14. "Where the Blame Lies for Movie Sex Stuff," *Literary Digest*, February 12, 1921, pp. 28–29.
15. "How Motion Pictures Promote Crime," *Review of Reviews*, LXIII, Number 5 (1921) , 55.
16. *New York Times*, May 10, 1917, p. 12.
17. *Ibid.*, April 13, 1921, p. 14.

18. *Ibid.*, April 28, 1921, p. 12.
19. "No Censorship," *Independent*, March 30, 1914, pp. 432–433.
20. "Blame . . . for Movie Sex Stuff," *loc. cit.*
21. "Schoolteachers as Film Censors," *The World's Work*, XLVIII, Number 3 (1924), 248–249.
22. "The Motion Pictures—The Good and the Bad of It," *Outlook*, July 13, 1912, pp. 598–599.
23. *New York Times*, December 9, 1921, p. 19.
24. *Ibid.*, January 15, 1922, p. 1.
25. *Ibid.*, January 19, 1922, p. 17.
26. *Ibid.*, March 7, 1922, p. 5.
27. *Ibid.*, p. 5.
28. *Ibid.*, March 12, 1922, p. 1.
29. Federal Council of Churches Report, *op. cit.*, p. 16.
30. *Ibid.*, p. 16.
31. Will H. Hays, The President's Report to the Motion Picture Producers and Distributors of America, Incorporated, April 11, 1932, p. 1.
32. Hays, *op. cit.*, p. 335.
33. Federal Council of Churches Report, *op. cit.*, p. 19.
34. Hays, *op. cit.*, pp. 335–337.
35. *Ibid.*, p. 338.
36. Federal Council of Churches Report, *op. cit.*, p. 66.
37. *Ibid.*, p. 96.
38. *New York Times*, August 10, 1922, p. 5.
39. *Ibid.*, August 21, 1922, p. 6.
40. Hays, *op. cit.*, pp. 361–362.
41. Federal Council of Churches Report, *op. cit.*, p. 70.
42. Hays, *op. cit.*, pp. 331–333.
43. *New York Times*, March 23, 1925, p. 14.
44. *Ibid.*, p. 14.
45. Federal Council of Churches Report, *op. cit.*, p. 74.
46. Raymond Moley, *The Hays Office*, (New York: The Bobbs-Merrill Company, 1945), p. 141.
47. Hays, *op. cit.*, pp. 352–353.
48. *New York Times*, February 4, 1926, p. 20.
49. *Ibid.*, April 22, 1926, p. 19.
50. *Ibid.*, May 31, 1926, p. 2.
51. *Ibid.*, August 18, 1927, p. 25.
52. *Ibid.*, May 24, 1922, p. 21.
53. Federal Council of Churches Report, *op. cit.*, pp. 116–117.
54. *Ibid.*, pp. 118–119.
55. Moley, *op. cit.*, p. 64.
56. *New York Times*, October 11, 1927, p. 21.
57. Inglis, *op. cit.*, pp. 114–115.
58. *Ibid.*
59. DeMille, *op. cit.*, p. 298.
60. Hays, *op. cit.*, pp. 436–437.
61. *Ibid.*, p. 438.
62. *Ibid.*, p. 438.
63. *Ibid.*, p. 440.
64. Moley, *op. cit.*, p. 69.
65. Hays, *op. cit.*, p. 442.
66. *New York Times*, April 1, 1930, p. 1.
67. Federal Council of Churches Report, *op. cit.*, p. 140.
68. *Ibid.*, p. 140.
69. See issues of July 15, 1931; August 19, 1931; and October 21, 1931.
70. *New York Times*, June 1, 1930, p. 5.
71. *Ibid.*, November 19, 1930, p. 48.
72. *Ibid.*, September 27, 1931, p. 29.
73. *Ibid.*, May 26, 1932, p. 26.

74. *Ibid.*, October 1, 1932, p. 26.
75. *Ibid.*, July 15, 1934, p. 18.
76. *Ibid.*, p. 2.

iii

1. Ramsaye, *loc. cit.*, p. 9.
2. *Ibid.*, p. 14.
3. "Censorship of Motion Pictures," *DePaul Law Review*, III, Number 2 (Spring-Summer, 1954), 101.
4. *Ibid.*, p. 102.
5. John E. Harley, *World-Wide Influences of the Cinema* (Los Angeles: University of Southern California Press, 1940), p. 56.
6. Ford H. MacGregor, "Official Censorship Legislation," *The Annals of the American Academy of Political and Social Science*, CXXVIII (November, 1926), p. 164.
7. *Ibid.*, p. 164.
8. "Censorship of Motion Pictures," *loc. cit.*, p. 108.
9. *Ibid.*, pp. 108–110.
10. *New York Times*, May 8, 1916, p. 4.
11. *Ibid.*, p. 4.
12. U. S. Congress, House, Committee on Education *Federal Motion Picture Commission*, 64th Cong., 1st Sess., May 17, 1916, H. Rept. 679 to accompany H. R. 15462, p. 74.
13. *Ibid.*, p. 74.
14. *New York Times*, February 23, 1922, p. 18.
15. *Ibid.*, p. 18.
16. MacGregor, *loc. cit.*, p. 165.
17. *Ibid.*, p. 165.
18. *Ibid.*, p. 166.
19. Harley, *op. cit.*, pp. 57–58.
20. *New York Times*, June 10, 1934, p. 21.
21. Harley, *op. cit.*, p. 58.
22. MacGregor, *loc. cit.*, p. 166.
23. *Ibid.*, p. 167.
24. *Kansas Senate Journal* (1913), p. 136.
25. *Ibid.*, p. 845.
26. *Kansas House Journal* (1917), p. 103.
27. *Kansas Laws* (1917), p. 452.
28. *Mutual Film Corporation* v. *Industrial Commission*, 236 (U.S.), 239 (1915).
29. *Mutual Film Corporation* v. *Hodges*, 236 (U.S.), 249 (1915).
30. Harley, *op. cit.*, pp. 69–70.
31. "Film Censorship: An Administrative Analysis." *Columbia Law Review*, XXXIX (1939), p. 1384.
32. *New York Times*, March 18, 1922. p. 6.
33. "Film Censorship: An Administrative Analysis," *loc cit.*, p. 1384.
34. *Ibid.*, pp. 1384–1385.
35. "The Legal Aspect of Motion Picture Censorship," *Harvard Law Review*, XLIV, (November 1, 1930), p. 116.
36. Harley, *op. cit.*, p. 64.
37. "Film Censorship: An Administrative Analysis," *loc. cit.*, p. 1385.
38. "Entertainment: Public Pressures and the Law," *Harvard Law Review*, LXXI, Number 2 (December, 1957), pp. 326–328.
39. *Ibid.*, p. 352.
40. "Film Censorship: An Administrative Analysis," *loc cit.*, pp. 1385–1386.
41. "Chicago's Movie Censorship," *Literary Digest*, March 28, 1914, pp. 702–703.
42. *New York Times*, May 10, 1914, p. 15.
43. *Ibid.*, May 19, 1914, p. 8.
44. *Ibid.*, May 18, 1916, p. 9.
45. *Ibid.*, October 22, 1916, p. 20.
46. *Ibid.*, June 19, 1920, p. 23.
47. E. P. Oberholtzer, "The Censor and the Movie Menace," *North American Re-*

view, CCXII, Number 780 (November, 1920), 643–644.
48. "The Nation Wide Battle Over Movie Purification," *Literary Digest,* May 14, 1921, pp. 32–33.
49. Quoted in "Motion Pictures and Crime," *Literary Digest,* May 7, 1921, p. 19.
50. "Censorship of the Movies," *Forum,* LXIX, (April, 1923), p. 1410.
51. *New York Times,* December 26, 1923, p. 10.
52. *Ibid.,* p. 10.
53. Federal Council of Churches Report, *op. cit.,* p. 106.
54. *Ibid.,* p. 107.
55. "Demand Growing for Social Control of the Movies," *The Christian Century,* October 21, 1931, p. 1301.
56. *New York Times,* September 27, 1931, p. 29.
57. *Ibid.,* June 1, 1930, p. 5.
58. *Ibid.,* November 19, 1930, p. 48.
59. *Ibid.,* December 16, 1930, p. 15.
60. *Ibid.,* May 26, 1932, p. 27.
61. Federal Council of Churches Report, *op. cit.,* p. 108.

iv

1. "The Legion of Decency," *Commonweal,* May 18, 1934, pp. 57–58.
2. *New York Times,* October 2, 1933, p. 5.
3. "Catholics Attack Obscenity on the Screen," *Literary Digest,* May 5, 1934, p. 22.
4. Hays, *op. cit.,* p. 454.
5. *Ibid.,* p. 451.
6. *New York Times,* June 26, 1934, p. 22.
7. "Legion of Decency," *loc cit.,* p. 58.
8. "Campaign Against Objectionable Motion Pictures," *Catholic World,* CXXXI, Number 833 (August, 1934), 617–618.
9. "The Progress of the Legion of Decency," *Commonweal,* August 17, 1934, pp. 375–376.
10. Moley, *op. cit.,* p. 81.
11. *New York Times,* September 28, 1934, p. 27.
12. *New York Times,* June 23, 1934, p. 1.
13. *Ibid.,* October 24, 1934, p. 1.
14. *Ibid.,* July 6, 1934, p. 3.
15. *Ibid.,* July 10, 1934, p. 1.
16. *Ibid.,* August 10, 1934, p. 21.
17. *Ibid.,* July 4, 1934, p. 16.
18. *Ibid.,* July 20, 1934, p. 13.
19. *Ibid.,* July 18, 1934, p. 14.
20. *Ibid.,* July 16, 1934, p. 11.
21. Hays, *op. cit.,* p. 453.
22. *Ibid.,* pp. 453–454.
23. *Ibid.,* p. 449.
24. *Ibid.,* p. 450.
25. Moley, *op. cit.,* p. 80.
26. *New York Times,* July 22, 1934, p. 1.
27. *Ibid.,* July 8, 1934, p. 1.
28. *Ibid.,* June 23, 1934, p. 15.
29. *Ibid.,* January 6, 1935, p. 5.
30. *Ibid.,* August 23, 1936, p. 18.
31. *Motion Pictures Classified by the National Legion of Decency, February, 1936–November 1950,* (1951), p. ix.
32. *Ibid.,* p. x.
33. *Ibid.,* p. 180.
34. Quoted in "How are the Movies?", *Commonweal,* August 4, 1939, p. 358.
35. Quoted in "The Encyclical on Motion Pictures," *Catholic World,* CXLIII, Number 857 (August, 1936), 618.
36. *Ibid.,* p. 618.

World War II and the American Film

Lewis Jacobs

Nearly thirty years after the publication of his Rise of the American Film, *Lewis Jacobs is still writing about films. In the following article he continues this personal commitment to the values of the movies by discussing the American film during World War II.**

In the late 1930's, the challenge of totalitarianism, followed by America's involvement in World War II, altered the aims and purposes of the American film and provided it with new subjects and themes. Until 1942, most Hollywood movies were escapist entertainment, which aimed to distract a spellbound public from agonizing radio and newspaper reports about the Axis partners' expansion in Europe. But in response to President Roosevelt's growing concern with foreign policy and his determined efforts in 1938 and 1939 to break the bonds of American isolationism, the screen began cautiously to report on fascism at home and abroad. In 1940 and 1941, as military events in Europe moved swiftly, bringing war closer to the United States, Hollywood stepped up its own belligerency and military spirit and became impatient for intervention. After the Japanese attack on Pearl Harbor, which catapulted the United States into a global conflict, the motion picture industry became totally engaged in the obligations and demands of a government at war. From 1942 until the end of the war three years later, the American film served as a potent instrument of national policy. With sweeping obeisance to military necessity, the screen helped to transform the social, political and military attitudes of an embattled nation, while promoting the aims and goals of the war effort.

Before the outbreak of war in Europe in September, 1939, the bulk of American movies consisted of musicals in various hybrid forms. The country was deluged with comedy and humor, with sophisticated ro-

* By permission from Lewis Jacobs, "World War II and the American Film," *Cinema Journal*, Volume VII, Winter, 1967–68. *Journal of the Society of Cinematologists.* © 1968.

mances, deft melodramas, adventure tales and Westerns, and only occasionally was there a glance at some serious domestic problem touching the lives of most Americans. The dangers of encroaching fascism as a dramatic subject for films was avoided as non-existent. Even when the fanatical dictatorships came to be recognized and labeled for what they were, American film-makers were reluctant to deal with the growing threat to the United States. Isolationist sentiment and potent pacifist groups, added to the government's pledges of neutrality, proved powerful restraining forces. No major film company, without the sanction of national policy, was bold enough to treat the subject of dictatorships and their aggressive atrocities, or the growing expansion of their ideological adherents.[1]

It wasn't until after Hitler had seized Czechoslovakia; Japan had taken over the Spratly Islands in the Pacific; Mussolini had snatched up Albania; Franco had captured Madrid; and Roosevelt had reacted by arousing the government to reexamine its neutrality legislation that the American screen broke its complacency about political events. In the spring of 1939, *Confessions of a Nazi Spy* struck out sharply against fascism. It was the first response to the political tensions of the time. It documented the spread of Nazi ideology in the United States and bluntly warned against a Fascist Fifth Column raising a direct challenge to democracy. The real dangers of the German-American Bund and the undercover activities of the German steamship lines were both underlined. So incendiary were the film's revelations that many people attacked it as propaganda and war-mongering, while others regarded its shocking disclosure as long overdue.

What made *Confessions of a Nazi Spy* so disturbing was its timing. American nerves were taut, and feeling was running high over Hitler's ruthless aggression in Europe. The F.B.I. had arrested a number of Nazi agents operating in the United States. Fritz Kuhn, head of the American Bund, threatened a $5,000,000 libel suit against the producers of the film. "We are loyal Americans," he claimed, "organized to uphold the Constitution of the United States." The German Consulate called the picture part of an American conspiracy. Many South American countries favorable to fascism immediately banned the movie. Its producers, the Warner Brothers, were said to have received murder threats for making it. The film's depiction of Nazi groups draping together the American flag and the swastika and saluting them with "Heil Hitler" at a time when the Third Reich's contempt for democracy was common knowledge came as a shocking provocation to that public which abhorred totalitarianism.

Despite this early attempt to deal firmly with material that was uppermost in the minds of millions of Americans glued to daily radio reports of fascist successes abroad, it was almost a year before Hollywood's neutrality finally began to fall apart. In the spring of 1940, Germany invaded Denmark, overran Norway, swarmed through the Low Countries, drove the British armies out of France, outflanked the Maginot Line and forced the Third French Republic to surrender. America was stunned. President Roosevelt called for a vast increase in armaments and a crisis-government of national unity. All illusions about pacifism, neutrality, and America's impregnability were shattered. Alarmed by the increasing signs of the coming showdown, Walter Lippman warned the nation: "Our duty is to begin acting at once on the basic assumption that . . . before the snow flies again we may stand alone and isolated, the last great Democracy on earth."[2] Thereafter, fascism would be attacked more and more on the American screen.

FROM NON-FICTION TO DRAMA

In a mild way, newsreels had already taken tentative steps toward revealing the Third Reich's ideology of assault. Throughout the late thirties, cameramen filmed first-hand reports of Hitler's take-over of Austria, Czechoslovakia and Poland; the British and French declarations of war; the German conquest of Norway, Holland, Belgium, France; and finally the beginning of the Battle of Britain. As events abroad brought the conflict closer to the United States, the early objectivity and neutrality which newsreel producers had maintained, collapsed. With the increasingly martial tone of the administration, they directed their cameras toward documenting the growing program of collective security and aid to Britain—toward informing, guiding and encouraging public sentiment to "defend America by aiding the allies." Every phase of United States preparedness began to be magnified with praise: military training, army and navy maneuvers, the air force's dive-bombing tactics. Nor was the labor front neglected, the production of tanks, guns and planes; civilian defense; USO activities. The fighting spirit of Roosevelt was praised as well as the High Command and the Allied prosecution of the war.

This was a period of "inspirational" and morale-building journalism which featured scenes of patriotic parades, town meetings, recruits leaving for camp, destroyers being launched, pilots receiving commissions, graduation exercises at West Point and Annapolis. Defense preparations were made to seem glamorous, fun, sporting, a kind of "national frolic." By contrast, British activities were reported to make a more pathetic appeal to the emotions. Prominent personalities, including Churchill, the Duke and Duchess of Windsor and others, were shown calling for our "unstinting help." Historic places of interest, Buckingham Palace, Westminster Abbey, Parliament, 10 Downing Street, various cathedrals were photographed accompanied by sad music. Pathetic shots showed London's populace crowded into subway shelters to escape German bombing, while the sound track pointed out the urgency of "all-out" aid to Britain.

Newsreels showing what the war overseas was really like, or the emotions of the man doing the actual fighting were understandably absent. Instead there were pictures of troops and materials in transport, "atmosphere" glimpses of the various fronts, political and military leaders addressing their people—tangible evidence of the urgency of the situation. Battle views and scenes of violence and death were scanty. The lack of such material was due less to the shortcomings of combat cameramen than to the various governments' control of what should be released and what should not.

A few white-heat documentaries did manage to break through the restrictions imposed on newsreel reporting to capture the human depravities and wreckage of war. *The Scuttling of the Graf Spee, The Siege of Narvik* and the *Retreat from Dunkirk* were vivid examples of superior camera journalism and gave American movie-goers sobering insights into war's grim reality and the course the conflict was taking.

Despite the fact that America was evidently backing the Allies, official neutrality was indicated by the showing of foreign documentaries based on current events, both those made by the Allies and those by the enemy. Four of the most impressive, two made by England and two by Germany, were given wide distribution in the United States. The British *The Lion Has Wings* (1940), showed the determination and courage of the R.A.F. to carry on with confidence despite the perilous situation; *London Can Take It* (1940), reported on the human fortitude and dignity of English people during a day and night raid on the British capital. The German *Baptism of Fire* (1940) presented a terrifying account of the blitzkrieg into Poland; *Victory in the West* (1941) dramatized the collapse of France and the triumph and march of fascism. Special versions of both these Nazi pictures were used by the Third Reich to celebrate German victories, emphasize Nazi invincibility, and impress foreign governments with the futility of resistance.

Nearly a year passed after the appearance of *Confessions of a Nazi Spy* before Hollywood finally found the courage to dramatize some of the "dreadful commonplaces" of the newsreels, printed pages and radio. *The Mortal Storm* (1940), adapted from a best-selling novel by Phyllis Bottome, threw a harsh light "upon matters of which most informed people had long since been painfully aware"[3] namely, the ruthless wave of barbarism set in motion by Hitler's legions. The plot dealt with a celebrated Jewish professor in a German university who, in the face of the rising tide of National Socialism, refuses to retract his scientific explanation that the composition of human blood is the same for all races. He is sent to a concentration camp and his own son turns against him. His daughter attempts to escape across the border to freedom, with the help of a friend who is in love with her. They are intercepted by a Nazi patrol led by the girl's former suitor, who has become a fanatic party officer. The girl is shot.

This was the first American feature with a story that took place inside Nazi Germany itself, calling Hitler by name, and showing the growing belligerency of National Socialism, the onset of oppressive measures against real or potential anti-Nazis, and the terror tactics and persecutions of the innocent by Storm Troopers during the early years of the Nazi regime. The prevailing temper of public opinion of that day was defined by Bosley Crowther, who asked: "Where was Hollywood when the lights in Germany went out? . . . The most distressing thing about this heart rending picture is that it reaches the screen so late, so unfortunately late . . . *The Mortal Storm* is the sort of picture we should have seen five years ago."[4]

Once a start had been made, however, other belated efforts to expose Nazi malevolence and speak out against German atrocities soon followed. *Four Sons* (1940) was an anguished account of the occupation of Czechoslovakia by Storm Troopers, pitting brother against brother with the swastika dividing them. *The Man I Married* (1940) stressed, through the eyes of an American woman, the difference between the old Germany and the evils of the Third Reich. *Escape* (1940), based on Ethel Vance's novel of Nazi Germany, indicted the authoritarian system by dramatizing the escape of a famous actress from a Nazi prison. *So Ends Our Night* (1941) was a compassionate drama of refugees fleeing from Hitler's persecution, forced out of one country after another for lack of passports, living in constant fear and suppression. *Manhunt* (1941), directed by Fritz Lang, exposed the international network set in motion against a man who had tried to assassinate Adolf Hitler, and thus showed the long reach of Nazi conspirators.

President Roosevelt's decision to "scrape the bottom of the barrel," in order to help England after the shattered retreat of the remnants of her army from Dunkirk, removed the last vestiges of strict American neutrality. The growing belligerency gave rise to movies that focused more and more on the need for readiness. From the pictorial rendering of the cruelties of the growing Nazi challenge, the screen moved to a more forthright demand for American preparedness.

A strong plea to get ready to go to war again against the old enemy was made by *The Ramparts We Watch* (1940), whose producers, The March of Time, believed "that the war shadow darkens America in 1940 just as ominously as it did in 1914." A foreword read: "The war we so thankfully consigned to history—the World War we wrapped in old newspapers and laid away for posterity to look back on—has suddenly become very much alive."

The picture itself was a reconstructed journalistic film-study of people in a typical American community (New London, Connecticut) during the World War I years, 1914–1918. It was composed of old newsreels and film from army archives, interspersed with shots of prominent personalities of the first world war—many from private collections—and scenes staged with non-actors from various occupations and social spheres. The film made a studious effort to be factual and informative. Its tone of objectivity, intended to give viewers "a clearer understanding of where America's foot belongs in the world today," was supported by a narration that described imperial Germany's overbearing arrogance until America's patience was exhausted and we were forced into the war to make the world safe for democracy. A final section made the point that Manchuria's invasion by Japan in 1931 sowed the seeds of World War II, for that led to Mussolini's grab of Ethiopia and Germany's rearming. There was no mention of the war in Spain, the Munich Pact, or other significant political developments that influenced the course of events leading to the current conflict. The focus was on military preparedness against a former foe.

Reinforcement of the same theme appeared in *The World in Flames* (1940), a "super-newsreel" made by Paramount and presented as "a documentation of events which set the stage for the present struggle." The political, economic, and sociological highlights of the past decades leading up to the war in Europe were reported. But like its journalistic predecessor, the past was arranged in a perspective that intended to give the public a "visual conception of the war's background" and make clear the urgent necessity to arm in defense of a democratic way of life.

The production of such "informative" pictures reflected the gradual shift in national temper toward intervention and belligerency. By the fall of 1940 events in Europe had moved so swiftly that the Burke-Wadsworth bill was passed, bringing in the first peacetime draft in American history.

HITCHCOCK AND CHAPLIN

Within months of each other, two films appeared clearly aimed at making the United States aware of the perils of isolation and the need to come to the aid of a nearly exhausted England in a common cause. *Foreign Correspondent* (1940), set in Europe immediately before the war and after England's declaration of war on Germany, had all the notable suspense ingredients that had won a reputation for Alfred

Hitchcock's direction in his earlier British thrillers. The story was of an American newspaperman reporting on the impending war in Europe. At a public ceremony, he witnesses what he thinks is the assassination of a famous Dutch statesman and peace crusader, who has information of a secret treaty which the Nazis are after. When the reporter tries to learn the truth of the killing, he becomes involved in a net of Nazi espionage. His life is endangered and he narrowly escapes being murdered several times. Finally he uncovers a Nazi spy-ring hiding behind a peace crusade. The film concludes with a fervent radio broadcast by the reporter in which he appeals to the United States to arm herself. "The lights are going out in Europe," he warns from a blacked-out London during a raid. "Ring yourself around with steel, America!" The film's release coincided with the air-blitz on London, giving it added urgency and authenticity.

Another forthright and more brilliant picture, with the similar purpose of arousing American public opinion against the fascist enemy, was Chaplin's *The Great Dictator* (1940). Through a comic approach, using mockery, irony and satire, the film attempted to dissect the Axis partners, Hitler and Mussolini, and their political ideology. Although the picture cost more than $2,000,000 and was financed by himself, Chaplin's motivation for making it, he declared, was not commercial but out of a sense of mission. "If I lose on this picture it won't matter," he told the reporter Ella Winter. "What have I worked for all my life . . . if not to gain the independence to make my own pictures as I like . . .?"[5]

Both people sympathetic to Hitler and well-meaning pacifists tried to exert pressure to stop the film's production. Friends and admirers of Chaplin wrote letters and made telephone calls saying it would be unwise "to hurt Hitler's feelings." Crank notes and threats to throw stink bombs in any theater where the film played, to shoot up the screen and create riots, were other common annoyances. There were also frantic entreaties from Chaplin's business office in New York to abandon the project because it was bad business and because the film would never be shown in America and England. But Chaplin ignored all endeavors to keep him from carrying through the picture's completion. "If they won't give theaters to show my picture," he said, "I'll show it myself. In tents. I'll charge 10 cents straight. I'd like to do that anyway, so that everyone can go and see it."[6]

Whether its making was an act of courage or not, *The Great Dictator* finally emerged from the welter of gossip and secrecy to be premiered simultaneously at two Broadway theaters on October 15th, 1940. No other film Chaplin ever made had roused greater expectations. The prospect of the little tramp with the small mustache—the most universally loved character in the world—using his talent to mock the abnormality of "the most dangerous man in the world"[7] loomed as a savage joke, a superb paradox. But Chaplin brought it off triumphantly. For the first time in his career, Chaplin no longer played the wistful jaunty figure who hopes for a pot of gold at the end of the rainbow. On the contrary, the dual role of barber and dictator was a new character, and tragically realistic. The subject, which many thought "too grim for jesting," expressed Chaplin's commitments in the political arena of the day. The film was his way of saying to the public at large in his own medium what he had been saying in speeches at rallies and to friends in private—commitments which were to bring him much personal abuse and criticism.

The story of *The Great Dictator* tells of an obscure Jewish barber who, as the result of a shock received in the first world war, becomes an amnesia victim. After a prolonged stay in an institution for treatment, he escapes and returns to his barber shop in the ghetto, not knowing that his country is now in the hands of a ruthless dictatorship. When he naively attempts to oppose the raids and persecution of Jews by storm troopers, he is beaten and sent to a concentration camp. Again he escapes and travels toward the border to try and cross into what he thinks is a friendlier land. When he is caught, he's mistaken for Hynkel, the tyrannical dictator whom he closely resembles, and who has just annexed the neighboring state. Pushed upon a platform to deliver the conqueror's speech, he makes instead an impassioned appeal aginst hate and dictatorship, urging people to unite in the name of democracy and "fight for a new world—a decent world."

The picture was a trenchant and grandiloquent satire—daring to lampoon dictatorship, tyranny, and oppression, and to strike a blow at Hitler's image at the very height of his seeming invincibility. At the same time, it was also a tragi-comic fantasy of man's inhumanity to man, with a passionate plea for the return of world sanity and an end to the barriers to universal peace. It tried to pillory the German and Italian dictatorships and their totalitarian philosophy by sheer ridicule. Chaplin, displaying brilliant comic verve, shifts back and forth from barber to dictator with bits of pantomime and withering mimicry, drawing violent contrast between the good little man and the evil tyrant. As the barber, Chaplin has a memorable scene in which he shaves a customer to the rhythms of Lizst's "Hungarian Rhapsody." In another comic conceit, the barber and four friends of the ghetto draw lots to decide who is to be the assassin by eating puddings containing coins in them.

But it was as the ranting and petulant dictator that Chaplin created one of his most memorable and devastating caricatures. With almost surgical precision he laid bare all the recognizable traits of Adolf Hitler in a ridiculous Adenoid Hynkel: the affected hand salutes, the ludicrous attitudes, the sudden maniacal fits of rage, the quick starts and jumps of piano-playing, the weeping, the delusions of grandeur, the mesmeric bursts of guttural oratory (a compound of double talk and nonsense).

One of the high points of Chaplin's performance was a plaintive dance done with a large balloon representing the globe, mocking Hitler's dream of world conquest. To the accompaniment of ethereal music, Hynkel playfully toys with the balloon, bouncing it into the air, pirouetting beneath it, caressing it with tender affection, until the balloon suddenly explodes in his face. At this, the would-be conqueror of the world bursts into tears, reminding us of the hysterical, slightly deranged malice of an adolescent unable to control his feelings. The sequence forecast what in a few years would in effect happen, even to suggesting Hitler's own demoniacal self-destruction.

In sharp contrast to the comic vein of the picture as a whole is the seriousness of the final scene—a four minute speech of Chaplin's credo and his belief in humanity—which aroused the ire of many critics. They called the conclusion "bewildering," "outright propaganda," "a shock," or complained that it "spoiled the unity of the picture." An unconventional social and political peroration to come from the screen, it was presumably addressed to the soldiers who were the victims of dictatorships. Yet it also served as a dramatic stratagem to strike at the conscience of America. England had been undergoing savage assaults by the Luftwaffe and anticipated an imminent invasion. The speech, delivered by Chaplin with great sincerity and feeling, was his way of articulating his hatred of warmongers and of appealing to America by playing on her sense of compassion and her common heritage with England, for immediate aid to embattled Britain. ". . . Brutes have risen to power," he says with vehemence. ". . . Dictators freed themselves but they enslaved the people!" Then, with passionate intensity, he pleads: "Soldiers! In the name of democracy, let us unite!"

Chaplin vigorous defended his ending of *The Great Dictator*. He said it was pretty much what he meant it to be. "I had a story to tell and something I wanted very much to say. I said it. . . . The picture is two hours and seven minutes in length. If two hours and three minutes of it is comedy, may I not be excused for ending my comedy on a note that reflects honestly and realistically, the world in which we live, and may I not be excused in pleading for a better world?"[8]

What Chaplin said in *The Great Dictator* was what he had been saying in his other films. "It is the story of the little fellow that I have told and retold all my life. But it has a viewpoint, as much a viewpoint as *Uncle Tom's Cabin* or *Oliver Twist* had in their time . . . I didn't pull punches . . . nor attempt to temporize with something most of us feel so deeply."[9]

As protests for neutrality faded and more of America began to favor all-out aid to England, a large variety of movies mirrored the determined national viewpoint. Melodramas, plots about spies, saboteurs, stories of manhunts, escapes, and also comedies and satires about military training became predominantly warminded. Pictures glorifying our combative deterrents—the new planes, tanks, dive bombers, anti-aircraft weapons—and the men serving in the army, navy, and air force now began to fill the screens.

Flight Command (1940) was produced with the "gratefully acknowledged cooperation of the U.S. Navy." The movie, though wrapped around a weak story of an ensign accused by his shipmates of carrying on an affair with the commander's wife, actually described the training of a fighter air squadron—zooming through maneuvers, performing target practice, taking off and landing on carriers, testing fog-landing devices. *I Wanted Wings* (1941), which depicted the training of army pilots, went into production right after Roosevelt's call for 80,000 planes a year and was made with the cooperation of the Army Air Force. In it, much of the government's new air equipment, including Flying Fortresses, was photographed for the first time. The story, which dramatized the military virtue of obedience, was plotted around the reckless stunts of three student flyers from three different walks of life—a socialite, a football hero and a mechanic—who were in training for their wings. *Dive Bomber* (1941) was concerned with research into the causes of "blackouts" in dive bombing and *Navy Blues* (1941) with gunnery practice and marksmanship.

The President's proclamation of an unlimited national emergency in April of 1941 set off a wave of pictures, aimed to help several million young men and their families accept agreeably the disruption in their lives caused by the Selective Service Act. Comedies and satires predominated. They carried such titles as *Buck Privates, Caught in the Act, You'll Never Get Rich, Call Out the Marines, Great Guns, "Tanks a Million," You're in the Navy, Keep 'Em Flying* and *Top Sergeant Mulligan.*

By the summer of 1941, American pictures had become more militant. Hitler's surprise attack on Russia, the Nazi U-boats' sinking of American ships, and the president's national broadcast ordering the navy to shoot on sight those "rattlesnakes of the Atlantic," had aroused public feelings to a fighting pitch. The screen began to share in the aggressiveness with stories calling for some form of counteraction. Both *A Yank in the R.A.F.* and *International Squadron* dramatized the careers of American pilots flying bomber ferries to England. They become so aroused at the bombing of England that they join the Royal Air Force in order to strike back at Germany. *Parachute Battalion, Flying Fortress,* and *Submarine Patrol* were "topicals" that gave a man and his country "the guts to fight, even against terrible odds," as one trade paper put it. *Voices in the Night* and *Underground* praised the virtues and bravery of rebel groups, operating clandestine radios within the captive nations, who stirred their people to acts of sabotage and resistance against the Nazi oppressor.

One of the most effective pictures in the movies' march to war—and perhaps the farthest removed from the typical recruiting poster—was *Sergeant York,* directed by Howard Hawks. The film was based on the true-life story of America's number-one hero of World War I, and it had a special relevance at a time when the nation was trying to balance a national antipathy to war with a conviction that the Axis had to be stopped. When the draft was called in 1917, York registered as a conscientious objector because his religion had taught him killing was a sin. But in a troubled vigil with himself in which he tried to reconcile his duty to his country and to his God, he came upon the Bible verse which said: "Render unto Caesar the things that are Caesar's and unto God the things that are God's."

Reassured by the holy admonition, York joined the army and went to war. In the battle of the Argonne, he killed twenty-five Germans, captured a machine-gun nest, took a hundred and thirty-two prisoners, and destroyed the enemy's position in a vital sector—practically single-handed. For this incredible feat, York received the highest American and French decorations.

Sergeant York became a kind of symbol for a public already deeply instilled with the idea of national defense. Appearing at the floodtide of pro-war films advocating preparedness, it was perhaps the strongest of them in preaching the necessity for taking up arms in the nation's defense. By showing what happened to an average American who, though he read his Bible and was a pacifist, yet became a war hero, the film subtly and astutely rallied popular feeling for participation in the war. The contemporary impact of the theme, the simplicity of treatment, the fidelity to a real event and a real person gave the picture conviction and made it an eloquent advocate for persuading pacifist-minded men to become war recruits.

Two months later the sudden and unforeseen attack on Pearl Harbor shocked America into the war and brought to an abrupt end any convictions favoring non-intervention. There was no opportunity now for isolationists—no matter where their political loyalties lay—to hold themselves aloof from the administration's program of internationalism.

The impetus of our involvement in war brought a new urgency to the role of the American film. It was no longer necessary for Americans to be told fascism was a threat to America: the surprise attack on December

7th had proved it. Overnight, film studios were mobilized for national defense. On December 18th, the President designated Lowell Mellett to act as coordinator of motion picture affairs for the government. His letter of appointment included the recommendation that he "consult with and advise motion picture producers of ways and means in which they can usefully serve the National Defense effort."

A War Activities Committee, made up of producers, theater owners, distributors, actors and labor unions, was formed to establish mutual cooperation in the national interest. The goal was to emotionalize and glorify "the blood, sweat and tears" of war, the sacrifices demanded, and the ends for which America and her allies were fighting. "Though the screen missed its chance to protest against fascism in a manner worthy of its might," wrote Cecelia Ager, film critic for PM, "now it got the opportunity to redeem itself. Now it got the opportunity to exalt democracy in a manner worthy of its might."[10]

Keeping in mind the aim of combining purpose with entertainment, six basic categories and themes were suggested by the government to serve as a guide for Hollywood's contribution to the all-out struggle: (1) The Issues of the War: what we are fighting for, the American way of life; (2) The Nature of the Enemy: his ideology, his objectives, his methods; (3) The United Nations: our allies in arms; (4) The Production Front: supplying the materials for victory; (5) The Home Front: civilian responsibility; (6) The Fighting Forces: our armed services, our allies and our associates. In treating these subjects, film-makers were advised that freedom of the screen, like freedom of the press and radio, would be respected. Nevertheless, there were certain responsibilities and obligations arising from the war, and the studios were expected to make the best possible use of the motion picture as "a weapon of democracy," as morale "vitamins," and "for the presentation of the government's message here and elsewhere."

The first pictures that tried to inject fact into fiction, with the aim of alleviating the emotional anxieties of a warring nation, were naive responses to the officially designated thematic patterns. Attempts to translate the meaning of war and stimulate audience awareness were crude, with the new themes thinned down to the old standardized plots and formulas. The first post-Pearl Harbor films, made in 1942, were still largely the old gangster or G-men melodramas, fitted out with Nazi soldiers, spies, or a war background. *Joan of Paris, All Through the Night, Salute to Courage, Dangerously We Live, Saboteur, The Lady has Plans,* and any number of other pictures flaunting exhibitionistic bravado failed to meet war on anything approaching serious terms. *Captain of the Clouds* and *To the Shores of Tripoli* which showed in detail the training methods of, respectively, the Royal Canadian Air Force and the United States Marines had all the familiar virtues and defects of those recruiting posters which aim to make men out of boys.

Nearly the entire spate of films immediately after Pearl Harbor undersold the issues of war for its sensationalism. By contract, the modest *Joe Smith, American* tried to express in homely terms some reason for the conflict. Its story was credible and stemmed from the government's category of production-front themes. A skilled aircraft mechanic who is selected to work on a secret bombsight is kidnaped by enemy agents. When attempted bribery fails to make him reveal the secrets of the new instrument, the worker is beaten and tortured. Eventually he escapes and helps round up his kidnapers. The method by which he and government agents retraced the road to the house where the mechanic had been held captive had the merits of originality, concision, and ingenuity in the use of sound effects. This picture was also the first to deal with defense workers, to show how they lived and felt under the stress of war's responsibilities; and, although it fell short of expectations, gave evidence of honesty, imagination, and awareness of what it was the civilian was fighting for.

Two other serious dramas made at this time illustrated the courage of "our allies in arms" in facing up to their war responsibilities. *This Above All,* based on the war's first best-selling novel, by Eric Knight, told the story of a disillusioned English hero of Dunkirk who deserts to figure out what he was fighting for. He wonders whether he has been risking death for officers who have no right to command beyond the right of birth; and whether the war is not just another "imperialist hoax" that will result in preventing his class from gaining a greater stake in the country they are defending.

The picture is centered around a romance and social debate between the low-born soldier who had gone AWOL and an aristocratic girl who had joined the WAAF. It gave strong expression to the soldier's questions of whether he was fighting for a just cause. The answer that brought him back to duty, however, was the oversimplified argument that "England must first be saved before she can be reformed." If the picture was weakest in its case for blind patriotism, it did argue vehemently against the Cliveden set's reactionary attitude toward the war, and against snobbish, superior members of the upper class. Unfortunately, the involved subject of social classes in war was focused in speeches rather than in any kind of authentic action.

If *This Above All* missed the high goal for which it aimed, *Mrs. Miniver* didn't fumble in its aim or message and emerged as one of the most articulate pictures of the day. Without talking or preaching about upper class snobbery, heroism, British tradition, or patriotism, it quietly dramatized these qualities through the humor and pathos of a middle-class family in war-time England. When Mrs. Miniver's husband was awakened at two o'clock in the morning to help in the rescue of the

British army from Dunkirk—when she watched her son, a pilot in the RAF, fly across the channel each night toward Germany—when she unexpectedly captured a sick and starving German pilot who had crashed and who reminded her of her son—when she witnessed her son's bride of a few weeks shot down by a stray bullet—when she comforted her two small children in an air-raid shelter while her home was bombed—the audience felt the quiet courage with which the people of England were meeting the onslaught. Mrs. Miniver's family became the audience's family. And in its own poignant way, William Wyler's picture underlined the things that not only the British but the Americans and the Allied forces were fighting for. It articulated the meaning of a "people's war" most forcefully and through the most potent kind of propaganda.

But for one *Mrs. Miniver,* there were dozens of films that contained less truth, much less discretion, and little respect for war's gravity. Pictures that dealt with the enemy's aims and methods, of which there was a preponderance in the first six months of 1942, unwittingly fostered misconceptions about the real character of the foe as well as the sober facts of war itself: *Berlin Correspondent, United We Stand, A Yank in Libya, Danger in the Pacific, Sabotage Squad, Counter-Espionage, Cairo, Submarine Alert, Journey into Fear, Texas to Bataan.*

Nor did the movies that depicted the production front, such films as *Wings For The Eagle, Girl Trouble, Swing Shift, The Tank Called John* and *Alaska Highway,* do justice to America's determination and vigor in a war which differed in character from any war in history. The problems of the home front were treated superficially with light-minded pursuits of women and trivial personal complications. The contents of *Blondie For Victory, Tomorrow We Live, The War Against Mrs. Hadley,* and other similar films attempting to build morale were hardly commensurate with the motives and issues of the conflict. An exception was *Journey For Margaret* which treated the sobering subject of England's uprooted children with uncommon perception and sensitivity.

As the war grew fiercer, films about the fighting forces became more numerous, sterner and harsher. They tapped all services and covered the world wide arena. *Atlantic Convoy, The Navy Comes Through, Flying Tigers, War Dogs, Army Surgeon, Thunderbirds, Suicide Squadron* and others of their kind made during 1942 tried to keep abreast of current events. In some instances there was an attempt to reconstruct history, to make the performers act like soldiers and not actors—even to make no compromise with an easy and happy ending. *Wake Island,* a reenactment of the heroic resistance by American Marines on that Pacific island, stood out for its lack of bluster and bravado and for its harsh expressiveness. But most often these attempts to dramatize war in clear and serious terms had all the authenticity of a recruiting poster.

Few of the war films made during the first year of conflict—whatever their category—focused sharply on their themes, or clarified thoughtfully the values of the agony and the effort. The majority, combining propaganda with entertainment, were flagrantly puerile. Most often they reflected the inherited points of view of the first world war or were obvious transformations of melodramas of the past with their leading figures now in uniforms. Training camps, military installations, flying fields, jungles, ships, and other war-time locales replaced the western range, the cattle towns, the big city clubs, bars, streets, penthouses, offices, and apartments. The two-gun fighters, the sheriffs, the private eyes, the executives, the racketeers, and the politicians now wore G.I. fatigues, a sergeant's stripes, or officer's bars. The blonde in the silk negligee, the sophisticated wife in the evening gown, and the sweet girl next door were similarly transformed into the Wac, the Wave, the nurse, the USO entertainer, or the factory doll in overalls.

In the rush to translate the shock of war into stories of dynamic action —to serve both the national purpose and entertainment—stock patterns and formulas became the rule. The preponderance of shoddy plots, the similarity of situation and action stirred up protests in trade papers and from exhibitors who told Hollywood that the public was fed up with war films. By the spring of 1943, the rising agitation had stampeded many producers into scheduling programs heavy with musicals and other frivolous films, advertised as having absolutely nothing to do with war.

Hostile to the wishful complacency of his colleagues, Harry M. Warner, president of Warner Brothers Pictures, Inc., denounced any abandonment of war movies. "A small group of entertainment appeasers are trying to keep the truth from audiences," he declared.[11] Bosley Crowther, who reported the executive's concern over the urgent need of war films, held much the same opinion. "The public is not tired of war's realities, but of woefully cheap make-believe," he wrote. "What we want in our war films is honest expression of national resolve and a clear indication of realities unadorned with Hollywood hoop-la."[12]

THE DOCUMENTARY INFLUENCE

Lowell Mellett, chief of the Office of War Information's Bureau of Motion Pictures, deplored the emphasis that film-makers had laid on the melodramatic aspects of the conflict, without conveying what the war was all about, or what it meant "for a great democracy to commit itself to war." He told the National Board of Review of Motion Pictures: "Somehow it is almost impossible to feel the war here in America where we seem to be safe. We are still in a state that makes it necessary for us to keep telling ourselves that it is true, that it is real, that we are part of it."[13]

Mellett's dissatisfaction with war films led to the army's deciding to show Hollywood its own viewpoint and thinking on war by giving the film capital the same indoctrination it administered to soldiers. In a series of evening screenings, conducted for producers, directors, writers and the press, the army showed a program of orientation films and documentaries, among which were the *Why We Fight* series. These included *The Prelude To War, The Nazis Strike, Divide and Conquer, The Battle of Britain* and *The Battle of Russia. (Battle of China* and *War Comes to America* were still in production.) Individually and as a series these military films were sharp and quick in impact, penetrating in persuasiveness. They were imbued with a clarity of meaning seldom approached by Hollywood, and set a challenging standard for studio-made products.

The *Why We Fight* series was produced under the supervision of Lieutenant-Colonel Frank Capra with the assistance of skilled Hollywood as well as documentary film craftsmen. The events leading to the war, the battle scenes, the intensities of combat were all treated on a very high level. There were no heroics, no romantic conceptions of war, and these pictures, in their vividness and technical proficiency and in their doctrine of total war—accepted both by the fascist countries and the democracies—were a powerful embodiment of the War Department's concern for "interpretation of the causes of war, the evidence on which the interpretation is based, and the events which combined to produce the present state of conflict."

The Capra series was made in the belief that if a man knows his enemy, the reasons for war, and why he is fighting, he will make a better soldier. Similar viewpoints and ideas were expressed in related informational and educational films, produced by the War Department, Army Pictorial Services, the AAF First Motion Picture Unit, the U.S. Navy, The U.S. Marine Corps, and the OWI in cooperation with the British Ministry of Information. Among the best were William Wyler's *Memphis Belle* (1944), John Ford's *Battle of Midway* (1944), *The Battle For the Marianas* (1944), John Huston's *The Battle For San Pietro* and *Let There Be Light* (1945), *Fury In the Pacific* (1945), and *The True Glory* (1945) directed by Carol Reed and Garson Kanin. All were striking studies of men preparing for, engaging in, or suffering from combat. Their intense, intimate, authentic tone, like the *Why We Fight* pictures, had an enormous effect on film-makers, inspiring them with a constant urge to make their own war pictures more genuine and meaningful.

Imbued with a new spirit, indoctrinated Hollywood responded more authoritatively to the need for weightier themes and to the demands of the democratic ethos. Pictures dealing with the nature of the enemy became marked by a deepening of the sociological and psychological issues. From stock portrayals of the enemy as a buffoon, a sentimentalist, a coward or a brutal gangster (in such pictures as *To Be or Not To Be, The Devil With Hitler, Once Upon a Honeymoon* and *Margin For Error*) a handful of subsequent pictures focused on revealing the enemy's disregard of moral precepts and ethical sensibilities, his calculated cruelty, his cunning, and his actual strength. *Keeper of the Flame* (1943) warned against Fascists in America, who masqueraded under Americanism but were plotting to destroy democracy. *Hitler's Children* (1943) revealed the training and indoctrination of German youth scientifically subjected to Nazi ideology. *Watch on the Rhine* (1943) dramatized the struggle for power in an American household in Washington between an anti-Fascist and a Fascist and its central conflict was the strategy of ideologies. A somewhat similar struggle informed *Tomorrow the World* (1944). Here a well-meaning American family was caught between its own liberal principles and the cynicism of Nazi-trained youth. *The Hitler Gang* (1944) portrayed the brutal nature of the Nazi leaders and their ruthless methods of achieving power.

One of the more ambitious and controversial films was Hitchcock's *Lifeboat* (1944). Here was an effort to create an allegory of world shipwreck, in which a deliberate attempt was made to give a more realistic complexion to the strengths and weaknesses of those responsible for the debacle, and to examine, at the same time, varieties of democratic egalitarianism.

The entire action of the picture takes place in a drifting lifeboat containing a group of eight Americans, survivors of a torpedoed freighter, and a Nazi commander, whose U-boat gunned down the freighter before it was itself hit and destroyed. The survivors seemed deliberately chosen to serve the ideological as well as the dramatic needs of the plot. Among them are a millionaire shipbuilder with all the virtues and vices of capitalism, a cynical lady journalist who believes in nothing, a religious Negro steward who loves all humanity, an engineer with liberal views, and the cold-blooded, arrogant U-boat commander. Each of these particular people takes his own particular view of their situation and brings to bear his own kind and degree of moral courage. The Nazi functions as a point of reference in relation to which the other types fix their moral attitudes. Together the occupants form an adroit microcosm of the two warring societies.

Lifeboat posed the problem of survival when social patterns begin to collapse, and when men (or nations) can only survive if they have strength and resourcefulness. In the life and death conditions that prevailed, the Nazi captain was deliberately portrayed as a resolute and cunning figure because, Hitchcock declared, "In the analogue of war, he *was* the victor at the time."[14] He manipulated the Americans' weakness for his own purpose. He was more competent and showed more skill and initiative. He was the only one who knew anything about sailing. He knew where he was heading for, could take command, plan for survival, and even cope with disastrous emergencies—in this case the amputation of the gangrenous leg of one of the crew members from the freighter.

By comparison, the other survivors "representing the democracies, hadn't gotten together yet, hadn't summoned their strength."[15] They seemed weak, poorly prepared to cope with their dangerous situation, and couldn't act as a group. Not until they discovered the Nazi's treachery were they able to act as one and oppose him. They learned that he had been secretly navigating the boat toward a Nazi supply ship, using a compass he had concealed from them; that he had stolen a bottle of water for himself while they were suffering from thirst; that his apparently superhuman strength had come from food tablets and energy pills; and finally, that he had drowned a member of their group, who had surprised him at his trickery. Outraged, and in a burst of common fury, they collectively beat the Nazi to death. Afterwards, still united and determined in purpose, they fish together.

The picture ends in a kind of allegorical epilogue. The survivors, having drifted in sight of a Nazi supply ship, prepare to die as it attempts to run them down, when, from beyond the horizon, comes a volley of fire, and the Nazi boat is destroyed. As the Americans begin planning their rescue, a Nazi sailor from the sunken supply ship attempts to climb into their lifeboat, precipitating a quarrel over whether to save the German or not. The sailor suddenly confronts them with a gun. The others respond by a group attack and take the weapon away from the Nazi. The last scene leaves them quarreling over whether any German can ever again be trusted or should be treated humanely.

Made at a crucial period in the war, at a time when many people were calling for a second front and the danger of German rocket and missile attacks from the French coast was imminent, *Lifeboat* was a grim reminder against underestimating the resourcefulness and power of the enemy.

ALLIES AND ACTUALITIES

Hollywood also deepened its treatment of the theme in many pictures coming under the classification of "our brothers in arms." These were mainly inside stories of the conquered people in Nazi-occupied Europe. In the past only surface reference had been made to any conflicts raging within individual characters, the films being largely stories of escape, intrigue and espionage. Seldom had any attention been paid to making the background real or saying anything about how the occupation affected the ordinary citizen. Now such pictures not only began to probe deeper into their characters, but also argue the political aspects of fascism in addition to its barbarism, and to dramatize the craving and need of human beings resisting Nazification for freedom. Beneath the exterior melodrama of underground plots, sabotage schemes and commando raids, the best of them tried to convey the reason some men resist and fight on moral grounds, and others don't.

The Moon is Down, This Land is Mine, Hangmen Also Die, The Commandos, Edge of Darkness, Cross of Lorraine, Song of Russia and *North Star*—a vintage crop from 1943—were grim and brutal stories of destruction, torture, heroic resistance and death. But they also tried to get underneath the externals of their action and to probe the feelings of individuals, to examine the conflicts between truth and hyprocrisy, good will and selfishness. The enemy was called by name—fascism. American and Allied nationals were shown fighting together in plots that graphically illustrated the possibility of victory over the "invincible" enemy, once questions of conscience had been resolved in the determination to win for a just cause.

One of the most outstanding pictures in this category, and one whose story was not set in occupied territory was *Mission to Moscow* (1943). The picture followed the book of the same name by our former Ambassador to Russia, Joseph E. Davies, and made use of confidential reports to the State Department, selections from the Ambassador's diaries, and official correspondence during his two-year mission in the Soviet Union. Its purpose was clearly to speak out against anti-Soviet prejudice and isolationist feeling in the United States with the object of promoting good will for America's ally.

Mission to Moscow had no plot or story line in the usual sense. It attempted to be a documentary of living history. Its events, presented more or less chronologically, began in 1936 at the Geneva Conference when Haile Selassie appealed for action against Italian aggression, and continued up to the time of Roosevelt's appointment of lawyer Davies to Moscow in 1937, where he was instructed to get the facts about the famous purge trials, and to assess Russia's strength and her attitude toward war or peace in Europe. Every important character in the picture was a counterpart of a real person on the stage of world events. Real names were used—Roosevelt, Churchill, Stalin, Litvinov, Trotsky and others. These roles were enacted by performers chosen for their likeness to the real person, with the exception of Ambassador Davies, who was portrayed by Walter Huston.

The realism given by such casting was reinforced by an introduction featuring Davies himself, who said: "There was so much prejudice and misunderstanding of the Soviet Union, in which I partly shared, that I felt it my duty to tell the truth as I saw it, for such value as it might have. . . ." Thereafter the picture loosely followed the approach of the book, recreating pictorially the diary and journal entries, plus numerous official reports, in an effort to present a strong case for the Russian system and its rulers. The Ambassador was shown touring Russian factories, both civilian and military, standing with the political elite at a May Day spectacle, attending an exhibition of Russian Army maneuvers, and conferring with Stalin about a united stand by the democracies against Hitler's aggressions. The Ambassador's wife and daughter were also pictured with Russian friends and with women in business and industry.

Among sequences arousing dispute (such as those criticising the Chamberlain government and the Congressional isolationists) by far the most controversial was the film's visual re-enactment of the famed Bukharin-Radik trials of 1937. Using what Davies reported to be the actual transcripts of the trials and the defendants' confessions of guilt, the picture followed the Stalinist contention that Trotsky and the men on trial had conspired with Germany and Japan to sabotage Russia's defenses, partition the country, and take over the government.

The picture's missionary zeal to approve the famous Moscow purge trials and to celebrate a country "long maligned and disgracefully minimized in our press and cinema."[16] evoked a sharp storm of debate. Divergent opinions evaluating the film ranged from "an epoch making film for America"[17] to: "The film is anti-British, anti-Congress, anti-Democratic and anti-truth."[18] One group of sixty-six distinguished and prominent commentators, including Anne O'Hare McCormick, Dorothy Thompson, Sidney Hook, Eugene Lyons and W. E. Woodward, took strong exception to the film and sided with the comment expressed by John Haynes Holmes: "As history it is a lie, as propaganda it is a scandal of the first order."[19] Another group of equally prominent Americans representing all fields of endeavor, among whom were Representative John M. Coffee, Senator Claude Pepper, Walter Duranty, Theodore Dreiser, Fritz Mahler and more than two hundred others, issued a signed statement denouncing the attacks as a "distinct disservice to the cause of American-Soviet unity during the war and afterward." *Mission to Moscow,* they declared, "is more than a motion picture; it is a gesture of international friendship made at the most crucial period of American history with the highly laudable and important object of promoting trust instead of distrust in the Soviet Union."

By the end of America's second year of involvement in the war, films about the "fighting forces" began to disassociate themselves from their romantic military heritage. In this period just prior to the invasion of Europe and the Allied advances in the Pacific, any focus on the romantic involvements of soldiers faded, and the enemy was treated with much less compassion. The typically chauvinistic values and verities of military romanticism and flag-waving, which had commonly inspired and molded war pictures, became increasingly rarer. G.I. audiences had pointed out the obvious phoniness of settings and surroundings in many combat films. Books by war correspondents and soldier novelists made a mockery of scenes that showed soldiers preoccupied by trivial anxieties and sentimental aspirations, or that showed the "beautiful" death of the fighting men. Documentaries by the armed services and newsreels by the Signal Corps had by now painfully familiarized film-makers with the truth and conviction of combat and violent death. Shaped by the dynamic interaction between America's grinding military advances and the rendering of deeper war-like images, the screen reached out for the heart and essence of war's reality.

Movies began to serialize the butchery and profanity of war, its soberness and attrition, the fighting man's dignity, his acts of conscience and personal decision, his fulfillment in group responsibility. In every section of the globe, on all battle-fronts, on bomber fields, in merchant ships, in submarines, in the skies, jungles, beaches and prisoner-of-war camps, the camera became an articulate and penetrating witness to the pain, bitterness, and horror of war. *Bataan* (1943), *With the Marines at Tarawa* (1944), *Guadacanal Diary* (1944), *The Battle for the Marianas* (1944), *Attack: Invasion of New Britain* (1944), truthfully projected the dirty business of fighting. These pictures were imbued with conviction and unavoidable horror. They documented unflinchingly the desperate involvement of men in close quarters with each other, the shattering muteness of men before the anonymity of death, and the bewildering sense of war's toll and waste.

INDIVIDUALISM AND IDEALISM

Among films that were preoccupied with the deep emotional crisis and individual agony of the average Joe, anxiously examining his own conscience, were *Action in the North Atlantic* (1943), *Destination Tokyo* (1943), *Sahara* (1944), *Air Force* (1944), *A Walk in the Sun* (1945), *The Story of G.I. Joe* (1945), and *The Purple Heart* (1945). They showed the perilous journey of a bomber or convoy bringing its lethal cargo safely through Axis flak or "wolf-packs" to its destination, the enforced quiet of an improvised hospital bed, the tension and tribulations of a march through enemy-controlled sectors, the humbled faces of men in prison compounds, the obstinate doggedness of prisoners refusing to divulge information to their brutal captors, and the fury and turbulence of actual combat itself. But there were vivid flashes and undercurrents of the human obsessions and depravities that war evoked. In the best of these films, there was implicit a rationale that attempted to define the moral consequences of the fighting and dying.

At the same time, the retreat from the war film as a glorified poster involved also the condemnation of old assumptions. To express the imperatives of an ideological and global war demanded scripts with characters coming from every economic level and representing almost every racial strain in American society. The ethnic composition of soldier groups was stressed, and they invariably included a Jew, a Negro, an Irishman, an Italian, a Pole or Swede—a choice obviously meant to present the microcosm of America. This kind of national collective hero, who wanted the Axis destroyed and a good society created, clearly sprang from the liberal social attitudes of the Thirties that questioned prejudice and social injustice and focused attention on those wronged or victimized by society. Unfortunately, the recognition of democratic and humane conceptions often was not in itself sufficient to convert psychological and sociological truths into imaginative truth.

While combat films had developed greater realism, those movies dealing with the home front applied the salve of humor to ease the pain of innumerable petty annoyances, anxieties, and other more profound changes in American life. Comedies and farces proved enormously helpful in alleviating the irritations of well-fed Americans whose menus were curtailed by food rationing, their mobility restricted by gasoline rationing, their jobs and wages frozen, and their income taxes and living costs raised. *Hail the Conquering Hero* (1944), *The Miracle of Morgan's Creek* (1944), and *See Here Private Hargrove* (1944) were among the best of a sundry output of farces, which, with irrepressible impudence, extravagant action and wild travesty, mocked some of the cherished notions and practices of a public now caught up in the frenzy of wartime living. The tongue-in-cheek sentiment and racy humor of *The More the Merrier* (1943) and *Princess O'Rourke* (1943) distinguished them from dozens of less successful films that mocked the irksome tribulations of a people who had to put up with seemingly endless scarcities and inconveniences and had to stand in line for almost everything.

Also intended to ease the uncertainties and anxieties of a home-front public were a number of pictures that attempted to pay tribute to the radiance of faith and to satisfy the craving for spiritual sustenance. The expert blending of comedy with religious virtue in *Going My Way* (1944), and the more sober pieties of *Song of Bernadette* (1944) set a trend for soothing the apathy and despair of mixed peoples held together by common sacrifices and common anguish.

A picture that was tradition-breaking and quite different from those made to fulfill the government's wartime demands appeared some months after the Allied invasion of Europe when the final phase of the war was already under way. *Wilson* (1944) paid homage to a man who tried to prevent a second world war, but it had a sharp relevance to the current war's end and to the impending Grand Alliance. The film was less a biography of a wartime President than an effort to show how politics relate to war and peace, and a reminder that the very war in which the world was then involved need not have happened but for the failure of others to recognize and act upon Woodrow Wilson's plan for world peace.

The story of *Wilson* was the dignified record of a champion of democracy. From the introduction of Woodrow Wilson at a football game in 1909 as president of Princeton to the closing scenes of his death as President of the United States in 1921, the film characterized him as a crusading American dedicated to democratic principles. He was presented not as the politician, the President, or the war-time Commander-in-Chief, but as the singular idealist.

The War Department banned the picture under Title V of Senator Taft's Soldier's Vote Act which forbade the distribution to the troops of any material "containing political argument or political propaganda of any kind designed or calculated to affect the result of any election." Hollywood saw the action as a serious threat to freedom of the screen and was preparing "to mobilize for broad action" when the ban was suddenly removed and Congress "set about repealing the censorship section of Taft's Act."[20]

Film reviewers also reacted strongly. James Agee wrote: "Pictures like *Wilson* have little if anything to do with mature serious cinema as such, and those who think of *Wilson* as a mature film are not in the least concerned with its liveliness or deadness as a work of art; they are excited because serious ideas are being used on the screen."[21] Bosley Crowther asked "whether this is not truly a picture with an importance far beyond the theater, a film with the impulse to action of a popular battle cry?"[22] Then he went on to add: ". . . The fact is too plain for disputation that there is heady special pleading in this film—special pleading for an international ideal envisioning permanent peace."

In the array of pictures dealing with the war and world events, *Wilson* stood out for its pervasive idealism. It appeared as victory neared in both the Pacific and European theaters, and when allied leaders were soon to meet in San Francisco to establish the United Nations and give increasing attention to shaping the post-war world. The picture's pro-international sentiment and its implied warning against repeating the foreign policy mistakes of the last world war gave it a residual influence, the impact of which could not be readily measured.

By 1945 the rising tide of Allied victories and the prospect of a sudden termination of the war shifted producers' interest away from war pictures. Martial subjects in production were hurried to a desperate conclusion. Those in planning stages were quickly abandoned. On the assumption that movies with men in uniform would become "box-office poison" after V-Day, there was a wild scramble for post-war themes as Hollywood beat all other industries to reconversion.

Energized by the demands of war, the motion picture during these war years gained point, purpose and direction. They provided entertainment to those hammering out the weapons of war as well as to those fighting the battles. They furthered the military effort by conveying information about war and increased the public's awareness of what was going on. Their real opportunity came in emotionalizing the war situation. This led to an exposure of the nature of the enemy and his assaulting ideology, a more realistic treatment of Allied efforts, and a more dignified portrayal of the fighting men. In dramatizing the stories of conquered countries and attempting to tell what Americans and their allies were fighting for, the screen psychologically and materially met the crisis persuasively and with an urgent sense of its obligations.

Of the more than seventeen hundred features made during this period, more than five hundred were directly concerned with some aspect of fascism and war. A good many were trite and superficial, aimed to keep civilian and military morale high and satisfy the home front about American and Allied struggles "out there." Others were of another sort —opportunistic responses to the need of the moment—either earnest or patriotically stimulating. Yet buried in this vast serialization of evolving history were a small number of notable films that sharply reflected the varied aspects of war and heightened our understanding of it at that moment. The best of these broke through the barriers of propaganda and entertainment to penetrate the truth of the terror and insanity let loose by fascism and by war itself.

NOTES

1. During this same period however, a number of independent documentary film makers were reporting on the rising threat of fascism abroad. Joris Ivens and Ernest Hemingway made *The Spanish Earth* (1937), behind the Loyalist lines during the Spanish Civil War. Herbert Kline and Alexander Hammid in *Crisis* (1938), reported the disintegration of Czechoslovakia after the Munich pact. The same team documented the hostilities in Poland and their effect on London in *Lights Out in Europe* (1939–40).
2. *New York Herald Tribune*, June 23, 1940.
3. Bosley Crowther, *New York Times*, June 23, 1940.
4. *Ibid.*
5. *Friday* Magazine, August 30, 1940.
6. *Ibid.*
7. *New York Times*, October 20, 1940.
8. *New York Times*, October 27, 1940.
9. *Ibid.*
10. *Variety*, January 7, 1942.
11. *New York Times*, May 23, 1943.
12. *Ibid.*

13. Reported by *New York Times,* November 11, 1942.
14. Peter Bogdanovich, *The Cinema of Alfred Hitchcock,* page 25.
15. *Ibid.*
16. From a letter by Clifford Odets, *New Republic,* June 14, 1943.
17. From the text of a statement by 266 leading Americans denouncing disruptive attacks on the picture.
18. From a letter by John Dewey and reported by *The Hollywood Reporter,* June 2, 1943.
19. *Hollywood Reporter,* June 8, 1943.
20. *Los Angeles News,* July 21, 1944.
21. *Nation,* August 19, 1944.
22. *New York Times,* September 10, 1944.

National Types
as Hollywood Presents Them

Siegfried Kracauer

Siegfried Kracauer came to America in 1941 and served as special assistant to the Curator of the Museum of Modern Art Film Library. His book, From Caligari to Hitler, *is acknowledged as the leading study of the German film. The following essay is a psychosociological study of American films through the 1940s.**

UNESCO has begun to inquire into the nature of tensions inimical to mutual understanding between the peoples of the world. Part of this "Tensions Project" is an analysis of "the conceptions which the people of one nation entertain of their own and of other nations."

It seems likely indeed that international understanding depends to some extent on the character of such conceptions—particularly if they assert themselves within the media of mass communication. Among these media the film is perhaps the most impressive.

If we are to study national images as presented in films, two broad areas for research immediately confront us. How do the films of any nation represent their own nation? And how do they represent others? The first of these two problems, increasingly dealt with in current writings, can be dismissed here in favor of the second which seems to me more important for UNESCO's quest. It is a new problem, not yet posed in a general way. Along with a whole family of similar problems, it has come into focus only now that world government is a possibility and world domination a threat. Only now, in fact, has the goal of mutual understanding through knowledge changed from an intellectual pleasure to a vital concern of the democracies.

* By permission from Mrs. Lili Kracauer and the *Public Opinion Quarterly.* "National Types as Hollywood Presents Them," *Public Opinion Quarterly,* Vol. 13 (1949), Princeton University Press. © 1949.

The following study is by no means intended to provide a comprehensive analysis of the various screen images which the peoples of the world have formed, and continue to form, of each other. It is a pilot study, and merely attempts to prepare the ground for such an investigation by examining a small sector of the total subject: the appearance of English and Russian characters in American fiction films since about 1933.[1]

In the universe of fiction films two types are of lesser importance—films about the past of the English and Russians, and screen adaptations of literary masterworks from the two countries. This is not to say that such films are rare. On the contrary, Hollywood finds Victorian England endearing and Catherine the Great amusing. Also, it often feels compelled to exchange entertainment for what it believes to be a culture, and thus it eagerly exploits Shakespeare's plays and Tolstoy's novels, trying to make of them entertainment.[2] No doubt both these historical and literary films are well-established genres. And of course I do not deny that they help build up the screen images of the foreign peoples to which they refer. Yet since they deal with remote events, they are decidedly less relevant to this study than films that have a direct bearing on present-day reality.

It is these latter films on which I am concentrating here—films, that is, which involve contemporary Russian and British characters in real-life situations. There has been no lack of them since 1933. I am thinking, for instance, of *Ninotchka* (1939), with its pleasantries at the expense of Soviet mentality, and of *Cavalcade* (1933), which follows the destinies of a well-to-do English family through two generations. What concepts the American screen entertains of the English and Russians can best be elicited from such more or less realistically handled comedies and dramas.

OBJECTIVE AND SUBJECTIVE FACTORS IN NATIONAL IMAGES

In the case of individuals and peoples alike, knowledge of each other may progress from a state of ignorance to fair understanding. It is, for instance, a far cry from what the average American knows about the Japanese to Ruth Benedict's recent disclosure of the set of motives that determine Japanese attitudes and actions. Her study, *The Chrysanthemum and the Sword,* marks progress in objectivity; it challenges us to dispose of the familiar notions and common prejudices which help fashion our standard images of that people. Generally speaking, any such increase of knowledge is identical with a closer approach to the object we seek to penetrate.

This approach, however, is bound to remain asymptotic for two reasons, one of which lies in the object itself. An individual or a people is not so much a fixed entity as a living organism that develops along unforeseeable lines. Hence the difficulty of self-identification. It is true that the successive images a people creates of its own character are as a rule more reliable than those it forms of a foreign people's; but they are not complete and definite either.

The other obstacle to perfect knowledge, alone important in this context, lies in ourselves. We perceive all objects in a perspective imposed upon us by our environment as well as by certain inalienable traditions. Our concepts of a foreigner necessarily reflect native habits of thought. Much as we try to curtail this subjective factor, as we are indeed forced to do in the interest of increased objectivity, we still view the other individual from a position which is once and for all ours. It is just as impossible for us to settle down in a vacuum as it would be to fuse with him.

Any image we draw up of an individual or a people is the resultant of an objective and a subjective factor. The former cannot grow indefinitely; nor can the latter be completely eliminated. What counts is the ratio between these two factors. Whether our image of a foreign people comes close to true likeness or merely serves as a vehicle of self-expression—that is, whether it is more of a portrait or more of a projection—depends upon the degree to which our urge for objectivity gets the better of naïve subjectivity.

MEDIA INFLUENCES ON OBJECTIVITY-SUBJECTIVITY RATIO

The ratio between the objective and the subjective factor varies with the medium of communication. It is evident that within the medium of the printed word objectivity may go the limit. In the radio, also, objective information plays a considerable role, even though it is hampered by various restrictions, most of them inherent in the nature of this mass medium. Yet for all its limitations the radio registers any signal increase of knowledge. I do not doubt, for instance, that the evolution of modern anthropology—resulting from the necessities of psychological warfare and this country's engagements in international affairs—has been instrumental in bringing about recent radio programs which surveyed living conditions in other countries, and in particular focused on "the character and ideals of the Russian people."[3]

And what about the film? Hollywood's fiction films are commercial products designed for mass consumption at home and, if possible, abroad. The implications of this overall principle are obvious: Hollywood must try to captivate the masses without endangering its affiliations with vested interests. In view of high production costs it must try to avoid controversial issues lest box office receipts fall off. What the latter "must" means for the representation of foreigners is classically illustrated by the setback which the Remarque film, *All Quiet on the Western Front* (1930), suffered in Germany after a few Berlin performances, in December, 1930. This film, with its emphasis on the antiwar mood of German soldiers in the years of trench warfare, stirred the Nazis to violent demonstrations which in turn caused the German government to suspend its further screening.[4] Similar experiences, made with vaguely anti-Fascist films in neutral countries shortly before World War II, have corroborated the sad truth that foreign peoples are as touchy as domestic groups, professional or otherwise. The film industry therefore "remains afraid of portraying characters or situations in a way which will offend its existing foreign market: why jeopardize a source of revenues?"[5]

Hollywood, then, is faced with the task of producing films that draw the masses, in particular the American masses. The problem of how it measures up to this task has long since been a subject of discussion. Many hold that Hollywood, with the support of its affiliated chains of movie houses, manages to sell films which do not give the masses what they really want. From this viewpoint it would seem that Hollywood films more often than not stultify and misdirect a public persuaded into accepting them by its own indolence and by overwhelming publicity. I do not believe that such a viewpoint is tenable. Experience has taught us that even totalitarian regimes cannot manipulate public opinion forever; and what holds true for them applies all the more to an industry which, despite its monopolistic tendencies, still functions within the framework of a competitive society. The film industry is forced by its profit interest to divine the nature of actually existing mass trends and to adjust its products to them. That this necessity leaves a margin for cultural initiative on the part of the industry does not alter the situation. To be sure, American audiences receive what Hollywood wants them to want; but in the long run audience desires, acute or dormant, determine the character of Hollywood films.[6]

The audiences also determine the way these films picture foreigners. The subjective factor in any such image is more or less identical with the notions American public opinion entertains of the people portrayed. It is therefore highly improbable that a nation popular with the average American will be presented unfavorably; nor should we expect currently unpopular nations to be treated with condoning benevolence. Similarly, screen campaigns for or against a nation are not likely to be launched unless they can feed on strong environmental moods in their favor.

Yet its surrender to such moods need not prevent Hollywood from volunteering information about foreign people. It is true that we usually want to understand other nations because of our concern with mutual understanding; but fear and distrust of a people may no less urgently compel us to inquire into the motives behind its aspirations. The desire for knowledge, an essentially independent inner drive, thrives on both antipathy and sympathy. To what extent do Hollywood films satisfy this desire? Or, more specifically: what is the ratio between the subjective and the objective factor in American screen images of foreigners? And has this ratio been stable so far, or are we justified in assuming, for instance, that the images of 1948 surpass those of 1933 in objectivity?

HOLLYWOOD'S ESTIMATE OF ITS AUDIENCE

Without anticipating answers, I wish to formulate a principle derived from the all-powerful profit motive. Hollywood's attitude toward the presentation of any given piece of information ultimately depends on its estimate of how the masses of moviegoers respond to the spread of that information through fiction films. It seems to me important in this connection that the film industry calls itself an entertainment industry—a term which, whatever it connotes, does not precisely make one think of films as carriers of knowledge (nor as works of art, for that matter). There has indeed been a widespread tendency not only to equate screen entertainment and relaxation, but to consider anything informative an undesirable admixture. This entertainment formula, championed as late as 1941 in the sophisticated Preston Sturges film *Sullivan's Travels,* rests upon the conviction that people want to relax when they go to the movies; and it further implies that the need for relaxation and the quest for knowledge oppose rather than attract each other. Of course, as always with such formulas, they characterize the mental climate without being strictly binding. Many a prewar film has defied the usual Hollywood pattern and has deepened our understanding of the world.

Only since the end of the war have ideological conventions undergone a change; and again this change must be traced to mass moods. Obviously inspired by the general desire for enlightenment in the wake of the war, spokesmen of the industry now advocate films that combine entertainment with information. "Motion pictures," says Jack L. Warner, "are entertainment—but they go far beyond that." And he coins the term *"honest entertainment"* to convey the impression of a Hollywood fighting for truth, democracy, international understanding, etc.[7] Eric Johnston, President of the Motion Picture Association, lends his authority to this view. In his statement, *The Right To Know*—which is none the less pertinent for referring to fiction films and factual films alike—he contends that "the motion picture, as an instrument for the promotion of knowledge and understanding among peoples, stands on the threshold of a tremendous era of expansion."[8]

Whether the American motion picture has already trespassed this threshold remains to be seen. On the purely domestic scene it has done so—at least up to a point and temporarily. Attacking social abuses, such films as *The Best Years of our Yives* (1946), *Boomerang* (1947), and *Gentleman's Agreement* (1947) reveal a progressive attitude which undoubtedly owes much to wartime experiences.[9] They still play to full houses, even though political pressures have meanwhile caused the industry to discontinue this trend. Will Hollywood revert to its old entertainment formula? For the time being, we must remain in suspense.

THE TIME ELEMENT

Such foreign peoples as one does see on the American screen do not appear consecutively in films about present-day life.

The English were featured in a number of prewar films succeeding each other closely—among them were the above-mentioned *Cavalcade* (1933), *Of Human Bondage* (1934), *Ruggles of Red Gap* (1935), *The Lives of a Bengal Lancer* (1935), *Angel* (1937), *Lost Horizon* (1937), *A Yank at Oxford* (1938), *The Citadel* (1938), *The Sun Never Sets* (1939), *We Are Not Alone* (1939), *Rebecca* (1940), *Foreign Correspondent* (1940), and *How Green Was My Valley* (1941). No sooner did the United States enter the war than the frequency of topical films about Great Britain and her people increased, as is instanced by *Mrs. Miniver* (1942), *The Pied Piper* (1942), *Journey for Margaret* (1942), *The White Cliffs of Dover* (1944), etc.

This vogue broke off immediately after the war. To the best of my knowledge, the British postwar generation would be nonexistent in the cinematic medium, were it not for *The Paradine Case* (1948), a murder story without any bearing on current issues, and the international-minded melodrama *Berlin Express*, released as late as May, 1948. Between 1945 and 1948, there was a gap spanned only by a few films that focused exclusively on the past—Lubitsch's *Cluny Brown* (1946) which satirized prewar attitudes, fashionable or otherwise; *So Well Remembered* (1947), a social-minded chronicle of small-town life between the two wars; *Ivy* (1947); *Moss Rose* (1947); and *So Evil My Love* (1948). The last three were mystery thrillers playing in turn-of-the-century Britain, if not earlier. Though three years may not be a long period, this sustained unconcern for the present still seems a bit strange.

During the thirties, contemporary Russians were less in view than the English, without, however, being wholly neglected. I have already mentioned *Ninotchka* (1939). Other films of the period were *Tovarich* (1937), and *Comrade X* (December, 1940). In the war, when Stalin joined the Allies, Hollywood permitted no one to outdo it in glowing accounts of Russian heroism. *Mission to Moscow, Miss V. from Moscow, The North Star, Three Russian Girls, Song of Russia*—a veritable springtime of pro-Russian films—flooded the movie houses in 1943 and 1944.

Then, exactly as in the case of the English, the Russians disappeared for three years. They disappeared even more completely than the English, for I do not know of a single, halfway important film since Lubitsch's resurrection of Catherine the Great (*A Royal Scandal*, 1945) which has dealt with their literature or past. Of course, I discount the "mad Russian," who re-emerged in *The Specter of the Rose* (1946); this stereotyped favorite of American audiences—usually a Russian-born artist having sought shelter in the West—is on the whole too estranged from the country of his origin to be identified as a Soviet citizen. It is true that Russians were also rare on the prewar screen, but in those days they were not featured in other media either. What makes one wonder at the absence of Soviet Russia on the postwar screen is just the fact of her omnipresence in speech and print at this time. Between 1945 and 1948, the films alone seemed unaware of a mass obsession.

That Hollywood behaved true to pattern in thus ignoring the Russians is proven by its equally conspicuous silence about the Nazis in the years preceding 1939. It is not as if Germany had played any noticeable role in American films prior to 1933. Yet precisely in the critical years 1930–1934, two grade-A films turned the spotlight on her— *All Quiet on the Western Front* and *Little Man, What Now?* (1934), a screen adaptation of Hans Fallada's pre-Hitler novel about unemployment in Germany. Hollywood, it appears, had become mildly interested in things German. And what came out of it? During the subsequent year Hitler was a topic everywhere but on the screen. If I am not mistaken, only two films with Germans in them appeared in this interval: *The Road Back* (1937) and *Three Comrades* (1938). Both were adapted from novels by Remarque, whose name meant business, and both were laid in the early Weimar Republic, which was dead and buried at the time of their release.

TIMES WHEN SILENCE SEEMS WISE

This temporary withdrawal from certain peoples at certain times can be explained only by factors affecting commercial film production. Significantly, prewar Germany as well as postwar Russia provoked impassioned controversy in the United States. Before the war the country was divided into isolationists and interventionists; immediately after the war it heatedly debated the problem of whether the United States should be tough or soft in her dealings with the Kremlin: I believe it is this split of public opinion which accounts for Hollywood's evasiveness in both cases. Hollywood, as I have pointed out earlier, is so sensitive to economic risks that it all but automatically shrinks from touching on anything controversial. Germany and Russia were tabooed as "hot stuff"; and they were hot stuff as long as everybody argued about them and a decisive settlement of this nation-wide strife was not yet in sight. They disappeared, that is, not in spite of their hold on the American mind, but because of it.

There has been no such controversy with regard to Anglo-American relations. Why, then, the scarcity of postwar Britons in Hollywood films? Considering the impact of mass attitudes on film content, this scarcity may well result from the uneasiness with which Americans react to Labor rule in Britain. Their disquiet is understandable, for what is now going on in Britain means a challenge to American belief in free enterprise and its particular virtues. In the United States any discussion of British affairs is therefore likely to touch off an argument about the advantages and disadvantages of the American way of life. But once this kind of argument gets started you never know where it will lead. The whole matter is extremely delicate and involved, and it is for such reasons, I submit, that Hollywood producers currently neglect, perhaps without consciously intending it, the living English in favor of their less problematic ancestors.[10]

. . . AND TIMES TO SPEAK OUT

These periods of silence may suddenly come to a close, with mimosa-like shyness yielding to uninhibited outspokenness. In the prewar era, the years 1938–39 marked a turning of the tide. At the very moment when the European crisis reached its height, the American screen first took notice of the Axis powers and their creeds. *Blockade* (1938), a Walter Wanger production, initiated this trend. It denounced the ruthless bombing of cities during the Spanish civil war, clearly sympathizing with the Loyalist cause—which, however, was left unmentioned, as was France, the villain in the piece. Hollywood soon overcame these hesitations. *The Confessions of a Nazi Spy* (1939), a realistic rendering of Nazi activities in the United States, overtly stigmatized Hitler Germany and all that it stood for. Then came the war, and anti-Nazi films, less realistic than well-intentioned, grew rampant.

During those fateful years 1938–39, other national film industries began to speak up also. The French released *Grand Illusion* (1938), which resurrected World War I in a pacifistic spirit, and *Double Crime in the Maginot Line* (1939) whose German characters were indistinct. Even though both these films shirked any direct mention of Nazi Germany, they effectively conjured up her giant shadow. A similar device was used by Eisenstein in his *Alexander Nevsky,* shown in the United States in 1939. In picturing the defeat which thirteenth-century Russia inflicted upon the Teutonic Knights, Eisenstein—and through him Stalin—warned Hitler not to try the old game again.

Shortly after the release of *Blockade,* John C. Flinn, a *Variety* correspondent, emphasized Hollywood's vital interest in its career: "Upon its success financially revolve the plans of several of the major studios heretofore hesitant about tackling stories which treat with subjects of international economic and political controversy."[11] This expert statement sheds light on the motives that prompted the film industry into action. Despite the protests of certain Catholic groups, *Blockade* was a success financially; and though Hollywood might have felt tempted to produce anti-Nazi films even before *Blockade,* it did so only after having made fairly sure that they would be accepted on a nation-wide scale. The appearance of Nazis on the screen was connected with the evolution of public opinion in the United States. They appeared when, after the debacle in Spain and Austria's fall, the time of wavering controversy was practically over. Isolationism, to be sure, persisted; but the whole country bristled with indignation against the Nazis, and there was no longer any doubt that some day the world would have to stop Hitler and his associates. Since this conviction also prevailed in Britain, France, and elsewhere, Hollywood did not risk much in expressing sentiments so universally popular.

What happened in 1939, repeats itself in 1948; after a lull of three to four years, Russians now begin to reappear on the American screen as abruptly as did the Germans. The parallels between *The Iron Curtain* of May, 1948 and *The Confessions of a Nazi Spy* are striking. Like the latter film, this new one is a spy thriller—a pictorial account of the events that led to the discovery, in 1946, of a Russian-controlled spy ring in Canada. Both films are based on scripts by the same author; and both are narrated in documentary fashion. Should these similarities be symptomatic of analogous situations, as I believe they are, then *The Iron Curtain,* with its avowed hostility toward the Soviet regime, would indicate that American public opinion has come out of the controversial stage in favor of a tough stand on Russia.

TREATMENT OF ENGLISH CHARACTERS

For a long time Great Britain and the United States have been entertaining an alliance founded upon the community of race, language, historical experience, and political outlook. Interchange has been frequent; processes of symbiosis have been going on. To Americans the English are an "in-group" people; they belong, so to speak, to the family, while other peoples—"out-group" peoples—do not. Where such intimate bonds exist, knowledge of each other seems a matter of course. American screen images of Britons might therefore be expected to be true likenesses.

Hollywood has tried hard to justify such expectations. Many American films about the English are drawn from their own novels or stage plays; and the bulk of these films are shot on location, involving genuine mansions, lawns, and London streets. In addition, there is rarely an important English part in an American film that is not assigned to a native Briton.

This insistence on authenticity and local color benefits films which cover a diversity of subjects: middle-class patriotism (*Cavalcade, Mrs. Miniver*); empire glorification (*The Lives of a Bengal Lancer, The Sun Never Sets*, etc.); Anglo-American relations (*Ruggles of Red Gap*); upper-class ideology (again *Ruggles of Red Gap*, then *Angel, The White Cliffs of Dover*, etc.); sports (*A Yank at Oxford*); social issues, such as the status of physicians (*The Citadel*) and of coal miners (*How Green Was My Valley*), and so on. Strictly personal conflicts prevail in *Of Human Bondage* and *Rebecca;* public school life is featured in *Goodbye, Mr. Chips* (1939), a retrospective film.

The wealth of themes engenders a wide range of types. I dare say that, taken together, American films offer a more complete cross-section of the English than they do of any other people. From night club musicians to Kiplingese colonels and from workers to diplomats, nearly all strata of the population are presented on some occasion and somehow. Frequent among these types are well-to-do gentlemen and their manservants—a couple of figures forever illustrating the Lord-Butler relationship, which has been so delightfully patterned in *Ruggles of Red Gap*. (Incidentally, in any film about foreigners the minor characters tend to be more true to type than the protagonists, because they are less deliberately constructed.)

In short, the English are rendered substantially as befits the prominent place they hold in American traditions. The result is a fairly inclusive image of their national traits, an image which for all its emphasis on snobbish caste spirit permits the audience to catch glimpses of British imperturbability, doggedness, and sportsmanship. *The Lives of a Bengal Lancer,* which initiated a trend of cloak-and-dagger melodramas—films playing in an India or Africa faintly reminiscent of the Wild West—points up the frontier bravura of English empire-builders and their soldiery;[12] *The Pied Piper* in a highly amusing sequence shows members of a London club indulging in the native penchant for understatement, while German bombers noisily drop their loads.

This many-sided approach further testifies to Hollywood's concern with the British way of life. Small wonder that several prewar films succeeded in reflecting it faithfully. A model case of objectivity is *Cavalcade,* the well-known screen version of Noel Coward's play. Before this film with its English cast went into production, its original director filmed the whole London stage performance of the play so as not to miss any of those minutiae upon which the impression of genuineness depends. Such efforts paid: *Cavalcade,* according to a report from London, "convinced the most skeptical Englishmen that the American film capital can on occasion produce a much better British picture than any English studio has yet managed to achieve."[13]

At this point the problem of the ratio between the objective and the subjective factor arises. Can the latter be neglected in the case of the English? Or, rather, does experience show that in the long run subjective influences—influences exerted by American mass attitudes—win out over that urge for objectivity of which *Cavalcade* is so impressive an instance? I wish to make it clear from the outset that all the measures Hollywood has taken in the interest of authenticity do not suffice to eliminate distortions. A script may be one hundred per cent British and yet materialize in a film imbued with Hollywood spirit. Nor do views of the Tower or a Tudor castle warrant accuracy; documentary shots, as is proven by many propaganda films and newsreels, can be juxtaposed in such a way that they falsify the very reality which they candidly capture. But are not English actors a guarantee for the truthful representation of English life? They are not, for two reasons. First, the screen appearance of any actor results not only from his own acting, but from the various cinematic devices used in building up his image on the screen, and because of their share in its establishment this image may well express other meanings than those conveyed by the actor himself. Secondly, even though an English actor is under all circumstances an Englishman, he may have to appear in a film so little suggestive of typically English behavior and thought patterns that he finds no opportunity of substantiating them. He will be neutralized within such contexts. In other words, whether or not screen portrayals of a foreign people are convincing does not solely depend upon their being enacted by native actors. What counts most is the whole film's susceptibility to the characteristics of that people.

THE SNOB

The influence of American preconceptions shows in the selection of English character traits. Hollywood films establish a hierarchy among these traits in which snobbishness, as I have indicated, figures foremost. Inseparable from class-mindedness, snobbishness pervades the servant's quarters in numerous films, confers upon screen aristocrats an air of inimitable superiority, surrounds as a palpable halo all those Englishmen who by provision of the plots defend advanced colonial outposts or mingle with Americans and Frenchmen, and makes itself felt everywhere not only in the manner of speaking but at decisive turning-points of dialogue. It is the one British characteristic which American movies never tire of acknowledging, ridiculing, condoning, or repudiating, according to the views expressed in them.

No doubt this trait actually exists. The English writer Margaret Cole, who is all against snobbishness, nevertheless admits that much in her recent *Harper's* article: "The British have a pretty lively sense of birth and upbringing: they like titles and honors, and they like to know people who have titles and honors . . . they are, most of them, pretty good snobs."[14] Yet this does not mean that the English are primarily snobs. Like any other people, they have a complex character structure; snobbishness therefore need not appear as their main trait. As a matter of fact, it could easily be shown that the films of different nations have conceived of Englishmen in quite different ways.[15] Take the German cinema: for all their surface similarities, the German and the American screen Britons are by no means counterparts. Such German peacetime films as dealt with the English at all paid tribute grudingly to their way of life. Among the traits featured, however, correctness and decency (e.g., of British navy officers) were more conspicuous than snobbishness —a trait whose social implications eluded a people which had never had a society in the Western sense. And when war came the Germans expressed their pentup resentments against the British Empire in films which made no bones about the ruthlessness of the English and about their alleged hypocrisy. The latter characteristic, passed off as an English cardinal vice by the Germans, is practically nonexistent in American films.

Any nation, it appears, sees other peoples in a perspective determined by its experience of them; and, of course, its cinema features those character traits of theirs which are an integral part of this experience. Hence the emphasis on English caste spirit in Hollywood films. To Americans this trait stands out among others because it affected them deeply under British rule. And since nations, like individuals, tend to build on their early impressions, the mass of Americans, among them swarms of Irish immigrants, took it for granted that the typical Briton is essentially a caste-proud snob. They reacted to him in two opposite ways—a further symptom of the imprint which his conduct, or, rather, their conception of it, had left on them. On the one side, they condemned British snobbishness for offending their sense of equality; on the other, they admired and imitated it. American snobbery contributes much to stabilizing the English snob on the screen; his recurrent image is both a reflection of and a protest against native cravings for nobility, Oxford, and authentic manners. This is confirmed by *Ruggles of Red Gap*, which mingles gentle gibes at the foreign idol with a solid satire of its Middle-West worshippers. Another case in point is Preston Sturges' brilliant comedy *Lady Eve* (1941). Even though this film does not include any Britons, it does show a cute American girl who reconquers her lover by posing as Lady Eve, the daughter of an English aristocrat.

The American screen image of the English is more or less standardized. True as this image is to reality, as a stereotype it has also a life of its own, a life independent of that reality. The English snob, as he appears in Hollywood films, is a figure which has in some degree drifted away from its original to join those mythological figures that people the world of American imagination. Whether angry at him or fond of him, Americans consider this kind of Briton one of theirs. He "belongs"; like Huckleberry Finn or Mickey Mouse, he is part of their universe.

This permanent preoccupation with British snobbishness is not the only subjective element in Hollywood's portrayal of the English. Other influences, equally instrumental in its composition, arise from changes on the domestic scene. In prewar days, when relations between the United States and Great Britain developed along traditional lines, there was no reason why these changes should interfere with an objective rendering of Britons. Domestic mass desires asserted themselves merely in the preference given to such film subjects as were likely to draw American audiences at a specific moment. *Cavalcade* was particularly well-timed. This film, with its unflinching belief in Britain's greatness, appeared at the depths of the Depression, a comfort to all those Americans who despaired of the predicament they were in. Many wept when seeing the film, and more than one reviewer declared it to be a tribute to what is best in all national spirits. Two years later, *Ruggles of Red Gap*, a comedy about the molding of a class-conscious English butler into a free American, struck that tone of self-confidence which by then filled the air. And so it goes. It would, by the way, be tempting to inquire into the causes of the enormous popularity which films about British imperialism enjoyed for a stretch of years. That they had a definite bearing on domestic issues is evident even in their casting: the elder colonels in *The Lives of a Bengal Lancer* and *Gunga Din* fell to the charge of English actors, while the young protagonists, heroes or cowards, were played by stars genuinely American.

BRITISH CHARACTERS IN WARTIME

Once the war was on, national exigencies encroached on the tendency toward objectivity. American public opinion endorsed the war effort, and Britain was now an Ally. For these reasons Hollywood could no longer afford to approach the English in that spirit of impartiality which is indispensable for an understanding of others. Rather, it was faced with the task of endearing everything British to the American masses. The task was not simply to represent the English, but to make them seem acceptable even to the population whose pro-British feelings were doubtful.

Significantly, most Hollywood films about Britain at war attempt to weaken the existing antipathies against English snobbishness, thus reaffirming American obsession with this trait. *Mrs. Miniver,* representative of the whole trend, shows wartime Britain undergo processes of democratization tending to transform her national character. In this film, as a reviewer judiciously points out, "even Lady Beldon, the aged, local autocrat, finally realizes that her class-conscious, if gracious, civilization has been forged into the practical democracy of an entire country united against the enemy."[16] *The Pied Piper* features an old English gentleman whose noble impulses increasingly get the better of his outward standoffishness; *The White Cliffs of Dover,* a sentimental retrospect which tries to enlist audience sympathies for British upper-class people, ends with hints of their readiness to conform to more democratic standards. It is not that such motifs had been entirely omitted in prewar films; but during the war they grew into leitmotifs, coloring all films of the period and serving as their very justification.

Produced in response to powerful domestic urges, these films, I assume, would have misrepresented English reality even if they had been shot on location. To what extent they actually distorted it can be inferred from the criticism with which they were received in Britain itself. *Mrs. Miniver,* though recognized as a laudable American tribute to English war heroism, was nevertheless blamed for "its faults and frequent air of English unreality."[17] Of *The White Cliffs of Dover* the London *Times* said that it "misses the tones and accents of the country in which the action passes."[18] And with regard to *Random Harvest,* another Hollywood wartime production, a polite reviewer remarked that "Greer Garson and Ronald Colman act away the frequent obtrusion of error in English detail and behavior."[19]

ABSENCE OF THE POSTWAR BRITAIN

The war over, one might have expected Hollywood to resume its relatively objective approach to contemporary Britons. Yet it preferred, and still prefers, to ignore their existence. Nothing proves more conclusively the overpowering effect of domestic influences in the field of screen entertainment. Now that the English in some respects really live up to the image drawn up of them in all American war films—class-mindedness is on the decline and snobbery less domineering—it would seem natural for Hollywood to acknowledge what it praised only yesterday. Instead, it resolutely turns its back on Britain, for reasons at which I have made a guess in earlier contexts. During the war, folks at home took delight in a Lady Beldon who proved herself a convinced democrat; at present, the peculiar flavor of English democracy so little pleases many Americans that the Lady Beldons are being held incommunicado until further notice.

The meaning of this temporary blackout—all the more striking in view of the influx into America of English films about postwar life in Britain —is enhanced by those Hollywood productions which introduce British characters of the past. They not only re-establish the stereotype of the English snob (*Cluny Brown*), but draw on other familiar prewar patterns as well. All of them could have been made before 1941. In thus combining disregard of the present with uninhibited rendering of the past, Hollywood follows a rule of conduct which it has already practiced before. Nor is this treatment of foreign peoples unknown to other national film industries: at a time when the German pre-Hitler cinema was completely oblivious of Soviet Russia, it elaborated profusely on the blessings of the Czarist regime. I have reason to believe that in all such cases the emergence of films about the past of a people betrays discontent with its present state of affairs. What makes these films into vehicles of indirect criticism is the fact of their appearance at a moment when any direct mention of that people is strictly avoided. They manifest apprehensions not so much through their content as their sheer existence. Only occasionally do they come into the open, picturing past events for the thinly veiled purpose of dealing with present ones. In *Alexander Nevsky* the eyes that gleam through visors of the Teutonic Knights are unmistakably the eyes of contemporary Nazis.

In sum, the objective factor in American screen images of the English is extremely vulnerable. Much as the age-old intimacy of Anglo-American relations favors its growth, the impact of subjective influences invariably tends to stunt it. Domestic needs and mass desire have on more than one occasion caused Hollywood to portray the English inadequately or not to portray them at all, which amounts to the same thing. There is no progress of knowledge noticeable as these portrayals succeed each other—in fact, *Cavalcade*, released as early as 1933, has probably never been surpassed in objectivity. Everything, it appears, hinges on market necessities which may or may not permit Hollywood to reflect the English closely.

RUSSIAN CHARACTERS

In their *America in Midpassage* the Beards mention the success of the first Russian Five-Year Plan among those foreign events which augmented American anxieties in the spring of 1933. "Still Russia was far off," they remark before turning to the more stirring repercussions of Hitler's rise to power, "and could be discounted as a bit oriental in its ways and values."[20]

To Americans the Russians are an "out-group" people indeed. There is a pronounced lack of traditions common to both countries, and there has never been an intermingling of their nationals as in the case of the English. The chasm separating the two countries is deepened by the antagonism between their regimes—an antagonism so laden with dynamite that it predetermines all popular notions Americans and Russians hold of each other. Unsustained by experience and inevitably biased, these notions are outright clichés. The average American has incorporated the figure of the "mad Russian" into the collection of his pet stereotypes; he knows that Russians are fond of music, ballet, and vodka. And, of course, innumerable editorials and the like have impressed upon him fixed concepts of Bolshevism as something with collective farms, secret police, and purges. Most of it is sheer hearsay, however true.

Hollywood, always inclined to capitalize on existing clichés, is not in the best of positions to breathe life into them. For obvious reasons American films about Russia are studio-made; and because of the scarcity of Russian actors in this country their native characters are as a rule assigned to Hollywood stars—or to German actors, who seem to have a knack for portraying Russians. In *The Last Command* (1928) Emil Jannings was a very convincing Czarist general. I have pointed out that even films with English actors in the cast may misrepresent the English; conversely, actors in the roles of foreigners need not, under all circumstances, miss the essentials. Nevertheless it remains true that the reliance on outside portrayals in imitation settings thwarts, rather than facilitates, an objective rendering of other peoples.

Such scattered Hollywood films about contemporary Russia as did appear between 1927 and 1934 frowned upon the Soviet Union with an air of grave concern. Most of them were laid in, or referred to, the early days of the Russian Revolution when everything was still fluid. Even though they did not pass over the disastrous abuses of Czarist rule—how could they?—yet they managed to make you feel gloomy about the victory of a cause so obviously barbarian. I am thinking of *Mockery* (1927), *The Tempest* (1928), *The Last Command,* and *British Agent* (1934). Except for Sternberg's *Last Command,* each of these films culminated in a romance between a Russian Red and his, or her, class enemy, which drove home the humanly destructive effects of Bolshevist class hatred. *Forgotten Commandment* (1932), "a sermon on the evils of Soviet Land,"[21] accused Russia of having forsaken Christianity. Of these productions only the Sternberg film and perhaps *British Agent* had some merits. The Beards are right: "Russia was far off . . ."

She did not come nearer after her recognition by President Roosevelt late in 1933. Yet American attitudes changed. After a period of silence filled in by several films which involved Catherine the Great, Tolstoy's *Anna Karenina,* and Dostoievsky's *Crime and Punishment* (like the current films about the English past, these may have conveyed polite discontent with the stubborn survival of Russian Communism), this change showed in Hollywood's transition from serious criticism to critical comedy. *Tovarich,* I believe, was the first film to endorse the fact of political recognition by substituting light skirmishes for heavy attacks. Hostilities continued, but they adjusted themselves to the improved relations with the Soviet Union which after all was here to stay. Lubitsch's *Ninotchka,* with Garbo in the title role, also marked a precarious rapprochement. This amusing piece of raillery which showed Marxist-trained Russians succumbing to the frivolous attractions of the West, viewed Soviet life with the condescension of an adult who watches fledglings romp. It was a sort of shoulder-patting; why not finally grow up, the film seemed to ask. Its success bred other films in this vein: *He Stayed for Breakfast,* "a gay spoof of the Communist camaraderie that flourished in Paris before the war,"[22] and *Comrade X* which, laid in Moscow, equally jeered at the conversion of rabid Communist. Released in 1940, both films not only lacked Lubitsch's finesse, but struck a tone of poignant aggressiveness absent in his *Ninotchka.* Of *Comrade X,* Bosley Crowther says: ". . . seldom has a film . . . satirized a nation and its political system with such grim and malicious delight as does this . . . comedy."[23]

THE WARTIME RUSSIAN

The English characters in American war films about Britain still resembled their predecessors of a few years before, but no such resemblances connected the intrepid Russian woman fighter glorified by Hollywood between 1942 and 1944 with the yielding Ninotchka so popular shortly before. This was not simply a shift of emphasis as in the case of the English, but a radical change of scene, with Stalin becoming Uncle Joe and collective farming a source of happiness. I scarcely need elaborate on characters and situations in *Mission to Moscow, The North Star,* and so on. All these films sprang from the overwhelming desire, on the part of the home front, to keep Russia in the war. The surprising thing is their unconcern for continuity: they idolized what had been condemned in times of peace, or winked at it unashamedly. It was a complete turnabout.

In thus wooing Russia for reasons of domestic self-interest, Hollywood ignored its otherwise guiding rule of leaving controversial issues untouched. Opposition against the Soviet regime was too stable a factor of American public opinion to be eliminated by the necessities of the war. Subdued as it was, it continued to smolder. This accounts for the criticism which in particular *Mission to Moscow,* with its indulgent references to the Moscow trials, met from diverse quarters. And about *The North Star,* which in its opening scenes extolled the insouciant life of Russian villagers before 1941, the *Daily News* wrote that this film is more Communistic "than the Russians themselves who have never pretended that pre-war Russia was a musical-comedy paradise."[24]

. . . AND THE RUSSIAN OF TODAY

Now that the spell of amnesia from which Hollywood suffered in the postwar years is over, we are witnessing another turnabout. Gone are the brave Russian women fighters, the happy villagers, and the democratic allures of the rulers. In their places somber bureaucrats, counterparts of the Nazis, spread an atmosphere of oppression. This at least is the way *The Iron Curtain* pictures Soviet officials—they appear as ruthless totalitarians obeyed by devout slaves. And the only "good" Russian is a man who so firmly believes in the superior value of Western civilization that he deserts Communism and betrays his country. Similar types were also advertised in American prewar comedies; but unlike *Ninotchka, The Iron Curtain* avoids any satirical overtones that might weaken the impact of its accusations. Other current films draw no less determinedly on the anti-Communist sentiments of American audiences. In *The Fugitive* (late 1947) —a deliberately fantastic film with exotic settings—humble priests are wantonly persecuted by all-powerful authorities which everybody is free to identify as Communists. The Russian black-market racketeer in *To the Victor* (April 1948) is no endearing figure either. And we may soon see more anti-Soviet films; two or three have already been scheduled for production. This general insistence on toughness, however, seems to be slightly mitigated by the fearful prospect of another war: *Berlin Express* and *A Foreign Affair* (June 1948) , both laid in Germany, indulge in a relatively amiable approach to their Russian characters, thus intimating that we should not give up hope for an understanding after all.

DOMINANCE OF THE SUBJECTIVE FACTOR

All this illustrates Hollywood's unconcern for Russian reality. Unlike the English characters in Hollywood films which at least give one a taste, however faint, of genuine life, American screen portrayals of Russians conform to what Americans imagine far-away Russians to be like. Even

Russian-born actors are strangely colorless in plots based upon such subjective concepts; and, of course, Garbo in *Ninotchka* always remains Garbo in the guise of Ninotchka. The objective factor in these portrayals is negligible—they are not experienced, but constructed. Hence their remoteness from the originals they pretend to portray. Commenting on *The North Star*, Archer Winsten, one of the most observant New York film critics, states that its characters are "single-plane cutouts rather than those deeply modelled characterizations of the best Russian films . . ."[25] He might have added that the many Russian films shown in the United States have not in the slightest stimulated Hollywood to relinquish its home-bred notions of Russia.

These notions are of a political nature. All Hollywood films about Russia raise topical issues, and many of them, I presume, would have never been produced were it not for the purpose of externalizing American attitudes toward the Soviet regime. This explains why the characters in them are so poorly instrumented. As compared with English screen figures, Hollywood-made Russians are sheer abstractions. Instead of being introduced for their own sake as are the English in many cases, they merely serve to personify pros and cons in the ever-fluctuating debate on Russian Communism. It is as if they were drawn from editorials. They resemble marionettes, and you cannot help seeing the strings by which they are pulled.

And finally these marionettes lack the relative stability of English characters. The English snob has survived the war, while Ninotchka was popular only for a transient moment. Her ephemeral vogue is symptomatic of the frequent, occasionally hectic changes which Russian characters undergo in American films. They succeed each other with a disregard for psychological consistency which again testifies to their function of conveying domestic views of Russia. In 1941, when these views changed so abruptly that films in keeping with the latest developments were not yet available, Hollywood tried to adjust an existing film to the new situation. Under the heading: "Whitewashing Reds," *Variety*, of October 22, 1941, published the following notice: "Reflecting the changed public opinion in this country towards Russia, Metro has added an explanatory foreword on the film *Comrade X* to make clear that any spoofing of Russians in the picture was entirely intended as good clean fun." Metro simply was loath to shelve *Comrade X*, a film released only a few months before Hitler's invasion of Russia; yet this grim satire of Soviet life could not be kept in circulation unless it was made to appear as a meek banter among friends.

Russian characters in American films are projections rather than portraits. Chimerical figures, they unhesitatingly change with the political exigencies of the moment. Russia is far off.

The film industries of other democracies, I assume, behave in much the same way as Hollywood. Fiction films are mass entertainment everywhere, and what information they include is more or less a by-product. Any national cinema yields to the impact of subjective influences in portraying foreigners; these portrayals, that is, are strongly determined by such audience desires and political exigencies as currently prevail on the domestic scene. There are different degrees of subjectivity, though: peoples intimately connected by common experiences can be expected to form more objective screen images of each other than they do of peoples with whom they have little or nothing in common.

In other words, images of "in-group" peoples surpass those of "out-group" peoples in reliability. But even they are halfway reliable only as long as public opinion in the country of their origin does not interfere with their relatively unbiased approach. And under the pressure of alienating developments this may happen at any moment, as is instanced by Hollywood's conspicuous neglect of postwar Britons. On the whole, screen portrayals of foreigners are rarely true likenesses; more often than not they grow out of the urge for self-assertion rather than the thirst for knowledge, so that the resultant images reflect not so much the mentality of the other people as the state of mind of their own. International understanding is in its infancy.

Or, rather, does it begin to show signs of growing up? I have not yet mentioned a new international film trend which seems to justify Mr. Johnston's contention quoted above that the motion picture is on the point of becoming "an instrument for the promotion of knowledge and understanding among peoples." This trend, a spontaneous reaction to the effects of the war, originates in Europe. Representative of it are the somewhat sentimental Swiss pictures *Marie Louise* and *The Last Chance,* and the two Rossellini films, *Open City* and *Paisan*—wartime and postwar semi-documentaries much acclaimed by American audiences. In a similar vein is *The Search* (1948), a Metro-sponsored film about European war orphans which has been made by the producer of *The Last Chance* and his associates in collaboration with a Hollywood director. Hollywood seems to be interested in this genre.

It is by no means a new genre. D. W. Griffith, great innovator as he was, developed some of its inherent potentialities, and his ideas were followed up by Eisenstein and Pudovkin in their classic screen epics—masterful blends of reportage and fiction, matter-of-fact statements and emotional appeals. What is new in the most recent semi-documentaries is their content: a changed outlook on the world which, of course, entails changes of cinematic approach. All these films denounce Fascist lust for power and race hatred; and whatever they picture—Nazis torturing their enemies, scenes of heroic resistance, abandoned children, indescribable misery in bombed-out cities—is rendered with profound compassion for the tortured, the killed, the despondent. They are films with a message. They not only record the frightful encounters of persecutors and victims, masters and slaves, but glorify the bonds of love and sympathy that even now amidst lies, ruins, and horrors connect people of different nations. Their goal is mutual understanding between the peoples of the world.

I do not know a single prewar film which is so deliberately international as is any of these semi-documentaries. All of them reflect, in loosely knit episodes, the vicissitudes of the war, featuring chance meetings between soldiers and civilians of diverse countries. German refugees join company with a British officer; an American G.I. makes love to an Italian girl; undernourished French children regain health in Switzerland. And most of these figures are fashioned with a minimum of subjectivity on the part of the film makers. Instead of serving as outlets for domestic needs, they seem to be elicited from reality for no purpose other than of mirroring it. They tend to increase our knowledge of other nations out of an overwhelming nostalgia for international co-operation.

CAN HOLLYWOOD AFFORD THE INTERNATIONAL TREND?

The whole trend, provided it is one, proves that screen portrayals of foreigners need not under all circumstances degenerate into stereotypes and projections. At this point the problem arises of what can be done to improve these images. It is a vital problem in view of the influence which entertainment films exert on the masses. There is no doubt that the screen images of other peoples help to weaken or strengthen popular interest in mutual understanding.

This does not contradict the fact, emphasized throughout my study, that entertainment films on their part are strongly influenced by actually prevailing mass desires, latent tendencies of public opinion. Such desires and tendencies are more or less inarticulate, and do not materialize unless they are forced out of their pupa state; they must be identified and formulated to come into their own. Film industries everywhere, as I have mentioned earlier, are therefore faced with the task of divining audience expectations at any particular moment. Sometimes they miss their opportunities. The response which the Swiss and Italian semi-documentaries have found in the United States, for thematic rather than for aesthetic reasons, reveals a disposition in their favor on the part of American audiences which Hollywood has hitherto failed to recognize. On the other hand, Hollywood films occasionally react to well-nigh intangible emotional and social constellations with such a promptness that they seem to create desires out of nothing, especially in the dimension of taste. Characteristically, the trade has coined the term "sleeper" for films which are believed to be flops and, once released, prove themselves as hits. Film making involves constant experimenting—and many surprises.

What matters most in this context, then, is the essential ambiguity of mass dispositions. Because of their vagueness they usually admit of diverse interpretations. People are quick to reject things that they do not agree with, while they feel much less sure about the true objects of their leanings and longings. There is, accordingly, a margin left for film producers who aim at satisfying existing mass desires. Pent-up escapist needs, for instance, may be relieved in many different ways. Hence the permanent interaction between mass dispositions and film content. Each popular film conforms to certain popular wants; yet in conforming to them it inevitably does away with their inherent ambiguity. Any such film evolves these wants in a specific direction, confronts them with one among several possible meanings. Through their very definiteness films thus determine the nature of the inarticulate from which they emerge.

Once again, how can screen images of other peoples be improved? Since film producers, for all their dependence on current main trends of opinion and sentiment, retain some freedom of action, it may well be that they will find a more objective approach to foreign characters to be in their own interest. Hollywood is presently undergoing a crisis which challenges producers to probe into the minds of weary moviegoers, and documentary techniques, much-favored in Hollywood since *Boomerang,* lends themselves perfectly to objective portrayals. And has not *The Search* been a success? There is no reason why Hollywood should not explore this success and try its hand at films, semi-documentaries or not, which in however indirect a manner serve the cause of one world. U.S. audiences may even welcome a comprehensive rendering of Russian problems, or of life in Labor-governed Britain.

Or, of course, they may not. And Hollywood (any national film industry, for that matter) has some reason to believe that in the long run it knows best what spectators look out for in the movie houses. I doubt whether it will follow suggestions inconsistent with its estimate of audience reactions. Therefore a campaign for better screen portrayals of foreigners—portrayals which are portraits rather than projections—carries weight only if the motion picture industry is made to realize that the broad masses care about such portrayals. This accounts for the primary importance of mass education. Unless organizations such as UNESCO can stir up a mass desire for international understanding, prospects for the co-operation of film producers are slim. *The Last Chance* and *Paisan* came from countries where this desire was overwhelmingly strong. Can it be spread and sustained? Films help change mass attitudes on condition that these attitudes have already begun to change.

1. Films of fact—documentaries and newsreels—will not be considered here, even though they frequently picture foreigners and events abroad. To exclude them is not to belittle their significance as a means of conveying information, but is simply acknowledgment of the fact that they all but disappear in the mass of fiction films. Except perhaps for their transitory wartime vogue, films of fact still belong among the sideshows, at least in the United States.

2. Professor Robert H. Ball, of Queens College, is presently preparing a survey of the innumerable American and European screen versions of Shakespearean plays. In it he plans to comment on the national differences between these versions as well as on the changes they have undergone in each country with the passing of time.

3. *You and the Russians: A series of five programs presented on the Columbia Broadcasting System* . . . A pamphlet issued by CBS. The programs were broadcast in November 1947.

4. Siegfried Kracauer, *From Caligari to Hitler: A Psychological History of the German Film*. Princeton, 1947, p. 206.

5. Leonard W. Doob, *Public Opinion and Propaganda*, New York: Henry Holt, 1948, p. 507.

6. For the whole argument, see Kracauer, *op. cit.*, pp. 5–6.

7. Jack L. Warner, "What Hollywood Isn't," publicity sheet issued by *Hollywood Citizen News and Advertiser*, 1946.

8. *Motion Picture Letter*, issued by the Public Information Committee of the Motion Picture Industry, June 1946, Vol. 5, No. 6.

9. See Kracauer. "Those Movies With a Message," *Harper's Magazine*, June, 1948, pp. 657–72.

10. More immediate reasons for Hollywood's conduct may be found in the "cold war" between the American and British film industries and also in the gloomy aspect of life in Britain, hardly attractive to a screen infatuated with glamor. But what weight these reasons carry accrues to them from the atmospheric pressures on the political scene.

11. John C. Flinn, "Film Industry Watching 'Blockade' as B.O. Cue on Provocative Themes," *Variety*, June 22, 1938.

12. Other films in this vein: *The Charge of the Light Brigade* (1936) , *Gunga Din* (1939) , *The Sun Never Sets, etc.*

13. Ernest Marshall, "Featured Players and Costly Set . . . ," *New York Times*, April 9, 1933. (Quoted from a clipping which does not include the rest of the title.)

14. Margaret Cole, "How Democratic Is Britain?," *Harper's Magazine*, July, 1948, Vol. 197, No. 1178:106.

15. It even seems that the images which one and the same nation form of a foreign people in different media of mass communication are far from concurring with each other. In American radio comedies, as Mr. Oscar Katz of Columbia Broadcasting System has informed me, the English are typecast as dull-witted fellows unable to understand a joke.

16. "Mrs. Miniver's War," *Newsweek*, June 15, 1942.

17. Evelyn Russel, "The Quarter's Films," *Sight and Sound*, Winter 1942, Vol. 11, No. 43:69.

18. Quoted from Lewis Gannett, "British Critics' Storm Lashes 'White Cliffs,'" *New York Herald Tribune*, August 20, 1944.

19. Evelyn Russel, "The Quarter's Films," *Sight and Sound*, Summer 1943, Vol. 12, No. 45:17.

20. Charles A. Beard and Mary R. Beard, *America in Midpassage*, vol. III: The Rise of American Civilization, New York: The Macmillan Company, 1941, p. 201.

21. "It Isn't the Screen; It's the Story," *New York World Telegram*, June 4, 1932.

22. Quoted from Kate Cameron's review of this film in the *New York Daily News*, August 31, 1940.

23. Quoted from Bosley Crowther's review of this film in *New York Times*, December 26, 1940.
24. Quoted from Kate Cameron's review of this film in *New York Daily News*, November 5, 1943.
25. Quoted from Archer Winsten's review of this film, *New York Post*, November 5, 1943.

Part II
Retrenchment and Renewal
1950-1969

The Decline of Hollywood

John Howard Lawson

John Howard Lawson was one of the most successful screen writers in America during World War II. He was a founder of the Screen Writers Guild and was one of the first Hollywood writers to defy the House Un-American Activities Committee. For this he was blacklisted. In the following essay he discusses the postwar American film.*

The invigorating emergence of new ideas and talents in Italy, and more recently in other countries, has not stimulated any similar development in Hollywood. In a recent book, *The Fifty Year Decline and Fall of Hollywood*, Ezra Goodman paints a gloomy picture of the industry's dwindling economic and artistic effectiveness. One can question whether the decline covers a fifty-year period, and it may also be an exaggeration to speak of the "fall" of Hollywood. The vast sums invested in the film business make it certain that production will continue. But there is no doubt that there has been a steady decline during the past seventeen years, and that Hollywood has lost a good part of its prestige and international power.

A writer in the *Yale Review* points out that Hollywood "has long had an impact on the world, and now the impact is being felt in reverse. . . . Ten years ago, American motion pictures occupied from 80 to 90 per cent of the screen time in foreign theatres. . . . Today it averages 60 per cent in England, 50 per cent in Italy, 35 in France, 30 in Germany, 50 in Argentina, 30 in Japan."[1] There have been protests against the cruelty and violence of American films from India, Indonesia, Viet-Nam, the Middle East, Africa, and England. Unfortunately, there is no indication that American producers have heeded or understood these protests.

* From *Film: The Creative Process* by John Howard Lawson. Copyright © 1964 by John Howard Lawson. Reprinted by permission of Hill and Wang, Inc., from Chapter 13, "The Decline of Hollywood," pp. 154–164.

The industry can continue to make money by devoting a good part of its facilities to television, by reducing its yearly output of films, by investing capital abroad, and transferring production to other countries where costs are less. Hollywood has already tried these remedies and it will try others. But it cannot meet the problem of quality; it cannot endow pictures with meaning or creative fire, because the forces that control the industry cannot afford to let film-makers deal with the burning realities of life.

Hollywood's difficulties reflect and are part of a crisis in the cultural and political life of the United States. The industry is unstable because the whole culture is unstable, shaken by the growing contradiction between the democratic needs of the people and the powerful interests driving toward aggression and war. The policies of Hollywood are determined by these reactionary interests; the declining prestige of the American film is a replica of the decline of the prestige of the United States as a result of aims and purposes which are reflected in cultural terms in cinema.

The cultural change at the end of World War II—after Franklin D. Roosevelt's death and the mushroom cloud that rose over Hiroshima—is already apparent in *The Best Years of Our Lives* (1946). The film has a restrained and troubled mood, stemming from the unwillingness to abandon fervent hopes of the previous period and the impossibility of finding equivalent values in the postwar situation. Robert Sherwood's skillful script and William Wyler's subtle direction conceal the fact that the story has no positive center, and that the four men trying to adjust themselves to civilian life find nothing which offers an answer to their search for dignity and hope.

A year later, Chaplin faced the basic problem of the time with relentless urgency. In an interview before the opening of *Monsieur Verdoux,* Chaplin remarked, "Von Clausewitz said that war is the logical extension of diplomacy; Monsieur Verdoux feels that murder is the logical extension of business. He should express the feeling of the times we live in. Out of catastrophe come people like him."[2] As in *The Great Dictator,* the pressure of the creator's feeling explodes in direct statement at the end of *Verdoux*. The force of Chaplin's indictment of war must be judged in terms of the historic moment when Hollywood was beginning to adopt a more favorable attitude toward war, moving to the callous defense of mass slaughter that would characterize pictures of the Korean conflict.

Arthur Knight describes *Verdoux* as "probably the most non-conformist picture ever made"; Chaplin, according to Knight, "brazenly attempted to shock and outrage virtually every section of every American community, with his pragmatic, unconventional morality."[3] This comment is astonishing from a critic as perceptive as Knight. One can hardly imagine his failing to grasp the satirical intent of such a work as Swift's *Modest Proposal*. His blindness to Chaplin's appeal for moral sanity must be attributed to the pressure of the cold war. The picture could only "shock and outrage" people whose opinions coincided with those of Verdoux. Unfortunately, the masters of Hollywood were in this category.

In the same year, 1947, the "investigation" of films by the Un-American Activities Committee of the House of Representatives was held in Washington. It established a climate of fear in all aspects of American culture; the cold war blew like an icy wind across the country to the Pacific Coast. I have strong feelings about the blacklist—my name heads the list—since I was the first of the "unfriendly witnesses" called to testify at the Washington hearings—but I do not think I am swayed by personal considerations in my belief that the blacklist is the main cause of the decline of the industry.

The 1947 hearings caused a national sensation. The charge that American films contained "Communist propaganda" was so absurd that it occasioned frequent laughter—one of the friendly witnesses called attention to a "Communist" line inserted in a Ginger Rogers picture, "Share and share alike, that's democracy." There was a memorable moment when Jack Warner was asked about Warner Brothers' films and parried with another question: "Do you want me to answer that as a motion picture producer or as an American?"

The proceedings were as comic and as fraught with social meaning as a Chaplin film. The chairman who presided at the hearings was Congressman J. Parnell Thomas, who was convicted a short time later of mishandling public funds and served his prison term along with some of the men indicted for "contempt" of his committee. The investigation was by its nature irrational and stupid, but it had tragic consequences. The danger was recognized by leading film directors, actors, and writers, and a large number of them joined in attacking the witch hunt. Judy Garland said, "Before every free conscience in America is subpoenaed, please speak up." Among those who spoke vigorously were William Wyler, Myrna Loy, Melvyn Douglas, Edward G. Robinson, Humphrey Bogart, Lauren Bacall, Burt Lancaster, Gene Kelly, and Van Heflin. Frank Sinatra asked, "Are they going to scare us into silence? I wonder?"[4]

Sinatra's words were prophetic: a resounding silence enveloped Hollywood. However, it would be a mistake to underestimate the significance of the fight conducted by the Hollywood Ten. Our attack at the Washington sessions was so widely publicized that it forced the committee to abandon the hearings after only ten "unfriendly witnesses" had appeared. The campaign against the committee continued; it was not until the Ten were finally sent to prison in 1950 that the committee felt able to resume its Hollywood trials.

From 1951 to 1953, the expansion of the blacklist coincided with the rise of McCarthyism. The House Committee followed a uniform procedure at its successive hearings: anyone who had ever engaged in progressive activity or expressed democratic ideas was called to testify. Witnesses were asked to name persons with whom they had associated as Communists. It did no good for the witness to deny that he had ever known any Communists: such an answer might be the truth, but was likely to bring a citation for "perjury." The unhappy victim was offered a simple choice: he could name names or abandon his professional career. Many witnesses displayed remarkably vivid memories. One Hollywood writer, Martin Berkeley, named 162 people as "Communists." The list included people of varied political convictions. Many were Communists. Some were persons who had happened to attend an anti-fascist meeting, or who had made some indiscreet remark indicating opposition to war or dissatisfaction with Washington policies.

The blacklist operates haphazardly, as an indiscriminate dragnet. It is designed to frighten everybody, warning them to do nothing and say nothing. The large number of persons who were driven from employment testifies to the severity of the witch hunt—and also to the widespread opposition to it. The blacklist constitutes a roll of honor of Americans whose patriotism was not for sale. They performed a vital service in demonstrating the continuity of the democratic tradition. A few of the blacklisted writers were able to sell material under assumed names or through persons who pretended to have written the work and offered it as their own. This anonymous outlet was not available for actors or directors. Most of the several hundred artists who were affected faced the wreckage of their careers. Many became truck drivers or warehouse workers or door-to-door salesmen.

The loss of these talented craftsmen was a misfortune for the American screen. Those who remained inside the studios suffered in a way that was less spectacular: they lived and worked under a ban on "dangerous thoughts"; private conversations were not exempt from the ban, which affected personal and political activity.

The most irreparable damage done by the blacklist is in its effect on the content of pictures. The climate of fear has discouraged experimentation, stifled initiative, and dulled moral sensibilities. In recent years, there has been some slight improvement in the blacklist situation, but the major studios continue to practice political discrimination, and creative endeavor is still to a large extent frustrated by the prohibition against serious confrontation with the great social and moral issues of our time.

However, throughout these years of cautious mediocrity, an ideological struggle has continued in Hollywood. The leaders of the industry attempted to follow the dictates of the Un-American Activities Committee, but the pressure of reaction was to some extent counterbalanced by the democratic and humanist traditions of the American people—traditions that affected audience attitudes and exerted an influence on film-makers. When a direct plea for American fascism was offered in *My Son John* (at the height of McCarthyism in 1952), it was one of the most costly failures in Hollywood history.

A considerable number of films during the fifties have presented serious themes relating to the real interests of the American people. Some of these offer a diluted and tentative humanism. Others have courage and a measure of creative vigor. The most inspiring film of the decade was made by blacklisted artists. *Salt of the Earth,* written by Michael Wilson, produced by Paul Jarrico, and directed by Herbert Biberman, was finished in spite of interference by the film industry and by the government. Portraying a strike of Mexican-American miners in the southwestern United States, it is the first major American film to deal honestly with labor struggle and the first to present a minority with dignity and understanding. In photographic composition and structure, *Salt of the Earth* inherits the tradition of *Grapes of Wrath*. It also shows the influence of the Soviet film and is linked with neo-realism.

Salt of the Earth has been honored for its integrity, but it has not been given its proper place in cinematic history as a work of art. It was not widely shown in the United States but it was duly noted by film-makers, and encouraged some of them to deepen the content of their work. *Salt of the Earth* played its part in the counteroffensive against McCarthyism that swept the country in the middle fifties.

The change was reflected in the emergence of a new type of film—a variant of neo-realism—depicting the lives of ordinary people with simplicity and winning tenderness. The genre originated in television, in the work of a talented group of young writers, including Paddy Chayevsky, Reginald Rose, Robert Alan Aurthur, and Rod Serling. Chayevsky's *Marty* is the prototype of the movement, and its film adaptation under Delbert Mann's direction was so successful that it brought a flood of similar subjects.

Aurthur's *Edge of the City*, directed by Martin Ritt, is a limited but honest portrait of a Negro worker; it would be stronger if it did not center attention on the neurotic and unstable white man who is the Negro's friend. The white man seems to represent the author's uneasy conscience, but his faltering will is given more weight than the Negro's heroism and death. In spite of its limitations, *Edge of the City* is the first Hollywood film to approach a Negro theme with respect.[5] A film _that deals incisively with another aspect of American life is *Twelve Angry Men*, written by Reginald Rose and directed by Sidney Lumet, a study of men locked in a jury room, exposing their social attitudes and class prejudices in their struggle over the fate of a prisoner.

The vogue of these modest studies of American reality was brief. They tended to deal with such "explosive" subject matter as racism, poverty, and labor discontent; the studios placed increasingly severe restrictions on treatment of these subjects so that it became almost impossible to handle them effectively. A few film-makers had the prestige and courage to ignore the restrictions. In 1956 George Stevens made *Giant*, a sprawling segment of recent Texas history, uneven and diffuse, but redeemed by moments of insight. In the following year, Kirk Douglas produced and acted in *Paths of Glory*, directed by Stanley Kubrick in a lucid style that is wholly different from the usual Hollywood technique. *Paths of Glory* attacks the wanton waste of lives by French military authorities in the First World War; it has unmistakable contemporary meaning for Americans.

In *The Defiant Ones*, Stanley Kramer broke several Hollywood taboos. He treated Negro-white relationships without condescension or reservations, and also had the courage to use material by a blacklisted writer. The unusually literate script was written by Nathan Douglas and Hal Smith, and it was well known and acknowledged by the producer that Douglas was really Nedrick Young, whose name had been on the blacklist for many years. Kramer followed *The Defiant Ones* with other films touching the large issues of our times—*Inherit the Wind* (screenplay written by the authors of *The Defiant Ones*) asserts the freedom of the teacher and the scientist to seek the truth; *On the Beach* warns of the danger of a thermonuclear holocaust.

These are not flawless works and Kramer is not a great master of film art. His limitations, as well as his merits, are evident in *On the Beach:* in depicting a world destroyed by atomic war, the story centers on a group of survivors whose petty personal emotions seem far removed from the horror that surrounds them. These are two-dimensional characters: no one among them has the intellectual curiosity to ask *why* this happened, or the emotional capacity to feel its horror. The film is more powerful than the Nevil Shute novel from which it is derived, and it ends with a sober appeal for peace. But it cannot escape the contradiction between the greatness of its theme and the lack of depth of passion in its treatment.

Kramer's concern with ideas makes him unique among Hollywood producers. His direction is thoughtful and honest, but he does not plumb the depths or scale the heights of human experience. Since his ideas never go beneath the surface of events, his technique is forced to be conventional. He cannot clothe his concepts in cinematic language. His use of the camera and microphone follows the custom of almost all Hollywood film-makers: it concentrates on the obvious aspects of the story and ignores the larger possibilities of audio-visual communication.

All this is simply to say that Kramer's outlook is psychologically and artistically conditioned by the commercial system within which he functions. If he ignored the restrictions imposed by the system, he would not be able to make pictures at all. He deserves credit for maintaining the moral integrity of the American film at a time when the main policies of the industry deny moral values and dishonor art. The hatred of war which motivates *On the Beach* must be contrasted to the glorification of war in other films.

Hollywood's attitude toward war is formulated with the advice and cooperation of the Pentagon. Robert Hughes, who has recently edited a book, *Films of Peace and War*, expresses regret that the book does not include an analysis of the relationship between the Pentagon and Hollywood:

> Four writers, including the present one, attempted to get sufficient information on this to present a thorough, incontrovertible brief. Perhaps some day soon a really imaginative, enterprising, and lucky reporter will get this story of the amount of tax money going to subsidize what amounts to propaganda for the military establishment. . . . Anyone who could get the whole story of Washington-Hollywood dealings, the dollars and cents of it, would deserve a Pulitzer prize at the least.[6]

Hughes quotes Dore Schary as having said that military "cooperation" can be worth the equivalent of between one and two million dollars worth of "free production values" in a big film like *The Longest Day*. "Mr. Schary also remarked," writes Hughes, "that the Pentagon was trying to persuade some studio to tell the glorious story of Wernher von Braun as far back as 1954."[7] Schary refused to have anything to do with the project, but the film, idealizing the former Nazi scientist who is now serving the United States, was duly completed in 1960; *I Aim at the Stars* had a gala Washington premiere, with the blessing of President Eisenhower.

Hollywood is engaged in revising the history of World War II so as to place the Nazis in a favorable light. For example, *The Young Lions* was adapted from a novel by Irwin Shaw in which a young German becomes a corrupt sadist in the course of the story. The film version, directed by Edward Dmytryk, turned the character into a sympathetic "patriot."

The disrespect for truth and lack of moral sensitivity in war films extends to other themes; every aspect of life is viewed in terms of personal brutality, social irresponsibility, and cynicism. This is general policy. Films that controvert the policy are still being made. The number of worthwhile films produced in the United States is not much lower than in other countries. The proportion of good pictures is small everywhere. The best work in Italy and France has more novelty and is more interesting cinematographically. The trouble with Hollywood lies in the declining level of artistry, or even competence, in the apparatus of production. This accounts for the statement of two French critics in reviewing the American cinema of the past twenty years, "The whole of a cinema we love with its qualities and faults seems about to disappear, if it has not already done so."[8]

In films like *Suddenly Last Summer* or *Butterfield 8* or *Return to Peyton Place* (to name only a few), there is a sense of exhaustion; the search for sensational effects seems to reach a dead end—the emotion is shrill and ineffective and the story structure is disorganized. The horror film also reaches an emotional dead end in *Psycho*. Alfred Hitchcock handles the material with his usual dexterity, and has designed his study of pathological violence for its maximum shock value. It is a cold and brutal film, almost devoid of human feeling.

The quest for sensation takes another form in the ornate spectacles on which vast sums are lavished in a desperate attempt to win back a dominant position in the world market. DeMille inaugurated the trend with the new and enormously successful version of his *Ten Commandments* in 1956. It ws followed by Wyler's *Ben Hur,* which cost fifteen million dollars and ran four hours. Other spectacles have been less profitable, but many have been made and many more are in preparation. The mammoth production of *Cleopatra,* announced as "the greatest picture ever made," brought Twentieth Century-Fox to the verge of bankruptcy. In spite of its banality, the costly grandeur of the production seems to promise a profitable return on the investment.

Hollywood has always exerted a corrupting influence on its most talented artists, but it has never enforced mediocrity so rigorously as it does at present. It is astonishing that a man of William Wyler's ability should be responsible for the dreary splendor of *Ben Hur.* It is tragic to find John Ford's name on *Two Rode Together,* which seems like a caricature of the worst Westerns of the last forty years. Promising young directors like Martin Ritt or Stanley Kubrick lose their promise in a few short years.

A belated and necessary rebellion against Hollywood has recently developed. A few striking films, made independently without the usual commercial restrictions, have appeared; these include Shirley Clarke's *The Connection,* John Cassavetes' *Shadows,* Lionel Ragosin's documentaries *On the Bowery* and *Come Back, Africa.* Less well known but significant in long-term possibilities is the proliferating production of experimental films made on small budgets or no budgets at all—personal testaments, poetic observation or avant-garde fantasies.

These artists represent conflicting tendencies, but they are united by their love of cinema and their determination to explore its creative possibilities. A number of them met on September 28, 1960, to form the New American Cinema Group. The twenty-three persons at the meeting adopted a statement, asserting that

> The official cinema all over the world is running out of breath. It is morally corrupt, aesthetically obsolete, thematically superficial, temperamentally boring. . . . We believe that cinema is indivisibly a personal expression. We therefore reject the interference of producers, distributors and investors until our work is ready to be projected on the screen. . . . We are not only for the new cinema; we are also for the New Man. . . . We are for art, but not at the expense of life.[9]

Excerpts cannot give the flavor or full quality of the statement. It is angry; it is hopeful; it is assertive, contradictory, overemphatic, rejoicing in its rejection of any specific program: "We are not an aesthetic school that constricts the film-maker within a set of dead principles. We feel we cannot trust any classical principles either in art or life."[10]

This declaration has not brought any tangible results. The New American Cinema Group has not been able to maintain a cohesive organization or develop effective activity. Nonetheless, the rejection of commercial sterility, the recognition that a viable aesthetics of film must be based on human values, reflect ideas and intentions that stir film artists in many lands.

NOTES

1. Richard MacCann, "Hollywood Faces the World," *Yale Review,* Summer, 1962.
2. Huff, *op. cit.,* pp. 293–94.
3. Arthur Knight, *The Liveliest Art* (New York, 1957), p. 45.
4. Gordon Kahn, *Hollywood on Trial* (New York, 1948), pp. 215–26.
5. I make no mention of the so-called "Negro interest" films made in 1949 and 1950, *Home of the Brave, Lost Boundaries, Pinky,* and *Intruder in the Dust.* These were of varying merit, but none of them can be regarded as a significant advance toward truthful treatment of Negro themes. See V. J. Jerome's illuminating pamphlet, *The Negro in Hollywood Films* (New York, 1950).
6. Robert Hughes, ed., *Film: Book 2, Films of Peace and War* (New York, 1962), p. 8.
7. *Ibid.,* p. 9.
8. Jean-Pierre Coursodon and Yves Boisset, *Vingt Ans de Cinéma Américain (1940–1960)* (Paris, n.d.), p. 3.
9. *Film Culture* (New York), Summer, 1961.
10. *Ibid.*

The Hollywood Blacklist
and the Hollywood Underground

Murray Schumach

Murray Schumach has reported on Hollywood for The New York Times *for many years. The following essay is his account of the infamous blacklisting procedure which occurred in the American motion picture industry in the 1950s.**

It is one thing to mature in response to valid criticism, from either individuals or groups. It is another to sacrifice artistic freedom out of fear of criticism. Terror of what pressure groups may do at the box office has been one of the main reasons that Hollywood has failed artistically. The most shameful illustration of artistic cowardice is the blacklist, a creature of Hollywood's terror of pressure groups at their worst. With the blacklist has grown up something unknown in any democracy today—an underground in movie-making that combines hypocrisy, greed, fear and art. Fear of group criticism has become so ingrained in the movie industry mentality that it has led to curious form of self-destruction that can be called pre-censorship. This is what prompts studio executives, producers, directors, writers to distort and water down the artistic merit of a script—not the industry's censorship code but fear that the original idea may somehow cause trouble, either with the code or with a pressure group. Coupled with this is that other manifestation of pre-censorship, the conviction that quality is inimical to box office.

* From *The Face on the Cutting Room Floor: The Story of Movie and Television Censorship* by Murray Schumach. Reprinted by permission of William Morrow and Company, Inc. Copyright © 1964, by Murray Schumach, pp. 117–140.

The most vicious form of censorship in the movie industry has been the result of cowardice. For it was fear, the offspring of greed, that produced the Hollywood blacklist, a form of censorship inherent in dictatorship but anathema to democracy. What the blacklist means, in effect, is that any actor, writer or director considered too radical politically shall not be employed. Every major movie studio in Hollywood keeps a blacklist. The movie companies insist that they do not conspire to maintain the same list. But no one familiar with the chicanery of the movie business believes this. Regardless of what courts may rule, the facts indicate, very strongly, that the blacklists maintained by each studio are sufficiently similar to have been produced on a single mimeograph machine, with a few names dropped from one or added to another.

The power of the blacklist was demonstrated when Frank Sinatra, in many ways the most courageous man in Hollywood, tried to fight it, for he is a tolerant man. In 1960, Sinatra, then at the peak of his power as a movie star, producer, recording artist, television notable and close friend of the then Senator John F. Kennedy, who was to become President later that year, took on the forces of the blacklist. He had acquired the movie rights to *The Execution of Private Slovik*, the nonfiction book, by William Bradford Huie, about the only American to be shot for desertion since the Civil War. He then revealed he had hired Albert Maltz, one of the best known of the blacklisted writers, to do the script.

The attacks came, as Sinatra had expected, first by the Hearst press and then by the American Legion. Pressure was brought on disk jockeys not to play his records, and the smear campaign went so far as to question the patriotism of Senator Kennedy, then trying to win the Democratic nomination for President. Producers, directors and stars who had often paraded their liberal beliefs for safer causes, remained silent, though privately they had often expressed a loathing of the blacklist. But Sinatra insisted he had the right to hire anyone he pleased to write the script. Days passed, the attacks mounted, and no support came for Sinatra from his friends and associates. Curiously, Sinatra was not even supported by Otto Preminger, the producer-director who earlier that year had hired Dalton Trumbo, the most famous of the blacklisted writers, to write the screenplay of *Exodus*. Just as silent was Stanley Kramer, another producer-director who had flouted the blacklist by hiring Nedrick Young, another well-known blacklisted writer, under the widely publicized pseudonym of Nathan E. Douglas. Sinatra capitulated. He fired Maltz and sold his movie rights to the book to George Stevens, Jr.

When the blacklist has been discarded—as it must, inevitably—it may seem strange that there ever was such a thing in our democratic nation. How did it happen, in a country where men and women cast secret ballots and do not hesitate to criticize their most important officials, that this instrument of dictatorship prevailed? How did a blacklist arrogate such power in a field that likes to think of itself as artistic?

The blacklist was an outgrowth of what was subsequently known as "The Battle of the Unfriendly Ten." Briefly, between 1947 and 1953, a series of investigations—Congressional, state and private—zeroed in on Hollywood. The avowed object was to expose Communists in the movie industry. Ten men—eight writers, a writer-producer and a director—were sent to jail for contempt of Congress when they refused to tell the Congressional Committee on Un-American Activities whether they were Communists or answer questions on communism in the movie field. Trumbo and Maltz were among the ten. Ironically, the chairman of this Congressional committee, Representative J. Parnell Thomas, later became a jail mate of some of these unfriendly ten, when he was convicted of payroll padding.

When the investigations began, the industry was at first eloquently indignant over the invasion of private rights. But the resistance soon crumpled and, late in 1947, Hollywood's leaders pledged publicly that the industry would not hire anyone considered politically dangerous. This pledge became known as the Waldorf Declaration because it was adopted at a meeting of fifty movie tycoons at the Waldorf-Astoria Hotel in New York. That the industry was fearful of what it had done was made clear by its then official spokesman, Eric Johnston, who said: "We are frank to recognize that such a policy involves dangers and risks. There is the danger of hurting innocent people. There is the risk of creating an atmosphere of fear. Creative work at its best cannot be carried on in an atmosphere of fear." The conservative *Los Angeles Times* quickly noted the inconsistency of the movie industry's position by saying: "First the [Congressional] committee was wrong in questioning, then the witnesses were wrong in not answering the question."

The timorous policy of the movie industry created the blacklist. And with it the dangers and risks that Johnston had feared materialized. How many innocent men and women were destroyed professionally by the innuendoes of unidentified accusers will never be known. The blacklist extended well beyond the 212 persons named in one fashion or another before the Congressional investigation. In an excellent study of blacklisting, published in 1956, The Fund for the Republic said: "It is apparent that studios now check the political record of their workers before placing them on the payroll." It was enough to have a name similar to that of a man named before an investigating committee to be blacklisted. One of the most vicious aspects of the blacklist was that the victim sometimes did not know his name had been placed on it.

Among the most pathetic cases is that of Louis Pollock, a writer who was condemned without ever knowing he had been tried. Louis Pollock's trouble was that a man named Louis Pollack, a California clothier, refused to answer questions before the House Committee on Un-American Activities on April 21, 1954. Until that day Louis Pollock, the writer, was doing well in the writing career for which he had forsaken newspaper work and then a $25,000-a-year advertising job.

"I was never a top price writer," he said. "But with each picture my price was going up and the best agents were interested in handling me. I was coming to where I was beginning to mean something. All of a sudden I could not sell anything. Fellows used to kid me. They would say: 'You must be on the list.' If I could only have believed this, I might have saved myself a lot of heartaches. How could I? I never belonged to any organization in my life except the Authors League and the Writers Guild and no committee had ever asked me for information."

The months and years passed—five years—and Pollock's scripts kept coming back. He had his only successes in magazine features, some of which he ghosted for famous Hollywood columnists. His house was mortgaged and then sold. A few times he and his wife were on the verge of divorce. He began to believe he had "lost the touch" and sometimes he thought "a clique was against me." He might have wondered indefinitely.

Then, in the fall of 1959, he met an important executive he had known when his fortunes were better. During a brief conversation he admitted to the executive tthat he could not understand why everything he wrote was rejected. That afternoon the executive phoned and asked him if he had been born in Hungary. No. The executive asked a number of other questions that seemed irrelevant. Finally the executive told him he was on the blacklist and that it might have been a mistake. Pollock rushed to a public library and, in a book on the hearings of the House Committee on Un-American Activities, found the name of Louis Pollack. On the advice of the Writers Guild he conferred with Martin Gang, one of the ablest Hollywood lawyers. Gang checked the story and then wrote to a local investigator for the Congressional committee. On December 3, 1959, the writer received a letter from Washington on the stationery of the Congressional committee. It was signed by Richard Ahrens, staff director of the committee. The last paragraph of the letter said: "The reading of the testimony of Louis Pollack indicates that he is not the same person as Louis Pollock and I very gladly point this out for your benefit and use."

After he received this letter the writer said: "Now I feel numb. But I can't help thinking that in those five years nobody ever asked me once: 'Are you this man?' 'Could you be this man?' Nobody ever asked me."

Though the ethical and legal aspects of the blacklist controversy have touched off moving essays and orations, the crux of the argument has become economics. The blacklist was not fashioned out of patriotism, but out of fear of boycotts and other forms of economic reprisal. And when the blacklist is finally abandoned it will be for profit.

Who frightened Hollywood into accepting the blacklist it hated? Most important was the American Legion. It was, for a number of years, enough for the legion to say that a man was suspect for a studio to refuse to hire him. The legion was relentless in its determination to impose its will on the industry. It organized boycotts and threatened to mobilize opinion against any movies written or directed by those it considered politically unsavory. Because of its dread of the legion, the movie industry sent one of its top executives to the legion's national convention in 1960 to head off a resolution accusing the industry of permitting reinfiltration by Communists and their allies. Neither the legion nor any of the investigating committees has produced evidence that any movie written or directed in Hollywood contained Communist propaganda. Throughout the turmoil about these allegedly dangerous radicals, their former movies were shown repeatedly on television—with screen credit given—without arousing the public.

Nevertheless, Hollywood remained afraid. It was concerned that the legion, through allies in Congress, could touch off an embarrassing Congressional investigation; that it might persuade the Hearst press and assorted gossip columnists to attack certain movies or studios. And at all times the movie industry feared the anti-Communist position of the Catholic Church favored a blacklist.

But as the years passed and some legion attacks—its boycott of *Exodus,* for instance—had little effect on the box office, movie companies became braver. But more important, the jungle competition of the industry tended to undermine the blacklist. Television had cut movie attendance in half. Every studio began living for the smash hit that would make up for the bulk of movies that did not make money. The quest for the cinematic gold mine compelled studio executives and producers to cast covetous eyes on the blacklist. As a top producer at one of the biggest studios put it: "There are not many first-rate writers, so why should we let the independent companies and the foreign companies grab off the cream of the blacklisted writers? Apart from the ethics, it's just stupid business. I want a good script and I don't care who writes it."

One of the most important forces in undermining the blacklist was United Artists, a company without a studio but with an idea. Its plan was to try to get the most creative talent in Hollywood by offering absolute freedom in making a movie. It was inevitable that the first breakthroughs would be achieved by independent producers making movies for United Artists release.

From the very beginning of its use of a blacklist, the movie industry found itself in a terribly embarrassing position. If it did not use a blacklist, it would be subjected to pressures ranging from snide allusions through vilification to boycott. If it did use a blacklist it might be sued for conspiracy in restraint of trade (as it was eventually anyhow). The solution was to have a blacklist but not call it a blacklist. How this was done was unwittingly spelled out by the late Benjamin B. Kahane, at the time vice president of Columbia Pictures. Kahane, incidentally, served on occasion as the liaison between the movie industry and the American Legion. In a letter to Paul V. Coates, a Los Angeles columnist and television commentator, Kahane wrote in 1959: "First, let me state emphatically and definitely that so far as Columbia is concerned, there is no so-called 'blacklist'.

"We at Columbia check on writers, actors and others before employing them. We started doing so in 1947 when the 'Unfriendly Ten' appeared before the House Un-American Activities Committee and shocked the country with the attitude they took and the intemperate statements they made which resulted in prison sentences for contempt of Congress. . . .

"With a desire to protect our large financial investment in films and yet to avoid doing anyone an injustice, we decided to engage a reputable firm of public relations men who could investigate cases that arose and report to us all facts and available information. . . .

"If we checked on a writer or actor, the report we received was not that he was on a blacklist or any kind of list, but a report setting forth the facts and information our public relations firm was able to collate. Such a report, for example, would state that there was no information that was found which linked him with the Communist party or any 'front organization' designated by the U.S. Attorney General as subversive.

"In other instances, the report would state that the person was identified as a member of the party or was involved in some way with suspect organizations. They would specify full details on the report. We would then examine the reports.

"In most instances we would discuss the report with the person's agent, who would in turn discuss the matter with his client. In the majority of cases, we would receive a letter or affidavit negativing or explaining the alleged connection with the party or party front organizations. We have kept a file of all reports. If that can be considered a 'blacklist' we are guilty."

Kahane's letter raised questions that showed how thoroughly the industry's conscience had been warped by fear. Why, for instance, was not the accused questioned directly? Why was there rarely any indication of the source of the accusation? Why, with an F.B.I., an Attorney General's office, numerous criminal enforcement groups, was it necessary to hire a "public relations" agency for this sort of work? How did it happen, if there was no collusion among the studios, that Louis Pollock was blacklisted throughout the industry? Or did all studios use the same "public relations" agency?

The fact is that the key to the answers to these questions was missing —the role played by Roy M. Brewer of the International Association of Theatrical Stage Employees and Motion Picture Machine Operators of the United States. This is the most powerful union in the movie industry. It attained nation-wide notoriety when its president, George E. Browne, and his personal representative, Willie Bioff, were sent to jail for extortion and conspiracy. Brewer was sent to Hollywood to lead his union in a fight against a rival union that claimed jurisdiction. Brewer told the House Un-American Activities Committee in 1947 that the rival union was Communist and called upon the Congressional committee to "destroy the Communist menace in the motion picture industry." Brewer, who had come to Hollywood in 1945, was to become the most important union official in Hollywood for nearly ten years. But more important, as far as the blacklist goes, he became known as "strawboss of the purge."

His labor power and anti-Communist campaign gave him influence with the House Un-American Activities Committee and the American Legion. With an ex-Communist as an assistant, Brewer set up a sort of "rehabilitation" technique for radicals who wished to recant and give names. Through friends in the movie industry, Brewer helped find work for admitted ex-Communists who admitted guilt and supplied names. Men who somehow became unemployable for political reasons were advised that if they could placate Brewer they would be cleared. Eventually Brewer's price for clearance was a letter of repentance that he virtually dictated. It is by following this technique in the case of Marsha Hunt, the actress, that one is led directly to Kahane's office at Columbia Pictures and to the meaning of his "public relations" agency.

There was never any question that Miss Hunt, a talented and very successful actress, was not a Communist. However, she was an outspoken critic of blacklisting. Soon Miss Hunt found work difficult to find. In 1952, after she was signed for a Columbia movie, *The Happy Time,* to be made by Stanley Kramer, she was asked to sign a loyalty oath. She refused, but offered to write a statement saying she had never been a member of the Communist party. Whereupon Sam Katz, chairman of the board of Kramer's company, expressed dissatisfaction with her statement and told her to sign another statement prepared by Columbia's legal department, in which she apologized for certain political activities. She refused. Katz told her: "You don't have to sign to make this picture, but you'll never work again in films if you don't." Miss Hunt offered a sentence that satisfied Katz. It was: "If any of these activities have furthered the cause of communism, I regret having done them." During shooting, Miss Hunt was badgered to crawl publicly. Again she refused. Suddenly no more movie parts were available. In 1954 Miss Hunt consulted John L. Dales, executive secretary of the Screen Actors Guild. In response to his question she told him she was not a Communist. He advised her to meet Brewer. After two long meetings Brewer told her: "If you want to, I will send your statement out to my people, but I can tell you now it won't do any good."

The investigation of Brewer's activities by The Fund for the Republic concludes: "Brewer denies that he kept people from working. But when he was not satisfied he would not help people find work, and many studio executives were loath to hire anyone who did not have his positive approval."

Gradually, the Hollywood climate for blacklisted writers changed, and 1960 was the key year. It was the year that Kramer disagreed openly with the head of the American Legion. It was the year that Dalton Trumbo's name reappeared on a movie screen as writer of *Exodus,* produced and directed for United Artists by Otto Preminger. It was the year that Sinatra, though defeated, showed it was possible to demand the end of the blacklist and still remain a great box office favorite, produce his own movies, put out his own records, stage television shows—all without retaliation from the forces that terrified Hollywood.

How much the Hollywood attitude had changed in 1960 was demonstrated when Jules Dassin, blacklisted writer-director, was guest of honor at a gathering of the Screen Directors Guild. There, after a showing of his *Never on Sunday* (also a United Artists release) , he was the subject of admiration and congratulation by many of Hollywood's top stars, producers and directors. The homage was not a form of apology for his blacklist status in Hollywood. It was a tribute to the fact that Dassin had written, directed and produced *Never on Sunday* for about $150,000 and would gross some $6,000,000 from the film. Dassin, a wiry, gray-haired man with sharp eyes and wry humor, was struck by the irony of these accolades to one blacklistee when so many others were still unemployable in Hollywood—even himself.

After the festivities had subsided Dassin described his feelings to an acquaintance. "About a year and a half ago," he said, "before the open-ing of my picture *He Who Must Die,* invitations went out to all the fine gentlemen of Hollywood for the same sort of screening—exactly the same. That movie, too, by the way, was made in Greece. As a member of the blacklist I could not have made a movie in Hollywood. I was amazed, therefore, to see that the R.S.V.P.'s showed that nearly everyone was coming. And then came the day of the preview. It was as though a secret button had been pushed. Hordes of men suddenly discovered unavoidable dinner engagements. There was this inexplicable epidemic of grippe and high fever. Of all my director friends—and I have friends —one came. Just one.

"Now things are different. The fact is that Hollywood has invested some $20,000,000 in blacklisted writers. The blacklist is unnatural to the American character. It was bad casting to begin with, and now it is in the throes of its last agonies. Most people in Hollywood are ashamed of the blacklist. I am talking about studio executives. Many of them now say: 'You know I am against the blacklist. I hate it.' Then comes the long series of 'buts.' It used to be difficult for me to persuade any American star to work for me. Now I get telephone calls from leading actors offering to work in my pictures.

"I do not believe that the American public ever created a blacklist. The blacklist was always a fraud, an extraordinary fraud."

In 1956, Dassin recalled, when his French movie *Rififi* won a Cannes Festival award, the French flag was presented at the ceremony. The picture was of course a French entry, and afterward someone said to him: *"Quelle belle revanche."* Dassin felt no sense of revenge. "The truth is, it made me sad."

But the blacklist, though weakened, is very much alive in 1964 and its advocates have no intention of letting it die. Consider a letter sent to Preminger on December 11, 1962, by the American Legion after Preminger had announced the employment of Ring Lardner, Jr., a blacklisted writer, to do the screenplay of *The Genius,* a novel by Patrick Dennis. This is not a political book. It deals with a flamboyant movie director determined to make a comeback in Mexico.

The letter from the legion's National Americanism Commission, written by its chairman, Daniel J. O'Connor, was not concerned with the subject of the book. O'Connor was interested solely in the fact that a man he considered politically radical was being employed to write a movie. His suggestion and the implied threat were very clear. "I believe," he wrote, "that it would best serve the interests of the theatre-going public if you would reconsider your decision to employ Ring Lardner, Jr., for the purposes indicated. There is extant an abundance of competent script writers whose loyalty, integrity, good taste and discretion have never been questioned."

Preminger, in his answer eleven days later, said he agreed with O'Connor in his opposition to communism, but not with his methods of fighting it. He urged strict adherence to legal methods and democratic principles. He opposed totalitarian means like boycott, blacklisting, usurpation of police or judicial powers. Then he stated his own case.

"Among the many writers I have employed are two who have been convicted for contempt of Congress, Mr. Dalton Trumbo and Mr. Ring Lardner, Jr. Both served their sentences and have, according to the Constitution, the right to work in their chosen profession. I believe that I have an obligation as an American citizen to respect this right without discrimination. If they should now, or in the future, violate the law again or if they should try to use their job for the slightest bit of subversive propaganda, I shall dismiss them at once.

"Until then I feel that I am serving the public by doing openly what other producers have done secretly for many years while giving hypocritical lip service to an illegal blacklist. Thus I make it possible for anybody who wants to discriminate against these writers to stay away from the films which list their names among the official credits."

In his short letter Preminger touched all bases. Blacklists do not belong in a democracy and certainly not in a field that is an art form and a mass medium. Once accepted, a blacklist will not just vanish by being ignored. It will not be eliminated by deals made in the shadows. The blacklist was born in cowardice and it can be destroyed only by courage.

2. THE HOLLYWOOD UNDERGROUND

Eeriest of the offshoots of the Hollywood blacklist is the Hollywood Underground. It is far more bizarre than any of the underground movements portrayed in the movies. The condition of its members ranges from poverty to affluence; from bitterness to compassion. Though the network of this underground extends to many parts of the world, it remains in effect an intellectual ghetto. Here live the men and women who were blacklisted by the movie industry solely for political reasons. Hollywood is not likely to make a movie out of them. Hollywood pretends that this underground, like the blacklist itself, does not exist. It is all part of the Big Lie that Hollywood has spun over its mansions, swimming pools, Rolls Royces and Impressionist paintings with its spidery blacklist.

With aliases, false fronts and a strict code, the members of the Hollywood Underground—they dislike thinking of themselves in this fashion —have created a world as carefully concealed and as labyrinthine as the accusations that forced them into this way of life. In a business where distrust of man for man is axiomatic, they trust one another. No matter where they are—New York, London, Paris, Rome, Mexico City, Ceylon—they keep in touch. They do not forget either those who informed against them or those who befriended them. They are alert for any harm that may threaten one of their number. For they have learned that for them the bell that tolls for one tolls for all. They never completely lose their suspicion of the outsider, nor the feeling that at any moment those blacklistees who are living in comfort, even luxury, could lose everything. In the wondrous history of show business there is nothing like this coterie of the Hollywood Underground.

Consider how they get work. First there is the use of the "front." A blacklisted writer does a script. He knows it will not be produced with his name on it. He approaches a "clean writer"—one who is not on the blacklist—and suggests that the latter's name be used on the script. For this the front usually gets a fee, sometimes running as high as 50 per cent of the sale price. The front generally does nothing more than lend his name to the script. There are some nonblacklisted writers who have refused to accept payment for this service, an admittedly risky undertaking in the timorous environment of Hollywood. Then there are fronts who do some of the writing with the blacklisted writer. If the blacklisted writer has a reputation, his agent may book the fronts for him.

The producer nearly always knows who the real writer is and often discusses rewrites with him in person. Sometimes stars, whose parts need changing, confer with the blacklisted writer. In the vast majority of cases, the studio that finances and releases the movie knows the identity of the writer behind the front. Nevertheless, a studio maintains, over and over again, the pretense that it is ignorant of the real writer. This requires a special kind of logic. The studio, since it claims there is no blacklist, cannot admit it is refusing to use certain writers. That would be an admission that there is a blacklist. At the same time it dare not admit it is using writers who are on the "nonexistent" black-list. That would antagonize powerful groups.

What happens in this world of the Big Lie is shown clearly by just a portion of the record of Hollywood hypocrisy.

One of the most ludicrous situations involved *Spartacus*. Dalton Trumbo, the best known of the blacklisted writers, worked on the script for many months. Kirk Douglas knew he was doing the writing, because the star's insistence was one of the main reasons Trumbo was hired. Nearly all the other stars in the movie discussed their roles with Trumbo. The top executives at Universal, the company that distributed the picture, knew he was doing the script. So did executives at the studio. Douglas wanted to say so openly but, though a courageous man, he encountered resistance among Universal executives who feared criticism and boycott of this $12,000,000 picture. Even after *The New York Times* said flatly that Trumbo had written the script, no one of importance connected with the movie would admit it. Then Preminger reaped enormous publicity by announcing he would give screen credit to Trumbo for *Exodus,* thus becoming the first producer to defy the blacklist. Only then did Universal, after much cogitation, decide to put Trumbo's name on the movie of *Spartacus.*

Others never were admitted. The name of Paul Jarrico, a blacklisted writer, never appeared on the movie *Jovanka,* released by Paramount. Michael Wilson, who left the country to escape the purge, has never been listed by Columbia as one of the writers of *Bridge on the River Kwai,* one of the biggest money-makers in movie history. Fox made many millions from *The Robe.* But it has yet to admit that one of the reasons for the success of this 1953 movie was that Albert Maltz, one of the "Unfriendly Ten," was one of the writers. Nor did the name of Ian McLellan Hunter, another blacklisted writer, ever appear on the screen of the enormously successful *Roman Holiday.*

As of 1964 there is only one unclaimed Oscar statuette at the Motion Picture Academy of Arts and Sciences. It was awarded to "Robert Rich" in 1957 for writing *The Brave One.* But no one ever appeared to claim this Oscar. That is because the script was written by Trumbo. Robert Rich was a relative of one of the three King brothers, who produced the movie. He was not a writer and had nothing to do with the script.

The use of fronts has produced other situations, none as extraordinary as the "Robert Rich" incident, but extremely interesting to those who seek skeletons in the Hollywood blacklist closet. One writer, whose output was neither substantial nor particularly good before the blacklist, has become an enormously prolific and successful producer-writer since the blacklist. Blacklisted writers say he has built his reputation and wealth by becoming a front for a "stable" of blacklisted writers.

There have been amusing aspects of the fronting business. The front for *Cowboy* was Hugo Butler. He was himself blacklisted for alleged radicalism shortly before the movie was released. Whereupon the studio removed the name of Butler from the credits. When Butler told Trumbo about this the latter said angrily: "They can't do this to you." Butler, who was not accepting a fee as a front, was astonished at this strange outburst. "Why, you damned fool," he exclaimed, "you wrote the script." Trumbo had forgotten that this script had come from his mill.

Then there was the rather inept writer who suggested a rewrite to the much more talented blacklisted writer for whom he was fronting. The blacklisted writer turned it down brusquely. The foolish front protested. "After all," he said, "my name is on this script and I have to consider my reputation as a writer." On the other hand, there were young writers of ability who fronted for blacklisted writers and thus received recognition on their own.

By an irony that Congressional investigators never anticipated, some blacklisted writers have profited from their stigma. There has grown up a widespread belief in the movie industry that all blacklisted writers are excellent. The top blacklisted writers say readily that just as there are good writers who are not blacklisted, so there are mediocre writers who are blacklisted. Yet, some producers, if they cannot get the services of the best of the blacklisted writers, will hire a blacklisted writer who is probably not as competent as some "clean" writer.

"It is a sort of mystique," said one blacklisted writer. "I, for example, am really nothing better than a competent hack. But because I am blacklisted I am now entrusted with enormous assignments that I might never have got if I were not blacklisted."

The most remarkable production record in the black market was established by Trumbo and Wilson. For eighteen months they turned out a script every five weeks. Their method was extraordinary. Wilson did the screen treatments in sections. This means he arranged plot, scenes, presented characters. As Wilson finished each section of treatment he sent it to Trumbo who supplied dialogue. Trumbo, while doing dialogue for one section, did not know what Wilson was preparing in the way of scenes for the next section. And Wilson, while writing ahead in his section, did not know what dialogue Trumbo had inserted in the preceding portion. In the end, of course, they would meet to unravel the knots.

In addition to the front there is the pseudonym. The best known of these is Nedrick Young's nom de plume, Nathan E. Douglas. Young's secret became known when the New York Film Critics chose *The Defiant Ones,* by Young and Harold J. Smith, for a writing award. The two writers—Smith is not blacklisted—received Oscars for this script. So idiotic are the blacklist pretenses that even after the Oscar award, when everyone in show business knew the true identity of "Nathan E. Douglas," the name turned up on the script of *Inherit the Wind.*

One of the sleaziest methods by which movie companies obtain the services of blacklisted writers without risking criticism has been to purchase pictures after they have been made abroad by independent companies.

Take the case of Warner Brothers, the company headed by Jack L. Warner, who never tires of making speeches about patriotism. This company bought a movie called *Moment of Danger* when it was made in England. When Warners distributed the picture in the United

States it was called *Malaga*. When the movie was bought its credits included the name of Donald Ogden Stewart, a very talented blacklisted writer, who has been living abroad since the blacklist. When the movie was shown in the United States the name of Donald Ogden Stewart was missing.

To make life easier for Hollywood studios, some foreign independent companies make contracts with blacklisted writers that include an unusual clause. It says that the writer will receive screen credit in the Eastern Hemisphere, but in the Western Hemisphere the distributor has the right to remove the credit.

In some cases the Hollywood studio does not have this right. It must then distribute the picture with the names of blacklistees who are unemployable under their own names in Hollywood. Thus, Metro-Goldwyn-Mayer purchased the distribution rights to the French film *Le Loi*—The Law. This movie was directed by Jules Dassin, the writer-director who, as we have seen, is unemployable in Hollywood despite his success with *Rififi, He Who Must Die,* and *Never on Sunday.*

Then there was the English movie *Blind Date*. It was written by Ben Barzman and Millard Lampell, and directed by Joseph Losey. All three are on the Hollywood blacklist. Nevertheless, Paramount bought the movie and changed the name to *Chance Meeting*.

As in any underground, an unwritten code is followed. It is a cardinal rule in the world of the blacklisted that a writer must not reveal he wrote a script unless the producer first agrees. Thus, after *The New York Times* printed the story that Trumbo had done *Spartacus,* another writer disparaged Trumbo's contribution to the movie. Trumbo could not, because of the blacklist code, defend himself. Another example occurred after it became known that Nathan E. Douglas was the pseudonym for Nedrick Young. The writer told reporters, falsely, that Stanley Kramer had not known it was his pseudonym when he signed him for *The Defiant Ones*.

Another rule of the blacklist underground is to try to help others on the blacklist. If one blacklisted writer is too busy to take on a project he will recommend another. If one blacklisted writer hears about a movie that is being considered abroad he will notify blacklistees abroad about this approaching venture. When blacklisted writers become directors abroad they try to hire blacklisted actors. London has become a refuge for the Hollywood blacklisted.

The fate of the blacklisted actors has been more grievous than that of the writers. When a face is, literally, a man's fortune it does him no good to change his name. Gale Sondergaard, an Oscar winner for her supporting performance in *Anthony Adverse,* never received another job after she was blacklisted. Other gifted performers, such as Ann Revere and Morris Carnovsky, returned to Broadway. Some, such as

Sam Wanamaker, became part of the English colony. Others managed to keep alive in their own field by directing community dramatic groups, giving readings or teaching.

Jeff Corey was making about $30,000 a year, with a good future, when he was blacklisted. Studios refused to hire him in Hollywood, though they invited him to study screen tests and paid him for his advice. Leading stars were sent to him, or went voluntarily, for coaching for special movie roles.

In its manner of life, as well as in its working habits, the Hollywood Underground is unique. In the financially stratified life of Hollywood, the community of the blacklisted is unexampled in its indifference to the income of its members. Prosperous ones share with those less fortunate. For example, one blacklisted writer who was doing well in Europe learned that a Hollywood blacklisted writer was hoping to write, direct and produce his own movie abroad. Without being asked, he sent to his Hollywood colleague his bank books, with power of attorney, and told him to use what he needed.

At a gathering of the blacklisted it is impossible not to sense the special kind of friendship that exists among them, though they argue about all sorts of things, sometimes with considerable heat. They rarely cry in each other's beer. Alvah Bessie, a writer who before the blacklist found no difficulty getting more than $1,500 a week, was handling the spotlight in a San Francisco night club in 1963. Others have worked as junkmen, bartenders, repair men. An ironic twist was that of the blacklisted writer who opened a television repair store. An employee of his, not knowing the boss's background, when applying for a civil service job that required security clearance, gave the blacklisted writer as a reference. The writer does not know if the young man got the job.

The underground was born in the early days of the blacklist. It became common, for instance, for a man dodging a subpoena to hide out for weeks. Friends helped the children of those seeking refuge. One child, knowing his father was lying flat in the bottom of a car parked in the neighborhood, would tell any stranger that daddy was out of town.

One blacklisted writer says: "We had a terrible sense of isolation for a long time. Even in the late fifties it was considered an act of courage by many in Hollywood to say hello to a blacklisted writer in a public place."

The common bond among the blacklisted is most noticeable in their dealings with those who cooperated with Congressional committees. One day a blacklisted writer and his young son entered a Hollywood restaurant. They almost collided with a man who had given names several years earlier to a Congressional committee. Before that the blacklisted writer and the witness had been good friends. The witness held out his hand to the blacklisted writer. The writer turned to his son and said:

"This is a stool pigeon." Not all of the blacklisted are so bitter. There are some who simply hope they never have to meet a "cooperative" witness, but who say that if they do they hope they will not be too cruel.

The writers who went to jail had the most vivid experiences. One writer sent a series of made-up stories from his cell to his seven-year-old boy. As heroes, he invented an Indian and a cowboy who served as confidential spies for Lincoln and sneaked behind Confederate lines. One day the warden of the southern jail summoned the writer to his office. The warden was furious. He waved a letter he had intercepted. It was the latest episode the writer had done for his son. The warden considered this glorification of Lincoln proof that the writer was a Communist. He ordered the writer to desist from any more such subversion. The writer refused and threatened to make a public issue of it. The warden surrendered and the Indian and cowboy continued to work for Lincoln for the rest of his jail term.

While Trumbo was in jail for contempt of Congress his daughter won and accepted a citizenship award at school for grades, leadership and cooperation. The prize was awarded by the American Legion. The legion knew she was the daughter of the man it had helped to send to jail.

Another writer recalled the reaction of other prisoners to the writers. "At first," he said, "we were regarded as weird. Then, when it became known that we had earned $2,000 a week in Hollywood, we acquired prestige. Then we acquired popularity because we wrote letters for uneducated prisoners to their wives, children or sweethearts."

But for all its pathos, personal tragedy, hypocrisy, the Hollywood blacklist and the Hollywood Underground represented the worst kinds of censorship because of what they did to the movie industry as an art form. If, in spite of the blacklist, Hollywood had grown artistically, it could be argued that the blacklist served the same healthful purpose as weeding out a garden; that without the strangulating influence of radicals in the industry, Hollywood's more beautiful plants had a chance to flourish.

This did not happen. Quite the contrary. For as the reign of terror spread through Hollywood with the growth of McCarthyism, even the most innocuous liberals became worried that their mild opinions would be construed as radicalism fit for blacklist purgatory. No job was considered too unimportant for judgment by the House Un-American Activities Committee, the American Legion and Brewer. Schary, who was boss of the Metro-Goldwyn-Mayer studio during much of this period, is convinced that one of the reasons he lost this job was that he was very enthusiastic in campaigning for the Democratic party.

None of the investigations into communism in Hollywood showed any evidence that Communist propaganda had been worked into films by radical writers—how actors could have done it has always been an unexplained mystery. Still the word passed like an epidemic through the movie industry that movies with serious themes were to be avoided.

Controversy was to be avoided at all costs. In 1947, Hollywood had filmed the delightful satire on national politics called *The Senator Was Indiscreet*. But after the blacklist atmosphere set in, such spoofs of politicians, a traditional form of American humor, were taboo in Hollywood. In 1947 the movie industry attacked anti-Semitism by making *Gentlemen's Agreement*. No more of that was wanted by Hollywood in the blacklist era.

Dorothy B. Jones, who made a study of the relationship between the investigations of Hollywood and the content of films, concluded that a decline began in serious themes in 1947, the first year of the blacklist, and continued to fall steadily into 1949, though "some social theme movies continued to be made." The years 1950–52, when the blacklist epidemic became most virulent, Mrs. Jones said, "can be described as a period when the industry radically reduced the number of social theme movies and devoted itself to escapist fare of all kinds."

Admittedly, it is difficult to say what is a "social theme." But a more explicit explanation of the kinds of pictures that Hollywood wanted was made during the blacklist heyday by Eric Johnston, as liaison between Hollywood and Washington and the official spokesman for the American movie industry. He made his point in a talk to movie writers. As one writer recalled it, Johnson said: "We'll have no more *Grapes of Wrath*. We'll have no more *Tobacco Roads*. We'll have no more films that show the seamy side of American life. We'll have no pictures that deal with labor strikes. We'll have no more pictures that show the banker as a villain." The memory of the writer could have been at fault, but the results have conformed to that talk. Hollywood was scared stiff.

In April of 1961 a movie star, known to favor freedom of speech and the United Nations, was asked to participate in a Hollywood rally to espouse both causes. It was not a meeting of radicals. Among the speakers were two United States Senators—Clifford P. Case of New Jersey, a Republican, and Eugene J. McCarthy of Minnesota, a Democrat. Important educators and clergymen in the Los Angeles area were behind it because it was a response to the bombing of the homes of two ministers who had praised the United Nations and criticized right-wing extremists.

Knowing this background, the star replied: "I don't want to get involved in anything more controversial than a charity for crippled children." This comment was typical of the answers of other Hollywood celebrities who declined to be at the rally.

What was true of the effect of the blacklist on the personal behavior of Hollywood was even more true of its artistic life. The blacklist paralyzed artistic growth. From this affliction, despite the worrisome competition of the serious movies made abroad, Hollywood had still not recovered in the early sixties. It was devoting the bulk of its money to such "safe" films as *Cleopatra, El Cid, Lawrence of Arabia.*

There is no doubt that Hollywood can bloom artistically without ever using a blacklisted writer, director or actor. But it is very unlikely that as long as Hollywood continues to tolerate a blacklist it will mature. Artistic integrity requires the sort of courage that is the natural enemy of a blacklist. Without integrity there can be no art in Hollywood. The atmosphere that produces a blacklist and has maintained it is the most terrible of censors precisely because it is a censor that hides in the minds, that cannot be refuted or changed like the written word of a censorship code or law. As long as there is a blacklist in Hollywood, there will be little stature to its art.

The Survivors

John Gillet

John Gillet suggests that many of Hollywood's most talented artists are in a state of decline. He steadfastly believes, however, that many of the "survivors" have a tenacious artistry that maintains the quality of American films. *

When a popular and distinguished director returns to the commercial cinema after an eight-year absence, one is bound to feel some qualms, especially as his best work belonged to a period far removed from the uncertain conditions of Hollywood in the late 1950's. But the first five minutes of *A Hole in the Head* were enough to dispel any lingering doubts. Stylistically at least, Frank Capra had returned—intact. Taking a play by Arnold Schulman as his starting point (necessitating an obvious and rather awkward switch from Jewish to Italian-American family comedy), Capra has embellished its lightweight and fairly predictable comic situations with his old, characteristic warmth and generosity, as well as some eccentric overtones reminiscent of *You Can't Take It With You*. The result is a fast-moving and cheerful *divertissement,* its artful combination of sentiment, comedy and child appeal all a little larger than life and thereby guaranteed to win an audience's approval.

Though the style is as personal and assured as ever, a noticeable change of emphasis in the subject matter reveals how far Capra has moved from his philosophy of ten or twenty years ago. His modern hero (Frank Sinatra) is no longer an innocent stubbornly pitted against a monstrous political machine, but a fast-talking Miami hotel proprietor plagued with money troubles and the necessity to "think big" and beset with quarrelsome relatives determined to marry him off to some nice, homely woman. Characters are introduced and then dropped after serv-

* By permission from Penelope Houston, editor *Sight and Sound. Sight and Sound,* Summer–Autumn 1959, London. © 1959 by the British Film Institute.

ing their purpose and there is little attempt at dramatic structure. Instead, Capra develops an inconsequential series of very funny character sketches and manages to include some late 'fifties references for good measure—the hero's scatty girl friend (Carolyn Jones), with her portable radio, surf-board and minimal beach wear, might be described as a "bongo beatnik," a modern sex symbol with an alarming appetite.

As in the old days, Capra retains the frankly theatrical tone of the original by shooting some of the long dialogue scenes straight on to the players; yet the effect is never stagy or boring. His control is so finely judged that there is always an onward movement, a crisp cutting edge (supplied by an old colleague, William Hornbeck) and a continuously lively surface action. A typical example is the quarrel between the brothers, with Thelma Ritter intervening, in which he actually manages to make funny the lame, repeated gag of a man sitting down on a broken chair. Most enjoyable of all, though, is the direction and shaping of the performances. Capra's effect on his players is rather that of a great conductor on his orchestra. Given reasonably pliable material, he is able to point a phrase here or accent a beat there, at the same time insuring perfect unanimity in timing and expression. It is not surprising that Frank Sinatra here gives his most human and easy performance, that Edward G. Robinson assumes the mantle of a dry, dead-pan comedian with monumental assurance, or that the hitherto mannered Eleanor Parker plays with a friendly and relaxed feminine charm. The tender little sequence in her charmingly cluttered flat is typical of this confident ensemble playing.

No characteristic Capra film would be complete without its demagogue or its final satirical scene of mass movement. Here, the figure of evil is a sharp-talking promoter (a harsh, edgy portrait by Keenan Wynn), who plays up to his old friend until he realizes that his main concern is money and the lack of it. Against the background of a gaudy dog-race track, with the Miami social set in full cry, Capra creates a typical set piece, with over-lapping dialogues and a screen full of jagged, gusty movement, beautifully captured in the camera-work of another veteran, William Daniels.

A Hole in the Head, then, is entirely professional entertainment in a familiar American style; it may not break any new ground, yet it is wholly alive and easily enjoyable. The final scenes—the reconciliation between father, son and attractive widow—perhaps belong to a more conventional tradition and are arbitrarily arrived at; but even the last minute decision of the staid, stolid elder brother to join the carefree vagabond life is so typically Capra in its joyous rejection of reality that one is really rather pleased when it happens. With the exception of the Keenan Wynn episode, there is little of the social moralising which made Capra a major spokesman for the American liberal spirit of the

1930's, for its fervent, sometimes muddle-headed New Deal optimism. But this, inevitably, is a film with a much lower ambition. Capra has clearly recognised the nature of his material and has contented himself with the opportunities afforded to rekindle his own world of wish fulfilment and sentimental fantasy. Always a shrewd showman, he has created a contemporary success-conscious hero who, for better or worse, probably suits the present mood as well as Mr. Deeds did that of more than twenty years ago. Deeds will remain longer in the memory; yet, in an age when the average Hollywood product is notable for its numbing anonymity, we should be grateful that he has been able to invest a relatively minor work with so much of his former panache.

Capra is not the only veteran to make a recent creative comeback, although he has remained silent for longer than the others—during the intervening years, he made science documentaries for television. The latest films of Ford, Hitchcock, Hawks and a few others confirm that some of the older generation have weathered the current Hollywood crisis, in a period when America is slowly losing her position as a dominant film power; and it is to these resilient survivors that this article is dedicated. But in order to see how this crisis has affected the entire structure and personality of the industry, one must look back to a more prosperous era, to the years before survival became a real issue.

2

1945–46. The Second World War was over, the major studios were returning to full production and the conscripted directors and actors were putting away uniforms and preparing to resume broken careers. In this atmosphere, Samuel Goldwyn and William Wyler made *The Best Years of Our Lives;* and today, despite its sentimental excesses, it still retains its vivid response to that post-war mood when old ideas were being challenged and new ones tested. The extent and range of available talent at this time can be seen in the following breakdown of prominent directors. Of the older veterans, some were nearing the end of their creative careers (Bacon, Fleming, Keighley, Lloyd, Lubitsch, Sam Wood). Others remained firmly on the active list: Capra, Curtiz, Dieterle, Ford, Hathaway, Hawks, Hitchcock, King, Lang, LeRoy, Mc-Carey, Milestone, King Vidor, Wellman, Wyler—a roster of Hollywood's dependable long-term talents. Those who had made, or were making, their names in America included Dassin, Kazan, Mankiewicz, Anthony Mann, Minnelli, Preminger, Preston Sturges, Welles, Wilder, Wise and Zinnemann. It is not surprising that these immediate post-war years seemed full of promise. It was the era of documentary realism, the taut location thriller, the journalistic social document (*Crossfire, Call Northside 777, The Set Up, Boomerang,* and Capra's own brilliant *State of the Union.*) It was the period when film-makers came back from the war to take a new look at their own domestic scene, to find a firmer, less glamorised response to people and characterisation.

But that was more than ten years ago. Looking back over this period, one realises that Hollywood has since passed through more radical (and disastrous) phases than at any other time in its history. The Un-American Activities Committee, for example, successfully drained off creative talent and corrupted the artistic climate for several years after its initial hearings. Many of those affected, like Dmytryk, Abraham Polonsky and John Berry, never recovered their former stimulus; and something vital disappeared from the American cinema when the independent spirit yielded to conformism. As the 1950's progressed, economic pressure vied with political expediency as the paramount talking point. The one-eyed monster of television was beginning to snatch away an audience hitherto considered untouchable. At the same time, the European and Asian cinemas were attracting a new kind of audience for a new kind of film, thus refuting the long-held view of Hollywood commercialism that the American film had a sovereign right to dominate all the screens of the world.

This battle, which still continues, is clearly manifest in the industry's desperate and often debased attempts to hold its audiences through a constant vulgarisation of subject matter and a faith in fabulously expensive blockbusters on ever widening screens. In these circumstances, it is not surprising that the personal film has become even more difficult to achieve. In a time of crisis, the director with a developed artistic personality may be faced with the prospect of retirement or compromise. Many of those mentioned earlier (Hathaway, Dieterle, Wellman and others) have slowly succumbed, due, in part at least, to a lack of suitable subjects. In any case, few of the veterans were likely to adapt themselves to Hollywood's unrestrained onslaught on the teenage market with its combination of horror, science fiction and beat generation gimmicks. Others have faltered owing to the absence of the kind of star material available in the 1930's. The successful commercial films of directors like Clarence Brown or George Cukor owed much to Hollywood's cult of personality: Garbo, Hepburn and other starry lights of the Dream Factory. Since the war, Brown has had only one substantial success (*Intruder in the Dust*) ; and Cukor, although he has added to his list of enjoyable theatrical comedies, has managed nothing of real note since his *A Star Is Born,* itself a tribute to a surviving star in the grand manner.

The effects of internal or external pressures have made themselves felt in the work of other formerly significant names. Anatole Litvak's last production, *The Journey,* revealed the souring of a liberal and intelligent talent. Leo McCarey, who seven years ago made one of the most dangerous of the anti-Communist sagas in *My Son John,* has recently returned, though not very happily, to the comedy field. Michael Curtiz, one of Hollywood's most glossy craftsmen, with a reputation for being able to handle any given subject, has lately shown a lack of interest in almost everything—the small virtues of his *The Hangman* were traceable to the script of another veteran, Dudley Nichols. Another European immigrant, Fritz Lang, achieved a few post-war successes only to fade away into routine thrillers; he has now returned to Germany and is there remaking some of his silent scripts, apparently with disastrous results. The long (and often inexplicable) career of King Vidor has taken him from pre-war social realism to a kind of post-war lunacy in films like *The Fountainhead* and *Ruby Gentry;* recently he turned to fashionable spectacles (*War and Peace*) and, not surprisingly, failed to respond. George Stevens' development must be placed slightly apart from the others, since films like *A Place in the Sun* and *Giant* have been much larger in scope than anything he attempted previously. But style is of little use when the subject is beyond its creator's imaginative range; consequently *The Diary of Anne Frank* fell a victim to Hollywood's craze for overblown portentousness as well as to its general miscasting. In a way, the sad failure of this film seems to sum up a whole epoch of Hollywood thinking.

3

How, meanwhile, has the younger generation been faring? The early films of Huston, Ray, Dassin, Wilder and Wise possessed a recognisably American technical adroitness as well as reflecting the violent restlessness of the society from which they came. Now, in the late 1950's, this whole American post-war generation seems broken up, its members scattered all over the world. Some are making films with exotic locations and foreign stars in yet another attempt to provide a TV-locked audience with a colourful, big screen eyeful. These productions, though they may have a certain cosmopolitan appeal, inevitably become progressively less American in feeling; and experience has shown that American directors are at their best on their home ground. This was demonstrably true in the case of an artist like the late Preston Sturges, one of the cinema's most brilliant satirists, whose sad post-war progress culminated in a comparative failure made in France and subsequent silence. Others appear to have left Hollywood for good, while Huston, Mankiewicz, Aldrich and Ray have wandered from country to country making a variety of subjects not always suited to their talents. The one influential director who has remained resolutely at home is Elia Kazan, and it seems significant that even he has not made a film for more than two years.

The peculiar problems and difficulties of post-war Hollywood have also affected those producers whose sheer professional knowledge and acumen have kept them in business for twenty or thirty years, despite changing fashions in politics, entertainment, exhibition policies and screen sizes. There is something almost gallant, in fact, in the way Sam Goldwyn has recently pinned his faith in a mammoth production of *Porgy and Bess*—hoping, presumably, that it will appeal to contemporary taste as much as *Dead End* answered the post-Depression mood of the 1930's. Sacrifices have had to be made, of course. Policy-making producers are subject to the whims of fashion as well as directors; and in the field of serious social drama, vulgarisation and compromise have affected even the most powerful. Nowadays, it is a little difficult to believe that Darryl F. Zanuck once produced *The Grapes of Wrath;* and even more difficult to understand why David O. Selznick, having surrounded himself with a polyglot and mutually incompatible array of talents for *A Farewell to Arms,* should have expected it to work. One of the old social crusaders, Walter Wanger, has however still managed to bring off the occasional half-success: *Riot in Cell Block 11,* for instance, or the best parts of *I Want to Live,* which somehow survive the fashionably jazzy and overwrought manner of presentation.

4

Altogether, this decade in Hollywood has been one of unease, insecurity, personal and creative uncertainty. Consequently it is now rare for Hollywood to commit itself to a weighty, socially responsible theme or a great subject. When it does so, it almost invariably veers towards mere portentousness, or a preoccupation with production values at the expense of content. A not unintelligent, very carefully made prestige production like *The Nun's Story* stops short of vulgarisation yet founders finally under its own weight and, more precisely, its lack of a strongly expressed personal attitude. A Bresson or a Buñuel, given this theme, would not have hesitated to explore its ultimate implications; a Hollywood director of 1959, however honest and talented, could scarcely be expected to attempt them.

All this is probably inevitable in a highly commercialised and competitive industry passing through a severe economic recession. But if Hollywood at present seems unable to produce works of lasting value, it appears to have recovered its talent for enjoyable, sometimes civilised, entertainment pictures with only mild intellectual pretensions but with a marked professional expertise. Recently, we have begun to see a renewed concentration on what the industry has always thought of as its family pictures—large-scale Westerns and outdoor dramas, comedy romances and thrillers laced with a contemporary element of intrigue. Not unnaturally, these have attracted veterans such as Ford, Capra, Hawks, Hitchcock and King, who have been working variations on these themes for many years and who, unlike their colleagues mentioned earlier on, have retained the kind of professional flair and authority essential for box-office success. These are the true survivors, and at the moment it looks as though they have the field to themselves. The younger directors have other preoccupations; they could hardly be expected to respond powerfully to a style of film-making which owed its inspiration to the more relaxed and confident conditions of twenty years ago. The strong degree of independence now enjoyed by the major producer-directors, many of whom maintain their own companies, has also strengthened their position within the industry.

Many directors understandably prefer to work with old and trusted associates: Ford, for instance, gathered together a marvellous cast of veteran character players for *The Last Hurrah,* with its vivid mixture of old-fashioned idealism and sentimental nostalgia. Though their material has its roots in the past, most of the artists I am concerned with here have equally retained their shrewd awareness of an audience's expectations: they know better than to disregard the teenage public, so that *A Hole in the Head* has its bongo drums and "beat" slang and *Rio Bravo* its Ricky Nelson ballads.

Of all the classic American styles, the Western has probably passed through more varied phases than any other. At present, acute psychological disorders, as much as Indians and outlaws, are among the hazards the Western hero has to contend with. Yet, despite these often unwelcome complications, the old fascination remains: here is a safe and well-tried world where the experienced craftsman can feel entirely at home—and among friends.

Perhaps the most striking aspect of John Ford's new Civil War Western, *The Horse Soldiers,* is its attitude towards the war itself. Amongst all the paraphernalia of battle, with its blazing bugles and daring cavalry charges, there is a sharp awareness of the aftermath in terms of pain, blood, terror, and the moral bitterness inseparable from any civil conflict. All this is interlarded with some pawky humour and a spasmodic romance between a rebellious Southern belle and a cavalry hero fashionably afflicted with a psychological hatred of doctors. Most of the elements of latter-day Ford are present in bewildering profusion, in fact—and yet the familiar magic works again. Ford's response to the spirit of his material can be found in the way each episode is composed (often in terms of the silent cinema), in the rich, romantic images of horsemen passing through fields and rivers, and in the masterly way in which the battle scenes, such as the attack on Newton Station, are grouped and constructed. Never ostentatiously composed, these images possess the strength and clarity of Ford's most personal films, such as *Wagonmaster* and *The Young Mr. Lincoln.* With all its perverse changes of mood, this is unmistakably the work of an artist who has never lost his instinctive response to the medium he has served for forty years.

Watching these films by directors of Ford's generation makes one

realise how the years of professional, practical experience tell in their
work—in the freshening up of variable scripts or done-to-death subjects.
An unerring judgment for the right kind of camera set-up gives their
films a visual distinction not easily achieved by the more technically
conscious younger generation. Henry King's *The Bravados*, for instance,
is a violent, only medium quality Western handicapped by some excessively maudlin religious sentiment; yet it is always alive and compelling
to look at. Even when one acknowledges the differences in tone and
content, the feeling for landscape and the open air is not so far removed
from the spirit of *Tol'able David*, among the most beautiful of all American films and directed by King nearly forty years ago. (It is regrettable,
incidentally, that this director so rarely finds a subject which interests
him throughout; his latest, *This Earth is Mine!*, is a lethargic family
chronicle with perhaps two or three scenes hinting at a degree of personal involvement.)

Although Howard Hawks has returned to Western themes less often
than Ford, his ventures into this territory possess a distinctive quality of
their own, with less mellowness and rather more acid. His recent *Rio
Bravo* is a long, leisurely affair which mixes most of the standard ingredients—very black villains, a stalwart sheriff hero, a frightened community—and erupts suddenly into fierce action whose very terseness makes
it all the more effective. Aided by clear-cut characterisation, the old
Western myths survive through Hawks' deceptively relaxed direction;
and the atmosphere of his little town is enhanced by a precise geographical placing of the action. William Wyler's *The Big Country*, on the
other hand, is even longer and more conscious of its size and prestige.
Wyler's later work has become increasingly academic in tone, and his
formidable capacity for careful craftsmanship now seems to dominate
other aspects of his talent: survival, for him, might appear to have involved a certain withdrawal.

Reminders of earlier methods and inspirations can be found outside
the Western theme, in the latest films of directors such as Billy Wilder
and Alfred Hitchcock. In many of his later works, Hitchcock's unique
talent for wringing the nerves of his audience has become a little lost
amidst a welter of romantic flummery and over-blown effects. His *North
by Northwest* still suffers from excessive length; there are the familiar
inflated close-up love scenes and a tiresome woman of mystery (is she
or isn't she a spy?). Nevertheless, the film marks a return to a more
strongly personal style, with terror striking from the most unlikely surroundings and in the least expected forms. Again, much of its mixture
of old-fashioned suspense and double-cross works because Hitchcock
knows exactly how to arrange his effects—the murder in the U.N., for
instance, and the strafing plane sequence. Sometimes he pushes an incident a little too far, then recovers by pulling a trick out of the bag, and

ends up with a cliff-hanging climax whose very ludicrousness suggests that the Old Master has not lost his special talent for self-parody.

Parody of another kind makes Billy Wilder's *Some Like It Hot* his most uninhibitedly and raucously vulgar comedy to date. Determinedly German in its leering awareness of the perils of female impersonation, it recalls the hard sophistication of Wilder's pre-war scripts and, unlike his recent lukewarm romantic fables, has an engagingly dark humour all its own. With its private film jokes, its brilliant performance by Jack Lemmon, and the funniest fade-out line in years, *Some Like It Hot* has that terse, intimate ruthlessness characteristic equally of its director and of a type of comedy one thought Hollywood had forgotten.

5

A last example is far removed from the Western, comedy or thriller, the three genres into which the American cinema has poured so much money and talent. The war film, with its inflated heroics and coarse sensationalism, is now almost equally firmly established as part of Hollywood's staple diet. But the American cinema's compromised treatment of this subject is part of its whole, hesitant attitude towards the contemporary scene. Lewis Milestone's "war" career provides an acute example, when one considers the marked shifts of viewpoint between the raw pacifism of *All Quiet,* the compassionate acceptance of *A Walk in the Sun* and the sentimental jingoism of *Halls of Montezuma. Pork Chop Hill,* the film with which Milestone returned to the American cinema after several years of inconclusive work in England and Italy, displays more creative drive and control than any of his recent pictures, yet presents us with a new enigma: a film whose images tell a different story from the words. From the very outset, these images communicate Milestone's highly distinctive view of battle: once again, there are the great tracking shots across grey, desiccated landscapes; some trench groupings are identical to those of *A Walk in the Sun;* and there are many small but recognisably personal touches, such as the soldier lamenting over the body of his friend, or the cold faces of the men as they grudgingly watch the empty transports returning to the rear areas.

Then, as the film progresses, so do the doubts. The story, set at the time of the Panmunjom peace negotiations in Korea, makes a point of the uselessness of Pork Chop Hill: the war is nearly over, but both sides must strive to hold it, if only to save face. For the American unit's leader, it is a symbol of what his men have been fighting for; as for the negotiating generals, the situation is complicated by dark political hatreds. There are many conflicting allegiances, in fact; but none is emphatically stated, except the necessity for heroism, honour, and duty, expressed in an uneven and equivocal script. Also, the film admits some inexcusable clichés which seem quite alien to Milestone's sombre presentation. In particular, the cowardly Negro who, revived by a quick pep talk, is greeted with a brusque "welcome back to the club," belongs to another and painfully familiar type of war fiction.

As it was produced by Gregory Peck's own company, the film presumably is what he wanted. Nevertheless, it seems legitimate to speculate on whether it is entirely what Milestone wanted. Judged purely as a piece of film-making, it is clearly the work of an old professional. And the last image of the unit, begrimed and dead on its feet, staggering down the hill, seems entirely worthy of its creator. Why, then, do the preceding scenes and the final commentary contrive to soften and distort what this image is telling us? We want to like its creators, and we would like to know.

6

In this article, I have tried to suggest reasons for the decline of so many of Hollywood's most talented artists, and to show how resilience and sheer professional know-how have simultaneously enabled others to retain their recognisably individual qualities as artists. I have mentioned only a proportion of those who have found themselves unable to respond to the current commercial pattern; others (like Milestone) have retained their technical prowess at the cost of some earlier convictions. In view of the fact that the younger generation is so scattered and, more important, so unequal in creative range, there appear to be few replacements available when the still active veterans finally disappear. This is not to deny the presence of several potentially important and talented artists—Kubrick, Lumet, Kramer, Ritt, the younger television writers and directors—but have they the same staying power?

Hollywood, though, is often a law unto itself—it has taken some hard knocks in its time and has always refused to go down for the full count. Nevertheless, it seems to me that we are nearing the end of an era in which the veteran craftsmen, at any rate, are trying to revive Hollywood's familiar traditions with some of their former vigour and style. In his notes for *The Last Tycoon*, Scott Fitzgerald remarked that "there are no second acts in American lives." For many artists in the American cinema, the curtain fell irrevocably after the first act, whilst a tenacious few have achieved a second or even a third. Let us praise and encourage these survivors—before the theatre goes dark on them for ever.

The End of the Assembly Line

Richard Dyer MacCann

Richard Dyer MacCann, a professor of film at the University of Iowa, served as the Hollywood correspondent for The Christian Science Monitor *for nine years. In the following essay he discusses the transformation that has taken place in American film production.**

> "Why don't we put some sprocket holes in the
> press book and throw the picture away?"
>
> *Steve Broidy, president of Allied Artists*

The theatrical motion picture producer is now in a very special position.

He doesn't have to see to it that all the small-town theaters have a new bill twice a week. He doesn't have to fill a newspaper every day, a magazine every month, or an hour on a TV network every week. Like a book publisher or a play producer, the Hollywood film maker can take his time, choose what he wants, start when he's ready. He has, if he can only learn to accept it, a new and responsible role in the communication system of his country. It is a more comfortable role than it used to be. He can concentrate on one good thing at a time. He doesn't have to be in a hurry any more.

THE OVERPRODUCED PICTURE

The Hollywood producer's new position has been forced on him by two historic circumstances.

In the first place, the anti-monopoly decisions by the courts (ranging

* By permission from Houghton Mifflin Co. and Richard Dyer MacCann. *Hollywood in Transition*, Chapter 6, "The End of the Assembly Line," pp. 104–115. © 1962 by Houghton Mifflin Co., Boston, Mass.

over the period from 1940 to 1950) which resulted in the divorcement of theaters from production-distribution companies, also resulted in the abolition of block-booking. The theaters no longer had to take what they were offered, in large and sometimes unidentified packages. The distributors, on the other hand, because they no longer owned theaters, felt no financial obligation to provide a steady stream of "product." Thus Hollywood began to cut down on its schedule of pictures long before TV pulled the bottom out of the market and sent countless theaters into bankruptcy.

In the second place, Hollywood's slow acceptance of television, beginning with transcontinental TV in 1951, has meant that the new system of electronic distribution has taken over the mass production of cheaply made films. Often the frantically busy TV producer works just across the hall, or down the studio street, from the office of the theatrical producer. The latter can say to himself thankfully: "There, but for the grace of God, go I."

For the individual film producer the combined effect of theater divorcement and the rise of television has meant freedom from the tyranny of the assembly line. It is no longer necessary for a studio to make 52 pictures a year—or for Hollywood to distribute 500 or more. Individual films are prospering in long-run engagements, and box-office grosses are increasing. In 1951, American motion picture companies produced 391 features. By 1954, the number had declined to 253. In 1960, after an upturn to 300 in 1957, annual production was down to 154.

The theatrical motion picture today stands somewhere between the stage play and the television show. This is not merely a description of box-office status and audience size. It is also a key to its creative freedom. The old deadlines of mass production are lifted. A producer can choose the script he wants, wait for the right cast, and release when circumstances are most favorable.

But has he really accepted his freedom? Has he been emancipated from the assembly line only to be frozen into a frantic kind of slow motion?

The curious thing about the now unblocked producer is that his freedom has increased his tensions. His new artistic advantage—his reduced work load—carries with it a heavy economic strain. His concern has become more and more fixed on one picture at a time, and for a longer time. Instead of taking the opportunity between productions to breathe the air of the changing world outside of Hollywood, he closes the windows, calls in the writers, and sets to work to polish his next script some more. The result often is a kind of overproduction, which weighs down the whole film with constant changes and takes away the natural freshness and flow of ideas and images.

Part of this persistent preoccupation with the present task is a natural outcome of the kind of work he does, and its traditional intensity. It has always been true that nothing seems to matter to a film maker except his latest picture and the way his audience is going to respond to it. During preparation and shooting, it is almost impossible for him to discuss anything else. But this habitual state of mind, arising from the complexity of film making, has been made more obvious by the cut-backs in production. The typical Hollywood artist has few outside re-sources. He doesn't have anywhere to go except back to work—or to parties where work is the main topic of conversation.

The new varieties of independent production, of course, only add to the strain. The independent producer usually has to stand or fall by the success of his latest film. He sees the whole world through the win-dow of that one enterprise.

A man like Samuel Goldwyn, the perennial independent, has usually limited himself to one or two pictures at a time, sometimes paying con-secutively for a dozen scripts of a story before he was satisfied. But now that films are more "special" than ever before, Mr. Goldwyn declares he must spend four years on one motion picture—two years in prepara-tion and production, two years in exploitation and distribution. This was one of the reasons for the tired look of *Porgy and Bess* when it finally appeared.

Spectacle films have always been carefully prepared and zealously overproduced. But now the hazards of the foreign market made it even more important to remove from these harmless extravaganzas any thorns that might annoy some segment of the world audience. The hesitations and revisions on *Ben-Hur* were only exceeded by the constant rewrit-ing job on the remake of *Mutiny on the Bounty*—in this case to please the star.

Normally, a little more time to think about a picture should improve it. But there is a crucial point of diminishing returns, especially when the story itself needs simplicity and spontaneity. The saddest example of over-production in recent times was George Stevens' production of *The Diary of Anne Frank,* in which a first-rate director somehow lost sight of the delicate tragedy of that spirited little girl in a welter of traditional Hollywood tactics: a worldwide search for a "new star," a sound-stage contraption to shake the whole cast with a representation of an air raid, and the introduction of even more cumbersome plot mechanics to shake the audience with suspense.

Overproduction is not irrational. Its purpose is to draw a big audi-ence. The more elaborate the preparations for a picture the greater the "talk-about"—according to Sindlinger opinion tests—in the press, the fan magazines, and the women's clubs. The more ribbons a picture is tied up with, the more likely it is to draw people who don't usually go to the movies—that extra audience which brings in extra profits. But the kind of ribbons that attract attention are getting more expensive all the time.

Overproduction is also an attempt to catch the salesman's eye. He has to be persuaded, long before the release date, that the producer's year-long effort will amount to a special event in the theatres. Whether the salesman is an independent himself or an employee of a major company, he is attuned primarily to money as a standard of judgment. If the production budget is big (he reasons) the exploitation budget has to be big enough to fit. If the production is planned from the beginning as a financial blockbuster, then it has to have special plans for release.

In the major metropolitan centers, the idea of a pre-release long run is increasingly accepted by distributors and exhibitors for the big spectacles and costly star-studded stories. But such farsighted faith in the "product" is seldom bestowed on the good little film which deserves a wider audience than a quick week in town will bring it. It is a historic irony that the salesmen—and also the top executives—had no faith whatever in *Lili* and grave doubts about *Marty*. Sure pictures are not as big as a house. They are only rare, like diamonds.

One way of setting budgets at blockbuster levels, right from the beginning, is to buy recent best sellers and hit plays. This pleases the salesmen because sometimes the high purchase price is itself a publicity point. And of course a "pre-sold" product is much easier to sell.

Original screenplays are not a totally lost art in Hollywood. The statistics usually look good on an annual basis. But it turns out that most of the originals are small-budget westerns, horror pictures, or science fiction films. A major picture like *The Apartment,* based on a script by Billy Wilder and I. A. L. Diamond, is a rarity indeed.

Top budgets are reserved for unoriginal films. The salesmen assume they are easier to sell. The producers, in turn, assume that the salesmen will give these used plots (which cost so much money to buy in the first place) a top priority in publicity and advertising. There is no particular conviction anywhere along the line that the film medium has anything unique to offer. The purpose of the film is to re-enact the play, reshuffle the novel. The purpose of Hollywood is to be a used plot lot.

THE GRAY FLANNEL MEN AND THE DECLINE OF STYLE

Colossalism is a familiar nostrum in show business. Once more it is becoming a substitute for the vitamins of story sense and film sense. This is partly because of a slow, historic change in Hollywood's leadership.

The era of the hard-fisted, colorful pioneers is past. They lived and worked for an extraordinarily long span of time, but Cecil B. deMille,

Jesse Lasky, Louis B. Mayer, Harry Cohn, and Joseph Schenck are gone. Everywhere the producers—whether independent, semi-independent, or staff—are beginning to have a gray-flannel look. Even the actors are sweating over taxes and account books.

The daring, irascible bosses of Hollywood's first fifty years had the excitement of show business in their veins. They gauged public taste in their own instinctive ways, having been only recently part of the public themselves. They may not have had much formal education, but for that very reason they were in tune with the audience of their time.

To a great extent, today's producer has grown up in the Hollywood scheme of things, under the shadow of the first, flashy entrepreneurs. Whether or not he is "second generation" by blood, he is at least the protected heir of an older order. He may know his way around the studios, and he may know all about the supposed special interests in the hard-core movie audience. He is likely to have a more educated alertness to the opinions of educated men. But he may be efficient without being effective—a calm, well-informed coordinator, making films without passion and without distinction. His formula, if he has any, is to remake old successes and spend a lot more money on them. What was box office for the older generation should be box office again, if it's modernized, with the right trimmings added. The used plot is even better if it has already been made, once or twice before, into a successful movie.

This formula usually requires little explanation to New York bosses and bankers. Bigness goes over big in traditional financial circles. Bankers can only respond with blank stares and long silences to the earnest plea: "It's a great story! It's different!" Investment money goes for "star values" and "production values."

A new generation of film makers, torn between the vivid remembrance of their swashbuckling predecessors and the sober actuality of accountants, bankers, and salesmen, finds it hard to insist upon the new and untried, either in stories or in techniques. The result is a widespread lack of pride in the film medium—in film as film and the things it can uniquely accomplish.

Outside of Hollywood, cinematic ingenuity seems to grow and flourish. The world has been pleased and astonished by a few quick cuts in *Hiroshima, Mon Amour* which brings the past suddenly in view—by a dizzy camera movement in *The Cranes Are Flying* which suggests death in battle—by the shadowy, unexpected introspections of *Wild Strawberries*—by the almost palpable color in *Gate of Hell*—by the close observation of family life in *Pather Panchali*—by the brilliant directorial authority of *La Dolce Vita*—by the confident buildup to a final slapstick scene in the Peter Sellers comedies—by the peculiar insouciance of objects and gadgets in *My Uncle*.

Why should the film makers of France, Russia, Sweden, Japan, India,

Italy, and England monopolize the praise of critics and the attention of much of the public? Why should foreign films be carrying on the heritage of America's D. W. Griffith in extending the resources of film in new-old ways?

The vice of the assembly line system was its tendency to spin off so many cheap films that were so poor from a critical standpoint. The vice of the post-television system of "fewer and better" pictures is its tendency to magnify to such a degree the importance of expensive films. If *Ben-Hur* had failed, M-G-M would have gone bankrupt. If *Spartacus* had failed, Universal would have been in a very shaky condition. The budget of *Cleopatra* carried with it the fate of Twentieth Century-Fox.

"Fewer and better" is more of an incantation than a fruitful policy. What Hollywood really loves to do is to make pictures bigger. When the chance came to make fewer pictures, it was inevitable that some of them would get bigger, more expensive, more overloaded with "production values," and the public went along. Ever since the 8-reel *Quo Vadis* was first imported from Italy in 1913, it has been clear that the public enjoys bigness.

With high stakes, of course, there is more margin for profit. Why labor to bring forth a nice little $500,000 picture on the chance that an advertising and distribution budget of $800,000 will bring in a net of $300,000? Why gamble on a reasonable return when you can just as easily wait around for a couple of top-ranking stars and a best-selling book—and then gamble on a $2,000,000 profit instead?

Colossalism is supposed to keep the community prosperous, too. In many ways, despite the everpresence of upheaval and change, Hollywood has become a conservative, settled town. Every major guild now has a new building of its own. The International Alliance of Theatrical and Stage Employees has won power and position since the jurisdictional strikes of the late forties. Contracts are ever fatter and more favorable to individual workers. Pictures have to be expensive to keep both the workers and the stars in the style to which they have become accustomed.

Yet costliness and the rigidity of guild and union rules have begun to drive creative people away. "Runaway" production is partly the result of restless, independent, creative people trying to get away from Hollywood's overpowering budgets. Foreign locations may be costly, too, but the controls are often looser and the chances greater for the kind of filmic excitement that artistry alone can achieve.

The art of the film has fallen by the wayside in Hollywood. There seems to be less and less opportunity for the passion and persistence of young people willing to make pictures for small stakes. Often the youngest people don't have as much taste or ability as they think they have. But they may have freshness and style and surprise. New young directors might make the mistake of under-producing a picture now and then. Inevitably they will waste money somewhere along the line. But out of the $20,000,000 invested in *Mutiny on the Bounty*, fifty low-budget films could have been made. Who is to say which proposition is more wasteful?

One of the best answers for the runaway production problem is low-budget production here at home. When Val Lewton and Orson Welles had a free hand for a while at RKO in the 1940's, they trained two young film editors who have turned out to be leading directors today. These two men, Mark Robson and Robert Wise, have kept a lot of people busy and well paid in the 1950's. They learned their trade and developed their art by making "little pictures."

Bigness isn't everything, and its appeal doesn't last forever. Bigger doesn't necessarily mean better, any more than fewness guarantees goodness. Quality is not achieved by subtracting from the total number of productions and multiplying the number and cost of people and things in the remaining productions on the list. Quality has nothing to do with either multiplication or magnification. It is something that sneaks into a film as a reflection of somebody's quality of mind and heart. It comes from the long-range commitments of specific human beings.

The men behind the screen, the men with the power to decide, may never feel secure enough to insist upon art. But they need not be so short-sighted as to squeeze out of American films all uniqueness and sense of style. The ones who love the medium most are the ones who work with it most intimately—the writers and directors who have to make the story come to life on the screen. If Hollywood is to come alive again, the men with the power to do so must find and cherish a group of writers who can develop stories directly for the screen and a group of directors who want more than anything else to use the unique resources of camera, editing, and sound.

Then it will be possible to have more "faith in the product" because there will be, in the first instance, faith in the creative art of the film.

Are Foreign Films Better?:
Show of Strength Abroad

Hollis Alpert

Hollis Alpert is a novelist and film critic for the Saturday Review. *In the following article, written in 1960, he discusses the changing role of the American film in relation to the international films.**

Hollywood has been banged on the head so often by its critics that it seems a little unfair to take similar advantage of it at a time when it is becoming increasingly clear that American movies are suffering by comparison with current European films. Having just glanced at the movie pages of *The New York Times,* I see that such entries from abroad as *Hiroshima, Mon Amour, The Entertainer, The Virgin Spring,* and *General Della Rovere* are having their runs simultaneously with *Butterfield 8, The World of Suzie Wong, The Alamo,* and *Surprise Package.* While *Sunrise at Campobello, Spartacus,* and *Ben-Hur* are also running, and while I wouldn't dissuade many of my friends from seeing them, I doubt that any of the American films I have mentioned would stand up, on the basis of quality, with most of the foreign ones we have seen here recently.

A snobbish attitude? Even in Hollywood, opinions on this would differ. One director of note went to see *Hiroshima, Mon Amour,* expecting one more overeulogized film, and was astonished to find himself admiring the technical gifts of its director, Alain Resnais, as well as being profoundly moved by its story. "Resnais has shown us a few things," he commented.

On the other hand, an equally well-known director, having seen

---

Wild Strawberries, said: "We stopped doing that sort of thing in Hollywood thirty years ago." My own memory may be faulty, but I couldn't recall a film of the same type, and, at any rate, the answer to that director from those who did find *Wild Strawberries* a remarkable film experience might well be: why did you stop?

Bergman, so far as technical aspects are concerned, is probably a traditionalist. His equipment is said to be antiquated, and he works on a budget that might pay for the services, alone, of one third-rate Hollywood star, prices for stars being what they are these days. Yet audiences have found moments of beauty in his moody landscapes, and his camera is able to accentuate the meaning of his story subjects. Such landscapes are not particularly new; neither are some of his surrealistic and dream passages, nor the trick effects he occasionally tries. But his expressiveness, his personal visions, his storytelling ability—these are another matter. To overlook them, and scoff at his use of camera, boom, and dolly, is pure and simply a Philistine attitude that has been long oversubscribed to by far too many American film people. Our own screens become wider, the images on them clearer, and, all too often, emptier.

Up until recently, enough films of impact came from Hollywood to keep alive the belief that Americans were pre-eminent in the motion picture field. Some of us were willing to disregard the prevalence of the meretricious and the mediocre, the dozens of shoddy little items made solely for the object of milking the box office, and to point with pride to directors such as George Stevens, Fred Zinneman, Elia Kazan, Billy Wilder, John Huston, Robert Wise, and perhaps three or four others who have brought enormous respect around the world for the American film industry. We could also rest on the vaunted superiority of our technical resources. American films, it was clear to almost everyone, were simply better made than the foreign product, by and large.

But it now appears that even this last assumption is not true. More is being attempted and achieved elsewhere. A British film, *Room at the Top,* was largely the work of an untried director, Jack Clayton. It was clearly the best-directed film of its year, even though Hollywood lavished its awards on *Ben-Hur.* You can be sure that a good many conscientious people in Hollywood devoted some study to *Room at the Top,* just as a good many more devoted study to the box office statistics for *Ben-Hur.*

Playing successfully in England right now is a movie called *Saturday Night and Sunday Morning,* with a screenplay by Alan Sillitoe from his novel of the same title. Due to open here in a month or two, it can be safely said about the movie that its direction, writing, acting, and editing are so exciting and fresh that our own movies, particularly in the black-and-white category, are bound to look stodgy and old-fashioned by comparison. It may be time to begin wondering if we aren't going to be left far behind in the international arena of quality, unless we begin paying more careful attention to what is happening abroad. While we have been searching for gimmicks and clues to public preference, others elsewhere have been exploring the film medium to find its essential vitality, and to discover more of its potentialities.

Barriers of finance, of star systems, of distribution setups have proved insufficient to check the growing body of unusual work in films abroad. Last year it was the French New Wave, this year the Italians are coming back. Bergman has functioned in Sweden, Fellini in Italy, Richardson in England, Ray in India. The Poles have made some fine films, the Soviet Union has perked up, the West Germans are by no means quiescent. Movies elsewhere have managed to emerge, to engage our serious attention, in spite of the enormous expense of production, and the fear of not recouping at the box office.

The director of *Saturday Night and Sunday Morning* was Karel Reisz. His previous experience was in the documentary field. He had also been a film critic and editor of a film magazine, noted for his grasp of the technical details of movie-making. How did he get his chance? Richardson had formed a small company, Woodfall Productions, with the playwright John Osborne. The company made films out of two Osborne plays, *Look Back in Anger,* and *The Entertainer. Saturday Night and Sunday Morning* was financed out of the usual channels, and Richardson this time served as producer, Reisz as director. The budget was naturally low, actors were chosen for their ability and suitability for their parts, and—lo and behold!—a fine movie.

It must not be assumed from the foregoing that youth is everywhere having its day. The New Wave has already subsided in France, the enthusiasm for it has begun to wane. But it would be wrong to dismiss the wave as more *vague* than *nouvelle.* What it did show was that several young people could conceive and make movies with individuality and effectiveness, that they could sometimes find new subjects and sometimes handle old subjects in such a way that they looked new. Young intellectuals in France have taken to the film form as nowhere else. Instead of writing novels and plays, they wrote scripts. If they couldn't direct, they wrote film criticism. They studied techniques. They went behind cameras with a bland disregard for traditions, and while they stumbled often, they also got crowds to line up before the marquees on the Grands Boulevards.

France had a subsidy system for quality film-making that helped to a degree. While it still has this system, there is word to the effect that several of the new directors are being denied subsidies because of their position on the Algerian question. But only a few weeks ago a new

French film called *The Love Game* came along, directed by another youthful newcomer, Philippe de Broca. This time Claude Chabrol, of *The Cousins* fame, was the producer. The movie is a minor comedy, but made spritely and joyous by the sheer exuberance of its direction and performance. Mr. de Broca obviously would not be downed. His story may be a wisp of a thing, but the camera follows the antics of a delightfully mad young man, Jean-Pierre Cassel, and his beguiling mistress, Genevieve Cluny, and somehow convinces us that they are entirely real people and worth knowing. I was also struck by the look of intelligence on the faces of the performers, as though it were no crime to be intelligent, unconventional, animated, and charming. It would be pleasant, for a change, to see more intelligence, more life, in the faces Hollywood puts on the screen. Even our most intelligent actors are generally used to portray painfully groping neurotics, the stupid, the mental incompetents.

When our own little new wave gets going, what is its direction? *Private Property,* with its pretty but dull housewife, an idiot of a husband, and two goons who lasciviously peep and plot a seduction. Also, *The Savage Eye,* a look, without purpose, at human wreckage. Another of these unconventional American attempts will shortly be unveiled: *The Connection.* Dope addicts, again! There is some basic misunderstanding about realism that we appear to have here. It can exist on many levels; it need not be confined to human blight and morbidity. I hope I do not sound too reactionary.

If movies can be made against the commercial tide abroad, why not here? Why this continual pouring of millions into more Biblicals, into comedies without style or wit, into pallid soap operas in wide screen and primary color? Why not an occasional off-pattern movie, one not backed up by smash-hit status on Broadway, or best-sellerdom? Of the close to 200 films made in Hollywood in the past year, hardly a half-dozen are worthy of notice. *The Apartment* had the canny direction of Billy Wilder, but a confused theme that failed to sort out the values of the characters who eventually found happiness. Zinneman's *The Sundowners* is one of the more encouraging of the year's offerings, but was made entirely in Australia. *Swiss Family Robinson,* a genuine delight for children and their families, was directed by an Englishman, made on location on the island of Tobago, and completed in an English studio.

There is some reason for the belief that Hollywood, as Hollywood, is in its decline. We know, of course, that the studio system has undergone vast changes within the past ten years, that some of the lots have been taken over by television performers, others by MCA, an agency with an octopus grip on much of the production—so Hollywoodites complain—and that stars have been making inordinate salary demands. But stars make more than demands for 10 per cent of the gross, or a cool million in cash. Because producers, hoping to play it safe, seek them, they have been able to corner stories for which they are often not suited. A Hollywood screenwriter said: "Half the scripts out here start out with Elizabeth Taylor and Rock Hudson in mind for the leads. The rest are naturals for Gary Grant and Marilyn Monroe."

The more inventive film-maker is discouraged before he can begin. He knows he hasn't a chance unless he has a star who wants to do the story. One of the most powerful movies of recent years, *Paths of Glory,* was rejected by every studio until Kirk Douglas took it under his personal wing. "The movie didn't make money," Douglas commented, "but it made Stanley Kubrick." (Kubrick then made *Spartacus.*)

In the mid-Fifties a movement away from Hollywood began, to locations abroad, and to New York. The results were promising at first, but it soon became apparent that what was sought abroad was what might be termed locale color, and that New York was just as expensive as Hollywood. *On the Waterfront* started the rallying cry "Keep 'em in New York," but the low-budget *Twelve Angry Men* proved a disappointment at the box office. *Baby Doll* ran into censorship difficulties, and the recent *The Fugitive Kind* demonstrated that a million dollars paid to Marlon Brando was not enough to bulwark a soggy script and the miscasting of Anna Magnani. The film unions wanted parity with Hollywood, and these days a producer needs unusual courage to buck the formidable array of charges that New York film-making can entail.

Because everyone involved in feature film production is caught in a cost vortex—for which creative and technical personnel are alike responsible—our film-making allows for little in the way of new ideas and new blood. Only the most established directors can still make reasonably satisfactory movies, and they too, John Huston and George Stevens among them, have had their flops. They can't keep the costs down, and a picture can bring in $5,000,000 at the box office and still lose millions.

The American film is losing such world-wide respect as it once had. The facts that Mankiewicz has made the sound track crackle with wit, that Huston and Stevens have filled the screen with fluid movement, are only of historical interest now. What is happening that is new? What is new is what is happening abroad. What is new are Truffaut, Richardson, Bergman, Camus, Resnais, and many others, who are charging the screen with a new look at people, with acting that reflects our time, with themes that have meaning, with styles that are distinct and individual. These people are in full cry against the glib slickness that the American movie has made its trade-mark. They study the techniques of our movies, then turn their backs on us, and show us how these techniques can really be used. And they are amused by the surface gloss we carefully apply on our movies, as though that would hide from any discerning eye the relative worth of the product. Since it is believed, even by governments, that movies are important not only as a medium of entertainment, but because they share, or should share, a place in the cultural sun with other arts, popular and fine, something of import is happening if we can no longer keep pace with the films of other nations. If for no other reason, the situation should be scrutinized with care.

Growing Pains of a Shrinking Industry

Arthur Mayer

Arthur Mayer, a respected film historian, is the author of Merely Colossal *and co-author of* The Movies. *The following essay is his view of the
American film industry through 1960, and what have been the effects
of independent production upon Hollywood.* *

"A little rebellion now and then," Thomas Jefferson once remarked, "is
a good thing." He was referring to cataclysms "in the political and
physical worlds" but his views are equally applicable to disturbances in
other spheres. They are particularly relevant to our mass communication
media, which require constant reassessment, revision, and an occasional
revolution if they are adequately to fulfill their informational, educational, and entertainment functions.

In the past decade TV has done to the movies even as the movies in
their precocious youth did to the legitimate theatre. Offering the public
the ultimate in convenience, economy, and banal entertainment, almost
evernight it cut motion picture theatre attendance in half. Ten thousand
of the 22,000 old "hard top" theatres have been converted into super-
markets, bowling alleys, or garages. Formerly every major company-
produced film made a profit unless it was unfortunately labeled "ar-
"tistic" or "experimental." Today some 75 per cent of the pictures
released are losing money. The huge studios, formerly exhibit A of
Hollywood's hegemony, have become, like the dinosaur, too cumbersome to survive in a changed world, and the more prosperous companies
are those unencumbered either by realty or by fealty to traditional
production procedures. The picture makers who have been exhorted so
often in the past to raise their sights may also have to raze their sites.
Indeed, it is probable that eventually studio facilities will be rented

* By permission from Arthur Mayer, "Growing Pains of a Shrinking Industry,"
Saturday Review, February 25, 1961. © 1961.

by producers anywhere from Culver City to Capetown only if and when they are required.

Twelve years ago Hollywood appeared impregnably entrenched as the cinema capital of the world. The profits of its seven major producing companies were running over $200,000,000 annually. Ninety million Americans, or so it was claimed by movie press agents (who rarely exaggerate more than 20 per cent), were attending motion pictures weekly. To satisfy their seemingly insatiable demands 400 pictures were being mass-produced every year. The industry's mores as well as its movies were dictated by a handful of survivors from the pioneer days of dog-eat-dog who had proved most proficient at devouring rather than being devoured. They were men of incredible acumen, ambition, and avarice whose pre-eminence, rudely speaking, was attributable to their faith in sentimental, escapist entertainment and their lack of faith in the intelligence of the public. Of any social responsibility to portray the nation's needs realistically and to foster its faith in human dignity and democratic institutions they were utterly unaware. And yet, in spite of the commercialism and cynicism of Beverly Hills and Broadway and the readiness of Main Street to accept whatever film fodder it was proffered, so great is the vitality of the medium and the skill and dedication of its creators and craftsmen that every year a considerable number of films of genuine merit were produced.

Suddenly, however, the movie makers were faced with a form of competition unprecedented in industrial annals. Thirty-four million Americans, it is estimated, are looking at motion pictures every night but 28,000,000 of them are watching them gratis in their living rooms rather than paying to see them in theatres. The ancient practice of regular weekly or twice-a-week attendance is as alien to the way of life of our young people (who constitute over 50 per cent of present theatre patronage) as wearing corsets or holding hands in the front parlor. It has been replaced by a more selective, though not necessarily a more discriminating, approach that confines theatre patronage to a limited number of productions which for reasons still undetermined stimulate the public's salivary entertainment glands. Some of the playing time formerly monopolized by Hollywood has not been pre-empted by foreign films—not primarily cinematic achievements of the caliber of *Wild Strawberries* or *Hiroshima, Mon Amour* but fatuous spectaculars like *Hercules*. Moreover, the industry's much-prized glamour is fading. It badly needs new personalities to replace the balding, face-lifted gods and goddesses of the Forties, but the younger generation sometimes seems more productive of juvenile delinquents than of juvenile stars and starlets.

Confronted by such catastrophes, producers proceeded to bolster their dwindling bank accounts by disposing of their pre-'48 negatives to their TV competitors. In this fashion they inadvertently nullified the efforts of a few video craftsmen to develop their own indigenous art, at the same time demonstrating their complete indifference to their own cultural heritage by permitting the classics of their past to be shown nightly, brutally chopped and interlarded with paeans of praise for detergents, deodorants, dentrifices, and depilatories. "It was," said Spyros Skouras, president of 20th Century-Fox, "a tragic mistake." But Mr. Skouras, along with his fellow presidents, is now repeating the tragedy by selling his post-'48 features.

Indeed, it can safely be predicted that in a belated effort to make show biz businesslike, anything that the companies possess that is not nailed down, whether old films, old studios, or old relatives, will be jettisoned. It is also evident that they will resort to any form of diversification that promises to make a buck, such as the production of quickies for video, of calculating machines (colossal, of course) or toll-TV electronic devices designed to replace the theatre box office with a box office in every home.

Meanwhile, the movie executives proceeded with considerable courage, foresight, and ingenuity to revolutionize completely the processes and practices of picture making through five drastic reforms: 1) Old-fashioned major company assembly-line procedures wehe replaced by independent production; 2) an ever-increasing percentage of pictures was shot away from Hollywood, particularly on foreign locations; 3) the number of films produced annually was reduced by 50 per cent, with the bulk of the industry's resources and showmanship concentrated on unprecedentedly costly features known as block-busters; 4) new wide-screen processes were introduced; 5) story material for plots and dialogue supposedly more sophisticated and mature than had formerly been regarded as suitable for mass entertainment replaced the so-called family pictures, bucolic comedies, and saccharine romances. The future may be fraught with perils and complexities but we have at least said a final farewell on the theatre screen to Ma and Pa Kettle and to Francis, the talking horse. We have also, at least temporarily, said goodbye to the grave-diggers who prematurely pronounced the industry on its deathbed. Theatre recipts in 1960 amounted to $1,375,000,000, a figure only barely exceeded in three halcyon years of the late Forties, and the stocks of all of the major producers surged upward in a depressed Wall Street market.

Independent production, of course, is nothing new. Over the years such pioneers as Goldwyn and Selznick concentrated their activities on a limited number of pictures produced slowly with meticulous care.

Naturally, the batting average of their product was considerably higher than that of the major companies which were each turning out some fifty-two pictures annually and which put a new production into work every week regardless of whether a suitable story, star, or director was available. Only one company, United Artists, founded by Chaplin, Pickford, Fairbanks, and Griffith, through the years operated exclusively as a distributor of independently made pictures. Of it, one industry wit wisecracked: "The lunatics have taken over the asylum."

The show-wise young attorneys who took over United Artists in 1951 after it had long teetered on the edge of bankruptcy were, however, far from lunatics. They reduced its overhead, undersold their competitors, ingratiated themselves with bankers, and enticed top-notch producers by extending them something previously unknown in the industry— almost complete autonomy. As a consequence of these innovations, with amazing speed they dispensed with red ink and within ten years were showing an annual profit of over $4,000,000.

Nothing is as persuasive to magnates, movie or otherwise, as a balance sheet which each year shows the assets increasingly outbalancing the liabilities. Today practically every other picture company has adopted to a substantial degree United Artists' production policies. This industry-wide acceptance was also accelerated by our tax laws, which make it more lucrative to be an entrepreneur who can pay a capital gain of 25 per cent on stock sales rather than a wage slave sweating beneath the yoke of a 90 per cent income tax. The good news spread rapidly among the unhappy upper-bracket set of the West Coast.

Independent production has failed, like most other panaceas, to live up to its advance publicity. In the case of a few gifted individuals such as Kramer, Spiegel, and Jerry Wald it has achieved a considerable advance in individual initiative and in freedom of subject matter and treatment. There is, however, a plethora of other independents no more encumbered by humanitarian or artistic ideals than were their big-studio predecessors. Certainly the 1960 record furnishes no occasion for complacency in American cinematic circles. In selecting the ten best pictures of the year the critics of *Saturday Review*, the New York *Post*, and the *New York Herald Tribune* included only two American pictures in their lists. Bosley Crowther expressed the sentiments of most of his confreres when he accused Hollywood of "extravagance, bad taste, and vulgarity."

Actually the major companies have practically abdicated their producing functions and are now primarily investors, distributors, and landlords. As investors they advance to independents all the finances required to make their pictures, receiving in return—depending upon whether they are dealing with John Doe or John Wayne—anywhere from 75 to 10 per cent of the profits, if any. They levy a fee of approximately

30 per cent for their distribution services, calculated to assure them a profit even on unprofitable pictures, and charge rent for their studios as and when they are used.

More and more films, however, are being made in alien locations formerly of little repute. The independents seem to have a special penchant for islands—the Canaries, Rhodes, Cypress, even Manhattan. Approximately 40 per cent of the movies made or financed by the majors last year were shot abroad, and in spite of the wails of the West Coast unions the trend is certain to continue, and possibly to expand. The industry stumbled onto this bonanza more through good luck than good business judgment. In the postwar years the only way it could utilize its unconvertible foreign currency earnings was to produce pictures where the funds were accumulating. Possibly because of the authenticity and the novelty of the locations, possibly because of increased American awareness of the charms of the Old World, possibly just because they were excellent pictures, such productions as *Three Coins in a Fountain, The Third Man,* and *Roman Holiday* proved, to everybody's surprise, to be smash hits. Generally speaking, production costs were and still are considerably less in such countries as Yugoslavia or Greece than at home. Extras for big spectaculars come a drachma a dozen, armies of rival nations compete for the glory of appearing in a block-buster, and no sets need to be constructed for ancient castles, awesome cathedrals, or authentic chateaus.

Moreover, there are special advantages to be gained from subsidies and preferential treatment provided by practically every government in the world except that of the U. S. for productions made within their borders and utilizing some of their native personnel. American producers have on occasion been sufficiently persuasive with local authorities to qualify for payments in three or four different countries! High-salaried performers took to foreign production like starlets to swimming pools. Some specialists in the role of the all-American boy, aged fifty or more, have resorted to the un-American expedient of numbered bank accounts in Switzerland that enable them to escape the clutches of the Collector of Internal Revenue while retaining their U. S. citizenship. Quite a few producers and directors aver that their artistic integrity and opportunity for self-expression are in direct proportion to their remoteness from Hollywood. More and more, these foreign-made films certainly represent the cream of the U. S. cinema crop. The 1956 Oscar was awarded to *Around the World in 80 Days,* surprisingly enough filmed around the world. The 1957 winner was *The Bridge on the River Kwai,* made in Ceylon. The Oscar for 1958 was voted to *Gigi,* shot to a large extent in France, and last year the award was given to *Ben-Hur,* made in Italy.

The independents, like their big-company predecessors, have displayed little zeal in developing literary material specifically designed for cinematic purposes but enormous energy in pursuing the rights for successful books and plays, frequently written by men whom Hollywood had previously hired and fired. Michener's *Hawaii* was sold prior to publication for $600,000. *The Sound of Music* was purchased for $1,250,000 guaranteed against 10 per cent of the gross, and this percentage of the gross formula, whether applied to authors, actors or directors, can prove, to put it mildly, quite costly. Bill Holden, for instance, received 10 per cent of the gross of *The Bridge on the River Kwai,* and *The Bridge* will probably wind up with world-wide rentals of some $20,000,000. Hitchcock's *Psycho* deal for 75 per cent of the profits should net him over $5,000,000. Marlon Brando, when he is not producing pictures for his own company, prefers to gamble on 50 per cent of the picture's profits but he does not gamble very recklessly as he demands a guarantee of $750,000. Marilyn Monroe is more conservative. She takes a straight million and comes to work late every day.

Instead of seeking to develop new talent, a task that requires a readiness to sacrifice immediate profits for highly speculative future earnings, the present breed of producers prefers to experiment with wide-angle lenses, 70 mm. film, or batteries of cameras handling different parts of the over-all scene, designed to give greater depth, vision, and clarity. Anamorphic lenses, which can expand and subsequently compress the image on the negative, have been available since 1927 when Cinemascope (under another name) was first demonstrated by a French inventor. It attracted little attention, however, until television made it imperative to achieve greater dramatic effectiveness than any little box in the living room could possibly afford. These so-called new techniques are immensely effective in spectacular scenes like the chariot race in *Ben-Hur.* On the other hand, the small attic in which Anne Frank and her family were hidden is now blown up to the size of Grand Central Station. Close-ups are frequently so magnified that susceptible patrons find themselves hypnotized by the pores of the heroine's nose or the gyrations of the hero's Adam's apple. As Cecil DeMille once said: "With Vista Vision I can show the Hebrews crossing the Red Sea, but I cannot adequately portray the Madonna fondling the Christ child." Another producer, deploring the new "letter-box" proportions of the screen, complained that he could show Gulliver in Lilliput prone but never upright.

Moreover, these wide-screen processes add tremendously to picturemaking costs already swollen by inflated salaries, story costs, and union demands. Last year only 224 pictures were released by American film distributors, but the total sum spent for their production and distribution was triple what it had been for the 368 pictures made in 1941. With the demise of block booking, movies entered the blockbuster ice age. The spectaculars, costing anywhere from $12,000,000 to $15,000,000, are proving treasure troves with unprecedented world-wide grosses of $60,-000,000 to $70,000,000. Many of the baby blockbusters, budgeted for only a negligible $2,000,000 to $5,000,000, are also doing quite nicely. Of the twenty-five highest-grossing pictures of all time, twenty-two have been released in the "depressed" years since 1950.

In sixty years of picture making we have, however, learned distressingly little about the qualities that make some pictures so popular and others so unpopular, not only from coast to coast but from continent to continent. In speaking of modern physics, the distinguished scientist Dr. Isadore Rabi once said: "We work with known laws in the midst of data unknown and unknowable." Motion pictures face exactly the opposite quandary. We know the data but the laws we work with are apparently unknown and unknowable. Certainly the favorites of the past year fail to furnish much guidance. The top twelve as listed by *Variety*, the industry's weekly Bible, are as follows: *Ben-Hur*, the epic to end all epics; *Solomon and Sheba*, a minor-league epic whose historical inaccuracies and ostentatious bad taste gave rise to rumors that Cecil DeMille must still be alive; Hitchcock's *Psycho*, an inexpensive chiller-diller, which in time will probably prove the highest-grossing black-and-white negative since Griffith's *Birth of a Nation; Can-Can*, a musical which neither Khrushchev nor the critics, but only the public, seemed to like; *Operation Petticoat, The Apartment*, and *Please Don't Eat the Daisies*, three comedies chockful of chuckles rather than belly laughs; two sex sizzlers, *Butterfield 8*, and *From the Terrace*, and the sizzlier if not sexier *Suddenly Last Summer*, which Eric Johnston, a connoisseur of movies if not of erotica, testified that he had seen three times without detecting any suggestion of homosexuality; *On the Beach*, a message picture of the type which exhibitors have for years claimed should be circulated by Western Union and not in picture threatres, and *Ocean's 11*, which at the very time that all authorities were agreeing that star value was waning, owed its popularity to the presence in the cast of members of the so-called rat pack, Frank Sinatra, Dean Martin, and Peter Lawford. So much for the experts!

Although "controversial" is still a dirty word in the motion picture lexicon, "mature" is for the moment the password. Unfortunately, many producers apparently suffer from the immature delusion that mature pictures are exclusively those dealing with sex in its more sordid aspects. They seem to be unaware of the many dramatic situations in a dynamic, democratic society and in a rapidly changing world order worthy of cinematic attention besides seduction and promiscuity. Until recently motion pictures were subject to the strict surveillance of censor boards in some dozen states and over fifty municipalities. A series of Supreme Court decisions, however, has so undermined the scope and power of pre-release censorship that only five state boards still survive, and they rarely, if ever, ban a picture; at the most, they insist on a few comparatively inconsequential cuts. A handful of municipal boards still occasionally make a local nuisance of themselves but if Memphis, for example, condemns *The Lovers,* this only serves to stimulate the citizenry in large numbers to cross the river to East Mehphis and see how wicked the picture might be—and to return home considerably disappointed.

A more potent control over picture content in the past was exercised by the industry itself through the Code Authority of the Motion Picture Association, which refuses to grant its seal of approval to any picture that might "lower the moral standards of those who see it." More specifically, it stipulates that "adultery and illicit sex must not be explicitly treated or justified" and "that the treatment of low, disgusting, unpleasant subjects should be guided always by the dictates of good taste." The terms of the Code have not been substantially altered since it was adopted in 1930. Like the United States Constitution, however, its enforcement varies greatly with their interpretation. What is good taste to one individual is nauseating to another. Men of good will can and frequently do disagee on whether certain subjects are "low and disgusting."

In the last few years the Code has, in the words of the National Council of Churches of Christ, "become increasingly ineffective." *Happy Anniversary,* for instance, dealt with a situation in which David Niven and Mitzi Gaynor, a happily married couple, unashamedly admit that they had had premarital relations. This is taboo, according to the Code, and at the last moment to pass the picture a speech was dubbed in in which Niven says (he was abroad and a substitute voice had to be used) : "I was wrong. I never should have taken Alice to that hotel room before we were married. What could I have been thinking of?" If the question arises of what the Code Authority could have been thinking of, the answer is that it was thinking of the independent producers who have proved far less tractable than the veteran presidents of the major companies to suggested sacrifices in behalf of "good taste" or the even more nebulous imponderable known as "public relations."

Even the Legion of Decency, the major religious pressure group, has shown a disposition to tolerate pictures that formerly would have been summarily banned as sacrilegious or pornographic. Only the American Legion remains to safeguard our patriotism if not our virtue. The power of the Legion was graphically illustrated when Frank Sinatra, declaring that he was "prepared to stand on his principles," hired Albert Maltz, one of the "uncooperative Hollywood ten," to write a screen treatment. So great was the outcry raised by the Legion, aided and abetted by the Hearst press, that Mr. Sinatra, who usually poses as a tough guy, quickly threw his principles overboard, discharged Mr. Maltz, and announced that he accepted "the majority opinion of the American public."

How Mr. Sinatra ascertained this "majority opinion" he neglected to reveal. It needs no public poll, however, to discover that there is a rising tide of disapproval of the "pathological preoccupation with sex and violence" of many of the current "mature" pictures. When Bob Hope cracked, "Our big pictures this year have had some intriguing themes— sex, perversion, adultery, cannibalism—we'll get those kids away from their TV sets yet," the laughter that ensued was less than hilarious. In forty state legislatures, measures are expected to be introduced this year calling for some form of censorship or at least classification of films suitable for children.

Statutory restrictions of this nature are in force in almost every country in the world except the U. S. The English system, which appears to function to the satisfaction of moviegoers without undue hardship to picture makers, classifies movies into three categories: those regarded as suitable for all age groups, those ecceptable for children only when accompanied by their parents, and those restricted to adults only. Personally, I object to the third category, feeling that the final responsibility for what their progeny see or hear should as far as possible rest with the parents. But the shrieks rising from Hollywood and New York that classification is only censorship in a new guise comes with ill grace from an industry that over the years has permitted the bulk of the battle against restrictions on the freedom of the screen to be borne by small, independent importers. Ephraim London, who, representing the importers, won both *The Miracle* and the *Lady Chatterley's Lover* cases and who is unquestionably the leading legal adversary of film censorship, is not an opponent of classification. Indeed, it is intellectually difficult to distinguish between it and other well-recognized government procedures for the protection of minors, such as their exclusion from bars, pool rooms, and restricted shelves in public libraries.

Every effort, however, should be made to avoid classification in the U. S., where it can safely be predicted that the boards that would make the rulings would be more apt to be composed of political hacks and the widows of police sergeants than of psychiatrists, educators, and social scientists. Nonetheless, legislation of this nature is, I fear, inevitable unless the Motion Picture Association and the Theatre Owners Association, when merchandising such films as *Strangers When We Meet, Butterfield 8, Happy Anniversary, the Bramble Bush,* and dozens more, make clear in their newspaper, TV, radio, trailer, and lobby advertising that such pictures are not designed for young and impressionable minds and that parents permitting their children to attend them do so at their own risk. Such advertising may occasionally prove costly but it is the industry's only protection if it desires, as it certainly should, to continue to produce pictures that deal candidly and with real maturity with the dramatic aspects of sex, violence, politics, and religious or medical quackery. Exhibitors must also exhibit restraint in not double-booking films appealing to children, like *Pollyanna* or *Swiss Family Robinson,* with such repulsive rubbish as *Night of the Blood Beast, The Screaming Skull,* or *Operation Dames.* The accusation, however, that motion pictures even as offensive as these produce juvenile deliquency is thoroughly unscientific. In a society where newspapers, television, radio, and the comics compete to feature sadism and brutality, it is impossible to isolate and measure the effects of any one medium. The furthest that responsible psychiatrists dare to venture is to suggest that in some cases certain pictures might aggravate antisocial tendencies.

In the long run, where an open market prevails and where the public pays the bill as it does in movies but not in TV, the country will get as good art or entertainment as it deserves. Walt Whitman once wrote: "To have great poets there must be a great audience." The same is true of motion pictures. A sluggish, apathetic people will be satisfied with sentimental, escapist movies. A strong, virile nation will demand and receive films warm with insight, tenderness, and power. If, Heaven forbid, the screen version of *Lolita* becomes fabulously profitable, this is the type of picture that will more and more dominate our screen. If, on the other hand, *Sons and Lovers* proves more profitable than early reports indicated, we will have more pictures of this high quality. You do not get good movies by staying at home and criticizing the offensive ones, but by patronizing the good ones.

Personally, I am a corrigible optimist, by which I mean I believe that we are making progress but making it in these critical times far too slowly and too intermittently. The old Mencken dictum that "no one ever went broke underestimating the taste of the American public" is still true, but it is also true that money can be made by having faith in the taste of a substantial segment of the public. It is a long stride forward from the dramatic and musical Broadway hits of my youth such as *Abie's Irish Rose* and *Capt. Jinks of the Horse Marines* to *The Miracle Worker* and *My Fair Lady.* I have no brief for the current best-sellers, such as *Hawaii* and *Advise and Consent,* but surely they represent an improvement in subject matter and skill over *Three Weeks* and and *When Knighthood Was in Flower.* More Americans are attending concerts than baseball games and over the week-ends the art museums are scarcely capable of accommodating the crowds. It is unfortunate that our most popular current movies fail to indicate similar progress in cinematic taste but the fine reception extended to some comparatively inexpensive English pictures such as *Room at the Top, I'm All Right, Jack, The Mouse That Roared,* and *Tunes of Glory* are at least an encouraging symptom.

Looking back over the past decade, the movie executives (at least those who know their Shakespeare) can with pardonable pride say with Hotspur: "Out of this nettled danger we pluck this flower safety." But while they have been preoccupied with plucking the flower, their old-time laurels have been withering. Surely it is not enough for any medium of communication to be safe in a world which calls for courage, beauty, gaiety, and truth.

The Death of Rastus:
Negroes in American Films Since 1945

Thomas R. Cripps

Hollywood has been criticized for presenting a false image of Negroes on film ever since the release of Birth of a Nation *in 1915. In general, Negroes were portrayed as lazy, pop-eyed buffoons and were confined almost exclusively to comedy or servant roles. Negroes started starring in films around 15 years ago. The following survey analyses the changing image of the Negro in the American movie.**

Students of the film have been divided over the issue of just what movies communicate. Those closer to the era of the behaviorists such as Lenin and Jane Addams believed that movies molded opinion. They held that films have a proven effect upon behavior because the experience of movie-going, unlike theater, is "extrasocial" and thus a clear identification takes place between filmed image and the mind of the viewer.[1]

More recent observers argue that the film is a kind of reflector of values. Siegfried Kracauer postulates a cinema as a social communicator of deep layers of Jungian collective meanings and psychological dispositions.[2] Given this assumption, each viewer's background determines what he gets from a film; that is, he captures what is usable to himself. "He utilizes the pictured situation," as Franklin Fearing puts it, "in the process of coming to terms with the larger environment."[3] Thus movies form attitudes in a chance way, depending on biases already held by the audience members individually. They have residues of imagery from older movies through which they view new images. Thus they may evade, misinterpret, or miss the point of a film's persuasion.

* By permission from Tilman C. Cothran, editor, *Phylon*, "The Death of Rastus: Negroes in American Films Since 1945," *Phylon*, Fall 1967, Atlanta, Ga. © 1967.

In some cases a boomerang effect is achieved: that is, the viewer comes away believing more strongly in the attitude opposite to the one presented by a film. German audiences, for example, missed the point of the problem movie, *Blackboard Jungle,* taking it to be a documentary with Glenn Ford the only professional actor.[4]

At least one critic, after seeing Stanley Kramer's movie about the hysterical paralysis of a Negro soldier, concluded that *"Home of the Brave* will convert no one; in some observers (because of the unintentionally implied cowardice of the Negro), it could have the effect of confirming prejudice." A social scientist who studied the attitude creation of the movie biography of Sister Kenny found it a weak propaganda agent simply because the audience respondents did not attribute accuracy and seriousness of purpose to motion pictures. Other critics have pointed to ethnic and national attitudes and minority relationships as other factors in the successful transmission of images by the film. As Kracauer has put it:

> Hollywood and any national film industry for that matter is both a leader and a follower of public opinion. In portraying foreign characters it reflects what it believes to be the popular attitudes of the time, but it also turns these often vague attitudes into concrete images.[5]

Thus in American motion pictures in-group self-images will become the norm of behavior and all the jangling diversity of ethnic groups will round off into a broadly based white Anglo-Saxon Protestant type. Some minority groups have contributed to this kind of negative stereotyping by their protests against reprehensible typing. Witness protests by Italians against *The Untouchables* and protests by Negroes against *Birth of a Nation.* The result is not an elimination of the stereotypes but instead the continuation of the least objectionable of them. As Terry Ramsaye stated: "the multitude can chuckle at Step'n Fetchit and laugh with Rochester, but they will woo and win with the Gables, the Taylors and the Coopers." Thus villainous Negroes stay off the screen at the price of making "the negro [sic] so amusing and agreeable that an audience is always pleased at the appearance of a black face."[6]

The combination of these two factors produces a kind of selective censorship. The history of film censorship in America is a long, tedious tale of the suppression of the sins of the Puritans. As Sterling Brown has pointed out, seven stereotypes of Negroes can be isolated: the contented slave, the wretched freeman, the comic Negro, the brute Negro, the tragic mulatto, the local color Negro, and the exotic primitive. The elements of these types include laziness, filth, sensuality, and crime, so that it is as though white America is torn between two conclusions: Negroes are America's anti-democratic nightmare and Puritan conscience and must be suppressed, or they must be depicted publicly as the stereotype because it sustains the myth of Anglo-Saxon purity.[7]

In practice a compromise has been struck. The private censorship code of the motion picture producers of America prescribes all the vicious elements of the stereotype and tolerates the ridiculous elements. Thus, through the 1930's and 1940's, only racial comics such as Rochester, Willie Best, and Mantan Moreland (as Charlie Chan's valet) crept into American films.[8] The effect in recent films has been that Negroes must still remain segregated even as the imperatives of segregation diminish in reality. A normal sexual role, for example, continues to be denied to Negroes. Sidney Poitier, in the widely acclaimed *Lilies of the Field,* is as effectively denied a full characterization by the presence of the nuns as co-stars as, say, Lena Horne was in the musicals in which she was consigned to a vaudeville act that bore no relation to the plot line.

In a sense the producers' code makes movies a technological equivalent of folk art. Their dependence on the box office makes them, at the same time, a reflection, a distortion, and an exaggeration of American life. If "Hollywood is the mass unconscious," the theater is the place where wishes are gratified, where (according to Marlon Brando) "people . . . correlate what happens on the screen with their own experience." One of Walker Percy's characters expresses this mythical quality:

> Our neighborhood theater in Gentilly has permanent lettering on the front of the marquee reading: Where Happiness Costs So Little. The fact is I am quite happy in a movie, even a bad movie. Other people, so I have read, treasure memorable moments in their lives. . . . What I remember is the time John Wayne killed three men with a carbine as he was falling to the dusty street in *Stagecoach,* and the time the kitten found Orson Welles in the doorway in *The Third Man.*[9]

It can be seen that although movies are a "symbolic expression of life," they can shape "value patterns" to a degree only and then not in the efficient way assumed by the earlier observers.[10]

Socially conscious Hollywood producers have accepted this view to some extent. Many are self-conscious and guilty about the charge that Hollywood's achievements in race relations over the long run have been anti-Negro from *Birth of a Nation* to *Gone With the Wind.* But it would be difficult to imagine a different condition in view of the social scientists' vision of moviemakers as essentially followers of rather than creators of mores. They would have had to crusade, "which Hollywood seldom does except for the most certain and established causes."[11] What is basically a scientific argument has its layman's equivalent: that is the liberal position that movies should "both symbolize and effectuate a revolution in the imagination and behavior"; as opposed to the conservative notion that because movies are one of the "principal influences of the modern world in the determination of the character of our people and our society" producers have a moral responsibility to seek what is right—a consensus. Thus to the conservative "controversial pleading and the pursuit of theoretical and experimental causes should have no place in the theatrical film."[12]

Censorship has been one of the most persistent influences on the maintenance of stereotypes. Southern censorship has taken the most exaggerated stances. In Atlanta, *Lost Boundaries* and *Imitation of Life* were banned *in toto* as inciting to violence or lawbreaking. Of all the movies in the 1940's about Negroes only Faulkner's *Intruder in the Dust* was uncut. In 1945 *Brewster's Millions* was banned in Memphis because Eddie Anderson stood too close to, and seemed too friendly with, Helen Walker. Even an innocuous film such as *Island in the Sun* was either protested or banned in Memphis, New Orleans, Jacksonville, and Montgomery, because White Citizens Councils and the Ku Klux Klan saw it as "immoral and indecent" because of the implied equality of the characters of Harry Belafonte and Joan Fontaine.[13] Where there is no censorship on racial grounds, producers, sensitive to protest from both Negroes and whites, have reduced Negro roles to ambivalent ciphers. Otto Preminger's *Carmen Jones,* as James Baldwin has pointed out, is not believable precisely because the role of Joe (played by Belafonte) is reduced to a nullity for fear of stereotyping Negro sexuality. Typically, any breaking of the color line, perhaps expressing the unconscious reservations of liberal moviemakers, is met by violence. In Robert Wise's *Odds Against Tomorrow,* Belafonte is burned to death unrecognizably along with racist (played by Robert Ryan) whom he fought, the obvious implication being that to resist segregation is to die. In *Broken Lance,* Spencer Tracy dies pointlessly after his interracial marriage to Katy Jurado.[14]

Tragedy can be barely averted only when non-Negroes are involved, as in *Broken Arrow* (American Indians), *Bhowani Junction* (East Indians), and *Love Is a Many-Splendored Thing* (Chinese); or when Negroes are saved by the sacrifice of a white friend, a kind of symbolic atonement for lynching, as in *Home of the Brave* and *Intruder in the Dust;* or when white actresses play Negro roles, as in, most recently, *Kings Go Forth.*[15]

The story of Negroes in American films since 1945, therefore, is not only the story of the death of Rastus, or Sambo, or Uncle Tom, but the rebirth of a complete man as yet unnamed. The story, so far, has three parts: up to 1954, Negroes as a social problem; through the 1950's, Negroes as emerging characters yet bearing the vestiges of Rastus; and finally from the varied themes of the 1960's, the beginnings of the fully articulated character. The first intimations of the end of the Negro stereotype were seen in the anti-fascist war movies: Dooley Wilson's wise piano player in Warner Brothers' *Casablanca;* Rex Ingram's Senegal soldier in *Sahara;* and Canada Lee in Alfred Hitchcock's *Lifeboat.*[16]

Shortly after the vogue of war movies ended, the cycle of racial message movies began. Stanley Kramer's *Home of the Brave,* adapted from Arthur Laurents' polemic against anti-Semitism, was the first in 1948, followed by Louis de Rochemont's *Lost Boundaries* and Elia Kazan's *Pinky.* By 1952, with Clarence Brown's *Intruder in the Dust* the cycle had spent itself, not so much departing from the old stereotypes but creating a new one: that of Negroes who cannot be fulfilled without the sacrifice of or the support of white men. As a case in point, James Edwards, the Negro in *Home of the Brave,* goes on a mission to a Japanese-held island where his best friend, a white man, is killed. Edwards feels a dual guilt at his friend's death first, because he is glad that he personally survived and second, because he had wished his friend dead after an argument in which he had been called a racial epithet. Falling victim to hysterical paralysis, he is taken to the base psychiatrist who induces Edwards to walk again by hurling the same epithets at him, symbolically implying that Negroes can be fulfilled only on white men's terms. At the end of the film the audience sees a fraternal scene in which Edwards and a one-armed white man depart, suggesting Negro-white equality only as long as the whites are not complete. In *Pinky, Lost Boundaries,* and *Intruder in the Dust* the problems by Negroes are resolved in each case at the pleasure of upper-class white society. So little came from the cycle of problem movies that Negroes nearly disappeared from the screen completely in the early 1950's.[17]

By the mid-1950's the cycle had achieved only a few side effects. The all-Negro exploitation films such as Robert Gordon's *Joe Louis Story* and James Wong Howe's *Go Man Go,* a cheap program movie about the Harlem Globe Trotters, declined in numbers. The South's romantic "lost cause" mystique became tarnished and its decadence in the manner of Tennessee Williams was emphasized in a rash of movies. Indians began to get sympathetic treatment in several Westerns.

After 1954, cinema Negroes became, not a problem for whites to comprehend, but symbolic figures of the struggle against oppression. In the strident *Blackboard Jungle,* only Sidney Poitier is allowed to struggle successfully against the tide of urban poverty. In Darryl Zanuck's movie of Alec Waugh's *Island in the Sun,* it is Harry Belafonte, until then a popular nightclub singer, who plays the dynamic labor leader; and in Robert Wise's tightly directed crime thriller, *Odds Against Tomorrow,* it is again Belafonte who is the criminal at war with both society and his Southern racist accomplice.[18] Only occasionally did the old Negro intrude upon the new Negro tragic hero-as-victim, as in Otto Preminger's gaudy production of *Porgy and Bess* in 1959.

By the 1960's, institutional racial equality had become socially accept-able behavior in many areas of America. One heard occasional liberal voices even from a closed society such as Mississippi.[19] Churches began to break their long silence on the issue of race.[20] Professional associations opened their doors to Negroes. No longer news was the marriage of the famous Negro actor, Sammy Davis, Jr.; nor Lyndon Johnson, late of Texas, dancing at his inauguration with the wives of the various darker-skinned men in attendance. Such rapid change was accepted in varying degrees. The intellectuals and the well-to-do had nothing to fear from it. The middle-class houseowner nervously accepted it in every neighbor-hood but his own. Older people and working-class people tended to not accept it at all. These varying degrees of acceptance of change were reflected in a tripartite cinema of the 1960's. A comparable case can be seen in the film treatment of juvenile behavior in the highly literate *David and Lisa* by Frank and Eleanor Perry; the middle-brow, guilt-evoking *Rebel Without a Cause;* and the sensational exploitation movie, *Untamed Youth;* each one dealing with the same subject, but in three distinct styles. Similarly, as Negroes intrude upon the collective con-sciousness of America they evoke a similar set of divergent images.[21]

At the lowest level of exploitation of racial themes is Stephen Borden's *My Baby is Black,* which depicts a love affair between a Negro medical student in Paris and his white girl friend. The audience is titillated by shots of the two in embrace alternated with scenes of vicious rejection of the Negro by the girl's parents. Another cheap exploitation film of the 1960's was Larry Buchanan's *Free, White, and 21,* in which a Negro, Frederick O'Neal, is accused of rape and acquitted. The film's gimmick is that, near the end, the audience is asked to "vote" as jurors to deter-mine O'Neal's guilt or innocence, after watching a plot that clearly shows him innocent. After he is acquitted, a lie detector test showing the jury wrong is introduced into the film. The prosecutor, playing every string of the lurid rape theme, asks rhetorically whether we do not "love the Negro too much." Both films express clearly the undercurrent of white proletarian reservations toward the assimilation of Negroes into American life.

In the middle-brow movies of the 1960's, many New Negro social roles are depicted, usually no more than one in each film. In Hubert Cornfield's *Pressure Point,* Sidney Poitier plays a prison psychiatrist whose patient is a racial psychotic played by Bobby Darin, who is an anti-Roosevelt, anti-Semitic fascist. Thus the audience is led to accept a Negro as a doctor, if for no other reason than that the psychotic cannot. Another break from the stereotype is even more literally stated in Millard Kaufman's *Convicts Four.* The standard blues-humming Negro convict gives way to a prepossessing, aggressive convict played by Sammy Davis, who upon being assigned a new cellmate, a murderer, announces that he is not to be called "shine," that he is never to be asked to sing or dance, and finally that it is he to whom tribute is owed if the new man wishes to be protected from the hazing by the other inmates. The result is a unilateral white paper announcing that here-after Rastus is dead.

In many movies small chips have been made in the stereotype. In Robert Aldrich's psychological murder mystery, *Whatever Happened to Baby Jane?*, all the whites are afraid, psychotic, or cheap crooks. Only the Negro maid is a balanced human being. She is like an enduring Faulkner Negro moved to a Northern city. In John Frankenheimer's *Manchurian Candidate*, dignified middle-class Negroes appear as win-dow dressing. Warner Brothers announced that forty Negro extras ap-pear in their comedy, *Kisses for My President*. In Gordon Douglas' *Rio Conchos*, Jim Brown plays a courageous Negro soldier immediately after the Civil War. The only racial stereotype is a lazy, serio-comic Mexican played by Tony Franciosa. All of the Southerners in the film are outlaws whose commander is insane and lives in a mock-up facade of a Southern mansion which symbolically burns to the ground in the last scene in the picture.

Occasionally the old stereotypes recur. In John Ford's *Man Who Shot Liberty Valance*, Woody Strode plays an Uncle Tom who shuffled off camera after being hit with a bucket of whitewash. In three Frank Sinatra comedies, Sammy Davis has played comic Negro Sambo types, especially in John Sturges' *Sergeants Three*, in which he plays Kipling's Gunga Din renamed Jonah and moved to the American frontier.

It is in the so-called art movie, independently produced on a low budget for limited distribution in small urban theaters, where one finds the most sensitive view of Negroes in American life. Artistically, this kind of film attempts to deal with reality seriously, with little conces-sion being made to market conditions, profits, or mass taste. The first limited success of this genre was John Cassavetes' *Shadows* (1960). Using unknown actors, Ben Maddow's script attempted to show the world of Negroes as closed and esoteric by juxtaposing it with the world of whites through the medium of the anxieties of a young girl who has been passing. On the surface, it would seem that Lela Goldoni's role is simply a repeat of many other white actresses who have played Negroes, including Jeanne Crain's *Pinky*, Flora Robson in *Saratoga Trunk*, and Yvonne de Carlo in *Band of Angels*. There is not the cheap sexually charged situation of the earlier films, but only the contrast of two worlds and the need, in American society, to choose one or the other. Similar to *Shadows* was Shirley Clarke's *Cool World* which also used unknown or amateur actors and which was shot on location in Harlem from var-ious concealed angles. The result is a fast-paced film about the habitués of the cool world of small time gangsters, junkies, and prostitutes. The movie is not a racial message or a plea to white America to send aid, but a story that uses a real part of Negro America without apology. There are sensual scenes, shots of narcotics addiction, drinking, wrecked and poor families, but the film does not piously say "look at the way these Negroes behave." It is a film about poor people who live in a city. The failure of the film, if it has one, is that few people saw it, even though in the Negro neighborhoods it was retitled *Cool World in Harlem* and luridly advertised.

The best evidence of the death of Rastus is Michael Roehmer's 1965 production, *Nothing But a Man,* the story of a marriage of a Negro railroad worker played by Ivan Dixon and a Negro school teacher played by Abbey Lincoln. They live in a small Southern town which is seen as a physical, unnamed presence pressing upon them in dozens of small ways. The pressures seem about to destroy the marriage as they destroyed the life of the railroad worker's father. The theme is not what are Negroes like, which would be a return to the stereotype, but rather, how do people behave under strain; how they survive; how do they live as persons when the society sees them as types.

Social change has thus compelled a comparable change in some artfully made movies about Negroes; while a few other movies still deal in the old sensationalism of the contradictory stereotypes of comedy, sexuality, brutality, and laziness. Neither is the norm for American moviegoing behavior. In most middle-brow films of the 1960's, Negro characters had changed into perfectly abstinent, courageous paragons of virtue as stifling and destructive of mature characterization as the old Rastus stereotype. This new unreality is evident in the absence of adult sexual behavior in the films of Sidney Poitier. In *Blackboard Jungle* women characters were carefully segregated from Poitier; in *The Defiant Ones* he is chained to a male character and confronts no women; in *Raisin in the Sun,* he is married, but residing in his mother's crowded apartment; in *Lilies of the Field* his co-stars are a gaggle of nuns; in *The Long Ships,* he is an African prince who, despite his large harem, has taken an oath of chastity. One can still wonder when a commercial film will put all the parts of *the* Negro together into a whole man.

NOTES

1. Paul G. Cressey, "The Motion Picture Experience as Modified by Social Background and Personality," *American Sociological Review,* III, 4 (August, 1938), 516–25. For brief comments by earlier observers, see Thomas R. Cripps, "The Negro Reaction to the Motion Picture 'Birth of a Nation,' " *Historian,* XXV, 3 (May, 1963), 344–62.
2. For various shades of opinion on the effects of motion picture viewing, see Hortense Powdermaker, "An Anthropologist Looks at the Movies," 80–87; Norman Woelfel, "The American Mind and the Motion Picture," 88–94; Allan A. Hunter, "A Clergyman Looks at the Movies," 95–97; Leo C. Rosten, "Movies and Propaganda," 116–24, all in *Annals of the American Academy of Political*

and Social Science, CCLIV (November, 1947). For estimates of value transmission to various audiences, see Mildred J. Wiese and Stewart G. Cole, "A Study of Children's Attitudes and the Influence of a Commercial Motion Picture," *Journal of Psychology,* XXI (January, 1946), 151–71 (in which the authors found that a movie gave support to "their uncritical conception of an idealized America," 170); Siegfried Kracauer, "Those Movies with a Message," *Harper's,* CXCVI, 1777 (June, 1948), 567–72, who warns that message movies may show the fragility of that which they wish to promote. See also Frederick Elkin, "Value Implications or Popular Films," *Sociology and Social Research,* VIII, 5 (May–June, 1954), 320–22, who more recently and scientifically argues that even an Abbott and Costello comedy may have an unconscious "social function" of suggesting values, though less obviously with a problem or message film.

3. Franklin Fearing, "Influence of the Movies on Attitudes and Behavior," *Annals of the American Academy of Political and Social Science,* CCLIV (November, 1947), 70–79.

4. Russell Middleton, "Ethnic Prejudice and Susceptibility to Persuasion," *American Sociological Review,* XXV, 5 (October, 1960), 679–86. For arguments for the persuasiveness of propaganda films, see, among others, Albert L. Goldberg, "The Effects of Two Types of Sound Motion Pictures on the Attitudes of Adults Toward Minorities," *Journal of Educational Psychology,* XXXIX (May, 1956), 386–91; L. E. Raths and F. N. Trager, "Public Opinions and 'Crossfire,'" *Journal of Educational Sociology,* XXI (February, 1948), 345–63; Irwin C. Rosen, "The Effects of the Motion Picture 'Gentleman's Agreement' on Attitudes toward Jews," *Journal of Psychology,* XXVI (October, 1948), 525–36; and C. I. Hovland *et al, Experiments on Mass Communication* (Princeton, 1961). For statements critical of the efficacy of film propaganda, see, among others, Eunice Cooper and Helen Dinerman, "Analysis of the Film 'Don't Be a Sucker'; A Study in Communication," *Public Opinion Quarterly,* XV (Summer, 1951), 243–64; Eunice Cooper and Marie Jahoda, "The Evasion of Propaganda: How Prejudiced People Respond to Anti-Prejudice Propaganda," *Journal of Psychology,* XXIII (January, 1947), 15–25; S. H. Flowerman, "Mass Propaganda in the War against Bigotry," *Journal of Abnormal and Social Psychology,* XLII (October, 1947), 429–39; Herbert Hyman and Paul B. Sheatsley, "Some Reasons Why Information Campaigns Fail," *Public Opinion Quarterly,* XI (Fall, 1947), 413–23; J. E. Hulet, Jr., "Estimating the Net Effect of a Commercial Motion Picture upon the Trend of Local Public Opinion," *American Sociological Review,* XIV (April, 1949), 263–75; Hans Zeisel, "A Note on the Effect of a Motion Picture on Public Opinion," *American Sociological Review,* XIV (August, 1949), 550–51 (cited in Middleton). For the reaction to "Blackboard Jungle," see Joseph Axelrod, "German and Austrian Reaction to the 'Blackboard Jungle,'" *School and Society,* LXXXV, 2105 (February 16, 1957), 57–59.

5. Robert Hatch, "Movies: Good Intention," *New Republic* (May 16, 1949), 22–23; Hulet, *op. cit.,* 263–75; Siegfried Kracauer, "National Types as Hollywood Presents Them," *Public Opinion Quarterly,* XIII, 1 (Spring, 1949), 53–72.

6. Margaret Farrant Thorp, *America at the Movies* (New Haven, 1939), 130; for other popular criticisms of unintentional stereotyping in message movies, see Kracauer, *op. cit.,* 567; Dore Schary, "Our Movie Mythology," *Reporter,* XXII, 5 (March 3, 1960), 39–42; Hollis Alpert, "D for Effort," *Saturday Review,* XLII (October 3, 1959), 29.

7. Sterling A. Brown, "Negro Characters as Seen by White Authors," *Journal of Negro Education,* II, 2 (April, 1933), 179–203. For the most recent studies of censorship and its effects, see Murray Schumach, *The Face on the Cutting Room Floor* (New York, 1964), pp. 279 ff, Appendix III.

8. See Cripps, *op. cit.,* for an earlier example of the striking of the bargain. For a copy of the Hollywood motion picture producers' code, see Schumach, *op. cit.,* Appendices. For a recognition of the compromise in advice given to young screenplay writers, see Walter B. Pitkin and William M. Marston, *The Art of Sound Motion Pictures* (New York, 1930), pp. 25, 62, one of several "how-to" books in which the authors advise young writers to "study closely the vogue in

pictures" in order to determine what sells. A handy chart delineating the various racial taboos is appended.

9. For development of the concept of the mass unconscious, see Siegfried Kracauer, *From Caligari to Hitler* (Princeton, 1947); the cinema criticism of Parker Tyler, especially *Hollywood Hallucination* (New York, 1944), pp. 231–238, 244; for the Brando comment, see Richard Dyer McCann, *Hollywood in Transition* (Boston, 1962), p. 187; for less technical comments, see Jean Benoit-Levy, *The Art of the Motion Picture* (New York, 1946), pp. 196–201, 217–18; Robert Hughes, *Film: Book I* (New York, 1959), pp. 3–24, 35–60; Gilbert Seldes, *The Public Arts* (New York, 1956), pp. 191, 210, 298; Henry James Forman, *Our Movie Mad Children* (New York, 1935), *passim;* Walter Percy, *The Moviegoer* (New York, 1962), pp. 12–13.

10. For fairly recent statements of the efficacy of film propaganda, see J. P. Mayer, *Sociology of the Film* (London, 1946), pp. 167–68, 49, 17–18, 25; Martha Wolfenstein and Nathan Leites, *Movies: A Psychological Study* (Glencoe, Illinois, 1950), p. 307.

11. Dore Schary, "Censorship and Stereotypes," *Saturday Review of Literature,* XXXII, 18 (April 30, 1949), 9–10; Louis Kronenberger and John T. McManus, "Motion Pictures, the Theater, and Race Relations," *Annals of the American Academy of Political and Social Science,* CCXLIV (March, 1946), 152–58.

12. Martin S. Dworkin, "The New Negro on the Screen," *Progressive,* XXIV, 11–12 (November-December, 1960), 33–36; Martin Quigley, "Importance of the Entertainment Film," *Annals of the American Academy . . . ,* CCLIV (November, 1947), 65–69.

13. Gerald Weales, "Pro-Negro Films in Atlanta," *Phylon,* XIII, 4 (Winter, 1952), 298–304 (reprinted from *Films in Review,* November, 1952); Philip T. Hartung, "Trillions for Brewster," *Commonweal,* XLII, 4 (May 11, 1945), 94–95; *New York Times,* July 4, 18; August 17, 1957; November 25, 1949.

14. James Baldwin, "Life Straight in de Eye," *Commentary,* XIX, 1 (January, 1955), 74–79; Martin S. Dworkin, "The New Negro on the Screen," *Progressive,* XXV, 1 (January, 1961), 38.

15. Henry Popkin, "Hollywood Tackles the Race Issue," *Commentary,* XXIV, 10 (October, 1957), 354–57; Martha Wolfenstein and Nathan Leites, "Two Social Scientists View 'No Way Out,'" *Commentary,* X, 4 (October, 1950), 388–91; Albert Johnson, "Beige, Brown, or Black," *Film Quarterly,* XIII, 1 (Fall, 1959), 38–43.

16. Dorothy B. Jones, "Tomorrow the Movies: IV. Is Hollywood Growing Up?" *New Republic,* CLX, 5 (February 3, 1945), 123–25; Dworkin, *Progressive,* XXIV, 10, 39–41.

17. See Dworkin, *ibid.* Except for this series of articles there is no treatment of Negroes in films after 1948. For an inadequate survey of the years before 1948, see Noble, *The Negro in Films* (London: Skelton Robinson [1948?]); for rather doctrinaire-Marxist comment on history and propaganda, see V. J. Jerome, *The Negro in Hollywood Films* (New York, 3rd printing, 1952); John Howard Lawson, *Film in the Battle of Ideas* (New York, 1953); and Gordon Kahn, *Hollywood on Trial: The Story of the 10 Who Were Indicted* (New York, 1948).

18. Dworkin, *Progressive,* 36–38.

19. For a recent example of liberal Southern comment, see James W. Silver, *Mississippi: the Closed Society* (New York, 1964).

20. For a criticism of the silence of the churches on social issues, see Peter Berger, *The Noise of Solemn Assemblies* (Garden City, 1961).

21. In dealing with the films of the 1960's, I have not supplied complete information about producers, releasing companies, and directors because they would be of little bibliographic value. Typically, in periodical indexes, films are listed by title, then journal in which a review or article appeared. Those few libraries which keep active files of film reviews also catalogue by title, as do the various Library of Congress film copyright volumes.

Character People: Faces from the Past

Arthur F. McClure and Alfred E. Twomey

The character actor is one of the most important and yet most elusive figures in American motion picture history. The following essay attempts to provide information on his contribution to American movies. *

"The real acting parts go to the character actors"

One of the most important aspects of the history of the American motion picture has been the contribution of the character actor. Not only has he had a great influence on the enjoyment provided by movies during the quarter century following 1930, but he also offered the student of American culture a unique picture. The movie fan came to be something of an authority on American character by seeing its facets isolated and embodied in character actors. Moviegoers could judge this character and weigh opinions in the light of their individual personal experience.

The actors creating these roles performed many of the same functions as stock characters in other art forms. The stock characters in any theatrical form generally remained constant. Movie character actors provided regularity and continuity to the films for audiences. It was not difficult for audiences to accept particular actors that played the stock characters with whom they had become most familiar, whether it was the banker, the drunkard or the cracker-barrel philosopher.

The movie character actor is someone who appears in a *kind* of role so frequently that his mere appearance practically creates the role itself. When a character's face is seen on a screen, it is possible to know the part he is playing. In many instances a star can be replaced by another

* By permission from Mr. Harry Smith, Arthur F. McClure and Alfred E. Twomey, "Character People: Faces from the Past," *Per/Se*, Vol. 3, No. 2, Summer 1968, pp. 34–39, Stanford, California. © 1968.

star, but the character actor was sometimes not interchangeable with any other character type.

It can be said that if plot is *what* happens in a movie, then character is *why* it happens. Plot gives movies their immediate sense of excitement, but movies are remembered for their characters. Movies derive a great deal of their intensity from the plot, but it is through the creation of character, the evocation of the various nuances of personality, that skillful actors win their audiences.

American movies made during the 1930–1955 period have often been criticized for their lack of experimentation. Many of these movie stories, however, if examined closely were distinctly different in style and in the approach to character and plot. One of the ways that moviemakers deviated from a standard plot formula was by outstanding acting. The action of hundreds of movies frequently gave way to character portrayal. The emotions and thoughts of these characters were often cunningly portrayed by "character people," who as specialists projected moods that had the texture of living experience. These actors, with all of their professionalism, helped to produce memorable glimpses of our life and culture.

As the United States plunged into the depression, political, economic and social problems were reflected in the movies; in the 1930's and after, the talking film became the vehicle that could provide audiences revenge, adjustment, repair of self-esteem, reconciliation, and acceptance. Audiences as never before found themselves deeply moved by the movies with an intensity that was difficult to measure. The trials of everyday living could be at least temporarily put aside in a darkened theater by identifying with the actors in the movies.

In addition to the social life, movies, and the characters in them, reflected in some way the unconscious conflicts of every individual in the audience. If a character behaved toward others in a way that the audience disapproved of, the viewer's identification with the actor was often rejected. But although the villainous character might be rejected, he was not *forgotten*.

The expectation of seeing the familiar faces of character actors was an important part of movie going for many years. Although each character actor may have played only one role, there were so many roles that there seemed to be an unlimited supply of parts for them to play.

Nearly every Hollywood studio in the 1930's and 1940's had its own group of character actors under contract, and they were used frequently and with great versatility throughout the company's products. The character actors were often listed as "featured players," in contrast to the stars whose names were listed above a film's title. The studios always made an effort to cast a "type" in various featured parts, thus making it necessary to define just what was the "featured" player. These characters were often more than supporting players. Frequently they were as important to the story as the stars, but their names were listed below the title rather than above. Many of them became entrenched in one type of role and repeated the same kind of portrayal over and over. But many character actors spanned a wide range of emotions with the versatility of their performances. These actors brought life to a given scene. Although many of the character roles had little to do with the plot, their technical important in terms of acting was considerable. The character actors were specialists in every sense of the word.

They also had the advantage of the opportunity to act much more often with the freedom to accept many roles. In addition, they could act in a flop and recover quickly to obtain a role in a film classic. A star's position was different because of the truism that he was only as good as his last movie! Dana Andrews was once quoted as saying that "The real acting parts go to the character actors."

In looking back at some of the great motion pictures produced during the period, particular roles by character actors stand out immediately. "Sergeant York," for all its gripping story and Academy Award winning performance by Gary Cooper, would have proved a lot less potent without a character actress of Margaret Wycherly's ability in the role of the mother. It was her deeply lined delineation that seemed to make the whole story right. The same sort of situation occurred in "Grapes of Wrath," in which Henry Fonda starred and gave an excellent performance. But where would that story have been without Jane Darwell as Ma Joad?

Although the actors' names may be forgotten—if ever really noted—moviegoers fondly remember their faces and the types that they played in picture after picture. How often has Ray Teal been seen as the local troublemaker in Western towns or Phillip Ober and Henry O'Neill as the executive types? Stanley Clements and William Benedict were called on dozens of times to play either bellhops, jockeys, or punks. Dick Foran or Jack Haley were often seen as singing cops, while Joseph Crehan and Edward Gargan were the non-singing desk sergeants. Noah Beery, Jr. and Henry Carey, Jr. were nearly always cast as the shy likeable friend of the hero in westerns. English character actors who usually gave a picture elegance, dignity, and aristocratic snobbishness included Alan Mowbray, C. Aubrey Smith, Reginald Gardner, and Reginald Denny. Hattie McDaniel, Louise Beavers, and Butterfly McQueen were usually seen on the domestic staff of wealthy families as philosophical servants, and Montan Moreland or Willie Best were comic chauffeurs and houseboys.

During the 1930's and 1940's every good movie, and most of the bad ones, had several vivid portrayals by character actors that literally *supported* the entire production. The young stars were backed up by these

very proficient actors who could make the stars and the pictures themselves highly successful. In recent years, when motion pictures have
aimed much of their appeal toward younger audiences, there has been
a gradual but steady disappearance of many good, competent character
actors. Many of the familiar actors are dead, while others, aging, are in
a state of retirement or semi-retirement. Many have moved on into
other fields of employment. Motion pictures have therefore suffered
greatly in a generation filled with conformity and sadly lacking in the
picturesque individuality that was often supplied by a favorite character actor.

Alan Napier has been a familiar face to movie fans for nearly thirty
years, and he has recently achieved fame as Alfred the butler on TV's
"Batman."

His career parallels that of most character actors and actresses and
demonstrates the pattern of transition they made from one entertainment medium to another. The usual route followed began with the
legitimate theatre, followed by the motion picture and ending with
television.

Napier was born in Birmingham, England, and was the first member
of his family to go into the theater. He was educated at Clifton College
and trained for the theater at the Royal Academy of Dramatic Art in
London. His first engagement was with the famous Oxford Players
which also gave a start to other unknowns at the time: John Gielgud,
Flora Robson, Margaret Webster, Robert Morley, and Tyrone Guthrie.
Napier graduated to the "West End" and the Old Vic in 1929, where
for ten years he played featured roles with all the great stars of the
time. He was brought to New York in 1940 to play opposite Gladys
George in "Lady in Waiting" by Brock Pemberton. He first went to
Hollywood in 1941, although he had previously made some pictures
in England.

With the advent of television and the increased demand for character
actors by that medium, he began to make numerous appearances on
various TV shows and eventually the Batman series, his acting career
now being divided between motion pictures and television.

Napier recently imparted some telling observations on the plight of
the current quality and quantity of character actors in the American film.

The source who told you that things aren't what they used to be
is right—the pool is depleted. And for a very good, typical American
reason. There is a parallel in agriculture—the exploitation of virgin
lands with no thought of replenishment. Hollywood dug deeply into
the great pool of theatre-trained character actors: they are dying off
and nothing is being done by Hollywood to replace them by training
the young talent coming up. Aging leading men sometimes make

good character actors, but not always, nor do they cover a wide field. Good character actors—little men, fat men, ugly men, come out of stock companies where the exigencies of putting on a new play every week or fortnight with a company of only 10 or 12 souls makes roles for which they are not obvious types. From this necessity you get acting . . . in place of the comparatively sterile practice of behaviorism.

It has been asserted on frequent occasions that the reason for the tremendous success of foreign films at the box office in recent years is the concerted effort of foreign film producers to "people their films." A splendid current example of this effort in Europe is the English movie "The Wrong Box" in which every performance is a character performance. Napier correctly maintains that the story "is a wild farce, yet every character is fantastically believable, down to the bit players."

It has been established that there is a correlation between the time when American film studios dropped their large lists of contract players in the 1950's and the dullness of American movies. A few American moviemakers, however, still stubbornly make valuable use of some of the great character actors that are still available. John Ford, Frank Capra, Jerry Lewis, and Walt Disney supplement their movie casts with some of the familiar faces of the 1930's and 1940's, and generally with great success resulting at the box office.

There is a tragic element in the loss of so many of these faces that were familiar to a generation of moviegoers. Harry Antrim, William Newell, Verna Felton, George E. Stone, Nestor Paiva, Sig Rumann, Mischa Auer and Jane Darwell all died during the past year. As these people drift away, unrecognized, from the movie industry either by entering other vocational fields or by dying off, a great part of the history of the American motion picture fades away and will never be able to be reconstructed adequately.

Ironically, it is television, with its insatiable appetite for movies on the "Later than Late Shows," that has created a whole new generation of movie experts. Regular viewers of these shows, young and old alike, are able to recall with great affection these players who help to strike a familiar chord, or oftentimes mirror a nostalgic facet of their own lives. In this way, their performances will always have a value. And their place will be assured in the history of the American film.

The Outlaws

Steven Farber

In the following essay Steven Farber, Los Angeles editor of Film Quarterly, *discusses the "artful use of violence" in films.**

In the early sixties the heroes of many of the most interesting or most successful American movies—*Psycho, Lolita, The Manchurian Candidate, Whatever Happened to Baby Jane?, The Haunting, Lilith*—were insane. The criminal heroes of the key new movies—*The Dirty Dozen, Bonnie and Clyde, The Flim Flam Man, Point Blank, Cool Hand Luke, The Incident, In Cold Blood*—are often close to insane too, but the emphasis has changed. Humbert Humbert and Clyde Barrow are both neurotic killers, but Humbert was a killer only incidentally, while Clyde Barrow is primarily a bank robber and killer, only incidentally neurotic. The madman and the criminal, of course, share the world beyond the fringe of normal society; they are the two most radical outcasts from respectability. But if the aim of both sets of films is to challenge socially accepted distinctions of sanity or morality and to locate value in the outsider, the new movies have a greater aggressiveness and determination in their challenge of the ordinary. Criminals to some extent *consciously* reject the ordinary by attacking it. Perry Smith in *In Cold Blood* knows that he is a psychopath.

Cool Hand Luke is probably the first important chain gang movie since Mervyn LeRoy's *I Am a Fugitive from a Chain Gang*, made during the Thirties, when a chain gang movie seemed an appropriate genre for social protest. And it was in the Thirties, too, that the criminals were last heroes of a major series of American films, the Cagney-Robinson-Raft gangster movies. Probably no one needs to be persuaded that there was a relationship between the social despair of the Depression

---

* By permission from Penelope Houston, editor, *Sight and Sound*. *Sight and Sound*, Autumn 1968, London. © 1968 by the British Film Institute.

and the movies' celebration of the gangster-killer. Neither, I imagine, does anyone need to be persuaded that the mood in America during the last couple of years has turned less hopeful, and the protests more violent, than at any time since the Thirties. (I understand there are even polls that 'prove' this.) So it seems fitting that the most controversial of the new outlaw films, *Bonnie and Clyde,* is set in the Thirties, in a Depression landscape.

Before looking more closely at the criminal heroes of a few of these movies, I'd like to consider the attitude toward authority that runs through all the new films. There's a chilling moment at the end of Larry Peerce's *The Incident* which curtly summarises this attitude. The film concerns a couple of hoods who terrorise the passengers in a subway car on a late night ride into New York City. One of the passengers has finally beaten the two of them down, and as the train pulls into Grand Central, another passenger calls out for help. Two policemen rush into the car, and without even hesitating, throw the one Negro passenger (who is well-dressed) up against the wall and frisk him brutally. This happens in an instant, and in the background, at one corner of the screen; what makes the audience gasp (and also laugh rather bitterly) is the casualness of the moment. The director simply *assumes* that police are ignorant and brutal—and is sure that we assume so too—and doesn't feel he has to belabour the point.

Police are unsympathetic in most of these movies. *Bonnie and Clyde* and *The Flim Flam Man* both stress the stupidity and vanity of police officers; the films even contain intriguingly similar scenes of policemen preening for photographers on the scene of the crime. In *The Flim Flam Man* the chief of police is morbid as well as self-indulgent—in one of the film's wittiest, sourest scenes he slavers excitedly as the confidence man's young accomplice tells him some phoney stories of their grisly murder of helpless old ladies. At the end of *Bonnie and Clyde* the police sneakily, viciously murder the buoyant young criminals: the slow motion death sequence, which everyone has praised, painfully intensifies our feelings of revulsion and hatred for the executioners.

Cool Hand Luke is notable for its total, unrelieved hostility toward the prison warden and guards. The movie has been compared more than once to *From Here to Eternity,* another study of an uneducated non-conformist in a repressive environment. But the differences are more striking than the similarities. *From Here to Eternity,* despite its sympathy for the loner within the army, is hardly uncharitable in its treatment of military authority as a whole. When the generals learn of the way in which Prewitt has been abused by his commanding officer, they immediately discharge the tyrant. The message seems to be that although there may be nasty individuals in the army, the establishment itself is benevolent: kindly, humane generals will uncover the culprits and clean things up for the good soldiers.

Cool Hand Luke shows none of this piety. The system in the prison camp is hopelessly perverted—when Luke most needs compassion, after his mother dies, the guards lock him for days in a grim, wooden outhouse to make sure he won't try to escape for her funeral. One guard, called The Man with No Eyes because he never removes his sunglasses, works in the film as an almost archetypal, effectively sinister emblem of totally unfeeling police brutality; and the moments when, without speaking, he lifts his rifle to shoot a bird or a snake or a turtle, are terse visual confirmation of his cruelty. Even the one guard who seems at first to be more sympathetic reveals his stupidity when he turns coldly against Luke after learning that he doesn't believe in God. And there is no higher authority to whom the prisoners can appeal.

The comparisons of *Cool Hand Luke* to *From Here to Eternity* have a certain subliminal validity, because the prison in *Cool Hand Luke* looks so much like an army barracks; the sterility of the camp routines and the desperate, parasitic camaraderie of the prisoners seem pretty clear allusions to the suffocation of military life. And none of the 'prisoners' seems to have committed a very serious crime. A minor moment in *In Cold Blood*—Dick shrewdly impresses a smarmy sales clerk by lying that Perry's motorcycle accident wounds won him a bronze star in Korea—represents the casual irreverence toward army and patriotism that would not have been tolerated in an American film several years ago. The army, though in the form of a nineteenth-century cavalry, is openly and mercilessly mocked throughout *Waterhole 3*. And in *The Dirty Dozen*, admittedly a badly confused movie, Lee Marvin says that the general who planned the mission he is to head 'must be a raving lunatic.' Except for Marvin, the army officers in the film are all presented as ruthless or incompetent.

But the anti-social bias of these films is even more conclusive than this antagonism toward authority. All of the films express disillusionment with the normal life choices and life styles of American society. They do this, first, by asking us to observe how little difference there is between the criminals and the respectable. The flim flam man has long ago observed that all people are petty and greedy and dishonest—the respectable folk we see are hysterically protective of their cars, anxious to cheat whenever they can—and he proceeds to teach the lesson to the young army deserter who temporarily joins up with him. The subway passengers in *The Incident* are, with a couple of exceptions, concerned about nothing besides money, status, securing or maintaining well-regarded careers. We feel they almost deserve to be tormented by the two hoods whose brutality and selfishness caricature the meanness of their own lives. All of the characters in *Waterhole 3*, sheriff, thieves, innocent shoemaker alike, hunger after gold. And the robber-killer is the most sympathetic character in the film because, like the flim flam man, he's perfectly honest about his criminal desires instead of hiding them behind a badge or a uniform. One of the reasons for the resurgence of the criminal hero is this observation that in a world totally depraved anyway, only the criminal's frankness and vitality retain appeal and value.

This is nowhere clearer than in John Boorman's *Point Blank,* which celebrates its criminal hero as the only live wire in an inert mechanical universe. The American reviews have given the film short shrift, admitting its visual authority but complaining of its banality and violence. Probably even now most people don't know that *Point Blank,* though uneven, unclear in intention, sometimes superficial and lurid, is also, at moments, the most imaginative, startling, *exciting* American film of the year—perhaps of the last few years. The basic story—a man agrees to help a friend in a robbery, then is shot and left for dead by the friend and his own wife, and, after recuperation, sets out to kill the friend and recover his share of the loot—would look creaky on television. But it has been dressed up in considerable cinematic elegance, and the plot line has also been intriguingly blurred, so that we're deliberately confused about some of the key episodes. The robbery, for example, takes place during some mysterious exchange of funds (never explained) on a deserted Alcatraz. And the man needs the money to pay his debts to an undefined Organisation (like the criminal organisation in Arthur Penn's *Mickey One*), some sort of crime syndicate obviously, though what they're involved in exactly, or what kind of front they're using remains cryptic. To somebody who doesn't respond to *Point Blank* this obscurity will seem only maddeningly pretentious, but I think Boorman and his writer Alexander Jacobs were trying to work some interesting variations on straightforward gangster material.

For instance, none of the hostile reviews has paid much attention to the strange, apparently incongruous touches with which *Point Blank* is filled. Just as we've accepted the film as a typical, if visually alluring and confusing revenge-and-sadism story, there's a scene that jars us by asking for rather different responses. The hero, Walker, is trying to find Mal, his betrayer, and has been led to a car lot whose owner may have a lead for him. And the film suddenly turns bizarrely comic. The car lot is plastered with freakish, ridiculously oversized billboards; as Walker approaches, we overhear the conversation of an unctuous salesman and a platinum blonde customer. (He: "I know the poodle's name is Lola, but what's your name?" She: "I *love* to go to the beach.") At that moment Big John, the owner, sidles up to the girl and flirts a little before coming over to Walker and beginning his best factory-

polished hardsell. Walker is pretending to be a prospective buyer, and
they get into a new convertible for a spin. Big John wants to listen to
his own commercial on the radio, but Walker wants information, and
to get it, he keeps smashing the car against the poles beneath the Los
Angeles freeway, remaining utterly cool himself (Lee Marvin's casual
brutality can be 'done' for comic or shock effect—here it's quite amusing), until he has frightened Big John into talking. Finally satisfied,
he leaves Big John bloody and panting in the wreck as his oily commercial twirps from the radio, the only part of the car that is still
working. It's a very funny sequence, from the first shot of the car lot,
but people seem to be bewildered until the last few moments, when
they can't help laughing openly. We aren't used to seeing satire and
brutality linked so outrageously in a movie (though they *were* linked
in *The Manchurian Candidate*).

The movie as a whole provides brilliant juxtapositions of the vapid
surfaces of our computerised world with outbursts of savage violence
and weird hints of omnipresent evil. Some examples: Mal walks into a
large, antiseptic office and stops to talk to a secretary, who has type-
writer, dictaphone, all the standard apparatus in front of her. Behind
her several women are chatting amiably by the coffee machine. Mal is
ushered into an inner office, but there the routine is jolted—he's searched
for a gun. Yet, in the background, our eye catches on the wall several
little coloured slides of an industrial product; the contrast between the
slickly mechanical and the potentially violent is arresting. Later in the
film, Walker is to pick up his money at a storm drain near one of the
freeways. He suspects a trap and forces one of the Organisation chair-
men to walk out for the money, where he is immediately killed by
a marksman concealed far away. The setting is a vast, interminable
terrain of concrete hills and bridges, a stream of water running through
the centre; through Boorman's camera it's a conclusive, powerful image
of the gleaming sterility and senselessness of the city. Everything's been
so neatly manufactured—everything is so *clean*—that it seems the last
place likely to be disturbed by violence; yet when two men are murdered
there, we feel it's somehow apt. The place has no conceivable purpose
but death. At the end of the sequence there's a superb black comic
moment. Walker goes out to retrieve the package of money, but on
breaking it open finds, as he expected, only paper. Desperately, he
takes a billfold from the dead chairman's pocket, but there are only
credit cards inside, and he leaves the string of them spread out over the
man's body, a grisly, funny summary of his corporation life.

Point Blank's juxtaposition of violence and satiric detail—its insistence that we laugh and shudder *simultaneously*—is not really such
a strange way of looking at our cities. We're all aware of the astonishing
contrasts—plush luxury apartments, shiny modern office buildings and

car lots, and frightening, reckless violence and corruption—presented by the film. And I suppose the film could be interpreted literally; one might say that it verifies our suspicion that the most successful business-men are often, in secret, quite ruthless and vicious, and that respectable industries sometimes cover for Mafia-like operations. But *Point Blank* is not a realistic social document; it's a fascinating film because it confirms some of our deepest, least articulate intuitions in the language of a witty, sadistic, hallucinatory pop painting—Dick Tracy in Eliot's Unreal City. (Boorman is British, and perhaps it takes an outsider to see the American city so freshly; the movie's treatment of Los Angeles is certainly the most interesting visual description of that city anyone has provided.)

As Walker lies half dead in a cell on a dark, uninhabited Alcatraz at the very beginning, he wonders if his betrayal has been a dream, and the movie as a whole is a kind of anguished dream of a man who's woken up one morning in a familiar city that somehow, for the first time, looks alien and threatening. An unending airport corridor, a discotheque of psychedelic montages and music that sounds like shrieks (so much so that when a girl discovers some beaten bodies and really does scream, no one notices her), a push-button office that contains almost nothing but aluminium window blinds, a modern ranch house filled with electrical appliances gone suddenly berserk—these are striking images of the commonest sights in our world twisted just slightly, so that they look oppressive. Everything we see in the film is either a gigantic tomb or a frenzied, mechanical dance of death. Only in the past, summarised for us in one lovely, indelible flashback of Walker and his wife walking and laughing in a misty rain, did Walker's life look any different; but now that seems as if it happened on another planet, in another existence.

Point Blank isn't a psychologically realistic film—there aren't clear or understandable motivations for anything—but that doesn't make it an empty film. The film is expressionistic, a portrait of a nightmare landscape that explains nothing literal about the complexity of people's inner lives, and a great deal, perhaps, about the perceptions that can drive a person mad—the devastating impact of really *seeing*. Because this is an American film, and because it's a variation on a gangster film, people aren't willing to think about it as they think about a movie like *Blow-Up*, which seems to me quite comparable—just as empty as a psychological study, understandable and satisfying only as an attempt to stylise and visualise the chaos of our times. *Blow-Up* shows us things that we already understand: the crazed rock and roll concert, the un-communicative pot party, the degenerate photographer's studio. We know how we're supposed to evaluate these things, and Antonioni hasn't done much to complicate the standard cultural weariness response.

But we haven't seen the bizarre juxtapositions of plastic and brutality that make *Point Blank* at times an electrifying, new experience. *Blow-Up* confirms what we already know, *Point Blank* changes us a little.

A few words about Boorman's artful use of violence. The violence all through the film is extremely sensuous. And I'm not talking just about the actual shootings and beatings (of which there are less in the movie than you'd think). What's persistently brutal about the film is the fierceness of Lee Marvin's every twitch, the passionate movement of his body when he fires the gun, even when he's firing at an empty bed or a telephone. The violence is overtly sexual at a couple of points —once when Walker rubs up against the Organisation's secretary, seeming to kiss her, but actually pressing a gun against her; again, in a curious homosexual touch, Walker pulls Mal, completely naked, out of bed, lunging on top of him in a kind of violent embrace, while Mal pleads seductively, "Kill me, kill me." The film is even violent in its editing: the establishing shots that we've come to expect in Hollywood movies are almost all omitted, and we're constantly being thrust into a scene before we have our bearings, forced to catch up with what's going on. The very rhythm of the film is that of an assault. Violence is presented so luxuriously because it's the only stance that has any meaning in Walker's world. At least violence, as Walker practises it, is alive and personal—even when he's threatening to kill someone, he wants to be close to him, unlike the Organisation marksmen who shoot men they can barely see. The Organisation men hide their violence and greed beneath the protective cover of business conferences and office memoranda, but Walker, essentially a 1930 gangster lost in a 1960 setting, insists on bringing his violence out into the open; he doesn't stifle his animal vitality in Ivy League courtesies that mean to turn even crime into a 9 to 5 routine. For him, at least, violence remains animated.

Liberals don't want to admit that violence can *ever* have value, but one reason these movies are exciting is that they disturb us, by undercutting those liberal pieties. In three of the new movies the best scenes are outrageous, full-scale, almost surreal destruction sequences. I've already described one of them, the wreck of the fancy convertible in *Point Blank*. In *The Flim Flam Man* Mordecai and Curley are riding through a backwoods Kentucky town in another new, stolen car; as they roar away from the police, they smash into buildings, monuments, gas stations, eventually wrecking not only their car and several others, but practically the whole town as well. And in the middle of *Waterhole 3* there is a wild and hilarious sequence that applauds the annihilation of the town's elegant Victorian bordello in a lively shoot-em-out.

Violence has always been presented as openly attractive in comedy, but these sequences in *The Flim Flam Man* and *Waterhole 3* are more than just funny: they have a piercing, almost painfully unrelieved intensity about them that distinguishes them from routine scenes in other comedies. The point of the scenes, as always, is the overthrow of the reputable. The whorehouse in *Waterhole 3* is the most lavishly decorated establishment in its ugly Western town, and the gunfighters relish smashing ornate doors, windows, and the expensive little figurines—"a vase brought round the Horn!"—that belie the earthly realities of the house. During the destruction of the town in *The Flim Flam Man*, the camera happily observes the demolition of an 'Uncle Sam Wants You' poster and a ceremonial cannon that stands proudly on courthouse square. In other words, details in these sequences, along with their general subversive energy, convey a violent antagonism toward authority, respectability, all gilt-edged, sanctimonious poses, and speak for a cheerful, spirited sort of anarchic brutality.

These films aren't, of course, made by protestors or for them, and I don't want to make them sound like self-conscious revolutionary manifestos; whatever revolutionary qualities they have are intuitive, indirect reflections of dissatisfactions only barely understood by audiences and film-makers. And I don't want to pretend that these movies are the only popular ones in America. On the same corner in Los Angeles where *In Cold Blood* was breaking theatre attendance records last winter and spring, *Guess Who's Coming to Dinner* was breaking records too, with even bigger crowds. The American public has always bought astonishingly different entertainments at the same instant. And perhaps audiences always respond enthusiastically to violence and crime—certainly our knowledge of psychology tells us so—but even a few years ago aggressive fantasies had to be disguised, washed with moral piety; the heroes of violent movies were the detectives, the secret agents, the unjustly accused. If moviemakers and audiences no longer need the disguises, that may be partly the result of a new urgency in the popular temper, as well as of a healthful new candidness in the American film.

Of course the compromises and cover-ups still *are* there in some of these movies; for some of the film-makers the hostilities they want to deal with are too radical and volatile to be presented straight. This is clearest in *The Dirty Dozen*, the most importantly confused movie of 1967 (also the year's biggest money-maker), which begins by asking us to identify with irreverent murderers and thieves who hate the army, and ends by asking us to applaud their reformation into frighteningly brave and efficient soldiers, who willingly and eagerly obey the army's orders (though even the ending is tinged with some uneasy strokes of irony). The movie only plays on the antisocial feelings that the film's director, Robert Aldrich, shrewdly recognised as contemporary. It finally, very moralistically, soothes the audience by saying, "Well, all of that irreverence was just fun, but we can be solemn and patriotic too, and look how nobly these men die for their country." The audience must be confused by the film's wavering between aggressive anti-authoritarianism and sugary, conformist platitudes about Men in War. But they're probably used to American movies that are confused in this way, and they may even like the confusion because it lets them have a good time without forcing them really to challenge the norms of their society that they're still, after all, committed to.

There's no such cop-out in *Bonnie and Clyde*. A lot of the favourable reviews of the movie have been phoney, because they wanted to answer Bosley Crowther's charge that the film romanticised the young criminals. So they have tried to say that the movie is not a celebration of gangsters or violence, that it is very moral really; even Warren Beatty, speaking as the film's producer, has said that Bonnie and Clyde are actually very *sick*. This is not entirely untrue, but it's camouflage. The movie *isn't* moral in any conventional sense, and Bonnie and Clyde are *very* attractive. That's the first thing we have to admit about the film, or we distort it badly. Even the defenders of *Bonnie and Clyde* have too often forced themselves into an unpleasant moralistic stance.

For whatever the limitations of seeing Bonnie and Clyde as heroes, the film, like *Point Blank*, provides no meaningful alternative to their inchoate, rather bumbling rebellion. They have impulse and vitality; they only want to be out of the ordinary, and when we see what the ordinary looks like, we have to appreciate their desire to escape. Arthur Penn's series of Depression tableaux are beautiful in a bleak, horrifying sort of way. The decaying towns, crumbling, boarded-up homes, a group of dispossessed families huddled together in a swamp—these glimpses of smalltown, rural America at its most hopeless are what Bonnie and Clyde turn away from. They travel across an American landscape that looks thoroughly gutted, and that they can manage, at certain moments, to maintain feelings of hope and even exuberance is remarkable, moving, beautiful. Why is it so wicked to present criminals sympathetically, unless you're committed to a milky liberal doctrine of social responsibility that has nothing to do with art? The film's celebration of the criminal is carefully considered, passionate, and seriously explored—all that we have a right to ask.

Pauline Kael was quite right to contrast *Bonnie and Clyde* with the Thirties version of the same story, Lang's *You Only Live Once*, to show that the current film no longer has a shrill, clear-cut social message. In the Thirties, after the New Deal anyway, the mood was optimistic in spite of widespread misery; everyone thought there were easy explanations and easy solutions. Even tragic stories were rather hopeful in lamenting the one identifiable, avoidable social mistake that doomed their heroes. David Newman and Robert Benton's script for *Bonnie and Clyde* expresses the mood of the Sixties: a desperate environment, with no suggestions of what causes or cures might be. No one is blamed for poverty or crime, and there is no neat, geometric relationship between the two. But there is a *feeling* in the film, rendered by Arthur Penn's evocative use of the settings and faces of poverty, of inarticulable, profound social dissatisfaction that does link the poor and the criminal in a dimly understood sense of a common plight. Bonnie and Clyde are not victims of Society as Thirties heroes were—they're not forced into crime by cruel officials who won't understand them and let them love. But they're victims of their society in a very different sense—they're led to crime because what's respectable and normal in their society is all so withering, so empty, so dull. Their surroundings are so bleak, contain so few possibilities, that extreme actions alone are meaningful.

And *Bonnie and Clyde* is popular with the young because it concerns young people with no future, who don't care about the future, who live for Now because youth is everything and there is nothing in the world to get older for. And if this ravenous hunger for life and excitement is what dooms them, well, that's attractive to young people too. The vision of youth consuming itself so quickly is a romantically self-pitying one, and I suspect we want to identify with Bonnie and Clyde as much in their untimely death as in their life. But the last part of the movie is upsetting; the deaths of Clyde's brother and of Bonnie and Clyde themselves aren't pretty. We may think we want to see them cut off while they are still young, before they have to compromise, but it's hideous when it happens. The sensation of the tremendous energy and yet the tremendous wastefulness of their violent, headlong rush at life matches youth's fantasies today, but *Bonnie and Clyde* criticises that fantasy even while celebrating it. The film makes us see the horror in the dream of dramatically burned-out youth, it scares us for wanting to be like Bonnie and Clyde.

The movie may sympathise with violent people, but it does not, finally, glorify violence. For one thing, though they take violence lightly, Bonnie and Clyde aren't aggressively violent. They kill only in self-defence, and they aren't in the least sadistic. (It's interesting that although Bonnie and Clyde kill a lot of people, and Walker in *Point Blank* doesn't actually kill anybody, Walker is the one who gives the impression of being a killer.) More important, the toll of their violence is on themselves. The sequence in which Clyde's brother Buck is killed by police bullets is the most powerful, excruciating film sequence I can remember seeing. The editing is superb, and the hysterical sense Penn gives of everyone talking separately but at once, is one of the finest achievements in overlapping dialogue since Orson Welles. We've enjoyed the violence in the early parts of the film, but in this sequence we're forced to pay for that enjoyment. We aren't allowed any 'tasteful' escape hatch from the intensity of their suffering; still, it's not gratuitously gruesome. When Buck, his head shot in, says to Clyde, "Clyde, I lost my shoes, I think the dog took 'em," it is a more searing, overpowering revelation of the horror of his death than any amount of bloody flesh could be.

After this sequence we can't simply identify with Bonnie and Clyde, we have to distance ourselves from the violent life they've chosen. But we distance ourselves not because of any discomfort over what they're doing to society, only because of the terrifying things they're doing to themselves. If banks and police suffer for their crimes, we certainly aren't allowed to feel concern about *that*. Even when *Bonnie and Clyde* is most devastating, most sceptical about the life of its hero and heroine, we always feel it's an antisocial film. We sympathise only with them, always with them.

In Cold Blood would not belong in this survey if it were only a replica of Truman Capote's 1966 best-seller. But Richard Brook's film is not an exact replica, it provides a very different experience, and the differences are revealing. The book, though consistently fascinating and provocative, was marred, it seemed to me, by its objectivity—Capote's dogged, almost perverse refusal to admit any personal involvement in what he was describing; it had no passion and no point of view. Brook's film does have a point of view, and thus, although most of it may be factual, it unfolds like a good drama, not like documentary reconstruction. It has lost some of the compelling detail, but it has a menacing atmosphere which the book did not have. Brooks unifies it with a mood of social desperation that distinguishes it from its source while linking it interestingly to the other current films.

Brooks even includes some bits of over-explicit dialogue to make his attitude clear—Dick telling Perry that there are different laws for rich and poor and that only the poor are executed, a detective interrupting his questioning of Dick to ask, with barely disguised revulsion, "Why do all of you people get tattooed?" That question is one of the best lines in the film, but when Dick angrily answers him, he's a little too articulate about the hypocrisy of the respectable people and their contempt for poverty. The film's imagery is more powerful than any such speeches in defining the deprivation in the killers' world. The very first images set the killers for us as outsiders—Dick helping his father out of a wooden outhouse on a lonely Kansas plain, Perry uneasy in the crowded Kansas City bus terminal, frightened away from a telephone twice, by a group of nuns and a soldier. This kind of precise observation is sustained. Throughout the film Conrad Hall's rich, controlled black and white photography perfectly captures the ravaged look of Midwestern and Southwestern America. *In Cold Blood* complements *Bonnie and Clyde* by reminding us that the poor rural America of the Depression still exists. The desolate Kansas farmlands, bleak small towns that are little more than railroad crossings, rundown hotels, truck stop cafés specialising in Mexican food, exemplify life that is as withered today as during the Thirties.

There is one marvellous, unforgettable vignette in the film that deserves more comment. After hitch-hiking across much of America, Perry and Dick have stolen a car and are driving west from Kansas City to Las Vegas. On the desert they stop to pick up a young boy and his grandfather, who have been surviving by collecting empty coke bottles from the side of the road and cashing them in for refunds. Dick and Perry join their scavenging for a while, and the scenes of their scurrying around the desert collecting the empty bottles from trash cans and abandoned picnic areas forcefully summarises the pathos of the poor in the American landscape at its ugliest and most obscene. I especially remember a brief shot of the old grandfather, toothless, distracted, very close to death, lying in the back of the car on top of hundreds of bottles, an emblem of an entire life of inescapable misery and coarseness. Yet this sequence is one of the most tender in the film too—the warmth struck up almost immediately between the killers and the boy is affecting, an intuitive community of the deprived.

Mocking the bleached, cruel America that the killers have known is the America of the Clutters, wealthy, religious, contented. Brooks provides only mercilessly clipped images of the Clutter family, almost snapshots from a family album, set, probably ironically, to sentimental music that intensifies the feeling of complacency. One of the important differences from the book is that in the film the Clutters are little more than cartoons (though sharp ones—the faces of Mr. Clutter and his son, especially, are exactly right). We know almost nothing about them. Some of the reviewers have objected to this, but Brooks didn't want to make the Clutters three-dimensional. We see them as the killers see them—simply as iconic representatives of a life utterly different from their own. The film is not an equally-balanced portrait of respectable and underworld America: it is *all* underworld, all from the perspective of the outlaws, and the brief alternative glimpses are only meant to tease us by their incongruity.

It's this reluctance to share the forlornness of the killers' world that people have really been objecting to. Richard Schickel admitted this when he criticised the film for *Life:* "In the book the victims, the residents of Holcomb, the detectives, the strangers whom the murderers met on their long flight all formed a collective antagonism who balanced the killers psychologically and whose ultimate triumph over them . . . granted the reader a sense of release, even triumph . . ."

It's exactly that sense of consolation that Brooks denies us by refusing to allow us to feel close to anyone but the killers. Capote even ended his book with a graveyard encounter between Inspector Dewey and a friend of Nancy Clutter's, intent on proving Hollywood-style solace; Brooks ends his Hollywood film grimly, with the hanging of Perry Smith.

Although the movie attempts psychological explanations for the murders, these are either oversimplified—Perry's love-hate relationship with his father—or not quite fully developed enough—the repressed homosexuality and rivalry in the tortured relationship of Dick and Perry. We're interested enough to wish we knew more; but the explanation that works most coherently in the film is a social one. It's interesting that *In Cold Blood* and *Bonnie and Clyde* both fail in their attempts at psychoanalysis (Clyde's impotence seems only a gimmick in Penn's film), succeed best as sophisticated, complex social commentary. And the sociology in *In Cold Blood* is like that in *Bonnie and Clyde*—far more equivocal than the neat kind of definition we would have had in a Thirties movie. The mood of the film, like the mood of most of these films, is despairing; its vision is of ineradicable blemishes in an America hopelessly devastated.

Almost everything that we know and see of the killers' present and past lives is sordid. Yet they have been nourished on the same air as the Clutters. One of the most interesting things about *In Cold Blood* is that it records a rural crime. It can be contrasted to *The Incident,* which seems to blame urban conditions for crime; the hoods appear to have grown out of the subways, and the passenger who finally subdues them is the one smalltown boy in the car. The film insists on the moral superiority of the countryside. *In Cold Blood* explodes that fantasy. Its killers, as well as its victims, are country boys; what's frightening about the crime is that it can't be explained away as a result of industrialisation or mechanisation. By choosing to write about a rural crime, Capote must have wanted to get at matters most fundamental to the American experience—most deeply-rooted, most inescapable. I have said that the film complements *Bonnie and Clyde* by bringing the Depression tableaux up to date; it also complements *Point Blank,* extending the American landscape of death beyond the city, to what Fitzgerald called "the dark fields of the republic [that] roll on under the night."

The killers have grown up with the same frontiersman's dream of wealth and success that the Clutters have realised. Perry still dreams of buried treasure in Yucatan just as Dick dreams of sharing in the wealth of wheat, oil, and gas—'the perfect score'. And if both dreams seem ridiculous and anachronistic, that's part of the film's criticism of

the American myth of endless opportunity—a myth that contrasts sting-
ingly with the actual barrenness of the American landscape they have
known all their lives. In one lyrical flashback sequence, of Perry watching his Cherokee mother, a rodeo rider, rope a calf, we can see, for a
moment, all that tantalised Perry: the beauty of frontier poverty, open
spaces, homelessness, and their promise of boundless freedom and
mobility. And so he went to Alaska with his father, the Lone Wolf
prospector, to strike it rich, and they opened a hotel, and waited and
waited until they realised no one would ever come. The world has
changed, but the killers don't know it; Farmer Clutter keeps no safe,
no cash, pays everything by cheque. But by the time Dick and Perry
are rummaging for empty coke bottles on the desert, Perry anyway has
learned where he is; at the thought of a three cent refund per bottle,
he laughs bitterly but heartily, "So this is the sunken treasure of Captain
Cortez."

Perry Smith, like Bonnie and Clyde, is essentially innocent, good,
hopeful—in impossible ways that can only lead to anguish, and eventually violence. He is the innocent American finally forced to admit
that his dreams and his treasure maps can end in nothing but death.
His crime (and it is he who commits the murders) is a consequence,
though he doesn't quite understand it consciously, of his recognition of
everything that separates him from the Clutters in a land that boasted
equal opportunities for all. His murders are a grisly conclusion to the
pioneer dream; they seem, almost, a requiem for America.

Something needs to be said about the final sequence of the film, the
hangings of the killers. Most people have regarded this sequence merely
as a shrill and heavy-handed attack on capital punishment. The ending
certainly is anti-capital punishment, but it has a dramatic inevitability
that no tract could have. We feel that their society has rejected Perry
and Dick all of their lives, was responsible for the agonised feelings of
frustration that made them killers, and now, with unbearable scorn,
the State goes one step further and takes their lives. It's worth men-
tioning that the hanging sequence is much more frightful and revolting
than the murder sequence, which is handled with relative restraint and
indirection. The hangings are filmed with much more intensity, merciless lingering over every detail—the clicks of the gallows as the minister
reads of green pastures, the trembling of Perry's hands, the movement
of his mouth as he chews his gum even under the black hood.

Yet the murder sequence is chilling too. Unlike *Bonnie and Clyde*,
where only once, for a moment—when Clyde shoots a pursuer in the
face—do we feel any horror for what the heroes do to others. *In Cold
Blood* forces us to ponder a horrifying act, and still retains sympathy
for the killers. Even though what the killers have done is intolerable,
we feel, by the end, such disgust at what is being done *to* them, that we

are enraged at the entire social rationale for their condemnation. Given all that Perry Smith has suffered, and his stumbling movement toward self-knowledge, he deserves help and freedom, not revenge of any kind; he deserves a chance to live. Brooks will not let us forget that he cut Herb Clutter's throat, for no reason, and still there is a moment, I think, when we don't want to see him suffer *anything* more, any kind of punishment at all, and that moment is a piercing one, a moment when we separate ourselves painfully, almost against our will, from the agencies of social morality, when we know that we are with the outlaw even when he is a psychopathic killer.

It's not a moment or a feeling that can possibly last, but *In Cold Blood* forces us to it, without glorification or falsification of the killer, and thus goes further than any of these films in its rejection of the norms of American society. There have been a lot of technical criticisms of the film—most of them valid—but they are niggling because, in the last analysis, the film does what only a few films do—it shakes us up a little. Some of it is clumsily done, but its insistence that we sympathise with someone who also appals us is truly unsettling. And the last moments of the film are hard to forget. Is it coincidence that in both *In Cold Blood* and *Bonnie and Clyde,* the two strongest and most searching American films of the year, the most forceful, indelible images are images of death—the death of guilty people, killers, murdered remorselessly by the society they have wronged—that leave us numb with grief and outrage? Where, if anywhere, can we go from here?

The Hollywood Screen Writers

Paul R. Reynolds

*In the following essay Paul Reynolds, a literary agent, describes the role of the screen writer in American films.**

There are some 1,500 working motion picture and television writers in Hollywood. Perhaps 100 of these writers work exclusively for pictures; 800 probably work exclusively for television. The others write for pictures when they can, but, more often than not, for television. These 1,500 writers create more than 90 per cent of the motion picture screen plays and 80 per cent of the television screen plays.

What is writing for Hollywood like? Who are the writers? In the first place, 90 per cent of them are men. Their average age is under forty. A few are former magazine contributors who have found writing for pictures or television more profitable; a few are dramatists who perhaps wrote one Broadway hit but could not repeat—or perhaps wrote one produced play that was a flop; some are former newspaper men; some are old pros who have been working in Hollywood for twenty years or longer. Quite a large number are younger aspirants attracted by the chance to write, by the alleged glamour, and by the possibility of making a lot of money.

About a dozen top screen writers live in New York or its environs and periodically fly across the continent; another dozen live in London; a handful, in Rome; and a few elsewhere. But Hollywood is the center for motion picture writing, and although television writing is divided between Hollywood and New York, four out of five TV writers work in Hollywood.

When a writer gets a job in Hollywood he is given what is called an assignment. He agrees in advance to do a specific writing job, and signs a contract that guarantees him the agreed-upon payment. His assignment may be to prepare a motion picture screenplay based upon a published book, a Broadway play, or an unpublished story, or to rewrite some one else's screenplay. Writing this motion picture screenplay, with revisions, may require six to fifteen or more weeks of work.

In television an assignment is different. Here the writer is usually paid to prepare a television screenplay based on an idea of his own. The writer describes his idea to a potential buyer, usually a producer or a story editor. If the idea is approved, the writer, for an agreed-upon price, then creates a television screenplay. Writing a half-hour television show usually requires at least two weeks; an hour show, three to four or even five weeks.

Every writer who gets a writing job in Hollywood must join a union, the large and powerful Writers Guild of America East and West. The only exception is the newcomer, the apprentice, who may work on assignment on his first job as a non-union man. Once in the union, a writer caught breaking union rules can be deprived of work indefinitely. A producer who violates the agreement can be blacklisted and prevented from hiring writers.

The Guild negotiates with both the motion picture and television industry, and contracts are agreed upon between the union on the one hand and the studios and independent producers on the other. The contract now in force for motion picture writers on assignment stipulates the following minimum payment:

For a motion picture screenplay
   (twelve weeks work at $375.38 per week) $4,504.56

The contract in force to date for all television writers on assignment stipulates the following minimum payments:

Idea and fifteen-minute screenplay	$ 612.61
Idea and thirty-minute screenplay	1,321.32
Idea and sixty-minute screenplay	2,402.40
Idea and ninety-minute screenplay	3,482.96

These minimum payments vary, depending on complicated factors. A writer gets more when he is working on a high-budget picture or television show; minimum rates also vary with the number of weeks guaranteed or worked, with the number of writers on the same assignment, etc.

Guild rules are almost never circumvented, with one exception: The Guild forbids a writer seeking a television assignment to do any speculative writing; when seeking an assignment, he is supposed to tell his story orally. In practice, the writer does tell his idea, but he also often gives the producer an outline to show his colleagues. Sometimes an outline even will be rewritten at the suggestion of a producer. The Guild now winks at such violations, and, ultimately, the rule that forbids outlines may be changed.

Only the beginning or relatively unsuccessful writers receive Guild minimum fees. Four-fifths of the writers receive more—perhaps one-third receive at least twice as much. However, few writers work all the time. A writer of half-hour television scripts rarely can dream up and sell twenty ideas a year. Often, he is lucky to sell ten, which may mean only twenty to thirty weeks' work a year.

The market for writers rises and falls. In 1965, the most writers working on assignment in pictures in any one month was 172, and the low was 125. In television the top was 726, the low, 370.

The two dozen or so top motion picture writers make enormous incomes. Dan Taradash, for example, obtained an assignment to write a screenplay based upon James Michener's novel, *Hawaii,* and he was paid a quarter of a million dollars. More than a dozen writers get $100,000 or more for an assignment.

Every Hollywood writer prefers to write for pictures rather than for television because pictures pay more. Also, the writer for pictures has more creative freedom. The television writer is cabined and confined. The length of a TV script is arbitrary (it cannot vary even a minute) ; the small television screen restricts the scenes that can be portrayed; a television show has strict financial limitations; and often the writer must use inexpensive backgrounds, and confine himself to a small cast of characters.

While most screenplays are written on assignment, a certain number are original screenplays—created by authors not writing on assignment or working with producers. These are written on speculation and sold to producers just the way a short story is written and sold to a magazine. There is no Guild minimum for an original screenplay—prices range from as little as $2,500 to more than six figures, with the majority selling in the range of $10,000 to $25,000.

In television it is also theoretically possible to write and sell an original screenplay, called a teleplay. However, only one show has been purchasing original teleplays, and this show bought only a few in the last few months. This situation is changing, and the market for original teleplays may expand in the future.

In the motion picture and television industry, unlike other writers' media, an agent is a necessity. Stars, directors, producers, and writers all have agents, or, in the case of a few top money-makers, an attorney who performs functions similar to the agent's. The agent business may not make much sense in a rational world, but this is beside the point. To the neophyte writer in Hollywood an agent is obligatory. Only through an agent can a writer obtain an assignment. No studio, and few, if any, producers, will consider an unknown writer's script unless submitted through an agent.

To the new writer, Hollywood seems the most difficult of all the great writing media to crack. First, there seems to him no way of obtaining an agent. In all probability no agent will look at the new writer's script or consider him for an assignment—the writer either receives a polite no, or his query goes unanswered. The writer may ask for a personal appointment and the agent refuses; the agent is too busy.

With agents remote, aloof, and completely uninterested, the barriers to breaking into Hollywood, then, seem insurmountable. Actually, this is not the case. Every writer's medium is extremely hard to crack; Hollywood is no more difficult than the others. The problem is just different. What steps must the neophyte take?

First, he must learn his trade. Screenplays have been published, and the writer can obtain some to study. Some articles and books on writing for motion pictures and television may be helpful. The neophyte, just for practice, can write and rewrite screenplays, struggling to get better and better.

Second, the neophyte can sometimes work in a local television station, not necessarily as a writer. Any job where at times he can watch the shooting of scripts will be helpful. Experience in a television station will add to his competence, and be a plus to his getting an assignment in Hollywood at some later date.

Third, once the neophyte believes that he has learned his trade he must go to Hollywood. Trying to sell oneself or one's scripts at a distance is a well-nigh hopeless proposition.

Fourth, arriving in Hollywood, the neophyte must talk some agent into reading his scripts, as examples and evidence of the writer's competence. The writer first may talk some producer or director or writer acquaintance into reading his scripts unofficially, and then recommending the writer to an agent. Some neophyte writers barge in cold on person after person until they find someone who will read their scripts and give them an introduction to an agent.

Number 4 of the above presupposes a smooth talker. Most successful Hollywood writers must not only have the competence (the first requirement) but also a glib tongue. If the neophyte is not good at selling himself, if he cannot describe a story well, he is under a handicap.

To the ordinary workaday writer living in the East, going to Hollywood to work for a studio is an extraordinary experience. Hollywood is not a town or governmental unit. It is a Post Office address and a telephone exchange in an outlying part of Los Angeles. Close by are residential areas such as Beverly Hills or Brentwood. The temperature is warm and constant, with little rain. Much of the land is fairly flat, but it is surrounded by mountains, hills, ravines, and canyons, with winding roads and abrupt climbs, and, often, gorgeous views. In this area, within a radius of four or five miles, are the Metro, Fox, Paramount, Columbia, Warner Brothers, Universal, and the United Artists studios plus NBC, ABC, and CBS, and several other TV studios.

The writer living in this charming locality has ideal physical working conditions. There is no clock punching; no five-day work week; no nine-to-five working hours. The writer can work at home on his own schedule. Ninety per cent of the television writers work at home; motion picture writers more often work in a studio office (perhaps because office conditions are so pleasant), but two-thirds of these work at home. Conferences are inevitable, and once or two a week the writer drives to the studio to confer with his producer or boss, but such conferences are informal.

Nevertheless the typical Hollywood writer, doing creative work of a fashion, living in a beautiful atmosphere, boss of his working hours, is a frustrated, unhappy man. His frustration begins because he is doing creative work, but his producer and others continually instruct him as to how to do it. It is as if a novelist had to devise his characters and his plot according to his publisher's instructions, then deliver his novel to the publisher chapter by chapter, and rewrite each chapter as bidden. Any novelist working under such conditions would be frustrated. The screen writer, required to work this way, lives with frustration.

There are other reasons for a screen writer's unhappiness. A motion picture is not the sole creation of a writer. The effectiveness of the picture depends upon the cast, upon the director, upon the composer (all pictures have some music), and upon the money spent upon sets, etc. The writer of the screenplay may be blamed when the failure of the picture was in no way his fault, or the praise for success may go to some star when the major cause for success was really the writer's. This situation gives any writer a basis for frustration.

Moreover, writers write for prestige as well as for money, and the writer of a screenplay gets almost no credit from the public. It is true that his name is flashed upon the screen as the author of the screenplay, but the public is uninterested. Who goes to a movie and says to himself, "My what a fine screenplay"? The only people who remember who wrote a specific picture are other writers and members of the industry in Hollywood.

The frustration of the motion picture writer is paralleled by the frustration of the television writer. Every television writer wants to write for pictures. If he occasionally gets motion picture work, he is unhappy when he has to work for TV. If he never is able to get motion picture work, he is all the more unhappy. There are dramas on TV that are good from a critical point of view, but nineteen of twenty are drivel, and the writers know it. There is at least local adulation for the writer of a successful motion picture screenplay; there is little adulation for most TV writers.

Idleness is another cause of the Hollywood writer's frustration. Few writers at the beginning of the year know how many weeks they will work or what their income is likely to be. They do not take vacations from work. Their idleness is interrupted by work.

There is another indirect but possible cause for a Hollywood writer's frustration. A writer on assignment is an employee, but an employee who changes his job a dozen times a year. Hence, he has little sense of loyalty to any studio or any producer, and less chance of making enduring business friendships.

Then there is the problem of living in a community where everything oozes money. In all walks of life people want all the money they can get, even though it is demonstrable that a group of rich people are no happier than a group of moderately rich. In Hollywood, the desire for money is carried to the extreme. Money is Hollywood's life blood, its only standard, its status symbol, the only desideratum.

Everyone talks of money. If a writer is out of work and broke each of his acquaintances knows it. When a writer is working, his acquaintances know about how much he is getting. A producer boasted to me that he could know within 10 per cent how much money any individual made. He said, "Tell me what a man does in the industry, and where he has last worked, and after a couple of telephone calls I can tell you his income."

In Hollywood, friends are in the approximately same financial bracket. A poorly paid writer (except in the case of long years of friendship) would not be seen lunching with a well-known, successful producer, director, or top writer who gets perhaps $100,000 an assignment.

On one business trip to Hollywood, I was told by a top screen writer —a woman whose fee for writing a screenplay was in six figures—that she wanted to give a dinner party for me, and was there any particular person I would like to have invited. I suggested a college classmate and close friend who was then writing TV Westerns at the Guild minimum. My hostess said she would be delighted to ask him. The next day she called me in great embarrassment. She told me that she had invited a certain motion picture star, the general manager of one of the studios, and various other well-known Hollywood characters, and that she hoped I would understand that my friend would be uncomfortable, and that she really should not invite him. My hostess had made inquiries and discovered what my friend was making. In point of fact, I was also ineligible for the dinner party on financial grounds, but as I came from New York no one knew.

Most writers in other media feel frustrated at one time or another. The feeling may be intense, but usually it is temporary. It is a feeling of frustration because the writer cannot reproduce on paper what is in his mind's eye, because a page or a chapter does not seem right. However, few writers of fiction or non-fiction or legitimate drama feel frustrated all the time, or feel frustrated because of the industry. They want to write. They continue to write even though the monetary return may be small, even though they are only partially successful.

The forty or fifty most successful Hollywood writers enjoy the occupation. In a money world they are at the top. They have prestige, at least in their own home town, Hollywood. Because of their names, their positions, their competence, they are given more freedom to write creatively than is the average writer. However, the great mass of Hollywood writers complain about the occupation, the industry, and their frustrations; their wives and their friends tell you, morning, noon, and night. Their money, whether substantial or not, is never enough in their Hollywood money world.

If the Hollywood writers are frustrated and the non-Hollywood writers are relatively happy, why do not the Hollywood writers enter one of the other writers' media? A handful, such as Irving Wallace, have become brilliant novelists. Many try, but usually they are unsuccessful. Writing for the films or TV reduces one's capacity to write good books or to publish in the top magazines.

There are many reasons. The writer for films does not have to show any great depth of characterization. The stars, with the aid of the director, do that. For the film-writer, much is plausible because one sees it happen on the screen. Motivation is less essential. A motion-picture viewer does not question whether a character would leave a room, because the viewer sees him leave. Furthermore, a film-writer rarely does intensive research work, such as is necessary for the non-fiction book and usually desirable even for the modern novel. Then again, a film-writer is dealing in a large part with other people's ideas. If he dramatizes a book, he is dealing with the novelist's idea. If he obtains a television assignment, his own idea is tailored to the concept of the TV show.

Finally, the film-writer deals with gimmicks, twists, and dialogue, occasionally just for their own sake. The successful film-writer has acquired great technical skill, great craftsmanship. He has special gifts. But when such a writer tries to be a novelist, he finds it difficult to abandon his film technique. He finds it difficult to show characters in depth, to probe motivations, to immerse himself in research dealing solely with his own ideas, to avoid the gimmicks and twists, the props of a film-writer. Most Hollywood writers have the time to write books. Many have the urge. But when they try, seldom can they shuck off the Hollywood influence.

The Living Legacy of Walt Disney

John Reddy*

The dissimilarity between W. C. Fields and Walt Disney could not be greater, either personally or in their effect on the history of the American film. The tremendous influence of both continues even after their deaths. The following two articles describe that influence. They collectively demonstrate the breadth of the American film which could embrace within its confines both a man of matchless imagination and one whose comic wit and irreverence was unforgettable. John Reddy is Roving Editor for The Reader's Digest. *Wallace Markfield is a writer and teacher who is the author of the popular novel* To an Early Grave, *adapted for film as* Bye Bye Braverman.

It was an unusual stockholders' meeting for a great far-flung enterprise. Many of the stockholders were children, and they whooped with glee at films in which Blackbeard's ghost played havoc with crooks, or Baloo the bear, from Kipling's *Jungle Books,* cavorted through a dance. The company, of course, was Walt Disney Productions, and the films were previews of its movies.

But no laughter greeted the final film that day, and tears glistened in many an eye. It was Walt Disney's last filmed appearance before his death on December 15, 1966. In this film he had outlined some of his plans for the future—plans which soared far above his finest imaginative achievements of the past. Most spectacular of his new ideas was a $100-million Disney World, including a glass-domed "city of tomorrow," to be built in Florida, near Orlando, on a site twice the size of Manhattan Island.

"On the day before Walt died, he lay in his hospital bed staring at

* By permission from John Reddy, "The Living Legacy of Walt Disney," *Reader's Digest,* Reader's Association, Inc., Pleasantville, New York, © 1967. (June 1967, pp. 1–6.)

303

the ceiling," his brother Roy, who succeeded him as head of Walt Disney Productions, recalls. "Walt envisioned the squares of acoustic tile as a grid map of Florida's Disney World. He'd say, 'This is where we'll put the monorail. And we'll run the highway right there.'"

Roy, a bald, folksy, 73-year-old man, has taken over the task of transforming Walt's last and biggest dreams into reality. He sits in an unpretentious office under a Karsh portrait of his famous brother and an Indian peace pipe given him by Walt after some long-forgotten argument. There he guides his management team full speed ahead through the worldwide Disney realm of movies, TV shows, comics and magazines, music and records. "It's strictly a team effort now," Roy says. "We're trying to be as smart collectively as Walt was individually."

EXPANSIVE AND EXPENSIVE

Although always in the public shadow of Walt, Roy Disney was by his younger brother's side through every step of the strenuous 40 years of building their giant company. "Roy used to push me around in a baby buggy," Walt once said, "and he's been taking care of me ever since." When Walt first tried his hand at cartooning in Kansas City, bank clerk Roy helped stake him. When Walt's cartoon business failed, Roy, then in California, helped set him up in Hollywood in 1923. It was Roy who borrowed $500 from an uncle to enable Walt to make his first film cartoon combining live action with animation. Roy acted as cameraman and rounded up kids to whom he gave a dime each for appearing in the film. As Walt's cartoons grew more ambitious, Roy's job of financing progressed, if that's the word, to tapping bankers for $5 million.

Ironically, though, initial success only compounded their financial difficulties. Even after Mickey Mouse, Donald Duck and the Three Little Pigs made Walt world-famous, the Disneys were still plagued by problems. Once Roy had to sell Walt's car to keep going. For years neither Walt nor Roy received a salary, drawing only expenses. If a cartoon did make money, they plowed it right back into the business.

THE HOUSE THE DWARFS BUILT

In 1937 Walt splurged $1,500,000 to make *Snow White,* the first feature-length movie cartoon. With its gross of $8 million, the brothers built the present studio in Burbank. The studio mushroomed to 1500 employees and a $5-million debt. When Roy worried, Walt laughed. "Roy, remember when we couldn't borrow one *thousand* dollars?"

Even though they sold stock to the public, their situation remained shaky. Between 1950 and 1955, Walt turned out three award-winning feature-length cartoons: *Cinderella, Alice in Wonderland* and *Peter Pan,* and the highly acclaimed but costly nature films such as *The Living Desert* and *The African Lion.* Yet every time Walt won a movie Oscar, the studio went deeper into debt.

Despite artistic success and world-wide acclaim, it wasn't until July 17, 1955, with the opening of Disneyland, that the Disneys finally struck solid pay dirt. When Walt first began talking about a new kind of amusement park, people thought he was crazy. "Dreams offer too little collateral," he observed. Eventually, Walt scrounged enough for a down payment on some orange groves near the town of Anaheim, 28 miles southeast of Los Angeles, and construction began. Walt wanted everything to be different from other amusement parks. "You're going to fall flat on your face," a veteran carnival man told Walt. "Maybe we will," Walt shrugged, "but we'll fall forward."

MAGIC WAND

The story of Disneyland's success is as fantastic as any of Walt's cinematic fairy tales. Over 60 million visitors from nearly every country have visited Disneyland. Walt called Disneyland his "magic kingdom," and suddenly it was as if a fairy godmother had waved a wand over all his undertakings. Walt took to television and was an instant hit. The Davy Crockett feature of his early shows became a national epidemic. Walt began making regular movies, and now 28 Disney "family movies," topped by *Mary Poppins,* rank among Hollywood's all-time high moneymakers. "Every time other films get dirtier, our box office goes up," Walt said.

After 30 years of precarious, cliff-hanging struggle, the Disneys were not only solvent, but had hit a parlay unparalleled in Hollywood history. This year Walt Disney Productions is turning out a half-dozen movies and 26 hours of new TV shows, pouring $45 million into additional attractions at Disneyland and launching work on Walt's new projects.

CONTROLLED CONFUSION

The nerve-center of Disney Productions is WED (for Walt E. Disney) Enterprises, Inc., where new projects for Walt Disney Productions are planned and built. WED is housed in a large, white two-story building in the shadow of the bald Verdugo Mountains. Step inside the door, and you are in a dream factory—a surrealistic scene of colorful and controlled confusion. On a floor the size of two football fields, architects, engineers, draftsmen, project designers and craftsmen of all types are working on everything from a lunar colony to a prehistoric Triceratops.

In one corner, a woman paints quietly on glass, using a technique that "died out" in the 13th century. In another, a small village burns briskly, but the flames do not consume the wood. "Walt used to call what we do here 'imagineering,'" says Orbin V. Melton, who presides over WED. It was here that Disney "imagineers" developed the amazing Audio-Animatronic system that brings to life the moving, startlingly lifelike human and animal figures that are among the chief attractions at Disneyland. "Our singing Audio-Animatronic birds seem so real that some people are afraid to sit under them," a staff member chuckled.

Among the many marvels conjured up at WED were the sketches and models for Florida's Disney World. Acquiring the 43 square miles of marshland and cypress forest in central Florida for this project was a cloak-and-dagger operation. "We realized that if word leaked out that we were buying up the land, prices would skyrocket," Roy says. The Disney brothers and their key aides flew to Florida in a company plane, landing at out-of-the-way airports, and staying at small motels. A "command post" was set up in a Miami hotel, and local realty operators, who didn't know the identity of their employers, would phone in each day with reports of their progress.

THE SPARK OF GENIUS

Last February, Roy announced detailed plans for Disney World. The theme park, similar to Disneyland but several times larger and more elaborate, is scheduled to open in 1970. Adjoining it will be a private jet airport, motels, golf courses, tennis courts and facilities for water sports.

The "city of tomorrow," called EPCOT (experimental prototype community of tomorrow), will be started, with the coöperation of leading U.S. corporations, after the theme park is completed. EPCOT will be laid out like a wheel, with a 50-acre, glass-domed and airconditioned hub. This hub will contain a 30-story hotel and convention center, with stores, theaters, restaurants and offices. Inside the hub, people will get from place to place on WEDway people movers, like the one currently planned for Disneyland. Outside the hub will be apartments and green-belt residential districts. "The idea of building a city of the future where there's nothing but marsh and cypress might seem crazy, but look what happened at Disneyland," Roy says. "When we went there, it was nothing but orange groves. Today Anaheim has become a major city."

Plans are also going forward for another of Walt Disney's dreams: a resort at Mineral King, a breathtaking valley nestled in the High Sierras, 225 miles northeast of Los Angeles. The master plan calls for an Alpine village with, among other attractions, 14 ski-lifts, two major hotels, ten restaurants and a snow play area, all designed to blend unobtrusively with the valley's natural contours.

Of all the upcoming projects, perhaps the dearest to Walt's heart was the new campus of the California Institute of the Arts. What he envisioned was a "community of the arts," a group of schools of *all* the performing and creative arts. Here young people not only would study painting, music, dancing and the other arts, but would mingle in an atmosphere of mutual creativity. The school would stress talent, rather than academic excellence. Walt donated 38 wooded acres from the Disney studio's sprawling Golden Oak ranch near Newhall, Calif., and left it 45 percent of his estate.

THE SHOW GOES ON

This year an estimated 250 million people will see a Disney movie, 50 million will watch each Disney TV show, 150 million will read Disney comic strips, 50 million will listen to Disney music and records, and seven million will visit Disneyland. The show goes on, as Walt planned it.

"Walt was proud of the team he gathered around him, the people who are carrying on now," Roy recalls. Yet so strong is the stamp of Walt's personality that a visitor to the studio still feels his influence everywhere. His name pops up in almost every conversation. "All we have to do," says Card Walker, a vice president, "is to remember what Walt wanted and then do it." That spirit, as much as the world of imagination he left behind, is the living legacy of Walt Disney.

The Dark Geography of W. C. Fields

Wallace Markfield[*]

FIELDS: *You remember the time I knocked down Waterfront Nell?*
BARTENDER: *Why, you didn't knock her down. I did!*
FIELDS: *Well, I started kicking her first . . .*

The scope of his hatreds, on and off the screen, was total and terrifying, taking in children, mothers, dogs, parvenu and proletarian, doctor and medicine man, city slicker and country bumpkin, the rich and the powerful, the insulted and injured, the fat, the lean, the flagrantly bearded, the fastidiously mustached, the midget and the giant, the lame, the halt and the blind; indeed, nearly everything human was alien to him. Physical contact—touch, jostle, embrace—caused him to flinch, gag and snarl, to swing wildly with cane or fist. His bigotry was pure, simple, uncomplicated by dogma or ideology, as obvious as the nose on his face. (Stage direction in one of his own scripts: *Enter Shine*). He feared most races, but mostly he feared Negroes, Chinese and Indians; they were hoarding razors, steam irons and tomahawks, he believed, and would one day march upon Washington. He was a misanthrope, a troublemaker, a cheapskate, a boozer and, most likely, somewhat paranoid. (Bank accounts he opened under assumed names may, 20 years after his death, still be drawing interest.) He was also one of the greatest comic artists to cross the light of the screen.

Buffs, Fields always had—perhaps even a cult—but his admission to camp ground was long coming. (Suddenly, surprisingly, his film festivals are doing at least as well as *Casablanca* or *King Kong;* cinema societies plead for prints, and anthologies of "Trivia" carry queries about the make and year of his car in *The Bank Dick*.) Film historians and critics, when they came to Fields—and a good many bypassed him altogether—

* By permission from Wallace Markfield, "The Dark Geography of W. C. Fields," *New York Times Magazine,* April 24, 1966. © 1966.

consigned him to the foot of their pages, somewhere among the first rank of the second-rate. A few, a very few, granted him his moments, his genius, his moments of genius—and went on to mourn that golden age of the silents, when comedy was king, writing prose-poems about Fatty Arbuckle's marksmanship with pies, Buster Keaton's hat brim, the way Louise Fazenda primped her spit curl or how the Keystone Cops fell on their backsides.

Mostly, though, they picked and puzzled over every last foot of Chaplin's films. Granted, it is virtually impossible to overrate Chaplin, but scores of critics came perilously close. (Wrote James Agee: "The Tramp is as centrally representative of humanity, as many-sided and mysterious, as Hamlet." And, compared to Parker Tyler, Gilbert Seldes, Arthur Knight, Theodore Huff and Siegfried Kracauer, Agee was positively tough-minded.) For Chaplin, unlike Fields, is easy to take. From two-reeler to feature-length comedy, he is appealing with all his might and all his art for love, and if not love, then compassion, and if not compassion, then justice in the face of a universe that is at worst murderous, at best governed by cruel chance. The appeal is reasonable, sweet-tempered, poignant, innocent; the very thought of rejection is enough to stop the hearts of most men.

Most men, that is, except W. C. Fields. (Field's private estimate of Chaplin: "A goddam ballet dancer.") He worked strictly and directly and mercilessly for gags, and his very best gags were milked till they drew blood. All those objects which compelled Chaplin's sympathy, love and sorrow—the waifs, the flower girls, the maimed, the displaced and dispossessed—Fields regarded with freezingly sinister disdain. When he had to—and he often had to—he gave them the back of his hand, the side of his mouth, or clobbered them with that cane he carried, which was so much thicker and more wicked-looking than Chaplin's cane.

Take, by way of contrast, Chaplin and Fields confronting blindness. There is Chaplin in *City Lights,* in that final fade-out when he reveals himself to the blind flower girl who has regained her sight, when she sees at last what her benefactor is. His soul is open and shines forth on his face which, within a half-dozen close-ups, manages to register compassion, anguish, exquisite gentleness, the power to endure, stating, with every lift of a brow, every flaring of a nostril, faith in and commitment to mankind.

And then there is Fields in *It's a Gift,* minding that store with its inventory of fiendishly breakable bric-a-brac. While buyers and browsers mill and shrill, Fields, feather dusters in both hands and one foot in a spittoon, dances around with elephantine grace. He is managing, just barely managing, to effect a *rapprochement* between chaos and anarchy as a blind and deaf man blunders smack into the middle of things.

This skinny, wretched, Lincolnesque croak—Charles Sellon, one of Fields's straight men—looking sick unto death, now and then uttering a strangled, pre-human cry, spins about like a cadaver divesting itself of a winding sheet. Everything is calculated and choreographed so as to keep him mashing and bashing with his weighted walking stick, always an inch and an instant away from the chair with which Fields is trying to engage his bottom.

"Sit down, Mr. Muckle," Fields blares. He is answered by the kind of sound a vampire is supposed to make at sight of a crucifix. Next, he piteously bleats: "Sit down, Mr. Muckle . . . Mr. Muckle, *please* sit down." His voice sinks and sinks, then faintly quavers over the chime of breaking glass. "Mr. Muckle . . . Mr. Muckle . . . please . . . sit . . . down . . ." By the tiniest alteration of pitch and stress from syllable to syllable, by the implacably malevolent line of his mouth (it gives a momentary illusion of frothing), by the quality of the smile it holds (the smile of a man standing belly-high in ice water), Fields tells us all we can bear to know about what he wishes upon the poor soul.

No other comic could have gotten that message across; as a matter of fact, no other comic would have been willing to deliver it. He may be insolent, outrageous, as nihilistic as Groucho Marx and Jack E. Leonard, or as scatological as Lenny Bruce, yet he takes utmost care to let us know that he is himself fundamentally decent, that his intentions are honorable, that the destruction of a few sacred cows does not endanger the herd. And who can blame him and who can complain if he hangs back and boggles at that line which is separated by the breadth of a hair from contention, unemployment and a shattered nervous system?

This line Fields stepped over as easily as he stepped over a cigar butt, or an accident case. For the simple, crucial difference between Fields and every other funnyman before or since resided in his creation of a comic identity more hateful than the objects of his hatreds. The realization takes time, and you must have all of Fields's work before you. When it comes, though, it is akin to learning that the Keystone Cops had been all along lacing their pies with sulphuric acid.

To serve that identity, Fields took beautiful care to devise the driest, most cerebral and satanic style in the business, one which demanded from the paying customer a great deal more than any other comic dared, or could afford to, demand—i.e., a good eye and a good ear for detail, very close attention, a fairly strong stomach, high intelligence and a *lumpen* outlook. Perhaps this is why he was, as Kenneth Tynan shrewdly observed, "pre-eminently a man's comedian," and why men took to him as they might take to a beloved, disreputable drinking companion. (By my own private poll women regard him as physically repugnant, a dirty old man, faintly sinister and, with justice, a mortal enemy to their kind.)

But even so it is easy—Fields *made* it easy—for the most addicted to forget just how superbly endowed Fields was with all the comic arts and crafts. When he had to, when he wanted to, he could do a dazzling recitation of comedy's basic physical vocabulary—pratfall, pantomime, mugging, double-take, deadpan—while he went about fighting that forlorn, foredoomed battle every great comic fights against inanimate things. Where Buster Keaton and Harold Lloyd needed the support of boats, locomotives, big clocks, wind gauges and dynamite, Fields managed nicely with a cane and a straw skimmer opening like a clam shell at the lid. Only Chaplin, I think, made his own stick and derby more articulate or got quite so much funny footage from a lighted cigarette. (Caught *flagrante delicto* by a cop or a monstrous mother-in-law, Fields first swallows the butt and after the swallowing he starts and sustains a windy sermon against smoking, and after the sermon he disgorges the butt, and after the disgorging he moves the butt by tics and twitches into and around every crease and aperture on his face, and after he has thus defied the rules of man and the laws of physics, when the butt is under his upper lip and he has finally spotted a place to ditch it, Baby LeRoy bops him on the nose and he is undone.)

Or, give him five fast minutes with a warped pool cue and he could turn it into a metaphor for a warped mind. Once in a while he juggled —fumbled, really—cigar boxes, keeping them aloft with a virtuosity born of the private desperate knowledge that one false move ushers in Armageddon. Heedless of script and story-line, he might play a protracted, seemingly pointless, game of ping-pong; as the volleying gets fiercer and faster, as Fields makes the transition from annoyance to aggravation to apoplexy, the sequence turns into more than your nerves can take: at the very least, an inhuman comment on the human condition. And the straw skimmer could be instantly converted into a lethal instrument, sometimes beating a bill collector to his knees, sometimes hurled like an assagai at Butch and Buddy or Baby LeRoy.

He spoke, though, and because he spoke . . . and spoke . . . and spoke, purists have not even at this late date forgiven him. And when he spoke it was in the most unlovely voice any sound track had ever carried.

It seemed to arise out of immense lethargy, the lethargy of a man too far gone to bother spitting out a few hairs or ashes. At best it was nasal, at worst it was nasty, and invariably it was monotonous, absolutely drained of every state and emotion Fields considered extraneous—pity, respect, good will, benevolence, trust, tenderness. This voice an ancient heathen idol might have used against a missionary.

Fields spoke slowly, slowly, taking his own sour time, allowing himself probably the longest pauses on record. Where modern comics never let you forget for a second how much effort they're putting forth, and at what expense of spirit and at what cost to health—Red Skelton, Danny

Kaye, Sammy Davis Jr. and Jerry Lewis seem to solicit applause, literally, by the sweat of their brows—Fields did all his work from way inside the dark geography of his mind. Though his movies abound with
memorable one-liners (Fields's cure for insomnia: "Get plenty of
sleep"), and two- and three-liners ("You're drunk," says Injured Party.
"You're crazy," says Fields. "You're drunk," says I. P. "All right," says
Fields, "but tomorrow morning I'll be sober and you'll still be crazy"),
he was by his whole style and nature a monologuist. Because of that
style, that nature, he had, from first to last, one, only one, vast, amorphous monologue in his repertoire.

Though it meandered like a young river, though half of it was in-
audible (the other half he seemed to be dictating to a sozzled stenographer), though it is all improvisation and accretion, it serves to establish Fields as the screen's supreme poet of petty harassment. He has
come to tell us all—all about carping mothers-in-law, tiny, nervous dogs,
sour landladies, half-daft boarding-house frumps, feisty babies, hash-house
harridans, fatuous barbers, dumb cops, blowzy beauticians, assorted
cranks, kooks and fanatics who have worn him down, bested him in
every engagement. (For no matter how many bottles of snake oil he sells,
or how he stacks a deck, inevitably he *is* worn down, he *is* bested; the
landlady keeps his bags, the brat pours the gin out of his hipflask.)
When last seen he is generally at the end of his rope, living, livid proof
that there is no spirit so small but that the world will seek to diminish
it further.

And diminished Fields was. For a good 50 years he had built up his
comic identity, nourishing it with consummate care and sustaining it
against all odds and all kinds of opposition. He demanded his own wild
way ("Fields's Way"), overrode studio big-wigs, made life miserable for
his co-stars, blithely ignored directors (notable exception: Gregory La
Cava, "that Dago bastard"). For "stories," "treatments," and "ideas"
scribbled on the backs of laundry tickets and grocery bills he demanded
and got screen credits (under the names Mahatma Kane Jeeves, Otis
Criblecoblis and Charles Bogle) and cold cash (as much as $25,000).
In a day and age when Hollywood salaries were high, his salary was one
of the highest. (High enough, it is said, to make Bing Crosby gasp.)

By 1941, though, when he finished his final feature-length film, "Never
Give a Sucker an Even Break," the stains and pains of his effort were
too visible, too much to take. Loaded as it is with beautiful bits of business—Fields delicately blowing the head off an ice cream soda, belting
out "Chickens have pretty legs in Kansas," mixing it up with a waitress,
diving out of a plane after his whisky bottle, wooing the matchless
Margaret Dumont—NGASAEB is simply Fields trying to turn himself
into a lovable old eccentric. This he wasn't, and this he couldn't do.

Then what was left for him, and where was he to go? Chaplin was artist enough to dissemble and displace his hatreds, to speak, finally, through a Monsieur Verdoux. But for Fields the dilemma was virtually insoluble. Not in a million years would he, could he, step out of character. Call it integrity, or call it spite; in Fields's case there is barely a difference.

Alcoholism (he drank two quarts of gin daily, plus wine, plus whisky), insomnia and terrible illness combined to ravage Fields during his last few years. When he could leave his bed he drove around in a huge car hunting pedestrians, or sat at his window with a rifle he had sworn to use on Deanna Durbin.

In 1944, he did his warped pool cue bit in *Follow the Boys* and a walk-on in *Sensations of 1945,* and then vanished altogether from the screen—though something like his voice might drone out of the mouth of an evil Merrie Melodies cat or a pompous Terry Toons rooster. Remember, Hollywood had entered World War II with all its might, and those mothers whom Fields despised were hanging service stars in their windows, those babies had grown up to become beach chargers, those frumps and harridans were working in defense plants, those *Bank Dick* boobs and bumpkins were now the "little people," the sturdy anti-Fascist folk who burst into song before Nazi firing squads.

Even if we were lucky enough to have Fields around today the most independent, intransigent producer wouldn't dare turn him loose. Consider, if your mind doesn't reel, what he would have done to, and with, say, National Brotherhood Week, the civil-rights movement, the spirit of ecumenicalism, folk-singers, the War on Poverty, permissive child-rearing.

They tell the tale of Fields on his death bed suddenly rearing up and calling his cronies to his side. Clearly, something is on his mind. "You know," he croaks, "I've . . . been thinking about . . . those poor little . . . newsies out . . . there. Peddling their . . . papers in cold . . . and rain . . . sole support of . . . their mothers. I . . . want . . . to do something for them."

He is answered, "Wonderful, that's wonderful, Bill."

Then, he lapses into silence. "Bill . . . Bill . . . ?" He rears up again and says, "On second thought . . . ——— 'em!"

Death, "that fellow in the bright nightgown," came, of all times, on Christmas Day, 1946. Which in itself could have been the basis for one of Fields's most inspired routines.

The Return of Busby Berkeley

William Murray

William Murray is a novelist and free lance writer who lives in California. In the following essay he analyzes the regenerated interest in the 1960's in the work of the master of film musical spectacular, Busby Berkeley.*

To any American moviegoer over the age of 40, the name Busby Berkeley has always been as much of a byword as that of Mickey Rooney, Judy Garland, Dick Powell, Ruby Keeler, James Cagney, Eddie Cantor, Joan Blondell, Ginger Rogers, Al Jolson or any of the dozens of other Hollywood personalities who starred in his films. We who sat enthralled in front of our neighborhood screens through what we've always thought of as Hollywood's golden years, the thirties and early forties, knew exactly what to expect from a Busby Berkeley picture, and we went to these films as much because they were *his* pictures as for any other reason.

Every dance and production number in all of the many musicals that he worked in over the years could only have been conceived and directed by him. And when, for a variety of related reasons—rising costs, the advent of television, the demise of the big studios—the Hollywood musical became rarer, as well as more realistic, more intimate, less spectacular in every way, we also realized we'd never see his like again and we stopped looking for his name on our screens. But though Hollywood cast him aside, along with so many others, *we* did not forget. Olympus may be no more, but the names of the old gods still trip easily off the tongue.

Ironically, television, which did so much to end the Hollywood we all knew and thought we loved, made Busby Berkeley famous again.

* By permission from William Murray, "The Return of Busby Berkeley," *New York Times Magazine,* March 2, 1969. © 1969.

Most of his movies, sandwiched between used-car pitches, diagrams of clogged sinuses and troubled digestive passages, have in recent years been gracing the late, late shows from coast to coast. Viewers of all ages have sat enthralled before such classics as *Gold Diggers of 1933, Forty-Second Street, Footlight Parade, Strike Up the Band, Babes on Broadway* and *The Gang's All Here,* marveling at the Busby Berkeley touch. That touch was nothing if not spectacular, a fantasy world, according to one film historian, of "kaleidoscopic patterns of female flesh, dissolving into artichokes, exploding stars, snowflakes and the expanding leaves of water lilies." No wonder the man lives on!

And then we discovered, somewhat to our surprise, that Busby Berkeley is actually, as well as figuratively, very much alive. Recently he's been popping up all over the place, here and abroad, to accept awards, deliver lectures, be interviewed on television and take a few well merited bows, between public showings of clips from his old movies. Newspaper photographs of these events have depicted for us a moon-faced, aging pixie with thinning gray hair, bobbing and smiling and shaking hands and clutching trophies and hugging old, equally delighted collaborators from the golden era, while audiences of young people applaud enthusiastically. It's nice to know he's still around, but what, we wonder, has he been doing all this time? The American impulse would be to think of him as retired.

Berkeley himself doesn't see it that way. For the past 10 years he has been living with his sixth wife, Etta, in a modest pink-stucco ranch house in Palm Desert, Calif., waiting for the phone to ring. Lately, despite the fact that no one from Hollywood has been bidding for his services, it has been ringing quite a bit. Etta, a plump brunette with the bland impersonal nicety of a nurse or an airline stewardess is quick to say "Oh, there isn't a week that he isn't being contacted for one thing or another." The contacts are mostly requests for personal appearances in connection with his past achievements and Berkeley grants nearly all of them. The result is that he and Etta have been traveling quite a lot recently. Etta, obviously her husband's greatest fan, has been keeping a voluminous scrapbook of his recent triumphs, including a series of interviews with him in a number of distinguished foreign journals. The Berkeleys do not speak a word of any foreign language; all they know is that these interviews are highly laudatory and fully appreciative of Berkeley's genius. "You have no idea of the enthusiasm, everywhere we go," Etta says. "People just stand up and cheer!"

Berkeley himself is gratified by all this attention, but he conveys the distinct impression that he'd much rather be back at work. He is a big man in his early seventies and the first adjective that comes to mind is "gray." Gray eyes, gray hair, a gray suit, gray skin. Much of the time, sitting or standing, he sags, somewhat in the manner of the late Wallace Beery, whom he slightly resembles. His stomach bulges, his lower lip is pendulous and his nose seems squashed against his face. In other words, he looks his age. But when he talks about his work, an extraordinary transformation takes place. Everything seems to lift into place. His stomach moves up into his chest, his lower lip tucks in under his upper one and his features seem to throb with suppressed energy. He speaks in a husky, booming baritone and emphasizes his points with heavy strokes in the air of big, thick-fingered hands. The realization comes abruptly that the man is a dynamo, ready to go into action instantly at the sight of a signed contract. "Hell, I've had loads of real big propositions, but they never get all the money up," he booms and the frustration of the long wait is evident on his face.

There's something obscene about the sight of an energetic man in full possession of his faculties forced to remain idle. Not since he was summoned back to direct the spectacle sequences in a disastrous film version of *Jumbo* in 1963 has Berkeley been able to work at what he likes best. When the adulatory trips are over and the television interviews have ended, he and Etta come back to Palm Desert and wait. They don't socialize much and, except for an occasional round of golf, Berkeley seldom leaves the house. He spends his time answering all of his fan mail personally, he reads a good deal and lately he has been working on his autobiography, mostly a reminiscence of his great Hollywood years entitled "Girls, Glamour and Glory."

The title is good vintage Berkeley, but not even this book seems to fill him with the enthusiasm he displays when he discusses his real work. The thought occurs that he could probably use the money, too, perhaps because the information that he and Etta are financially secure for the rest of their lives is volunteered gratuitously by each of them separately. The house is small, huddled low against the desert heat on a quarter-acre plot and, except for the inevitable swimming pool, utterly devoid of luxuries. "We's had our big houses, we're all through with that," Berkeley says, but without conviction. Etta, whose hobby is feeding the stray neighborhood cats, goes out to the patio to survey her dozen unpaying guests. "I never go anywhere now without her," Berkeley says and he begins to sag again. Out in the carport sits a sedan that is at least several years old and in which they drive to Los Angeles for the business meetings that now occur, one gathers, only infrequently.

If Busby Berkeley had never been imported from Broadway in 1930 to make his famous Warner Brothers musicals, it would have been necessary for Hollywood to invent him. The time was overripe. Ever since the advent of sound in the late twenties the big studios that dominated the film world had been looking to New York for salvation. Broadway knew all about the uses of sound, both words and music, and movie producers imagined that their new films, especially their big musicals, would benefit enormously from that knowledge. The immediate result was a series of attempts in which the camera stood still, much in the manner of a front-row spectator in a legitimate play-house. The producers had temporarily forgotten all about the camera itself as a creative factor.

Berkeley came west with impressive Broadway credentials. His parents had been touring actors and he himself had made his first stage appearance at the age of five. He had moved on from comedy acting and dancing to directing straight plays and musicals. By the time Sam Goldwyn hired him as a dance director, Berkeley had been involved in one capacity or another with 21 Broadway musicals.

His first job for Goldwyn was staging the dance and production numbers for an Eddie Cantor vehicle called *Whoopee*. "The first new thing I did," he recalls, "was film close-ups of the girls. They're beautiful girls, I told them, so why not show them to the public?" He also spent a lot of time wandering from set to set and finding out about the camera: "I soon realized that in the theater your eyes can go any place you want, but in pictures the only way I could entertain an audience was through the single eye of the camera. But with that single eye I could go anywhere *I* wanted to. You couldn't get any of my sets onto a legit stage, but I didn't care about that. To be entertaining and spectacular, that's what I cared about."

It was at Warner Brothers that his talent burst into awesome bloom. His first movie there, *Forty-Second Street*, included a production number featuring hordes of tap-dancing prostitutes and criminals, while Dick Powell, at the bar of the saloon, observed in song that "the big parade goes on for years/A melody of laughter and tears." In *Gold Diggers of 1933*, Powell and Ruby Keeler sang and danced through phalanxes of near-naked chorus girls and athletic-looking boys. In *Footlight Parade*, there was an aquaballet, photographed from above, featuring shifting patterns of interlocked female thighs, an opium-den sequence shot through swirling smoke, a barroom brawl, a lot of dancing throughout by Keeler and James Cagney, and a parade of soldiers blending into marching patterns featuring portraits of the N.R.A. eagle and F.D.R. By the time the forties came around, Berkeley had achieved true surrealism. His "Polka-Dot Ballet," in *The Gang's All Here* (1943), featured masses of girls twirling glowing metal hoops and revolving huge, multicolored polka-dots and ended with the tiny, disembodied heads of the entire cast bobbing about the screen while bursting into full-throated song.

In most of his early movies Berkeley only directed the dance and production numbers. It wasn't until *Gold Diggers of 1935* that he was hired as over-all director, but it's a tribute to his particular talent that every film he ever worked in survives today in our memories purely as a Busby Berkeley vehicle. Berkeley himself never cared much about the story line and regarded it merely as a convenient skeleton on which to flesh out his fantasies, much in the manner of Rossini draping his gorgeous solos, duets and ensembles all over the framework of whatever hack libretto an impresario handed him. "I did my numbers and the director did the story," Berkeley recalls. "Sometimes I'd even forget who was directing." No one ever knew exactly what would finally emerge from such a collaboration until the day of the first screening.

It didn't really matter because most of Berkeley's early films had the same plot. It almost always revolved around the epic struggles of a harried show-biz tycoon to produce some form of theatrical entertainment, always on the edge of disaster and under the most appalling handicaps. This basic story line has been perfectly recreated by a little Off-Broadway musical called "Dames at Sea," one of the hits of the current season, in which Ruby (Keeler) is a sweet, innocent chorine, Dick (Powell) is an aspiring songwriter, Joan (Blondell) is the wise-cracking babe who befriends them and it all ends with the cast tap-dancing like crazy all over a battleship. In every one of these movies there came a dramatic crisis resolved by the innocent chorine rushed in to substitute at the last minute for the incapacitated star of the show in rehearsal. The quintessential line of dialogue for all these films was delivered by Warner Baxter to Miss Keeler in *Forty-Second Street*. "You're going out a chorus girl," he told her, "but you're coming back a star!"

What made Berkeley's own work memorable was the sheer grandeur of his unique creative vision. "I never got any ideas from anyone," he claims. "I'd plot the whole thing out in advance and set every camera angle myself. Nobody but me ever knew what the number would look like on the screen until it was in the can." Someone once figured out that his big production numbers cost $10,000 for each minute of screen time, an awesome figure for that hard-money era. "But no one ever lost a dime on any of my pictures," Berkeley says, "because all of them were so great."

He invented a monorail to make his camera more mobile and devised the so-called top shot, the technique of filming from directly above the action. To get the distance and perspective he wanted on some of these shots, he forced the studio heads to let him bore through the ceilings of their sound stages, causing one angry executive to exclaim,

"Jesus, now Berkeley's going through the roof!" For an Esther Williams vehicle he built a swimming pool in the middle of a lake in Florida's Cypress Gardens. For Ann Miller he drilled holes through a stage floor and taught the startled orchestra musicians to play their instruments over their heads, so that Miss Miller could eventually dance on screen through a forest of disembodied arms sawing and tootling away.

None of Berkeley's production numbers were intimate nor were they encumbered by good taste. His routines always displayed swarms of performers as well as tremendous technical effects—50 girls playing illuminated violins, 100 babes banging away at pyramided stacks of grand pianos, 200 tap dancers for one night-club routine. "There weren't any union rules and work laws to worry about then," Berkeley observes. "We'd go on for 12, 16 hours until we got it right. It was nothing for me to be doing a close-up at 5 A.M. and sometimes I'd have two or three numbers in production at once."

His girls were noted for their beauty as well as their endurance. "I'd interview them through their eyes," Berkeley says. "They had to have good figures, of course, but I could tell more about them by looking into their eyes. And I didn't care if a girl could dance or not. If she had a good sense of rhythm, I could teach her all that." For a while he had 16 of his girls under personal contract to him, at $75 a week.

Berkeley's great value to the studio, of course, was as an idea man. He would sit alone for hours in his office at Warners' until, through intense meditation, a blinding vision of his next spectacle would suddenly overwhelm him. "I don't know where my ideas came from," he says, "but I never did the same thing twice." Orders would be dispatched to every production department, but no one was ever allowed to know exactly what Berkeley was up to until it materialized on the screen, not even the stars.

Ruby Keeler, Berkeley's favorite leading lady, would occasionally protest feebly that she simply couldn't do what Berkeley demanded of her, "I'd tell her just to go ahead and do it," Berkeley recalls, "and she always did." Cost-conscious executives were sometimes more persistent in their objections, but Berkeley shooed them away. After all, if the man could make money for the studio (and he made gobs of it during those early years) by insisting on 200 tap-dancers or a reproduction in miniature of all of Manhattan's skyscrapers, who were they to scream?

As for the dance routines themselves, Berkeley left the teaching of the actual steps to underlings. "Hell, I didn't know the first five positions of dancing," he admits. "I just picked it up." His great forte, in addition to the original concept, was his ability to move great masses of people in strict time all over his stages. This was a talent he developed during the First World War when, as a second lieutenant in France under General Pershing himself, he had taught his battalion first to order themselves about the parade ground, then to march and drill to band music, executing the most complicated maneuvers, in absolute silence. Berkeley discovered he had a natural talent for handling people, 5,000 or morely five at a time.

During these years of enforced exile in Palm Desert, Berkeley has managed to keep abreast of development in the entertainment work and he is not enthusiatic about much of what he sees. He bemoans the passing from the scene of the big studios, the soaring production costs and the consequent conservatism of the film industry. "You see, today it's different," he points out. "They wait until a show is a hit in New York, then they buy it and film it. In our day, we wrote original stories, we created our own material." Nor is he impressed by developments in the dance world, especially as they are reflected in current musicals and TV shows.

Here's his account of a recent routine he witnessed on his tiny screen: "They have these eight girls and four boys. You see them do this modern dancing. First the girls alone, then the boys alone. Then they all fall on the floor and hold their arms up and that's the end of the number." Berkeley takes a fairly dim view of choreography in general. "That's a word that came in with Agnes de Mille," he says. "Now they call everybody who kicks his foot a little a choreographer. Me, I was always a dance director."

Berkeley has no illusions about the realities of the movie business today and he admits that the grandeur that was the Hollywood musical of his time could only be duplicated now at a tremendous cost, but he claims to have devised a number of secret ways of keeping expenses down. It certainly does not occur to him that his style could in any way be dated and the term "camp" evokes from him only a slightly puzzled stare. What the man wants to do is go back to work at what he does best. "My philosophy was purely—call it gigantic entertainment," he says and proceeds to outline two big sequences he'd love to film. One would have the floor changing colors under the feet of his whirling dancers. The other would be an abstract ballet for 100 cuspidors and 200 black hands, "the dream of a Negro cleaning woman in an office building."

When Berkeley talks about working again, those big hands flail the air and rap-tap-tap on the arms of his chair. Etta comes back from feeding the cats and recounts how in Europe recently one question-and-answer session after a lecture went on so long that the audience was only finally persuaded to leave the building by turning the lights out.

Berkeley discloses that he is currently negotiating to do a Broadway musical that is supposed to go into rehearsal in the fall and that his greatest filmed dance routines are being assembled into a single full-length movie.

Because he is a showman who dates from an old tradition of the business—that the best movie or play is what is most entertaining and that, at any cost, it *must* go on—he admits only to being in his late sixties. Nothing must interfere with his ability to give it all he's got, certainly not anything as trivial as his age. "Theater and films—it goes in cycles," he says. "One of these days the spectacular will be back and I hope I'll be around to do it."

The Shock of Freedom in Films

Time Magazine

The following, a cover story in Time, *discusses the Hollywood "renaissance" of the mid-1960s.*

Two girls embrace, then enjoy a long, lingering kiss that ends only when a male intruder appears.

A vulpine criminal in a sumptuous penthouse pulls aside a window curtain to look down at the street. When he releases the curtain, he is abruptly in another apartment. He crosses the thickly carpeted living room to peer into a bedroom; when he turns back, the living room is empty and bare-floored.

In the midst of an uproariously funny bank robbery, a country-boy hoodlum fires his pistol; the tone of the scene shifts in a split second from humor to horror as the bloodied victim dies.

At first viewing, these scenes would appear to be photomontages from an underground-film festival. But *The Fox,* based on a D. H. Lawrence story with a lesbian theme, is soon to be released nationally, starring Sandy Dennis. *Point Blank,* with Lee Marvin, is in its plot an old-fashioned shoot-'em-down but in its technique a catalogue of the latest razzle-dazzle cinematography. *Bonnie and Clyde* is not only the sleeper of the decade but also, to a growing consensus of audiences and critics, the best movie of the year.

Differing widely in subject and style, the films have several things in common. They are not what U.S. movies used to be like. They enjoy a heady new freedom from formula, convention and censorship. And they are all from Hollywood.

* By permission from *Time,* December 8, 1967, pp. 66–76. Time Inc., New York. © 1967.

POETRY & RHYTHM

Hollywood was once described as the only asylum run by its inmates. It was the town where, as George Jean Nathan said, "ten million dollars' worth of machinery functions elaborately to put skin on baloney." There is still plenty of machinery out there putting skin on baloney. But the most important fact about the screen in 1967 is that Hollywood has at long last become part of what the French film journal *Cahiers du Cinéma* calls "the furious springtime of world cinema," and is producing a new kind of movie.

Newness is not merely a matter of time but of attitude. Despite the legacy of such rare masters as D. W. Griffith and Sergei Eisenstein, the vast majority of films a decade ago were little more than pale reflections of the theater or the novel. The New Cinema has developed a poetry and rhythm all its own. Traditionally, says *Cahiers* Editor Jean-Louis Comolli, "a film was a form of amusement—a distraction. It told a story. Today, fewer and fewer films aim to distract. They have become not a means of escape but a means of approaching a problem. The cinema is no longer enslaved to a plot. The story becomes simply a pretext."

Whether or not film makers want to tell a story, they no longer need adhere to the convention that a movie should have a beginning, middle and end. Chronological sequence is not so much a necessity as a luxury. The slow, logical flashback has given way to the abrupt shift in scene. Time can be jumbled on the screen—its foreground and background as mixed as they are in the human mind. Plot can diminish in a forest of effects and accidents; motivations can be done away with, loose ends ignored, as the audience, in effect, is invited to become the scenarist's collaborator, filling in the gaps he left out. The purposeful camera can speed up action or slow it down; the sound track can muddle a conversation or over-amplify it to incoherence. Black-and-white sequences intermingle with color.

Comedy and tragedy are no longer separate masks; they have become interchangeable, just as heroes and villains are frequently indistinguishable. Movies still make moral points, but the points are rarely driven home in the heavy-hammered old way. And like some of the most provocative literature, the film now is apt to be amoral, casting a coolly neutral eye on life and death and on humanity's most perverse moods and modes.

PROUST IS POSSIBLE

The New Cinema has been displayed on U.S. screens recently with astonishing variety and virtuosity. Michelangelo Antonioni parodied the modish artsiness of fashion photography to help create the swinging

London mood of *Blow-Up*. Italy's Gillo Pontecorvo faithfully reproduced the grainy style of newsreel footage to restage *The Battle of Algiers*—a pictorially harrowing exposition of war as an extension of politics. Czech Director Jiří Menzel leaped from tears to laughter in quick sequence to create the moody turmoil of *Closely Watched Trains*. The "undoable" film can now be done, as shown by the creditable and convincing movie versions of Joyce's *Ulysses* and *Finnegans Wake*. Even Proust is possible—if anyone wants to try.

It remains to be seen whether the new thematic and technical freedom is a cause for unrestrained rejoicing; there is the obvious danger that it will be used excessively for the sake of gimmickry or shock. But the fact is that innovation is no longer the private preserve of the art houses but a characteristic of the main-line American movie. *Two for the Road*, otherwise an ordinary Audrey Hepburn vehicle, has as much back-and-forth juggling of chronology as any film made by Alain Resnais—not to mention a comic acidity about marital discord that is as candid as anything the Swedes have said. Even a conspicuous failure such as John Huston's *Reflections in a Golden Eye* bleeds color images through black-and-white in a startling extension of the camera's palette. U.S. movies are now treating once-shocking themes with a maturity and candor unthinkable even five years ago; the life of drug addicts in *Chappaqua*, homosexuality in *Reflections*, racial hatred in *In the Heat of the Night*. And *The Graduate*, a new Mike Nichols film, is an alternately comic and graphic closeup of a 19-year-old boy whose sexual fantasies come terrifyingly true.

NO MORE HABIT

As in the days of Goldwyn and Mayer, the studio goal is to make money—but the customers are now willing to pay for a different product. "The main change has been in audiences," argues Robert Evans, head of production at Paramount. "Today, people go to see *a* movie; they no longer go to *the* movies. We can't depend on habit any more. We have to make 'I've got to see that' pictures."

As the studio heads have discovered, there is not a single cinema audience today but several. There is—and perhaps always will be—an audience for banality and bathos. But a segment of the public wants the intellectually demanding, emotionally fulfilling kind of film exemplified by *Bonnie and Clyde*. By now, television has all but taken over Hollywood's former function of providing placebo entertainment. Movie attendance among the middle-aged is down; yet box-office receipts are up—partly because cinema has become the favorite art form of the young.

The growing mass audience has been prepared for change and experiment both by life and art. It has seen—and accepted—the questioning of moral traditions, the demythologizing of ideals, the pulverizing of esthetic principles in abstract painting, atonal music and the experimental novel. Beyond that, oddly enough, younger moviemen credit television with a major role in paving the way for acceptance of the new in films.

"TV has changed the world by changing people's attitudes," says Polish Director Roman Polanski (*Knife in the Water*). "When they are born with a TV set in their room—well—you can't fool them any more." Or at least, it might be added, not in the same way. Director Richard Lester, who got his start on TV, believes that television's abrupt leap from news about Viet Nam to *Gomer Pyle* to toothpaste ads expands people's vision. "TV is best at those sudden shifts of reality. TV, not *Last Year at Marienbad,* made the audience notice them for the first time."

Undeniably, part of the scandal and success of *Bonnie and Clyde* stems from its creative use of what has always been a good box-office draw: violence. But what matters most about *Bonnie and Clyde* is the new freedom of its style, expressed not so much by camera trickery as by its yoking of disparate elements into a coherent artistic whole—the creation of unity from incongruity. Blending humor and horror, it draws the audience in sympathy toward its anti-heroes. It is, at the same time, a commentary on the mindless daily violence of the American '60s and an esthetic evocation of the past. Yet it observes the '30s not as lived but as remembered, the perspective rippled by the years to show that there are mirages of time as well as space. The nostalgic Technicolor romanticism alters reality, distorting it as a straight stick under water appears to be bent.

The story has its basis in fact. Clyde Barrow and Bonnie Parker were two veal-faced wrongos who rode out of Texas during the Depression, killing and plundering for fun and profit. The constabulary bushwacked them in May 1934 near Arcadia, La., firing a thousand rounds into the fugitives and their 1934 Ford De Luxe, which 18 years later was still touring auto showrooms as a ghoulist curio. On their own turf, Bonnie and Clyde passed from the front page into folklore; elsewhere, they were relegated to Sunday-supplement features, colorful figures of the gangland era. It is a measure of the movie's excellence that it has transformed those unlikely, unlikable criminals into the leading characters of an epic folk opera.

Bonnie, played by Faye Dunaway, is first glimpsed naked, a sensual Erskine Caldwell backwoods beauty imprisoned by her hot, airless room. Clyde, the jaunty, vacant car thief, played by Warren Beatty, offers her passage out of the Dust Bowl, with his gun as her ticket. To her dismay, she discovers that he is impotent. "Your advertising is just dandy," sneers Bonnie, after their first no-love session, "Folks'd never guess you don't have a thing to sell." Yet Clyde does have a salable commodity: movement in a time of inertia, elation in the midst of depression.

Although Clyde is a murderous ex-convict and Bonnie is his willing, amoral moll, they are essentially innocents: violence is something they can neither comprehend nor manage, and their dreams are always of settling down somewhere when hard times are over. When the two take up their aimless career as thieves, they try to see themselves as striking back at the haves on behalf of the have-nots—although there is no hint of ideology or social protest in their actions.

For a time they are cheered on by starving drifters who vicariously enjoy the cocky résumé: "I'm Clyde Barrow, and this is Miss Bonnie Parker. We rob banks." In an episode at once poignant and wonderfully funny, Clyde lends his .45 to a Texas-gothic farmer, who shoots his deserted farmhouse, repossessed by the bank. They speed away from their jobs in a succession of stolen cars—their Ford coupés, Essex tourer and Marmon Saloon are virtually living members of the cast. The sound track adds a further fillip to the humor; the exuberant banjo picking of Earl Scruggs playing *Foggy Mountain Breakdown* suggests a comedy chase.

"Though the boys throw stones at the frogs in sport," wrote an ancient Greek poet, "the frogs do not die in sport but in earnest." The Barrow gang—Bonnie and Clyde, his brother Buck and wife Blanche, their goofy, moon-faced driver, C. W. Moss—proves the truth of that maxim with its targets. At first, the shots are scattered in the air, like careless shouts. Then one lands point-blank in the face of a bank clerk. Blood bursts onto the screen, and from that instant, the audience is torn between horror and glee.

LIFE FOR A DEATH

The police pursue them relentlessly and, during one ambush, Buck's skull is split open by bullets. Blanche, wounded in one eye, turns into a shrill animal, incoherently rending the air with screams. Buck thrashes in agony, like a blind bull pierced with sword thrusts. Pain becomes palpable, and the actors become horribly real as the screen turns as bloody as a slaughterhouse floor.

The comedy is completely eroded now. Badly wounded themselves, Bonnie and Clyde escape to the sanctuary of C. W. Moss's home. C. W.'s father puts on a smarmy smile for the couple, but then arranges their execution by trading with the police; his son's life for the couple's death. The police arrange the ambush; and in what may be the most remarkable use of slow motion in cinema history, the bodies of Bonnie and Clyde writhe to earth in a quarter-time choreography of death.

The bloody ending is as inevitable as the climax of a Greek tragedy; yet to most audiences it comes as a shock, and there is usually a hushed, shaken silence to the crowds that trail out of the theaters. The reason is not simply the cinematic perfection of the death scene. It is also caused by the fact that Bonnie and Clyde are what Warren Beatty calls "ordinary people," whose curiously appealing lower-middle-class normality emerges between crimes—Bonnie's perpetual avian bickering with Buck's wife, the Barrow brothers' spirited roughhouse chaff. They kill and rob banks; but they share the common concerns of common men.

DRAMATIC IRONY

In portraying the archcriminal as the boy next door, *Bonnie and Clyde* displays a dramatic irony that gives the picture much of it vitality and stature. It is the irony that weds laughter and horror, belly laughs and bullets in the face, life and death. Clyde holds up a bank—which has failed three weeks previously. C. W. Moss's father belts him across the mouth, not for consorting with murderers but because he has got himself tattooed. Bonnie expresses her wish to settle down near her mother. "You try to live three miles from me," says the mother mordantly, "and you won't live long, honey."

There are maudlin flaws in the film, however, and the gore sometimes flows in almost absurd, Grand Guignol quantities. Buck's death goes on and on, long after the audience is fully aware of his agonies. One scene of an Okie auto camp, where the dispossessed farmers huddle together in the humiliating dawn, is posed with a self-consciousness that elicits admiration for the masterly photography but no emotion for the wretchedness of the humans within the picture frame. Yet many other passages could hardly have been bettered: the vaporous, honey-colored scene in which the movie enters Bonnie's simple, sentimental mind as she visits her mother for the last time; the low comedy of the first successful heist; the slow dance on the killing ground that ends the film.

It is little wonder that the picture has shaken up not only audiences but Hollywood as well, and elevated its principals to genuine star stature. Warren Beatty, a boyish 30, used to be known mostly as Shirley MacLaine's brother, an off-again-on-again actor who moonlighted as global escort of Natalie Wood, Leslie Caron, Julie Christie and Barbara Harris. A *Mondo* movie all by himself, he was like, wow, to the starlets but something else to the studios, which doubted his ability to produce the film. The studios now concede that as a producer Beatty was like, wow. He brought in the film on time and at its modest budget ($2,500,000). As for his acting future, he can pretty much name his own price and project.

Faye Dunaway, 26, the Florida-born daughter of a U.S. Army master sergeant, was an original member of Elia Kazan's Lincoln Center Repertory Company, and brought her special brand of sparkle to the off-Broadway hit *Hogan's Goat*. But in Hollywood Faye was indistinguishable from the rest of the bleachers in the crowd. One of 100 girls considered for Bonnie, she got the part a few days before shooting began. Today she is a suddenly recognizable presence as she strides through the fashion pages of the suddenly popular '30s-style dresses and suits like the ones she wore in the film. The supporting players were even more obscure than the stars. Michael J. Pollard, 28, had a few minor parts to his credit before *Bonnie and Clyde*, usually playing an ungainly amalgam of chagrin and Silly Putty; he is almost certain to get an Oscar nomination for his slobbery, hound-dog portrayal of C. W. Moss.

Bonnie and Clyde has also brought the metamorphosis of success to its scenarists, Robert Benton and David Newman. They began thinking about the movie four years ago in New York City, after mulling over the films of François Truffaut—*Jules and Jim* and *Shoot the Piano Player*. At the time, Benton and Newman were house satirists at *Esquire*, writing sophomoric advice to college boys like how to fake mononucleosis. *The Dillinger Days*, a book about crime in the '30s, crossed their desk. The way they like to tell it, a figurative light bulb appeared over their heads when they came to the section on Clyde Barrow.

YELLING THIRTIES

Benton and Newman were not the first to see the cinematic potential of Bonnie and Clyde. Back in 1937 the gangster couple inspired Fritz Lang's *You Only Live Once*, a fictionalized treatment of a man ruined by a prison sentence, starring Henry Fonda and Sylvia Sydney. As recently as 1958, *The Bonnie Parker Story* starred Dorothy Provine, a veteran of TV's *Roaring Twenties* turned into a Yelling Thirties girl.

None of these earlier reincarnations bore much relation to the true Bonnie and Clyde story, and they did not bother Benton and Newman. Frankly imitating the juxtaposition of dulcet tragedy and saline comedy that characterizes the work of France's François Truffaut, the two writers decided to write a script for him—even though they had never met him. In their original version, Clyde was a homosexual; he and Bonnie shared the favors of C. W. Moss in a weird *ménage à trois*. At the time, Truffaut was working on *Farenheit 451,* but he took a week off to teach the writers the grammar of film making, what the camera could see and say. After turning them loose, he then turned them down because he was still too involved in *Farenheit* to do the movie with them.

DO IT NOW

The script next went to Jean-Luc Godard. "He came over and said, 'Great, let's do it now,'" recalls Newman. "He wanted to leave right away for Texas and do the movie in two weeks." But the producers— two friends of Benton and Newman who had never done a movie before—procrastinated. The film was supposed to take place in summer, they argued, and this was winter. Godard abruptly cooled on the subject. "All they can think of is meteorology," he complained, and flew back to Paris. Exit Godard.

Enter Beatty, who had heard about the script in a Paris conversation with Truffaut. Beatty found Benton and Newman in New York City, liked their work enough to wait out the original producers' option, then bought the property for $75,000, intending to produce as well as direct under a contract with Warner Bros. Sister Shirley was to star as Bonnie. Eventually, he decided that he ought to play Clyde, which meant that Shirley had to go; after all, the picture featured more than enough gore and transgressions without seeming to add incest to injury.

As director, Beatty signed up Arthur Penn, 45, a narrow, sparrowish Broadway veteran (*Two For the Seesaw*), whose Hollywood record included a few hits (*The Miracle Worker*), several flops (*The Chase, Mickey One*). Penn wanted the film edited in Manhattan, which meant that the choice of which scenes would end up on the cutting-room floor would take place 2,500 miles from the home base of Warner Bros. To Jack Warner, 75, who liked to make his own pick of the rushes, everything but salami should be cut in the studio. More problems were to follow—arguments about sound, music, casting, script, going on location in Texas. To solve them, Beatty poured on the charm and indulged in some mock histrionics. During one argument with Warner, Beatty prostrated himself before the old man, dug his nose in the rug, and moaned: "Look, Jack, please do what I say. I won't waste your money." Warner looked down and grunted: "Get up off the floor, kid, you're embarrassing me." Beatty got his way.

NO TRAMPS

Most of the film was shot on location around Dallas. It was in a motel there that Beatty felt the first trickle of the torrent of controversy that would follow the film. "A huge waiter came in," he recalls, "and said to me 'Hey Warren, 'at trew yew gone play Clahd Barra? Sheee! I knowed Clahd Barra, and he wuz much better lookin' than yew are.'" As it happens, Clyde Barrow was not much better looking than Mr. Hyde.* The encounter was simply an initial indication that Texas folk heroes are never to be taken lightly—and that the story of Bonnie and Clyde had the power to shock and disturb anyone anywhere, from the simple to the most sophisticated.

It may have shocked audiences, but it brought them to the box office in record numbers. *Bonnie and Clyde* also stirred up a battle among movie critics that seemed to be almost as violent as the film itself. Bosley Crowther of the New York Times was so offended by it that he reviewed it—negatively—three times. "This blending of farce with brutal killings is as pointless as it is lacking in taste," he wrote. TIME's review made the mistake of comparing the fictional and real Bonnie and Clyde, a totally irrelevant exercise. *Newsweek* panned the film, but the following week returned to praise it.

The New Yorker ran a respectful appreciation by Guest Critic Penelope Gilliatt, followed nine weeks later with an ecstatic 9,000-word analysis by another guest critic, Pauline Kael. In Chicago, the Tribune's reviewer sided with the nay-sayers. He called it "stomach churning"; the American said it was "unappetizing." But the Daily News acclaimed it as one of the most significant motion pictures of the decade; the Sun-Times said it was "astonishingly beautiful." It seemed as if two different *Bonnie and Clydes* were slipping into towns simultaneously.

---

* Also outraged by the movie was Bonnie's sister, Billie Jean Parker, who lives in Dallas and had spent nine months in jail for sheltering Bonnie. She engaged Attorneys Jim Martin and Clayton Fowler (previous client: Jack Ruby) to sue Warner Bros. for $1,025,000. The film, it is alleged, "blackened" the memory of Bonnie and injured the reputation of Billie Jean, who offers some support of the claim: "One time Bonnie's leg was burned real bad in a car wreck. It took $9-a-day worth of Unguentine to put on her leg. Clyde *had* to rob places." Besides, she adds, "we used to take Bonnie pretty clothes. They didn't go around like a bunch of tramps."

One reason for some of the harsh reviews may have been that the critics were too aware of the movie's American origin. The homegrown skill displayed in *Bonnie and Clyde* may seem strange to Americans; it is no surprise to Europeans. To an extent, the American film was discovered by the French, who see things in U.S. movies no one else saw before. The directors who created France's New Wave openly imitated such films from the American past as the westerns of John Ford, the adventure flicks of Howard Hawks, and B-level gangster fray-for-alls of the '30s, like *Scarface*. French critics who have seen *Bonnie and Clyde* praised it enthusiastically—an American movie that started out as a film for a French director whose best works were echoes of American movies.

In both conception and execution, *Bonnie and Clyde* is a watershed picture, the kind that signals a new style, a new trend. An early example of this was *Birth of a Nation*, which still stands alone; it gave American cinema an epic sense of the nation's history. Orson Welles' *Citizen Kane* was another watershed film, with its stunning use of deep-focus photography and its merciless character analysis of that special U.S. phenomenon, the self-made mogul. John Ford's *Stagecoach* brought the western up from the dwarfed adolescence of cowboy-and-Injun adventures to the maturity and stature of a legend. Gene Kelly and Stanley Donen's *Singin' in the Rain* proved again the ingenuity of U.S. moviemakers to bring fresh style to the format of musical comedy, which, like jazz, remains an authentically American art form.

Even during the past decade, when the creative impulse in film has seemed to be the province of European directors, Hollywood has turned out movies that at least in retrospect, have the qualities of classics. Hitchcock's *Psycho* inaugurated America's cinema of cruelty, with a demonic amalgam of bloodshed and violence that was not equaled until *Bonnie and Clyde*. Stanley Kubrick's *Lolita* treated the forbidden subject of nymphet-mania with cool humor; his *Dr. Strangelove* demonstrated that the biliousness of black comedy was as American as the H-bomb. John Frankenheimer's *The Manchurian Candidate* was a flawed murder drama that explored the mind of a brainwashed assassin with psychological depth and technical brilliance.

OPEN CHECKBOOKS

In the wake of *Bonnie and Clyde*, there is an almost euphoric sense in Hollywood that more such movies can and will be made. The reason is that since mid-1966, the studios have opened doors and checkbooks to innovation-minded producers and directors with a largess unseen since Biograph moved from Manhattan to Los Angeles in 1910.

To be sure, these are different studios from the one-man autocracies that used to welcome creative geniuses like France's Jean Renoir with lavish contracts and then crush their talent with assembly-line production techniques. The old dinosaurs in the corner offices have finally given way to younger dinosaurs. Robert Evans of Paramount is 37. Richard Zanuck, Fox production chief, is 34. David Picker, United Artists' vice president for production, is 36. Today the studios are frequently packagers, providing money and facilities for small, independent production teams—which naturally insist upon artistic control. These film makers are not necessarily American. Hollywood is bankrolling movies all over the globe, and the cast and crew of a film can sometimes read like the attendance list of a U.N. committee meeting.

WELCOME TO MGM

Because of Hollywood's international outlook, Britain's Joseph Janni, producer of *Darling*, now looks there rather than to England. "If I go to J. Arthur Rank with a film idea, they consider me a nuisance," he claims. "If I go to MGM, I am welcomed." France's Claude Lelouch (*A Man and a Woman*) has been signed to a multipicture contract at United Artists, as has Polanski at Paramount. The Iron Curtain countries are a continuing source of new talent, and Hollywood studios have dangled fat contracts before Czechoslovakia's Jan Kadar, who made *Shop on Main Street*. Even the customarily aloof Antonioni has become part of the new Hollywood; his next film, *Zabriskie Point*, will be financed by MGM and shot in the Southwest. It will be, he says, about violence.

Hollywood is now so eager to experiment with young and untried directors and writers that some older, proven film makers are complaining about lack of work. Director Mark Rydell—one of a host of refugees from television—got the chance to do *The Fox* when a studio executive saw a segment of *I Spy* that impressed him. Francis Ford Coppola, 28, is a precocious graduate of the nudie industry who is now doing *Finian's Rainbow* for Warner Bros. Another untried talent is Faye Dunaway's fiancé, Jerry Schatzberg, 40, a still photographer of women's fashions, who is doing *Puzzle of a Downfall Child*.

So far, the freedom given to the new film makers is being expended largely on "adult" themes—which means, of course, lots of sex. But more than nudity and frankness is involved. A proliferation of new techniques—multiscreen, three-dimensional, the 360° projection of Expo 67—are already beginning to find their way into Hollywood productions.

The Boston Strangler is being shot with multiple images. One scene shows at the left an elderly woman watching TV; at bottom center, a detective interviews a witness; on the right, the strangler drives his car slowly through the streets to the elderly woman's house. Mary Ellen Bute's adaptation of Thornton Wilder's *The Skin of Our Teeth* will employ a wide screen, occasionally fragmented into a honeycomb of separate actions.

PATROLS AT THE FRONT

For all the new talent, new money and new freedom available, it is not certain that Hollywood can or will sustain the burden of living in a renaissance. Technical innovation does not in itself guarantee quality. There is some evidence already that the relaxation of censorship, for example, only replaces euphemistic clichés with crass clichés. Love scenes are not necessarily better because they are nuder. By getting close to graffiti, movie dialogue does not necessarily get closer to the truth.

Nonetheless, the best directors and writers are aware that cinematic freedom is a privilege that involves responsibility. Says Italy's Pontecorvo of today's film makers: "None of them knows where to go from here, exactly what the right direction is. They are searching, experimenting, feeling out here and there, like patrols at the front in war."

Those patrols have been annihilated before. For every bold, experimental foray there are bound to be many ambitious failures or cold, calculated imitations. Still, occasionally, one victory can change the world—or at least the part of it that produces films. *Bonnie and Clyde* is a conspicuous victory. It has proved to the industry that the "new movie" and "popular success" are not antithetical terms. Hollywood has sometimes acted as if money and art were incompatible. At worst, they can come together in a marriage of convenience. At best, they may even get to like each other.

The Falling Stars

Hollis Alpert

In the following essay Hollis Alpert describes the changing status of the Hollywood stars in the 1960s. *

In 1962, it still made some sense to say, as did Richard Schickel in his book, *The Stars*, that "the star stands at the very center of movie economics, and it is to his public image that all movies, no matter how high their artistic aims, are tailored. "Mr. Schickel exempted certain foreign films from his dictum, but, even so, one wonders if, today, he would want to withdraw it. Certainly, those at the very center of movie economics would not be likely to agree with him, especially after totting up the returns on such films as *Blow-Up, Bonnie and Clyde, The Graduate, Rosemary's Baby*, and *2001: A Space Odyssey*. These films and several others not tailored to any particular star image have caused Hollywood and that hyperactive branch in London to wonder if they've been placing their bets on the wrong stables.

The new "thinking" found its way into a *Variety* headline of a few months back: RISING SKEPTICISM ON STARS—OVERLY COSTLY, LACK B.O. PUNCH. In a free translation, this meant that the film companies are less inclined to base their production schedules on the availability of "important" stars or to pay them their astronomical fees (perhaps $1,000,000 or more), looking instead to other areas for the ingredients of a box-office smash. The development is an important one for the movie-going public, for it can mean—and has already meant—a fresher look for motion pictures.

It was only a few years ago that a would-be producer could babble to friends: "I've got myself a deal with UA if I can get myself a star." This meant that if Burt Lancaster, or Kirk Douglas, or Doris Day would agree to appear in his picture, the company would willingly

* By permission from Hollis Alpert, "The Falling Stars," *Saturday Review*, December 28, 1968.

provide him with a bankroll, with a hefty slice of the budget going to the star. The star would have consolidated his bargaining position during the dark Fifties, sometimes taking over the production reins himself. The banks that provided the loans for feature film production required the presence of a star in a film as a kind of mystical guarantee of its public appeal. Thus, Stanley Kubrick, before he was able to make his now classic *Paths of Glory* in 1958, had to shop around among the "bankable" stars before he could get his project approved. Kirk Douglas was the one who finally made the film possible.

More recently, when Kubrick made *2001: A Space Odyssey*, he had full freedom to choose his performers without regard to their public images, and, in fact, he gave a major role to a non-star and a non-human —Hal, the computer aboard the spaceship. Hal, perhaps symbolically, all but stole the show, and the film, in spite of its extremely high cost, is one of the most successful in MGM's recent history.

Yet, it was only two years ago that a highly placed executive in that same company told me that his own computer had reaffirmed his faith in the value of stars. "We ran through some figures on movies made without names," he said, "and compared them with movies featuring important stars. The costs of the latter were higher, but on balance they showed a higher profit margin." It is safe to say that MGM's computers are punching out a different message today.

In the *Variety* issue mentioned above, the reporter, Lee Beaupre, did some adding up of his own and discovered that many of filmdom's most sacrosanct star names had little, if any, interest for the movie-going public. He used the same criterion that the studios use: film rental returns. Heading his list of losers was Marlon Brando, whose films during the past ten years all went into the red ink column. Two of them, according to Mr. Beaupre, carried "history-making deficits." Included in the cross section of sometime flop artists were such well known people as Yul Brynner, Glenn Ford, James Garner, Brigitte Bardot, Tony Curtis, William Holden, Rock Hudson, Anthony Quinn, and Natalie Wood. Not all of their films came in at a loss, but their combined salaries could have reconstructed the blighted areas of Cleveland, and with considerably more profit.

In the industry, however, all it took to counter such facts was to mention the name of Elizabeth Taylor, a superstar if there ever was one. With a choice selection of film projects to choose from, with script approval, director approval, and co-star approval, Miss Taylor was certainly testimony to the importance of a star. But was she? A look at the recent record appears to show otherwise. *The Comedians* (with Richard Burton and Alec Guinness as co-stars) came out a loss, perhaps to be rescued by its television sale. *Reflections in a Golden Eye* (with Marlon Brando) glimmered faintly and sank. *Boom!* (again with

Burton) was a shuddering box-office bomb. And *Secret Ceremony*, buttressed with a supposedly vibrant and much talked-about new star, Mia Farrow, and with a solid one, Robert Mitchum, probably won't bring back the paper the contracts were written on.

The signs are all too apparent that the star system, on which the film industry once rose to its financial and mass-appeal glories, is crumbling, if not already defunct. The cultural signs, too, are all around us. Fabled favorites of past decades have become Madison Avenue camp, to be quaintly mocked in magazine ads and TV commercials. Former movie queens occasionally totter into films, but usually as grotesque caricatures in the horror genre. The vogue for Tiny Tim is, in a way, a horse-laugh at the star system. Michael J. Pollard is "in"; Cary Grant is "out." The over-thirties might still nominate Julie Andrews as a star of today, but her most recent effort *Star!*, directed by the fail-safe Robert Wise, looks as though it will wind up on the deficit side. Ask someone under thirty "Who is a movie star?" and you'll likely get the answer I got: "Dustin Hoffman. Maybe?"

Another sign of the changing times got dramatic attention some months ago when Richard Burton exhibited symptoms of tardiness during the shooting of a film called *Laughter in the Dark*. The director, Tony Richardson, peremptorily fired Burton when he showed up a half hour late and replaced him with a non-star, the presumably more punctual Nicol Williamson. Until that heretical moment, Burton had been regarded as the foremost male star of our time. Of importance is the fact that United Artists backed the director.

One reason the film industry had remained so loyal to its stars was the link they represented between the film present and the film past. They were a relatively stable element in a financially unstable medium. Hollywood folklore is full of stories about the girl discovered in a drug store who sailed on to film glory trailing profits in her wake. In the publicity apparatus developed by the studios, stars were the most exploitable items. The supposedly sophomoric public gobbled up the stuff, identified with the stars, dreamed about them at night. And, when movies were in their more primitive period, this, to an extent, was true. Movies were, indeed, tailored to their images. Stars were very handy for the kind of simplistic movies the studios preferred to make. If movies were made with and for stars, the clichés could be repeated endlessly. Stars were "types," and the type soon enough becomes the cliché.

But, with the emergence of the rival medium, television, the star system, as it had been developed over the years, was doomed, although it took some time to realize why. For one thing, the clichés were to be found on the home tube; for another, "personalities" appeared so thick and fast on it that stars lost their exclusivity and remoteness, their mythic configurations. But the most important development (and it took the rise of a whole new generation before it became apparent) was the visual training and orientation the young viewers received. The medium itself grew more addictive than the personalities, and it is to the visually dynamic film, the more "cinematic" kind of film experience, that our newly mature generation is more likely to respond. Many older film critics are finding it hard themselves to adjust to the new "style" that is more and more coming into being and principally espoused by younger directors, many of them trained in television. This accounts for the crusty critical greeting often given such films as *2001: A Space Odyssey*, or *Joanna*, in which subject, style, technique, and ambience loom more importantly than the display of personality or even "story." Younger viewers have little difficulty in jumping the "gaps." They don't require the familiarity of star faces and mannerisms in order to absorb meanings, for films to "speak" to them.

It is not that the public has tired of stars. They simply don't count for as much any more. An Antonioni insists on subordinating his performers, even his stars, to the demands of his visual and meaningful conception. The industry will insist on misinterpreting the significance of the box-office results of so admittedly difficult a film as *Blow-Up*. It will assume that it was the magnetic qualities of David Hemmings or Vanessa Redgrave that brought it through. But put those same new "stars" in a bloated, more traditional film, such as *Camelot*, and they seem to have not the slightest drawing power. Another misinterpretation is to assume that it is the "sex" in the film that attracts the public. But it is wishful thinking, indeed, to assume that a few moments of artistically nuanced eroticism is what causes audiences to sit through two rather subtle hours. There's always 42nd Street, and the grind houses everywhere, for a rawer kind of sex—and in infinitely greater measure.

An audience has emerged for the visually exciting film, and it is a large one that is often able to discern between the fake, the empty, and the newer and more challenging filmic conceptions. Today, the director who shows the ability to "style" his films and to communicate with cinematic directness, is the one most in demand. The director has virtually replaced the star at the center of movie economics. Mike Nichols, quite properly, has become the first million-dollar director. Until he demonstrates otherwise, it is assumed he knows the secret of this shorthand cinematic method. Critics and movie buffs may complain and lament that movies aren't being made the same way as they used to be in the good old days; aging producers may declare that there's nothing wrong with the movies that a crop of new faces (by which some of them mean new and bigger breasts and buttocks) won't cure; but the truth of the matter is that the old form of fan worship is unutterably square, espoused perhaps by today's lineal descendants of the bobby-sox screamers but with no discernible effect on what happens at the box office.

It is slowly being realized even in the financial bastions of the film industry that stars don't matter very much any more. Here's a recent quote by a major studio head: "Carefully choose your producers, directors, and writers, and the actors will take care of themselves." No one has any real objection to putting a big star name in a picture, but it had better be the right star for the right picture. It is the tailoring concept that has gone out the window. The canny star will seek the role for which he is right, the film to which his own style, perhaps talent, can contribute rather than stultify. It is the talented performer who is coming to the fore, and because of this the term "star" will take on a more genuine connotation. Such figures as Rod Steiger, Sidney Poitier, George C. Scott, and Anne Bancroft deserve their star designations. They are sterling, creative performers, able to subordinate their public images (although Sidney Poitier is beginning to show signs of typing himself) to the demands of a role. Ironically, the above were not even regarded as true stars by the industry, until recent box-office figures proved otherwise.

The more creatively gifted stars often appear ready to abandon their public images in order to make a more effective contribution to the film medium itself. Certainly Warren Beatty's instincts were correct when he rebelled against his "pretty boy" roles—which were getting him nowhere anyway—and decided to produce his own picture, *Bonnie and Clyde*. Suddenly it was Warren Beatty, the actor, the cinematic performer, who electrified the screen. Nor did he show any inclination to hasten into another picture. He didn't have to; *Bonnie and Clyde* made him wealthy. Paul Newman showed his dissatisfaction with his star image by directing a picture. A studio decided to "humor" him and *Rachel, Rachel* was the result, one of the biggest successes of the year. The cinematic language is by no means the sole possession of directors. There is no reason at all for an observant, intelligent actor, able to keep his ego under control, not to be able to learn directorial techniques while performing in films. Hollywood's tendency to categorize can prove a financial boomerang. And, meanwhile, having given Paul Newman his opportunity, another fine acting talent was thereby resuscitated: Joanne Woodward. Hollywood had all but given up on her, too.

Some do better by working outside the industry channels. John Cassavetes, not exactly an important star but one in demand because of his professional capabilities, seems to find the film-making process more challenging than acting. His *Faces* has its peculiarities and not altogether successful moments, but its concepts are light-years away from the stereotypes of the films on which the industry has invested its resources for so long. Nor can the industry point to *Faces* as an experiment for select and limited audiences, for it will out-earn many an expensive "commercial" Hollywood product. Cassavetes uses his actors not as types, or even as performers, but as contributors to the film reality he is attempting to achieve. This may well be a significant direction, once again pointing to the end of the dominance of the star.

Thus the film itself becomes the star, becomes the attracting force for the public, or at least one very important segment of the public. The more visually sophisticated the audience grows, the more it will ask that movies provide the kind of experience that is inherent in the medium. Whether it is the quivering excitement of *Bullitt*, the devilish fantasy of *Rosemary's Baby*, or the deft, cinematic fun of *Joanna*, these are basically films. Their inhabitants may be or become stars, but it is as films that they are successful.

The Moonchild and the Fifth Beatle

Time Magazine

*The following article is an intelligent view of the new "anti-stars" in American films.**

> **JOHN**
> *Sleep well?*
>
> **MARY**
> *Yes.*
> *(a small grin)*
> *What there was of it. I didn't wake you up, did I?*
>
> **JOHN**
> *No, you didn't wake me up.*

John and Mary pick each other up in a Manhattan dating bar. They never quite catch each other's name, but they go to bed (his place; she has roommates). They spend the next day finding out about each other, fall in love and that evening again head for bed. They speak their final dialogue as the camera follows a trail of clothes across the bedroom floor:

> **MARY**
> *My name's Mary . . . What about you . . . ?*
>
> **JOHN**
> *I'm John.*

Peter Yates, the British director who began filming *John & Mary* in Manhattan last week, calls it a "contemporary love story." It begins

* By permission from *Time*, February 7, 1969, pp. 50–54. Time Inc., New York. © 1967.

where romantic movies used to end—with the snuggling in the percales. After that, the script lightly flicks such switched-on subjects as astrology, hippies, fags, the Pill, Jean-Luc Godard's *Weekend,* May-September adultery, *cinéma vérité* film makers and, just for laughs, itself. From time to time, for example, it underlines the dialogue with subtitles:

MARY

You've got a lot of room here.

SUBTITLE

"Is your wife away for the weekend?"

Who are Mary and John? The ad announcing the new production says it in ideographs: Rosemary's baby carriage perched atop Mrs. Robinson's knee. Mia Farrow, 23, and Dustin Hoffman, 31. The wandering waif and the victim of the middle class. Mrs. Sinatra and Mr. Acne. Novelist Flannery O'Connor put it another way: "Everything that rises must converge." The casting together of the two fastest-rising performers in the business was inevitable—it always is. But it once took half a career to manage the box-office mergers of Jimmy Stewart and June Allyson or Spencer Tracy and Katharine Hepburn. The tempo of American cinema has speeded up; it happened to Farrow and Hoffman after one big hit apiece.

Those two hits themselves are significant: they are obviously part of their time and yet, in other ways, out of it. The era is supposed to belong to the politically active and the sexually liberated young; how could anyone hope to succeed with a picture about a male-virgin college graduate whose only politic problem was turning off Mrs. Robinson? This is an age dominated by science, which prides itself on being free of superstition; who would have thought that a story that takes the devil seriously could become a smash? Yet *Rosemary's Baby* was not only a bestseller as a book, but already ranks among the top 50 alltime movie hits. *The Graduate* has become the third largest money earner ($40 million) in movie history.

It is mainly the kids who made the success of these films, suggesting that the image of the new generation free of sexual hang-ups and fascinated only by reality is misleading. The young, in fact, have made a new cult of the occult. The cause, Psychologist Rollo May believes, lies in the disintegration of familiar myths that leaves individuals alienated and adrift. When the medieval myths broke down, he argues, people turned to "witchcraft, sorcery and, in painting, the wild surrealism of a man like Bosch. In our day it is LSD, hippies and touch therapy."

New myths for old. *The Graduate* and *Rosemary's Baby* spin a new myth of lost innocence, of the individual against the wicked system.

The new young actors themselves represent the death of many myths—among them, the one of the movie star. The big press buildup, the house in Beverly Hills baroque, the ostentation and the seven-picture commitment are giving way to a stubborn kind of performer who is as suspicious of the Hollywood system as a student rebel is of the university trustees. Many of the young stars are, in fact, anti-stars, who fight against the inducements and erosions of the big time. People like Olivia Hussey, Robert Redford and David Warner have nothing against fame, but they trade on it to gain freedom—the freedom to choose their roles and their directors. The once-desirable studio contract now looks like slavery.

DID YOU TOUCH HIM?

The anti-star attitude itself threatens to become a new pose or convention in which the Hollywood swimming pool is replaced by the interesting East Side pad, the Valley ranch by a Martha's Vineyard retreat, the antic table-hopping by frantic political activism. At any rate, both Farrow and Hoffman live and breathe the new freedom; both have opted for the small apartment over the big house, the East over the West. Both feel that though there may be New York and New York, and Chicago and Chicago, there is only one Los Angeles. "I'm not connected with it," says Mia, who was born there. To Dustin, who was raised there, "there's this great emphasis on the external; the automobile you drive, the house you live in. The day *The Graduate* was finished shooting, I flew back to New York. I just couldn't wait to get back."

Together, Mia and Dustin represent a coincidence of other myths: the airborne colleen and the earthbound Jew, Peter Pan and Peter Schlemiel, the miserable winner and the happy loser. Like most myths, they contain an indissoluble grain of truth. Mia Farrow has been cowering from show-business success like a cornered rabbit. Hoffman has been swimming backward in it like a lobster. To Mia, life is colored with pastels and studded with magic stones; to Hoffman, it is a black-and-white documentary. She can skip down Manhattan's Third Avenue without creating a ripple. When Hoffman is recognized, he becomes a fifth Beatle; every night outside his dressing room is a hard day's night. Girls choke up and babble when he walks by: "Oh my God, it's him . . . What a groove, look at that nose . . . It's so beautiful. Did you dig those muscles? . . . Did you touch him? Yes. Oh my God . . ." Dustin hates it, he says, yet stays the departure of his manager's limousine to scribble his name on *Playbills* slipped through the crack of the electric window.

The distance between Mia and Dustin was apparent during the first few days of location shooting for *John & Mary*. Between interminable rehearsals and takes at an East Side "singles" eatery called Maxwell's Plum, Hoffman hied himself off to mumble inconsequentially with the bit players and extras clustered around the bar. Mia sat tensely at the table that was the focus of the sequence, fiddling with a fork, making conversation with two other actors, and once breaking into a high, put-on Southern accent. The few times that Hoffman lingered at the table to make a time-killing joke, he addressed it to the table at large, not to Mia; except when the action called for it, he never even looked at her. Obviously—and very tentatively—they were getting to know each other, sizing each other up both in the plot and in reality.

GO INSIDE YOURSELF

At first, Dustin comes on all of a heap. His stance is simian, his face an *objet trouvé*. The hair is from a thatched roof in Cambodia, the nose and chin from a 1948 Chevrolet, the hooded eyes from a stuffed hawk. Even the voice seems assembled, an oboe with postnasal drip. It all appears a shambles—until it begins to work, stunning audiences with articulate force. His current comedy, *Jimmy Shine,* is a mere vaudeville of the absurd. But within it is the vortical power of Dustin, pulling in the laughs, the cast and the audience. He growls like Durante, drones like W. C. Fields, shambles like Groucho Marx, and dances like a good-natured puppy. Yet the elements are his own—so much so that other performers are already copying them.

The surprise is Hoffman's secret: it is because no one expects him to be adequate that he excels. From the beginning, he has been the Chaplinesque figure who makes progress through a series of falls. In his favorite posture, looking backward, Hoffman recalled his circular route from Los Angeles to New York in a series of interviews with TIME Reporter Carey Winfrey. Hoffman's father was a furniture designer, middle-class and Jewish. His mother was a movie fan and named him after Dustin Farnum, the silent-screen cowboy (his older brother is Ronald, for Colman). The game of the name made Hoffman a loser from childhood. "I always used to wish there was another Dustin in class," he recalls. "When you're poked fun at—they used to call me 'Dustbin'—you either go inside yourself or become a clown. In seventh grade, I played Tiny Tim because I was the shortest kid in the class. Because a ninth-grader dared me, in from of all the parents at the Christmas show, I said: 'God bless us every one, Goddammit.' I got suspended for that. In high school, the other guys had hair on their chests and played football. I played tennis, had a big nose and acne so bad my face looked like a rifle range."

It was only after a thoroughly unproductive year at Santa Monica City College that he decided to jettison ambitions to become a doctor and impulsively enrolled in an acting course at the Pasadena Playhouse. After a sketch in which he played an old man, his instructor took him aside and said, "Dusty, it may take you a long time—ten or 15 years— but you are going to have a life in the theater." Recalls Hoffman, ruefully: "He was sure right about how long it would take."

After graduation from the Playhouse, Hoffman, who at 5 ft. 6 in. would always be one of the shortest kids in class, collided with California. "Cowboys were the big thing then on TV, and all the guys at the Playhouse would practice drawing on each other in the hallways. I had to get away from all that."

He got 3,000 miles away, to New York, full of grim expectations. "I used to watch the *Dead End Kids* on Saturday afternoon, thinking wouldn't it be fun to swim in the East River and play in dirty streets." He never did dive from a pier or play stickball; for three weeks, in fact, he slept on the kitchen floor next to the refrigerator, in the apartment of his former classmate, Actor Gene Hackman (*Bonnie and Clyde*). "I was too afraid to face the fact that I had to go outside and become an actor," he confesses.

SHOW ME A HERO

The introvert overcompensated in public. Recalls Hackman, "Dustin wore very long hair, a sheepskin vest with no shirt, leather boots, blue jeans and had a motorcycle—the whole bit." Like all unemployed actors, Hoffman took a variety of offstage roles: attendant in a mental hospital ("Until my dreams got so bad I had to quit"), typist, weaver of Hawaiian leis, janitor at a dance studio.

Nothing succeeds like failure. His type was Out theatrically, but In socially. His ex-roommate, Actor Robert Duvall, remembers that Hoffman "had more girls than Namath ever had. He had a line standing outside his apartment even when he didn't have a name."

It was eventually Hoffman's anti-heroism that made him an anti-star. "If the hero is defined as an event-making individual who redetermines the course of history," wrote Philosopher Sidney Hook, "it follows at once that a democratic community must be eternally on guard against him." Said F. Scott Fitzgerald: "Show me a hero and I will write you a tragedy." Those aphorisms were a long time catching on in America, where the legend of event makers—the cowboy and the gangster, the self-made entrepreneur and the conquering soldier—are dominant dramatic myths.

As comedy grew steadily blacker and as audiences grew steadily younger, hipper and more draftable, the old concepts began to erode. The invulnerables like Peck and Holden and Wayne seemed lost in a country full of people whose destinies were not in their own hands. The nation of cities needed new images, and suddenly Hoffman became an archetype.

In 1967, he was offered the role of Zoditch, a misanthropic 40-year-old Russian clerk in an off-Broadway play, *Journey of the Fifth Horse*. He won the Obie award as the year's best off-Broadway actor. Typically, the play closed three weeks later. Next came the role of a beleaguered night watchman in the farce *Eh?*

TOKEN GESTURE

The sound of success reached Hollywood and Director Mike Nichols, who was then casting *The Graduate*. Summoned to Los Angeles for a screen test, Hoffman took a day off from *Eh?* and arrived at the studio the next morning, he says, "feeling awful. And paranoiac. I was sure the crew was asking, 'Jesus Christ, where'd they get him?' Everything Nichols told me to do, I did wrong." At one point, to prod some life into a love scene, he grabbed Actress Katharine Ross's buttocks and yanked her toward him. "When it was finally over I apologized to Nichols and to Katharine," Hoffman lugubriously remembers. "As I was putting on my coat to leave, a New York subway token fell out of my pocket. One of the crew picked it up and said, 'Here, kid, you're gonna need this.'"

Six days later, Nichols called Hoffman to tell him that he had won the part—which was to pay him a fast $17,000. "We're in business," he said. "You came up with just the kind of confused panic the character is supposed to have." The rest is mystery. Hoffman himself admits, "If *The Graduate* were better, it wouldn't have done as well." And neither would he. Today his film price is $425,000; for *Jimmy Shine*, he receives $4,500 a week against 10% of the gross receipts. But then, the cost of living has risen. The psychoanalyst that he started with four years ago used to charge him $3.50 a hour. His fees have risen considerably since then—and Hoffman sees him five days a week.

The anti-star occasionally flashes star temperament. Donald Driver, director of *Jimmy Shine*, remembers that "Dustin cut his finger on opening night in Baltimore. Long after it had healed, he insisted that the stage manager announce to the audience that Mr. Hoffman was appearing with a cut finger. It was a blatant bid for public sympathy." It also appears that Dustin never became too big to pick up small change. *Jimmy Shine* Producer Zev Bufman calls him "a hard bargainer who held us up for half the profits on the $1.00 souvenir programs because we didn't clear material about him, with him. Traditionally the money goes to the backers. The whole thing amounted to $100 a week."

Still, apart from the analysis, a new Greenwich Village apartment and a pool table, he remains a champion of inconspicuous consumption. The night of the Academy awards, Hoffman—nominated for *The Graduate*—called a friend, Actor Stanley Beck. "It was about 1 o'clock in the morning," says Beck. "The phone rang. It was Dusty. 'Hey, can you pick me up?' he says. There he is, out at the Academy awards the night he's been nominated for an Oscar, and he has no car, no driver, no place to sleep. I told him to take a cab and he could sleep in the living room. He came up, slept, left without making the bed, and I never saw him."

FOUR-LETTER INCANTATION

Hoffman's long ascent is, in its anti-way, heroic. But hardly atypical. For an actor, it is impossible to become a leading man until he has a face: that is his hardship. For an actress, it is possible to become a leading lady as soon as she has a body: that is her handicap. Mia Farrow's measurements are closely akin to a newel post's. "I look like an elephants' graveyard," she admits. Nevertheless, it is a body. The face is something else; the exquisite bone structure and the fine, flawless skin suggest an antique doll. But so do the faces of other girls. It is the immense, luminous eyes that make her unique, almost unearthly, like someone not born but drawn—perhaps by her old friend Salvador Dali, who calls her "a black moonchild, like Lilith. Her sex is not here," he insists, pointing to his groin, "but in the head, like a wound in the middle of the forehead." To Actress Shirley MacLaine she is "all turned in and vulnerable, a child with a highly energetic brain. From the neck up, she's 80." To Actor Roddy McDowall, "trying to describe Mia is like trying to describe dust in a shaft of sunlight. There are all those particles." Her conversation is clotted with such words as amulets, transcendentalism, utopia—and then, unexpectedly but inevitably, a choice selection of four-letter expletives. Only when Mia uses them, her friends feel, somehow she makes them sound like an incantation.

In a series of interviews with TIME Reporter Jay Cocks, Farrow, speaking in her *sotto voce* that raises "Good morning" to the level of a state secret, took some of those particles and put them together in vaguely chronological order. In nearly every respect, Farrow began as Hoffman's polar opposite. He was outside show business with his nose pressed up against the window. In Hollywood, Mia was Old Money: her father was Director John Farrow, her mother Actress Maureen O'Sullivan. The third of seven children, Mia was always the vulnerable one. "I got all the diseases," she recalls, "including polio when I was nine. The whole family had to be evacuated, and all my things burned. Even my magic box, full of things that were magical to me."

"Before I could talk," she says, "I had a private name for myself. And that was part of my magic kingdom." The name was Mildred, a stand-in *Doppelgänger* who took the blame when things went sour. "Sometimes, the kingdom would become very, very strong and I had to go away—it was a lot like *I Never Promised You a Rose Garden*."[1]

Mildred finally died an unnatural death one summer when Mia was six and the family was aboard a ship. Recalls her mother, "I said to Mia, 'I tell you what we're going to do. We're going to drown Mildred.' So we theoretically put Mildred overboard into the Irish Sea, and we drowned her. We never did see Mildred again." Not in that form, anyway.

Hoffman's education was entirely public; Farrow's completely parochial. She "had the screaming meemies" the first time she saw a nun— at the age of four. But at ten she decided to become one. "They told me they wouldn't have me. Incompatible and everything, you know. I really wasn't their type." Actually she wasn't anybody's type. Underdeveloped, undernourished, she found that only her family and her fantasies could tune in on her.

PLOTS OF SOIL

Even in Mia's childhood, moviemaking was a global business. The nine Farrows trooped from Los Angeles to Spain, then on to London, where a series of tragedies began. "You can't be Irish without knowing the world is going to break your heart before you're 40," goes the Gaelic lament. For Mia the time was halved. Although the Farrow family life was chaotic and neurotic, there were still close alliances within its framework. In London at 13, she learned that her brother Michael, with whom she had been closest, had been killed in a private-plane crash in California. "It quite simply destroyed the family," she says. "He had been my confidant, my idol. When my brother died, the rest of us just sort of fell into our own plots of soil and grew."

More pain was to come. At 17 she visited her mother—then playing on Broadway in *Never Too Late*. "It was while I was there that my father died. That was a very big blow." John Farrow's reputation as a roistering, reckless womanizer conflicted sharply with the strict, militant Catholicism he displayed at home. But Mia accepted what confounded his colleagues. "He was priest and lover, powerful and incompetent, strong and weak, a poet and a sailor. He was a very complicated man and I loved him very much." And her mother? "Well . . . like . . . my father was strict, and she was his wife."

"It was immediately after John's death," recalls Maureen O'Sullivan, "that Mia found herself a role in an off-Broadway production of *The Importance of Being Earnest,* which led to a part in a television show that we thought was dreadful. We all sat around and said, 'Now who's going to tell her?' We didn't tell her because she thought she was pretty horrible herself."

On-screen she may have been flat-footed; offstage she could have used some lead weights on her shoes. When she first met Dali, he gave her a bit of rock he called "a tiny piece of the moon." Shortly thereafter, the painter invited the young actress for tea. "That afternoon," he remembers, "I had received a beautiful box of butterflies, and I had them on the table when she came in. We had English muffins with honey, and as she talked she took one butterfly out of the box, put it on top of the honey and ate it. She finished all twelve butterflies by the end of tea."

MYTHICAL SUICIDE

The producers of *Peyton Place* saw more in Mia than she saw in herself. For two years as Allison MacKenzie, Mia made the soap opera one long disaster aria and attracted the attention of millions of viewers—including Frank Sinatra. It was 1964—a very good year for long-haired swingers and toupeed singers. The way the public pop-psyched it out, at 19, she was looking for a father; at 48, he was looking for his youth. Their life became about as secluded as an airport. The couple took the most curious romantic cruise since the owl and the pussycat, with much the same result: a mismatched marriage.

After the Las Vegas wedding—attended by 37 still cameras, 14 motion-picture cameras and seven writers—show business set in. "Hah!" chortled Sinatra's ex-wife Ava Gardner, "I always knew Frank would wind up in bed with a boy." The gossip columnists were scarcely kinder. The pair's every waking hour seemed to make the wire services. During the affair, when she lopped off her hair, Dali called it "mythical suicide." After the separation, her behavior seemed more of the same. She flew off to India with her flower-child sister Prudence[2] for a month of transcendental meditation with Maharishi, the groovy guru. "I got there," Mia remembers, "and it was just the same zoo all over again. It was scary in the Himalayas, although I was scared of just about everything at that time. There were even photographers in the trees. I was there for my birthday, and I had to wear a silver hat. Two days later, I left."

A disintegrating marriage has several breaking points: the most obvious occurred during the filming of *Rosemary's Baby* with Director Roman Polanski. Sinatra tried to get her to leave *Rosemary* and join *The Detective;* she wouldn't. By night he telephoned her to say that he couldn't live without her; by day he planned divorce proceedings. Mia heard about them not from her husband but from his attorney. Coolly she announced that she wanted no financial settlement—which apparently stunned the singer more than a countersuit for a million. After the lawyer's visit, she took Sinatra's private plane to Los Angeles—where she found an airport full of reporters who could only have been tipped off by Sinatra's associates. Terrified, Mia talked the pilot into taking off and depositing her at another airport miles away.

Like a child who insists on a happy ending for *The Red Shoes,* Mia remains transcendentally tranquil about the chairman of the board. Though the divorce decree is final, she still absently refers to Sinatra as "my husband," still remembers him wistfully as "a gentle, quiet man." Yet she offers the best clue as to why the marriage proved unworkable: "Maybe it bothered him not being young. He felt things getting away from him. My friends from India would come into the house barefoot and hand him a flower. That made him feel square for the first time in his life."

Hoffman has lived 31 years, and every month of it shows. Mia has crammed several lifetimes into one—and, on the surface at least, has the dewy quality of a maiden who has just learned that people do not conceive babies by holding hands. Hoffman has settled into a quiet domestic arrangement with ex-Dancer Anne Byrne, a divorcee with a 2½-year-old child. Since her divorce, Mia has been seen with a succession of rock singers and film stars—and, most recently, with Conductor-Composer André Previn.

Byrne admits that Hoffman lets the air out of his psyche offstage and retreats to his home and his pool table. "We almost never go out," she says. "He'd much rather come home, get into his bathrobe and lie in bed." Farrow is almost always up, out and on. "People have a tendency to look at Mia," insists Previn, "and say, 'Look at those funny clothes and the way she acts and the things she talks about. Compared, let's say, with Debbie Reynolds she's some kind of a freak.' But I think that Mia is the straight one. I think that Debbie Reynolds is the freak."

Hoffman tends to drone his conversation, compressing his replies into brief, considered phrases. Farrow is a quotable compendium with an entry on every subject:

On film nudity: "There's no need to show sex things graphically in films. It's not necessary to show it at all, especially when it will offend people. Why not just do it at home?"

On certain unprintable words: "I would like my children to have these as sacred words. If I cursed at you, it could be a compliment. Couldn't it?"

On Negroes: "Right now I'm in love with someone, and it wouldn't make the slightest difference if he was black. Someday it will have to happen that one and one will make two. Just two, no other thing about color or anything else. That's utopia."

On hippies: "They're great, gentle people. I slept with 16 different people in those communes, and nobody ever touched me."

On Hollywood: "The system is full of crap. They've got it in the darkest part of their minds that everybody's sleeping together. I just don't know where their heads are at all, and I've given up trying to find out."

On drugs: "They still haven't been able to prove that pot is harmful. You can stick it in your ear, sleep on it or do anything you want—it's a natural thing, a product of nature. Drugs like LSD can be harmful, since they are a product of man."

On *Rosemary's Baby:* "I liked it—the possibility of the Antichrist. It makes a stamp on you, the Catholic upbringing. It's tattooed on your soul."

On marriage: "You have to make these promises for the rest of your life. Who can do that? Who knows what's going to be next year, or even tomorrow?"

On psychiatry: "I know too many people whose use it as a crutch: 'Give us this day our daily analyst.' I'd rather do it myself."

PLASTIC WINDUP STARLETS

Different as they are in conversation, background and the life style, Farrow and Hoffman remain peculiarly identical in their view of films and their down-look on Hollywood. For the moment at least, they share a professional bond as foremost symbols of a freshening in American cinema. They are even valid sex symbols: the man with the post-graduate face, the mixed-up, half-hippie woman with fear in her eyes.

Not that the pneumatic uplift of a Raquel Welch is suddenly undesirable. But it is only one of many symbols. There have been haunted girls and unprepossessing men before—Audrey Hepburn was never known for her measurements, and Humphrey Bogart commanded affection even though he looked accident-prone. But there has never before been such a crowd of real faces, so many young actors resembling young audiences—and young audiences pay for 65% of the movie tickets in America.

To expect all the flimflam to be swept away is, of course, absurd. Pressagents and windup plastic starlets are as much a part of movies as acetate; in one way or another, they always will be. And no matter how actors and actresses play themselves down, their films play them up. Movies are wide-screened, stereophonic and 30 times larger than life—so are actors. What is important is that many of the young actors can separate the reflected face on the screen from the original in the mirror.

Wallace Stevens once wrote that a community of originals is not a community. But each year brings more originals, more actresses like Mia Farrow, who asks: "What does it mean to be a star today? The only real value it has is in being offered more and better parts." And Dustin Hoffman, who says, "I've always had this fantasy—every actor has, I guess—that when I made it, I'd be able to do whatever I wanted." Up in the Hollywood hills, the superstars may grumble at the youngsters who have turned their backs on the old values. But not so long ago, young audiences rebelled against the old ways by staying away from movie theaters. The new anti-stars might just be the prescription for the problem of the anti-audience.

---

1. Hannah Green's 1964 novel of an institutionalized schizophrenic girl who created a fantasy world where imaginary rules alternately punished and rewarded her.
2. For whom the Beatles wrote the song of the same name.

Part III
Whither, Hollywood?

Elegy for Wonderland

Ben Hecht

Ben Hecht wrote some of the finest and wittiest screenplays in the history of the American film including those for Front Page, Twentieth Century, The Scoundrel, Wuthering Heights, Spellbound, Gunga Din, Ride the Pink Horse *and many others. The following article is one that he wrote in 1959, in which he makes some telling observations about Hollywood and its product.**

I started an elegy for Hollywood with the title, Good-by, O, Wonderland. Doubt halted me. I hied me to the cinema capital for another, definitive look at the Great Celluloid Corpse. I am still with doubt.

Hollywood looks waxen and inert. The Great Halls of the Yes Men and the Throne Rooms of the Bosses where geniuses wriggled in and out on their bellies are *kaput*. But Hollywood has looked waxen, inert and *kaput* before, and come to life in the manner of a Kazatsky dancer.

I've seen Hollywood drop dead a half-dozen times. I was there when the Eastern bankers took it over, introduced financial sanity into the studios, and ruined them. There was another time when all the studios, driven nigh to madness by the persistent emptiness of the movie theatres, got together and offered a tremendous cash grand prize for the best slogan with which to bamboozle audiences back into their seats. I forget the winning magic words, but remember, happily, the slogan entered by screen writer Herman Mankiewicz:

"Let's show the movies in the street and drive the people into the theatres."

Before putting pennies on its closed eyes, honesty urges the report that Hollywood's silence is not quite tomblike. There are some Independents sawing away at some sure-fire flops. In the major studios,

* Reprinted by permission of Esquire, Inc. © 1959 by Esquire, Inc. (*Esquire*, March 1959) , pp. 56–60.

writers still stagger out of producers' doors, *hari-kari* knives in hand. In the gossip columns the Louellas still offer their daily swoons over the Wizard Bosses—the same ones who burned the Industry to the ground. Stars who used to get $200,000 to $300,000 a picture are suddenly working for nothing, having been cooed into Controlling Partnership by the surviving money men of moviedom. Controlling partnership means a lion's share of the nonexisting profits. But the stars are happy. They are finally able to use their minds—buying material, hiring other actors and telling writers what to write. Also, as Controlling Partner, they are in charge of the publicity departments.

And there is a group of die-hards making a last bid for the family trade with plots about the horrors of incest, nymphomania and kindred dangers which beset the Republic.

Surely death is more silent. But you must be wary of judgment here. Hollywood was always a little unreal. It could be that this tambourine-banging figure in red boots is actually a Hollywood cadaver.

The truth may lie in a single fact that is chanted and murmured nightly in the columned palaces—the one-time weekly American audience of 80,000,000 movie-goers is down to 49,000,000—and ebbing.

It is a fact hard to assay. It seems to spell doom. On the other hand, 49,000,000 people a week are twenty times more than the group who read books or go swimming. If 49,000,000 people went to the legitimate theatre every week it would mean the damnedest biggest Renaissance since Michelangelo.

THE UNQUESTIONING AGE

The fact of the vanishing movie-gaper indicates one thing I can put down without doubt. A certain Hollywood is dead, no question of it; the good old Hollywood of the $5,000, $10,000, and $15,000 a week salaries, of the Cockalorum Earth-shakers and their teeming harems.

During its rain-of-gold era, not only actors, producers, and directors but even writers received more money than has ever been flushed by any alleged artists. My own take reached $3,500 a day (from David O. Selznick). High though this seems, it was less spectacular than the weekly receipts of a Metro-Goldwyn-Mayer writer named Percy Wintoon.

My collaborator Charles MacArthur and I ran into this young man when we stopped at a Hollywood gas station for a fill up. A good-looking fellow with a thick English accent (early Noel Coward) pumped gas into our tank. We learned, in a chat, that the young man had quit school at fourteen, that he had never read anything but newspapers and bawdy magazines, that he could write a letter (with difficulty), but that his spelling was off.

MacArthur and I took him along to the MGM studio where we were employed. We told him we were going to get him a job as a scenario writer, and gave him instructions on what to say and how to act. We also thought up the name Percy Wintoon.

Percy went on the MGM payroll the next day for $1,500 a week. He remained at Metro for a year. During this time he wrote not a line and obeyed our instructions happily: to stay mum during all story conferences, except to ask, in his English brogue, for a cigarette or a light; to frown whenever pressed for an opinion and reply only (in full, clipped accent), "Don't know about that. Have to linger on it a bit."

Percy finally took his literary earnings and hopped back to London —without exposure. How could a writer, particularly an underpaid one at $1,500 a week, be exposed as an imposter in those lovely days merely because he couldn't write?

The greatness of Hollywood is so gone that it is almost impossible to be a great man there, as it was once almost impossible *not* to be one, given a bankroll and a press agent. Twenty years ago the achievements of Sam Spiegel (producer of *The African Queen, On the Waterfront, The Bridge On the River Kwai*), would have set him above Humankind in movieland. The Louellas would have simpered hosannas to him each daybreak, and his genius would have spread a hush wherever he passed.

Today Mr. Spiegel, whose pictures win all the Oscars and break box-office records and are even patted on the head by those terrible fellows—the New York critics—today Mr. Spiegel has as much trouble getting reservations at the Beverly Hills Hotel as I have. And I have seen him walk across its entire lobby without producing a single salaam.

Yes, it is gone—that Hollywood. In Romanoff's, Chasen's, The Brown Derby and La Rue's—which once crackled with Mad-Mullahs—the bragging is down to a whisper. Money is tight. Rumors of folding studios fly the night.

THE AGE OF THE CALIPHATE IS OVER

Jobs are rare and slippery. And the Founding Wizards have started departing the lots. I have no hesitancy in reporting that the days of the caliphate are down the drain.

What this new mutation is—this hard-up Hollywood, this dreamless place barren of grosses and lotus leaves—I am not certain. Experts tell me it's a new and healthier movie capital. Other experts tell me that its noises are only a death rattle, and that it and the four million miles of film on which it photographed some thirty thousand dramas will be as forgotten as Mycenae in a few years.

My own finding is that the new Hollywood, whether corpse or debutante, is a bore. The old one was a bore, too (if you happened to be a writer). But it was a wondrously lucrative bore. And there were times when its Soul-in-Bondage doings were more Fun than Art.

The factors that laid low so whooping and puissant an empire as the old Hollywood are many. I can think of a score, including the barbarian hordes of Television. But there is one that stands out for me in the post-mortem.

This factor has nothing to do with a changing world. It was a factor that I saw boring away at the movie vitals in the bonanza days, of which George Jessel said: "Nobody can stop the movies, not even the Tom Thumbs making them. If you smeared butter on the film, everybody would still make a fortune."

The factor had to do with the basis of movie-making: "Who shall be in charge of telling the story."

THE ERA OF THE WRITER DIMINISHES

The answer Hollywood figured out for this question was what doomed it. It figured out that writers were not to be in charge of creating stories. Instead a curious tribe of inarticulate Pooh-Bahs called Supervisors and, later, Producers were summoned out of literary nowhere and given a thousand scepters. It was like switching the roles of teacher and pupil in the fifth grade. The result is now history. An industry based on writing had to collapse when the writer was given an errand-boy status.

My own overpaid chores as a writer included keeping the producer company while he sat in the projection room looking at screen tests, "rushes," or sometimes other studios' movies whose plots he thought I could steal; going to the races with the studio heads, watching the L.A. police accept the death by gunshot of a movie factotum as a suicide rather than a murder. (Two days later the murderer jumped off a ferryboat in San Francisco Bay and drowned, so there was no real thwarting of justice involved.) As a writer drawing top pay—higher pay, in fact, than anyone except the head of the studio himself—I had no more authority over my script than a weather vane over the wind. Director, producer and even actors, half as munificently paid as I, could and did induce me to make changes in the script, to add nitwit scenes, corny endings and cut my pet dialogue (usually belonging to minor characters not allowed into story conferences) . I made the changes because if I hadn't the scenario would have been taken out of my hands altogether and gleefully mangled by a group of studio hacks, trained to read the producer's mind, without wince or backfire.

The problem for me from then on became a drawn-out battle with the Screen Writers' Guild to have my name removed from the film thus maltreated. I have only the vaguest knowledge of this Guild, and am thus unaware of any of its good deeds for writers. What I know is that its presidents were always denouncing me in press interviews for my disrespect for the writer's bosses. They called it "biting the hand that fed you"—a fine Hollywood picture of literary dog and master.

The writer is a definite human phenomenon. He is almost a type— as pugilists are a type. He may be a bad writer—an insipid one or a clumsy one—but there is a bug in him that keeps spinning yarns; and that bulges his brow a bit, narrows his jaws, weakens his eyes and gives him girl children instead of boys. Nobody but a writer can write. People who hang around writers for years—as producers did —who are much smarter and have much better taste, never learn to write.

The early collapse of the writer in Hollywood was as much his fault as anyone's. The writer, put in any active group of men, will always collapse as a dominant. He will be the least listened to in any mixed company. Even other writers shy at hearing a writer sound off.

The reason is sort of biologic. A writer's ego goes into the game of solitaire he plays with plot turns and speeches. He has, usually, little left over for the domination of the realities around him. A long-suffering wife or an aging concubine are usually the only human beings before whom he can strut successfully.

THE WAR ON THE WRITERS

I saw the writer's collapse happen in the early happy days of Hollywood. The eager bosses, often full of the finest literary bounderism, summoned to their golden lairs the fanciest scribblers of the world. Almost without exception disillusion smote these early double-negative bosses. Almost without exception the high-toned and high-priced literary nabobs were a moody, pallid, stuttering, droopy lot of ineffectual human beings. It seemed a rash thing to put a $2,000,000 project into such thin, wobbly hands.

The writer's collapse was not a generality alone. It was also a matter of individual casualty. Ernst Lubitsch, the director, boasted to me when I went to work with him on *Design for Living* that he had sent four writers to the hospital on his last picture. Most of my script-writing friends—I never had more than a handful—took eagerly to the bottle or the analyst's couch, filled their extravagant menages with threats of suicide, hurled themselves into hysterical amours. And some of them actually died in their forties and fifties. Among these were the witty Herman Mankiewicz and F. Scott Fitzgerald, the fine novelist. Scotty took a beating for a few years in Hollywood. The blow that knocked him out came on his last script job. He had handed in a scenario based on one of his great short stories, and he had worked lovingly on this script.

"I'd like to be remembered," Scotty said to me, "for having written one movie with nice dialogue in it."

The producer redictated the Fitzgerald script in three days, removing all its dialogue and substituting his own anacondian patter. Fitzgerald's note of protest, written shortly before he died (of many things —Hollywooditis among them) contained the line: "If there's anything I know about writing it's the sound of my generation and the rhythm of its talk." But the producer stayed unmoved and no single word of Scott Fitzgerald's dialogue remained in the last movie he wrote.

The bosses looked around for better insurance than the feeble-egoed writer—and the producer came into his own. He was no fumbler, like the writer. He had a firm baritone. He made quick decisions. One of the quickest was to acquire the bosses' mistake of confusing egomania with storytelling.

The producers, whose position was a reward for sharp personality, felt themselves always superior to writers. I have never known a single producer, however mentally helpless, who did not feel himself firmly my superior in "making up" a movie story. It is difficult to understand how a man who can't think, can't invent, and has little but fog in his head, can, nevertheless, regard himself as a prince of letters, or a final authority on drama. This incomprehensible situation has flourished for thirty years in Hollywood.

THE UNUSUAL PRODUCERS

I have known a handful of producers who actually were equal or superior to the writers with whom they worked. These producers were a new kind of nonwriting writer hatched by the movies—as Australia produced wingless birds. They wrote without pencils or even words. Using a sort of mime-like talent, they could make up things like writers.

When I come to put down their names, there weren't many. David O. Selznick, Sam Goldwyn, Darryl Zanuck, Walter Wanger, Irvin Thalberg seems to exhaust the list. They were not only producers, but heads of the studio in which they functioned. Lest it look as if I'm inclined to curtsey only to the highest, I recall other studio pharaohs who were as helpful on a job as so many Will-o'-the-Mills. Thirty, and forty years of overlordship in movieland left them inept and, of course, the last expert word on everything. Among these were Harry Cohn, L. B. Mayer, and the Warner brothers, Harry and Jack.

Ninety per cent of the producers I have known were not bright. They were as slow-witted and unprofessional toward making up a story as stockbrokers might be, or bus drivers. Even after twenty or thirty years of telling writers what and how to write, they were still as ignorant of writing as if they had never encountered the craft.

CONCOCTION: A BEGINNING AND AN END

The result of all this was—the Hollywood movie. It was a concoction wangled into being by weeks of inane dispute between producer and writer—sometimes three to six writers, but always the same mastermind stuttering on his throne stool. He was the one to whom the bosses looked as the literary hero who would be able "to lick the story."

Guided by the nonwriting producer, the Hollywood movie became a sort of unchanging story. All the big scenes remembered by the producer from other movies appeared, willy-nilly, over and over again. And this Hollywood product had an unwavering philosophical aim —the producer's major contribution. It was out to prove in a world decimated by villains and scourged by scroundrels that villainy was an impotent force. Virtue, with the right bust measure, must win.

Here is some remembered dialogue from one of the Metro story conferences.

PRODUCER: I want to say first I think you've written a fine, brilliant, powerful piece of work, Ben. I think it's a real movie masterpiece.

MYSELF: Thanks. (This is obviously going to be one of the tough ones.)

PRODUCER: I hope you don't mind a few little criticisms I want to offer.

MYSELF: Dying to hear them.

(A jewelry salesman is ushered into the producer's sanctum. The purchase of a diamond ring for the producer's wife takes twenty minutes. It is, alas, nearly always the producer's wife who gets the diamonds and fur coats. The largesse enables the producer to consort with his mistress with a lessened guilt complex.)

PRODUCER: Emmy's going to go nuts when I hand her this ring.
MYSELF: It's a beauty, all right.
PRODUCER: I won't beat about the bush, Ben. I don't care for the ending.
MYSELF: The last page?
PRODUCER: No—the whole last two or three reels. It won't work. You can't have the girl untrue to her soldier lover while he's fighting for his country—and then—

THEY CAN DO WITHOUT MR. BELL, TOO

(The talking desk begins: people from all over the studio can talk openly to the producer without the handicap of a telephone. They press a button and talk right out of the desk.)
VOICE: What time you going to the track?
PRODUCER: I ain't going today.
VOICE: You ain't going? You sick?
PRODUCER: No. Tied up in a story conference.
VOICE: I'll drop in in a half hour.
PRODUCER: Bring a couple of new card decks.
VOICE: Okey-doke.
MYSELF: If she's faithful to her soldier, there's no story.
PRODUCER: I disagree. I think we can "lick it" if we both concentrate.

(It goes on. Other people enter the conversation. The director doesn't like the beginning, the producer's mistress doesn't care for the heroine's character at all—and has some suggestions. I, the writer, have an appointment to go sailing off Santa Monica in a fellow-writer's new $50,000 schooner. I slide out as the producer starts playing gin.)

HOLLYWOOD REVIVED: EASTWARD TO THE WESTERN

The new Hollywood, the one I am told is on a healthier basis than our old Babylonian capital, has in a measure solved the writer problem. It concentrates on making movies so full of horses, bonfires, collapsing temples, Indian uprisings, wild beasts and uncovered breasts (the censor allows them to bob around in Biblical movies and *The Fall of Rome*) that a writer would actually be in the way.

At this point I feel it my duty to inform the reader that I have written some sixty or seventy movies for the screen, and that my musings on the death of Hollywood, therefore, may be a bit biased. Of my own work, I have enjoyed doing about a fourth. In this fourth—

due to the subject matter or the compatibility of producer or director or to my own enthusiasm—I wrote well, and the movies came excitingly onto the screen. The other three-fourths of my movie work seems as alien to me when I remember it (I try never to look at it) as if it had been done by some fellow with a pointed head. I know who this fellow is. It is I, in my Hollywood guise as producer-errand boy.

My fourth is not the only good work I've noted in the movies. In the four million miles of film shot by Hollywood there are many leagues of beauty and fine drama. The great Hollywood factories were interested only in turning out a standard product for mass consumption. But talent, brought to heel, did speak in this mass product. The world was given flashes of what might have been the greatest of the arts.

Out of the seventy movies I've written some ten of them were not entirely waste product. These were *Underworld, The Scoundrel, Wuthering Heights, Viva Villa, Scarface, Specter of the Rose, Actors and Sin, Roman Holiday, Spellbound, Nothing Sacred.*

And, perhaps, these flashes signal the future of Hollywood. At least, it pleases me to think so. It pleases me to think that when the greedy-guts money men have turned their backs on the industry they created and destroyed, perhaps a few writers will start the photographs moving again—and an Art will get born in place of a defunct grab-bag industry.

When I say writers, here, I mean writers who are able to direct. A writer who can't direct or a director who can't write is almost as big an amateur as the producer who can do neither.

So much for my Hollywood corpse. I am a bit surprised to find I have revived her, stuck a Van Dyke on her and renamed her Shakespeare.

What's Wrong with Hollywood

John Cassavetes

John Cassavetes, one of the American film's finest artists, wrote the following brief article in 1959. In 1961, he directed an independent film, Shadows, *which became something of an underground classic. Nearly a decade after making these observations about Hollywood, he starred in* Rosemary's Baby *and wrote and directed a much discussed film,* Faces. *Some of his thoughts have a prophetic tone when read today.**

Hollywood is not failing. It has failed. The desperation, the criticisms, the foolish solutions, the wholesale cutting of studio staffs and salaries, the various new technical improvements, the "bigger picture," and the "ultra-low-budget picture," have failed to put a stop to the decline.

The fact is that film making, although unquestionably predicated on profit and loss like any other industry, cannot survive without individual expression. Motion pictures can not be made to please solely the producer's image of the public. For, as has been proved, this pleasure results neither in economic nor artistic success.

On the other hand, the audience itself, other-directed and mass-minded as it is, may condemn pictures such as *Twelve Angry Men* or *The Goddess*. These pictures may lose money, but they have inspired applause from those who still think freely and for themselves. These pictures have gone beyond Hollywood "formulas" and "ingredients," and will affect strongly the future of American motion pictures.

More often than not, the mass audience will not accept a new idea, an unfamiliar emotion, or a different point of view if it is presented in one or two films only, just as it will not immediately accept new ideas in life. However, the new thoughts must eventually lead to change.

* By permission from John Cassavetes and *Film Culture* magazine. "What's Wrong with Hollywood," *Film Culture*, No. 19, pp. 4–5. © 1959.

364

This is not to say that individual expression need only be so called point-of-view films or films that stimulate thought. Certainly the standard of the musical can and must be improved too; the treatment of comedy should reach in other directions; the "epic" and "Western" pictures and the "love story" must also search for more imaginative approaches and fresher ideas.

However, the probability of a resurrection of the industry through individual expression is slim, for the men of new ideas will not compromise themselves to Hollywood's departmental heads. These artists have come to realize that to compromise an idea is to soften it, to make an excuse for it, to betray it.

In Hollywood the producer intimidates the artist's new thought with great sums of money and with his own ego that clings to past references of box office triumphs and valueless experience. The average artist, therefore, is forced to compromise. And the cost of the compromise is the betrayal of his basic beliefs. And so the artist is thrown out of motion pictures, and the businessman makes his entrance.

However, in no other activity can a man express himself as fully as in art. And, in all times, the artist has been honored and paid for revealing his opinion of life. The artist is an irreplaceable figure in our society too: A man who can speak his own mind, who can reveal and educate, who can stimulate or appease, and in every sense communicate with fellow human beings. To have this privilege of world-wide communication in a world so incapable of understanding, and ignore its possibilities, and accept a compromise—most certainly will and should lead the artist and his films to oblivion.

Without individual creative expression, we are left with a medium of irrelevant fantasies that can add nothing but slim diversion to an already diversified world. The answer cannot be left in the hands of the money men, for their desire to accumulate material success is probably the reason they entered into film-making in the first place. The answer must come from the artist himself. He must become aware that the fault is his own: that art and the respect due his vocation as an artist is his own responsibility. He must, therefore, make the producer realize, by whatever means at his disposal, that only by allowing the artist full and free creative expression will the art and the business of motion pictures survive.

Where Are the Stars of Yesteryear?

Eugene Archer

Eugene Archer writes of the specialness of some stars in American movies with their lasting individuality.*

Greta Garbo stopped acting almost a quarter of a century ago, and became divine instead. She was ready for immortality. Name any attribute of the legendary greats—Duse, Sarah Bernhardt, Réjane—and Garbo had it. She was beautiful, she was mysterious, she played tragic roles, she was imitated and endlessly analyzed and passionately worshipped by the intellectuals of her day. Most important of all, she quit while she was ahead—still at the height of her powers, at 36.

But Garbo had to cope with one problem Duse never encountered. Her work did not disappear. Instead of fading into a fond memorial haze, it is still very much on hand. Everybody knows that today's stars couldn't hold a candle to those of our parents' day—but now, disconcertingly, a new generation is finding out for itself.

Television is the villain, and the test is not exactly fair. A sensible viewer may well decide not to spend $2.50 on Kim Novak when he can look at Garbo on Channel 2, but he will still be subjecting the Adrian-styled goddess of the 1930's—all plucked eyebrows and sequined sheaths—to the scrutiny of a gaze attuned to Courrèges. Cold-war cynicism and a more liberal morality, too, sometimes make a 'Thirties heroine's most agonizing dilemma seem absurd. Television has a way of revaluating former favorites, and it can be cruel.

Who today can fathom the wartime popularity of the G.I.'s inverted pyramid, Betty Grable? Sarongs are as funny as ever, but Dorothy Lamour's penciled brows are painfully visible through the video blur. Noble Greer Garson, suffering through the blitz, was Hollywood's

* © 1965 by the New York Times Company, Reprinted by permission. (*The New York Times*, May 30, 1965.)

conception of the typical British housewife—and looks downright embarrassing today.

Television has clouded some bright reputations. It would be easier to accept John Barrymore as a great actor if he remained unseen. Paul Muni was capable of clean, forceful acting in *I Am a Fugitive From a Chain Gang,* but his celebrated gallery of biographical portraits hid his talents beneath a bushel of beards. That other historical scholar, George Arliss, is an antiquated mass of make-up and mannerisms. And double Oscar-winning Luise Rainer? In *The Good Earth* she was a Viennese Chinese.

Garbo, of course, survives. If she had come along in the 'Sixties she would have devastated her competition with one laconic Swedish syllable. Except for *Ninotchka,* most of her movies were pretty foolish, but Garbo stalked through them all with the same stoic aplomb. She was genuinely unpredictable. No matter how many times you may have seen *Camille,* she makes it new.

Personality is just about the only thing that penetrates the television snow, and Garbo was the personality supreme. Not all the actors who register strongest in the living room were so eminent in their own time.

Take John Garfield. From *Four Daughters* through *He Ran All the Way,* Garfield was always an interesting star. His acting was solidly grounded in the theater, and his tough-guy image earned him a certain following. At the box office he ranked below Bogart but ahead of Robert Taylor.

Yet today Garfield is one of the most arresting actors on the networks. He is the Depression hero personified, the East Side slum kid who came out swinging, ready to take on the world. As the disillusioned Spanish Civil War veteran of *The Fallen Sparrow,* the fast-talking lawyer who made it the wrong way in *Force of Evil,* the classic prizefighter of them all in *Body and Soul,* he camouflaged his vulnerability with braggadocio —but he never fooled Priscilla Lane.

Garfield foreshadowed the Brando type, but the latter-day mumblers never quite conveyed his cockiness and crushability. Garfield is missed. So is James Cagney, who preceded him. Cagney is a gentleman farmer in retirement these days, but to televiewers he is still rat-tat-tatting away with tongue and tommy-gun, the noisiest solution to a sleepless night. Bogart and Garfield brought sadness to the gangster hero, but Cagney was indomitable. When they blew him up atop an oil tank in *White Heat,* he was still screaming, "Top o' the world!"

There's nobody around like Ronald Colman, either. He was the only actor who could actually deliver the line "Tennis, anyone?" with the proper élan. Colman was an authentic matinee idol—handsomer than

John Gilbert, more romantic than Tyrone Power, a far better actor than Errol Flynn. He had the bearing of an aristocrat but the soul of an idealist. In *Beau Geste* he sacrificed his life for honor; in *A Tale of Two Cities* he did it for the woman he loved. Colman was the man who searched for Shangri-La.

They don't write roles for imperialist heroes any more. They do write parts embodying the Yankee pioneer tradition, but there's nobody around to play them. Certainly no one like Walter Huston, whose death in 1950 left a gap Hollywood has never been able to fill. A good look at his inimitable old prospector in the omnipresent *The Treasure of the Sierra Madre* explains why. Huston was an eloquent *Abraham Lincoln* for D. W. Griffith, a brilliant Devil in *All That Money Can Buy*. He was strong, shrewd and sinewy, characteristic of the self-made American male—and a type all to himself. Current casting directors sigh when they come across a Walter Huston role, for the only man who could possibly replace him is his director son John.

Carole Lombard might be the wrong kind of myth today if television had not made her something more. When she died in an airplane crash in 1942, leaving her last Ernst Lubitsch comedy unreleased, the sentimental obituaries obscured her most unusual quality.

Lombard was something very special, and recent airings of *My Man Godfrey* and *To Be or Not to Be* show just how extraordinary her talent was. She was a remarkably beautiful woman who would screech and claw and howl, and the contrast between her classic features and elastic grimaces was hilarious enough in itself. But Lombard had a rarer gift. She was able to shift instantly from laughter to tears, and to command the same response from her audience. High comedy has always been the most difficult, least appreciated form of acting. Lombard was quicksilver.

The television mines are rich, and everyone has his own discoveries. There is Mary Astor, the subtlest of *farceuses,* letting go and kicking Peter Lorre in the shins in *The Maltese Falcon.* Or Conrad Veidt, the last word in romantic villains, smiling at Joan Crawford's scar in *A Woman's Face,* and reducing her to Jello. Or Mae West, still a potent comedienne through the television blips, asking Beulah to peel her a grape. Or doughty old Florence Bates in *Rebecca,* trying to land Laurence Olivier, no less, for a dinner *tête à tête.* Or the young Katharine Hepburn, long before Bogart characterized her so definitively as a "crazy, psalm-singin', skinny old maid," revealing herself in *Morning Glory* and *Holiday* as one of the screen's most electric beauties.

In the long run it is not so much talent that lasts as individuality. The old-time stars who come over best today are the ones who depended least on the artifice of make-up and vocal mannerism and the tricks of technique, and concentrated instead on expressing strong personalities in the most direct style. Perhaps the most fascinating thing about the movies is the opportunity they give for reappraisal and revaluation from a modern vantage point—seeing a work in a new context without the gauze of nostalgic reminiscence, *exactly in its original form*. This has never before been possible with any of the performing arts—and the general public is finding it a lot of fun.

Can TV Save the Films?

Charles Champlin

Charles Champlin is Entertainment Editor of the Los Angeles Times. *The following is a sensitive article in which he writes of the relationship between the American film and television.**

One Sunday evening last September, an estimated 60,000,000 viewers in 25,000,000 homes sat down to watch one movie being televised by the American Broadcasting Company: *The Bridge on the River Kwai*. It was an event that Hollywood now regards as only slightly less epochal than the premier of *The Jazz Singer*. *Kwai* wiped out the competing programs in ratings and even reduced the attendance at movie theaters. For that showing and one to follow, ABC paid Columbia Pictures $2,000,000.

It did not escape Hollywood that even at that price the network got a bargain, while Columbia got a handsome helping of gravy from a film that long since had paid for itself—and, having leased rather than sold the film, Columbia retained control of it. The rush was on. Almost within hours of the *Kwai* screening, negotiations that had been in progress for some time culminated in three Hollywood studios' announcing new agreements with two of the networks for showing of movies not yet seen on television. The agreements cover 113 films—including eighteen which have not yet been made—and will fetch the three studios more than $92,000,000.

ABC will pay Twentieth Century-Fox nearly $20,000,000 for television rights to only seventeen films. The network is paying Fox $5,000,000 just for the right to screen *Cleopatra* twice, two or three years from now. Three other films are being leased for $2,500,000 each, the rest for $500,000 each. "God knows what we'll get for *The Sound of Music*," says

* By permission from Charles Champlin. "Can TV Save the Films?" *Saturday Review*, December 24, 1966. © 1966.

Richard Zanuck, Darryl's son and vice president in charge of production at Fox. That film, which has already brought the studio nearly $70,000,-000 in theater rentals, will probably command such a high price that it may have to await some kind of pay TV. ABC also will pay Paramount Pictures $20,000,000 under an agreement covering thirty-two films in the studio's recent library.

Metro-Goldwyn-Mayer, meanwhile, under an agreement with CBS, will receive some $52,800,000 for televising of forty-five existing MGM films starting next fall and, under a separate agreement, has guaranteed CBS the television rights to eighteen films not yet made. And NBC, which has locked up a good bit of feature product over the years, has an arrangement with Universal Studios for co-financing a number of two-hour-long feature films to be shown initially on television. For its money, NBC has the right to show each film twice. Under a separate agreement calling for an additional payment, the five stations owned and operated by the network are entitled to a third showing. Thereafter the films are Universal's, to be merchandised as the studio wishes.

The first of this World Premiere series of films, a slick, quick comedy mystery called *Fame Is the Name of the Game*, was shown Thanksgiving weekend in NBC's well-established *Saturday Night at the Movies* time period. It far outdistanced the competition, luring a bigger audience than any Saturday night film this season.

What do these developments mean to Hollywood?

"Television," says Lee Rich, a former Madison Avenue advertising man who now is a TV executive with the Mirisch Brothers, "has taken over the motion picture industry."

It hasn't, quite. But it has undoubtedly restored the bloom of economic good health to Hollywood.

At its pre-television peak, Hollywood made as many as 600 feature films annually and showed them to between 80,000,000 and 90,000,000 customers a week in this country. Then came the one-two combination which Hollywood itself was prepared to regard as fatal. The government forced the major studios to sell off their theaters, so they no longer had captive outlets for their product. And along came television, so the studios no longer had captive audiences, either.

Weekly audiences shrank to 30,000,000 customers. Feature production fell to fewer than 150 films a year. Even now, although film audiences are coming back, weekly attendance is still only half what it once was—about 45,000,000 admissions a week. Film production still stands at little better than 200 pictures a year, but this includes a heavy proportion made abroad and financed by the major distributors.

Thanks to a combination of customer choosiness and higher ticket prices, the most successful films do better than ever. Public willingness to pay $3 to $4 a ticket to see something regarded as special is making the picture which will attract this notable amount of cash an enterprise of magnitude. And the cost of tickets has risen so drastically in recent years that movie-making once more can be a highly lucrative enterprise. *The Sound of Music,* for example, though far from being the most expensive film ever made, will earn the most money of any movie in history. Fox, with *Dr. Doolittle* in production, is even rosier about its prospects. This Arthur P. Jacobs production, a musical extravaganza, is being budgeted in excess of $15,000,000, and cheerfully so.

But it also is true that no more than one motion picture in four—perhaps one in five or six—earns back its cost at the box office. As one film executive has said, "You can't fool audiences any more. They knew *The Russians Are Coming The Russians Are Coming* was a winner even before we could try to tell them it was. And they knew *Assault on a Queen* was a dog even before it was through shooting."

However, even for the "dogs" which may give the producer no more than his not inconsiderable producer's fee for his labor, the intricacies of distribution can make a picture that only breaks even, or does less than that, a profitable enterprise. This is because distribution fees of 35 per cent are charged off before the actual producers of the film ever see a penny of profit. (One executive of a major company, when asked how a chancy picture was doing at the box office, said, "Wonderful! We're breaking even.")

In many ways, television's projection into this situation is rich with ironies. When television was aborning, the major studios—to paraphrase a present-day mogul—sold off their existing libraries too cheaply (or so it seems in retrospect), pared their staffs, and were prepared to wither away. Legend has it that at one studio it was forbidden even to use the word *television* in executive conversation.

But if the studios sought to run away from television, an unslakable thirst for material sent television running after the film-makers. Today, Hollywood is turning out footage equal to 600 feature films a year. The industry is at full employment and, in fact, there are critical shortages of several kinds of personnel—even qualified press agents.

Through its outright sales of old films to television, through its leasing of films to television, through its production of all those series, and now through its production of features for TV, Hollywood is notably enriched—financially if not qualitatively—by the medium. Indeed, the recent rapid-fire takeover of several studios by outside financial interests reflects in considerable part an awareness of the television gold yet to be mined.

But the ironies continue. At odd moments Hollywood finds itself losing from one pocket what it is stuffing into another. Despite the stories about all those residuals, grinding out all those series is financially as risky as movie-making, and it is getting riskier each season because of the competition from the movies which make the other pockets jingle. A third of this season's new shows have already been sentenced to die, at great cost to their producers.

The rewards from a series come from the second and subsequent seasons, when there is enough product in the can to sell to independent and foreign television. If a series dies after only a season or part of a season, the producer may have lost as much as a million dollars. Fox saved $500,000 by urging ABC to kill this season's *Tammy Grimes Show* after only three or four episodes had been shown. The series was obviously going nowhere, and it was costing Fox $50,000 a week. *The Blue Light,* an unsuccessful entry last year, is believed to have cost Fox $20,000 a week net loss. On the other hand, when *Peyton Place* finally comes to an end, it will probably have 500 episodes on film, a veritable diamond mine for syndication sale.

Television, then, in a sense, has given Hollywood two shaky legs to stand on instead of only one. For the industry as a whole it means relatively more stability, but within the industry there are certain to be dazzling changes of fortune.

It seems clear—perhaps ominously clear—from the epochal showing of *River Kwai* that a sharp and arbitrary distinction between film-making and television-making is now, in Hollywood, virtually a thing of the past. The sense of the recent studio-network agreements, says Dick Zanuck, is that the *minimum* worth to television of almost any film is $500,000. This is an item no studio and few independent producers can afford to ignore.

One truth which Zanuck holds to be immediately self-evident is that no studio can any longer afford to make a black-and-white film, since the networks want color, color, color. (Billy Wilder's recent *The Fortune Cookie* is in black and white, of course, and it will be interesting to see how it makes out in the TV bargaining.)

While Zanuck himself foresees no changes one way or the other in casting policies, the prospect of the television increment surely will serve to reinforce the star system by putting an additional premium on the safe, known, proven, promotable names, as against the un- or semi-knowns. It might be thought that the star names television itself has created would have an enhanced value, but there are no signs of it. With a few male exceptions such as Dick Van Dyke, Steve McQueen, James Garner, and Rod Taylor—and no female exceptions—the giants of seriesland continue to be ignored by the film-makers. The television viewer seldom seems willing to spend money to see a personality in the theater when he can see that same person regularly in his living room, free. And even if this fact were debatable, the studios are unwilling to spend the experimental funds that would be needed to vault a television star into film stardom.

If the new dispensation seems likely to reinforce the star system, it seems equally likely to reinforce the story equivalents of the star system: the technically capable, handsomely produced, but less than innovating film, certainly not a controversial one that would alarm a network buyer or a network censor (although the network censors view features more permissively than they view their own series). Clearly, the prospect of a TV dollop beyond the box office will mean some upgrading of budgets, but it does not yet suggest an unfettering in other ways.

Indeed, from the evidence of the Thanksgiving weekend showing of *Fame Is the Name of the Game,* it seems that what may be reappearing is the B picture—long neither on imagination nor cash, skirting budget limitations, using able and familiar if not top-price names (Tony Franciosa, Jill St. John, Jack Klugman) from films and television, and showcasing the studio's promising unknowns (in this case, a plumply pretty young comedienne named Susan Saint James). It's not for the art houses, and while it does reveal its television derivation, it is long enough to qualify as a motion picture and therefore is marketable. And it could evolve into an interesting development, a kind of third form between television and film, if such a form is necessary. Since the two dozen top or so-called "bankable stars" are beyond price reach in any event, Universal may well be able to cast for performance. On both sides of the camera, the studio then can employ a mixture of new names, old names, film talent, television talent, the unknowns, and the underused. As Jennings Lang, Universal's senior vice president for television production, says, the first films have been "Hollywood classical in concept"—*the* western, *the* comedy, *the* war film and so on. But Lang hopefully says he has a couple of far-out scripts in hand and hopes to explore and experiment more as the series gets established.

This is a song we have, of course, heard before. But just as there were occasional gems among the B pictures, there is no reason why this venture, with its relatively low risk, should not produce some surprises. Perhaps more importantly, just as television took over many of the training-ground functions which the B's had in the days when the majors were major, these features can train some vigorous young talent.

One hope we can take from present-day Hollywood is its awareness—albeit reluctant—of the discernment of audiences at home and in the movie houses. If 60,000,000 people tune in *Kwai* of an evening they have tuned in to watch an excellent motion picture, and whether the picture is a well produced comedy or a more challenging film such as *A Place in the Sun,* the very fact that the audience will prefer a good old film over a mediocre new series gives the industry a sound reason to seek fresh new entertainment.

The success of films on television is an opting for relative excellence. Only at its peril will Hollywood take it to mean anything different.

Movies and Censorship

Bosley Crowther

Bosley Crowther was the motion picture critic of The New York Times *from 1940 until the late 1960s. He is the author of* The Lion's Share *and* Hollywood Rajah. *In the following essay he comments on the content of movies and their relationship to our society.**

"What in heaven's name is happening to the movies?" an anxious mother said to me recently at a private dinner party in a New York suburban home. "The other day I took my 15-year-old daughter to see one she particularly asked to see—an Italian movie about a mother and her daughter—and I was absolutely appalled. You probably know the picture. At the climax, the mother and daughter both were raped! No doubt about it! And by a gang of soldiers! I was never so shocked and embarrassed at anything!"

Of course, I knew the picture. It was a fine and successful Italian film, *Two Women,* starring Sophia Loren, which had been one of the outstanding dramas of the year. To be sure, it was intensely realistic, with no punches pulled, no curtains drawn, but it carried a powerful message of love and compassion. I asked my friend what she and her daughter thought of it.

"Well," she replied, with some caution, "it was a very moving, a very disturbing film. We were both rather deeply shaken. But, really, it's not the sort of thing I think a child should see. Where are the censors? Where is the Hays office? I'm surprised they permit such a thing. We never saw stuff like that in the movies of Ginger Rogers and Loretta Young when I was a girl!"

Here, in one sudden burst of feeling, was concentrated and conveyed

* By permission from "Movies and Censorship," Public Affairs Pamphlet No. 332, Public Affairs Committee, Inc., New York. © 1962.

a fair sample of sentiment towards the movies that many parents are expressing these days, disturbed as they are by the candor and rawness of some pictures and by the public objections of certain religious and civic elements. Here, too, was a typical example of the lack of understanding of the majority of people today about what is happening in the realm of motion pictures.

THE CHANGING MOTION PICTURES

For the fact is that large and significant changes in the culture of motion pictures have been occurring in the past decade—and these are but a part of and in line with a whole complex of developments and shifts in our ways of living, our facilities for pleasure, our educational expansion, and our intellectual growth.

The characteristics of the motion picture audience have changed considerably in the past fifteen years, due largely to the effect that television has had upon the American people and upon the use of our leisure time. The number of movies available each year for the theatre-going public to see has been steadily declining, as has the number of conventional theatres in which these films may be seen. The nature and quality of theatrical motion pictures have been changing perceptibly, and the level of sophistication of movies in general has shown an appreciable rise.

Parallel to these notable shiftings, there has occurred a revolutionary change in the legal status of motion pictures. The United States Supreme Court, which, in 1915, held that movies were no more than a form of commercial entertainment, in the nature of "spectacles," and thus were not to be regarded in a class with the other communications media, has reversed this judgment completely in the past decade. It has held that films are clearly conveyances of information and thought, and thus are entitled to guarantees of free speech and free press under the First and Fourteenth Amendments.

As a consequence, the many agencies for state and municipal censorship of films that had been erected upon the Supreme Court's early ruling and the prior restraint that these agencies imposed on films have been strikingly reduced, so that censor boards are maintained today in but four states and a few cities, and the only ground for prior restraint is now obscenity.

At the same time, and because of the recognized changes in the characteristics of the theatre-going public and its evolving sophistication, there has been a considerable "liberalization" of the American motion picture industry's own self-patrolling Production Code. This code and its administration, to which our friend at the dinner party applied the old colloquial and long-antiquated name of "the Hays office," have been readjusted to conform with the change in public attitudes. Most of its old taboos have been abandoned. The Code Administration now gives its seal of approval to many films that would have got a fast thumbs-down ten years ago.

In the light of these realistic changes, it is understandable that anyone (such as our friend at the dinner party) whose notions of the movies are based upon what movies were in the 1930's and the 1940's might be astonished and perplexed at the forthright nature of many pictures coming along these days. It is hard for one to grasp in a moment that the movies have moved a long way.

It is understandable, too, regardless of whether one is aware of change, that there should still be some serious critical questioning of the responsibilities exercised in the field of films. For despite the "maturing" of the medium, there are still many liberties taken in its commercial creation and merchandising that need to be better controlled to qualify it fully for its new cultural status.

BEFORE TELEVISION

To appreciate what has happened, one must cast back over the years to the time when there was no television, when the movies were the prime device for popular mass entertainment. Then the preoccupation of film-makers and merchants alike was upon the desirability of having all pictures suitable for a wide audience—for the entertainment of everybody "from 8 to 80." That was the perennial boast. The movie theatre was endowed with the image of a haven of safe excitement and escape. It was assumed to be an equally convenient place to take a "date" or park the kiddies, a sanctuary for "family" gathering and enjoyment.

Much movie-going was a matter of habit. People went to the theatre on certain convenient nights—children on Saturdays and Sundays—regardless of what was being shown. While there certainly was marked discrimination in favor of the more star-leaden and "stupendous" films, the general public was willing to give its patronage to a great lot of routine, hackneyed fare.

THE ADVENT OF TV

With the growth of television, all this was subject to change. In the decade from 1950 to 1960, the number of television homes in this country increased from roughly 5,900,000 to something more than 45,000,000. In 1962, some 90 per cent of all American homes were provided with this new entertainment device.

The consequence was startling. As the leisure time of increasing millions of people was devoted to the television screen, a heavy drop in attendance at movie theatres occurred. In 1947 the estimated average attendance was around 75,000,000 a week. This figure fell to a low point of 46,000,000 in 1955. Indeed, there were weeks during the winters, when the air was crowded with particularly popular shows, that attendance was half that figure. Theatre men bewailed the "lost audience."

Actually, it was not a matter of massive segments of the population giving up movie-going altogether while other segments remained true. What happened was that virtually the total "mass audience" turned to television for its "everyday" entertainment and greatly reduced its "habit-going" to movies. This was particularly the case with the young married population and the children born into the TV world.

While the average individual entertainment-seeker thus reduced the frequency of his movie theatre-going (it was fashionable for people back in the 1950's to boast, "I haven't been to a movie in six months"), it was noticeable that this average individual was still susceptible to the attractions of particular pictures that might attract his curiosity and suit his taste. He remained a potential customer for certain pictures —for a certain quality of entertainment—that he could not get from television. And he demonstrated his susceptibility by going in large numbers—extraordinarily large numbers, in some instances—to see films of particular attractiveness.

THE DISCRIMINATING AUDIENCE

Thus movie-going became more and more a matter of *discrimination*, so that movie patrons now merit the appellation of the "discriminating audience" rather than the "mass audience." To be sure, the word "discriminating" does not necessarily mean that the individual patron is exercising a particularly high degree of intelligence and good taste, but he is "picking his movies" according to his interests much more than he ever did before.

This inducement to picking and choosing, for which we have television to thank, has produced some marked changes in the trends and types of pictures now being made with reasonable hopes that they'll be successful—and in the organization of the film industry. The old low-budget, low-grade pictures—the "series" films, cheap Westerns, gangster films, and such—which now have their counterparts as staples on television are virtually gone from the theatres. The emphasis now is upon the development of dramatic material with elaborate and often spectacular graphic elements or upon realistic dramatic situations and forthright social themes. A film must have "oomph," "that certain something" of one sort or another to draw these days.

FEWER FILMS, FEWER THEATRES

This virtual elimination of the small films and concentration on the "block-busters" have caused the decline in the number of pictures made. Whereas there were 332 films produced by American companies in 1952, of which only one-tenth were shot either wholly or in part outside Hollywood, there were only 200 films made by American companies in 1961—and approximately one-fourth of these were made abroad.

There has also been a decrease in the number of theatres in this country, especially the famous old movie "palaces" that were show-places in the larger cities. While there are no reliable figures on this decrease, it is estimated that the drop has been from somewhere around 18,000 after World War II to no more than 12,000 today. This slack has been taken up to some extent by the development of nearly 5,000 outdoor drive-in theatres, mostly seasonal in operation, which are now the resorts of much "family" movie-going. This diminution of theatrical facilities is significant.

FOREIGN FILMS

Withal, there has been a marked expansion in one area of motion picture culture that was of comparatively little importance before the emergence of TV. That is the area of foreign pictures, those French, Italian, Swedish, and other films imported to this country. These films, which were generally imported in limited numbers and for only a limited audience until after World War II, are now a considerable element in movie culture and trade.

What happened was that, with the fall-off in attendance and the decrease in the number of American films, certain theatres in the larger cities turned to the exhibition of imported films. These pictures, distinguished by generally more realistic and sophisticated content than American films, attracted a more perceptive and demanding audience. Shown in what were at first called "art houses," they began pulling, indeed, a marginal element of the population that seldom went to films.

Now the Italian films of Roberto Rossellini, Vittorio de Sica, Federico Fellini, and Michaelangelo Antonioni; the films of the so-called French "new wave" directors such as Francois Truffaut, Roger Vadim, Alain Resnais; the films of the Swedish Ingmar Bergman and even Akira Kurosawa's Japanese films have opened new territories of thought and emotional stimulation for the American audience and have reached an opposite pole of cultivation from that of the cheap American "B" pictures, which they have in a sense replaced.

RISE IN AUDIENCE AGE-LEVEL

The consequence of these changes in the substance of theatrical films is reflected in a rise in the average age-level of the American audience. Statistical researchers find indications that the average age of movie-goers today is one to three years older than it was some fifteen to twenty years ago. The frequency of attendance of older people particularly is found to be on the rise.

Thus our motion picture culture is much different from what it was in the days when the medium was presumably channeled to the "family" trade and was kept in bounds, on the pretext of protecting the children, by rigid censorship.

Yet the notion that this culture should be disciplined by moral measurements and restraints of a sort applied to no other medium of culture in this country still prevails in the thinking of certain influential religious and parent organizations that continue to regard the motion picture as a menace to youth.

These elements follow a tradition that has extended from the infancy of films, when the moral indignation of many ministers and educators was initially aroused over the "lewd and corrupting" influences of the new entertainment device. Their beliefs are somewhat altered but still basically firm that censorship of some sort will keep the screen reasonably "pure" so that young people may be able to see motion pictures (or be forbidden from seeing certain of them) without peril of contamination.

HISTORY OF CENSORSHIP

Censorship has a lengthy and hoary history. It has been imposed as a prior restraint upon the motion pictures almost from the beginning of their commercial success. Back in the days of the nickelodeon theatres, which charged 5¢ and 10¢ to see little programs of films, no one of which was more than twenty minutes in length, the moral indignation of churchmen and others was aroused by the quality of the films—and also by the nature of the theatres—to demand official control and regulation of them.

The first ordinance empowering a censor to look at motion pictures in advance of their exhibition in theatres and determine whether they were morally fit for the public to see was adopted by the city of Chicago in 1907. The responsibility for making the determination was assigned to the police. (Censorship is still practiced in Chicago under a special Mayor's committee.)

New York City set up reviewing arrangements in 1909, and other cities followed. The first state censorship board was adopted in Pennsylvania in 1911; Ohio and Kansas came next in 1913.

At first, the theatre men were agreeable to the arrangements which they felt would provide them with a flow of pictures that had been officially approved and thus free them from the frequent harassment of censorious elements in their communities. But soon it was discovered by film producers and distributors that the practice was jeopardizing many of their films—and was also adding the heavy expense of the inevitable reviewing and licensing fees charged by the censor boards.

FIRST CHALLENGE TO CENSORSHIP

The first all-out formidable challenge to the system of censorship as a denial to motion pictures of the right of free press and free speech was taken to the United States Supreme Court in 1915 by a distributor in Ohio. Lawyers argue that pre-release policing of motion pictures constitutes illegal prior restraint. Such prior restraint cannot legally be imposed on newspapers, books, or magazines. This is the classic and continuing argument against censorship.

However, the United States Supreme Court did not take this view in 1915. In a historic ruling, it said: "The exhibition of motion pictures is a business pure and simple, originated and conducted for profit, like other spectacles, not to be regarded, nor intended to be regarded . . . as a part of the press of the country or as organs of public opinion."

This judgment put the stamp of legitimacy on film censorship and became the accepted doctrine during the next four decades. It left the motion picture, then growing by leaps and bounds, without legal safeguards or defenses against those that would impose restraints on it. Within a few years after that ruling, a succession of states passed censorship laws—Maryland, Virginia, New York, Florida, and Massachusetts.

Typical of their mandate was that of the New York law, which provided that a film be licensed "unless such film or a part thereof is obscene, indecent, immoral, inhuman, sacrilegious or is of such character that its exhibition would tend to corrupt morals or incite to crime." The determination of whether it contained these elements was left to a dubiously qualified panel of state-employed reviewers.

By 1922 there were censorship bills before the legislature of thirty-two states and a surge of moral indignation against the movies was once more billowing across the land.

THE MOTION PICTURE INDUSTRY'S CODE

It was at this point that industry leaders, well aware that there had been an excess of bolder pictures made after World War I—and also that the public had been excited and aroused with elaborate reports of a few private scandals that had occurred among the people of Hollywood—pulled themselves together and formed their own organization for the advancement of their public relations and the political protection of the industry. Will H. Hays, then Postmaster General of the United States, was prevailed upon to accept the position of chairman of the organization which was called the Motion Picture Producers and Distributors of America (MPPDA). Within a year, Mr. Hays, who was a remarkable combination of shrewdness and piety, succeeded in having all the pending censorship bills killed or pigeonholed.

With a great deal of skill and persuasion, Mr. Hays continued to stave off the objections of the screen's moral critics and the further spread of censorship all through the 1920's, but with the arrival of sound and talking films, which brought a new element of realism and theatrical sophistication to the screen, there were fresh assaults upon the medium for its exposures of "sex and violence."

To pacify these critics, Mr. Hays recommended to the MPPDA that it adopt a "code of morals" drawn up by a trade paper publisher and a Roman Catholic priest as a guide to what should and should not be in pictures. This was the origin of the so-called "Hays code," adopted in 1930. Significantly, the code was but an arbitrary restraint upon the operations of the member producers. They could abide by its regulations or leave them alone.

However, three years later, when the Roman Catholic Church, concerned about the content of motion pictures, established its Legion of Decency to play an active role in watchdogging the medium, the MPPDA found it expedient to "put teeth into the code." It set up a Production Code Administration which was organized to read all film scripts of its member producers, advise as to the undesirable elements in them, and then pass upon the acceptability of the finished films. Those acceptable were given what was known as the "seal," and were free to be released and shown in the theatres of the member companies that had agreed to show only Code-approved films.

Thus, under definite pressure, mainly from the Catholic Church, the motion picture industry established its own device of self-restraint, which was apart and different entirely from the various agencies of state and municipal censorship.

So, through the 1930's and 1940's, the American motion picture was under two moral controls of a generally rigid nature—the initial control of the Production Code, and then the second line of control in the state and municipal censor boards.

LEGION OF DECENCY

Beyond these stood yet another considerable barrier to be passed by the film seeking wide circulation. That was the "rating" of the National

Legion of Decency. Shortly after its formation, the Legion began a practice of reviewing and classifying films according to their moral content and their suitability for showing to audiences. These classifications now are: "A-1," films deemed morally unobjectionable for general patronage; "A-2," morally unobjectionable for adults and adolescents; "A-3," morally unobjectionable for adults; "B," morally objectionable in part for all persons; and "C," totally condemned.

These ratings, arrived at by a panel of voluntary lay persons (mostly women, members of the Motion Picture Department of the International Federation of Catholic Alumnae), receive wide circulation in the Catholic press, and annually members of the faith are asked in their churches to take a pledge to be guided by the recommendations in their and their families' film going.

Thus, while the Legion's ratings do not impose enforced restraints and are, of course, a legitimate service of the church to its parishioners, the effect of a "B" or "C" rating in many Catholic-populated communities has been found a liability to a film. Some theatres in such communities have refrained from showing "B" or "C" films, especially when priests in such communities have brought overt or subtle pressures to bear, such as threats of Catholic boycott of the theatres.

WEAKENING RESTRAINTS

Such was the general picture until after World War II. Then began the great change in the patterns of motion picture attendance described earlier, and the inevitable challenge to the whole structure of restraints was begun by new elements moving into the field of films.

One reason for the weakening of the structure of restraints was the long-threatened dissolution of the monopoly structure of the motion picture industry. When the major motion picture companies (which were the chief factors of intra-industry control) were forced in 1948 to divest themselves of their theatre holdings and stick solely to the production and distribution of films, the tight grip which had enforced the rulings of the Production Code was loosed. With the control of theatres by producers eliminated, theatres that chose to show films without the seal of approval could do so. And since many of the films imported from Italy and France did not have seals, there was an increasing temptation for the theatres to disregard that lack.

THE ISSUE OF FREEDOM OF THE PRESS

It was in connection with a ruling of the United States Supreme Court on "divorcement" of theatres that the first hint came that the court might now be ready to look upon motion pictures differently from the way it had looked upon them in 1915. In conveying the court's opinion, Justice William O. Douglas wrote: "We have no doubt that moving pictures, like newspapers and radio, are included in the press whose freedom is guaranteed by the First Amendment."

This was an open invitation to challenge statutory censorship, and the motion picture people moved to do so in several instances. But it was not until four years later that two cases ultimately came before the U.S. Supreme Court almost simultaneously. It is interesting that the first to be ruled on—and now the historic one of these—served to protect the right to show one of the new imported foreign films.

THE CASE OF "THE MIRACLE"

The film was a short dramatic fiction called *The Miracle,* made in Italy by Roberto Rossellini and having Anna Magnani as its star. It told a story of an unmarried peasant woman, a bit of a simpleton, who became pregnant by a passing vagrant and then thought, in her simple faith, that Saint Joseph had caused her to conceive. The manner in which she was taunted in her village and her later ordeal of the birth were the solemn and poignant substance of it.

This film, presented by Joseph Burstyn, an independent importer, was initially passed by the New York censor and opened at the Paris Theatre, a so-called "art house," in December, 1950. Twelve days later, the New York City Commissioner of Licenses informed the theatre that he found the film "officially and personally blasphemous" and threatened to suspend the theatre's license if the film were not stopped. In the course of the next few weeks, there were several new developments.

The film was temporarily removed, then reinstated, the action of the Commissioner was taken to court and, on January 5, it was ruled that the License Commissioner had no authority to stop the showing of a film he did not like.

Meanwhile, the Legion of Decency had condemned the film and formidable individuals and groups of organized Roman Catholics, including Francis Cardinal Spellman of New York, had expressed their contempt for it.

Now the film was re-reviewed by a three-man committee of the Board of Regents, under which the New York censor is maintained. This committee ruled it "sacrilegious." Hearings were then held on the authority of the Regents to revoke a license. They ruled they had the power. Burstyn now sued the Regents for denial of a license on constitutional grounds. The *Miracle* case dragged through the state courts and finally reached the top court in the land.

In the meantime, another case arose out of the censoring of an American film. *Pinky* (a film about a Negro girl who had "passed" for white in the North returning to her home in the South and being subject to strong racial discrimination) had been banned by municipal action in Marshall, Texas, as it had also been banned in other cities of the South. The manager of a theatre in Marshall was induced to make a test. He showed the film, was fined $300, and took an appeal. This case reached the Supreme Court simultaneously with the *Miracle* case.

DECISION OF U.S. SUPREME COURT

The Miracle was the first to be passed on. On May 26, 1952, the court handed down a unanimous decision which removed the New York ban, holding "sacrilege" not a cause for which a state could censor a film.

More important, however, the decision boldly proclaimed that motion pictures are a medium of communication and are entitled to the constitutional guarantees of free speech and free press under the First and Fourteenth Amendments. This finding, of course, reversed the previous ruling of the court in the Ohio case that had stood for forty years. However, it did not automatically render null and void all censorship statutes then in force. It simply stood as a judicial guide to state legislatures or courts. All that the *Miracle* decision specifically nullified was the validity of "sacrilege."

Indeed, the court stated clearly, "Since the term 'sacrilegious' is the sole standard under attack here, it is not necessary for us to decide, for example, whether a state may censor motion pictures under a clearly drawn statute designed and applied to prevent the showing of obscene films. That is a very different question from the one now before us." And this has remained the considerable and critical question ever since the revolutionary ruling in the *Miracle* case.

One week after that ruling, the decision in the *Pinky* case came through. It repeated the court's determination that motion pictures are a part of the free press and, in effect, held that a film could not be banned from showing because it might offend the prejudices of a community.

EFFECT ON CENSOR BOARDS

Thus the demand that all censor boards justify their rulings and themselves has been a persistent feature for the past ten years.

But censor boards and the censor-minded die hard, and the running battle to reduce the scope and authority of the censors has been tough. In a series of cases ruled upon by the Supreme Court since the *Miracle* ruling, the authority of the state censor boards has been whittled away to the point where it is limited now to the determination of obscenity. And the court has ruled that the test of obscenity must be "whether, to the average person applying contemporary community standards, the dominant theme of the material taken as a whole appeals to prurient interests."

The first state to give up censorship after the *Miracle* case was Ohio. In January 1955, the court of appeals in Franklin County of that state declared its censorship statute illegal and unconstitutional, and efforts to pass new censorship bills in the Ohio legislature have been unsuccessful. The Pennsylvania Supreme Court, in a six-to-one decision, declared the censorship act of that state unconstitutional on March 13, 1956. The state adopted a new statute in 1959, which provided for classification of motion pictures as to those unsuitable for persons under seventeen as well as those unsuitable for all audiences, and it was made a criminal offense to show a film that had been classified unsuitable. This statute, too, was killed by the State Supreme Court, which held that it violated the free speech and free press guarantees of the Pennsylvania constitution.

Massachusetts and Florida have also abandoned state censorship. New York, Maryland, Kansas, and Virginia are the only states that persist.

However, the practice of censorship on the municipal level remains and is a sporadic problem for film distributors. Chicago, for instance, still has its local censor. Although his power is limited to rulings on obscenity, he sometimes takes in a wider range with this power, compelling the film distributors to seek redress in the courts.

THE CURRENT SITUATION

An effort to get the United States Supreme Court to take the final step and rule all censorship—or prior restraint of movies—unconstitutional was made in 1960–61 by a foreign film distributor who applied for a license to distribute a film in Chicago but refused to submit the film for the censor to view. In a 5–4 decision, the court upheld the city's right of inspection on the ground that "it is not for this court to limit the state in its selection of the remedy it deems most effective" to cope with the problem of determining whether a piece of material contains matter against which the community should be on guard.

In a dissenting opinion, Chief Justice Earl Warren said of this reasoning, "It comes perilously close to holding that not only may motion pictures be censored but that a licensing scheme may also be applied to newspapers, books, periodicals, radio, television, public speeches, and every other medium of expression. The court in no way explains why motion pictures should be treated differently than any other form of expression."

Here the situation now stands, with censorship still being practiced, with the censor—particularly the one in New York State—often making rather broad interpretations of the prevalence of obscenity, but with lawyers generally expecting that, within the next few years, there may well be a Supreme Court ruling that will render unconstitutional the whole practice of prior restraint.

Of course, this would not mean that the showing of movies of a grossly obscene or pornographic nature—movies that are clearly designed to appeal solely to prurient interests—might not be challenged by the police and their exhibitors arrested and made to stand trial *after* they have shown the film. This would be consistent with the practice of safeguarding the community against the circulation of offensive materials in other media, including television and radio.

INDUSTRY CODE REVISED

In line with the steady erosion of the extent and effectiveness of censorship, there has been a parallel moderation of the restraints of the film industry's Production Code. Aware that the ideas and customs of society are undergoing change and that the spread of education and sophistication has been rapid since World War II, the Production Code administrators made an extensive revision of the code in 1956.

The previous absolute taboos against depicting narcotic traffic, prostitution, abortion, and kidnapping were removed. Miscegenation was no longer a forbidden topic. Ordinary profanity (such as "hell," "damn," etc.) was cleared when dramatically valid and used with discretion, and the code's administrators were allowed to be more "liberal" in interpreting the other guiding rules. In 1961, the code was further interpreted to permit reference to homosexuality, so long as it is treated "within the careful limits of good taste."

IS "CLASSIFICATION" THE ANSWER?

While the informed and comprehending public has generally accepted as the right and democratic thing the steady elimination of pre-release film censorship and has conceded the cultural desirability of liberalizing the code, there contains an intelligent and responsible segment which feels that some method should be found to differentiate between films that are suitable for everybody and those which only adults should see. This feeling is based upon the notion which seems ingrained in our thinking that children may be harmed by seeing films of a particularly candid or violent nature, just as the mother described previously assumed that something "bad" had happened to her daughter from seeing a drama which included a double rape.

In recent years there has been a growing sentiment on the part of parent organizations and church groups that "classification" is the answer—that in this procedure lies the best way of keeping children from seeing pictures the adults think they shouldn't see.

What is classification? It is the practice of estimating films on the basis of their moral and emotional content (not their artistic qualities) and grading them according to whether they are suitable for everybody or just persons over a certain age to see.

COMPULSORY CLASSIFICATION

Classification may be of two sorts—and in the difference between them lies a wide range of philosophical disagreement and likely impracticality. The first is compulsory classification. This would be a function of a state (or municipal) authority which would classify all films according to their suitability. Then its classifications would be enforced by law. A theatre manager who permitted a person under the legally established age to see a film classed as not fit for such a person would be subject to prosecution and penalty. This sort of classification would be perilously close to censorship.

ADVISORY CLASSIFICATION

The other sort of classification—the sort that is most widely advocated by the various organizations now leaning heavily towards this new protective means—is termed advisory classification. Under it, the classifying would be done by either a statutory agency or one acceptable to the populace, such as the Code administrators of the motion picture industry, and its advices on the suitability of individual pictures would be publicized with each one as it was released. Thus parents would presumably be guided by this advice as to what films were suitable (or unsuitable) for their children to see. No penalty would be imposed upon a theatre that admitted a child to a disapproved film.

The arguments *pro* and *con* classification are many and variable, and the individual's readiness to accept them seems to depend largely upon the slant of his sentiments. Here again the extent of comprehension is generally limited. Much more thought should be given to the matter before any big decisions are made.

For instance, a basic assumption by the advocates of classification, both compulsory and advisory, is that it is reasonable and practicable to pass a judgment as to the suitability (or unsuitability) of a picture for *all* persons under a certain age. Corollary to it is their assumption that it would be reasonable and practicable for *all* parents to accept this more or less official judgment as fitting for their children. The flaws in these assumptions are vigorously cited by those who oppose classification.

In the first place, they note that the establishment of a cut-off age would be completely arbitrary and unrealistic because chronological age is a hopelessly unreliable index to the intellectual, emotional, and social maturity of a person. There are as many youngsters at 16 who have the sophistication and stability of the average person at 21 as there are youngsters at 16 who have the emotional stability of the average person at 10. There is no scientific way of measuring the impact of dramatic and entertainment material upon the mind of a child.

The advocates hold that, regardless of the logic of this argument, the state nonetheless establishes age levels below which individuals cannot legally do certain things such as buy alcoholic beverages, obtain a license to drive an automobile, or be employed in a steady job. Therefore, there is no reason why an arbitrary age level should not be set for the suitability of viewing films.

The answer to this by the opposition is that the effect of film content cannot be measured and thus can in no way be compared with the measurable effect of alcohol on a teen-ager or the statistical incidence of automobile accidents involving young drivers. There is dependable medical and police evidence for the latter; there is no substantial evidence—only conjecture—as to the "harmfulness" of films.

WHOSE STANDARDS?

Then there is the question of the standards of suitability that would prevail. Whose experience—or taste—would determine the official judgment of a film? At present, the greatest anxiety of the advocates of classification is the moral content of pictures, the prevalence of "sensationalism" and "sex." These are the elements that are supposedly most insidious and harmful to young people.

But a frequent concern of parents and child psychologists is the occurrence of horror, violence, and other emotionally disturbing elements in films. These, say the child psychologists, are invariably more upsetting to a tot who is emotionally disturbed or highly sensitive than are adult presentments of sex. The latter are usually either meaningless or annoying to the younger child, they say.

The advocates of classification who have given the matter serious thought contend that this consideration of film content should be as much in the minds of the classifiers as are considerations of sexual excess and immorality. The younger child needs to be guarded from possible abrasion as much as the teen-ager.

The opponents of classification say that this theory would logically require the subdivision of classification into ratings of films suitable for children in different age groups, and they observe that such stratification would only make the judgments of the classifiers more delicate, esoteric, and confusing to the average parent and child. (Incidentally, it has been wondered whether any official classification board would have the nerve to rate such a "fright"-laden picture as Walt Disney's "101 Dalmatians" as unsuitable for children under ten?)

It is strongly questioned by its opponents whether classification would be of much use on the advisory basis and as a purely voluntary thing. The point is made that most of the conscientious parents who might avail themselves of it are already sufficiently sophisticated and generally well-informed by critics and existing film-rating services to know something about the current pictures and which ones are generally suitable for their children. Such parents usually prefer to make up their own minds and not have someone else make up their minds for them.

On the other hand, it is reasoned that labeling and finger-pointing to films that are suitable "for adults only," without any restriction on who can attend, only arouses the curiosity and attracts the attendance of those teen-agers who are looking for sensations and are not under parental control. Thus advisory classification might serve as much to guide the undisciplined to the "unsuitable" pictures as to keep the disciplined away.

THE BRITISH SYSTEM

In discussions of classification, the advocates usually point to what they understand is the "success" of a system of classification in England. The operation of the English system is generally misunderstood by people in this country.

Actually, the British Board of Film Censors, which classifies films in that country, is a non-governmental body financed by the motion picture industry. This board now rates films in three categories: "U" which is suitable for all (Universal); "A" suitable for adults, with under-16's admitted if accompanied by an adult; and "X" for adults only (no under-16's allowed).

These ratings are then passed along to local authorities who must decide whether they are to be made mandatory in the theatres in their areas. Most of the counties and municipalities impose them, but some do not. Oftentimes local authorities make further demands and classifications of their own, creating confusion and anomalies that are as absurd as some consequences of municipal censorship in the United States.

For instance the film *Saturday Night and Sunday Morning* was given an "X" certificate, but the Warwickshire County Council refused to let it be shown within its jurisdiction even with that classification unless two scenes were cut. The distributor refused to make them and as a consequence the film was banned in Warwickshire.

However, within the boundaries of the county are the cities of Birmingham and Coventry, which, under their municipal authority, allowed the film to be shown with an "X" rating. Thus anyone in the county over 16 could see the film by taking a trip to one of these nearby cities. And, ironically, the scenes that were banned by the county council were shown on a Midlands television program that went into all the county homes.

It is a recognized fact that "X" ratings are often boastfully advertised. One film was recently blazoned as "the X-iest film on the screen."

INDEPENDENT RATINGS

Instead of some official form of classification, administered either by the state or by the motion picture industry, opponents feel that the public is already provided with adequate guides to movie content in the existing independent rating services.

Best known of the existing agencies is the Legion of Decency, whose ratings and operation have been described. It is calculated that its recommendations are brought to the attention of most of the 43,000,000 Catholics in the United States.

It is true that the Legion is sometimes forward and has been known to suggest that, if certain cuts be made in certain pictures, a "C" (condemned) rating might be avoided. This has been remarked by some observers as having the effect of a tacit form of private censorship. But, of course, the Legion's answer is that no one is compelled to make the cuts it suggests; it is simply trying to be constructive—to help make films recommendable to persons of the Roman Catholic faith.

Perhaps the most objective of the film information services is that provided by *The Green Sheet,* a monthly publication of brief reports and classifications of current pictures, prepared by a large panel of voluntary women reviewers representing ten recognized educational and religious organizations. Suggested classification for all audience levels are provided in *The Green Sheet* reviews, which are published by the Motion Picture Association of America (522 Fifth Avenue, New York City) primarily for mass media dissemination and the use of educators, librarians, clergymen, theatre managers, and others who are able to circulate its information widely.

Ratings of films as to their suitability for different age groups and interests are also run in *Parents' Magazine,* the *PTA* (Parent-Teachers Association) Magazine, *Consumer Reports, Consumer Bulletin,* the *Protestant Motion Picture Bulletin* and the *DAR* (Daughters of the American Revolution) *Magazine.*

And, of course, many newspapers and magazines throughout the country carry, in addition to critical reviews, assorted thumbnail reports and recommendations on current movie fare.

Indeed, the amount of information about movies that is available—the news stories, critical appraisals, and rating services—should be enough to provide anybody who is genuinely interested in determining what films are suitable for children with all the information they need. And the notion of setting up another master agency for putting tags on pictures as a quick and easy guide for those comparatively few nervous parents who might use it seems patently superfluous.

In the new-blown sentiment for classification appears a curious carryover, indeed, of the old custom of putting the responsibility for "protecting" the public against "harmful" movies upon some remote higher authority such as the state. Just as it used to be argued that censorship was as much justified as a protective device against "poison" as the pure food and drug laws (an argument, incidentally, which is easily demolished by the point that it is impossible to make a chemical analysis of the dramatic contents of a film), so people are now devoutly arguing that classification is required to save our youth from corruption.

ROLE OF PARENT AND TEACHERS

What will best guard the youth of this country from those occasional perverse and seamy films that present a distorted, inartistic, and often untrue picture of life is intelligent guidance by parents and teachers who draw upon a wide range of information for their guidance and not on some agency's arbitrary tag. The latter dependence smacks too strongly of the Big Brotherism of George Orwell's *1984.*

Now, with the motion picture medium advancing into broader and deeper explorations of the complexities and meanings of life, it should behoove the public to greet its advancement gratefully, to encourage its explorations with excitement and eagerness, to be well informed about it, and to give it its full cultural due—not to be squeamish and suspicious about what it may do to youth.

The significance of this potent medium is that it is available to and embraces everyone. Only by personal investigation and discovery will the individual learn to appreciate and appraise it, to sense what he and his children should take and what he and they should leave alone.

Defunct Theater Was Once Grand

Rosalind K. Ellingsworth*

Every moviegoing adult who grew up in a city of any size laments the passing of the motion picture palaces, where going to the movies was an adventure among vast murals and marble halls. Many of these theatres have disappeared over the years as the structure of the American movie industry has changed. Two of the following articles describe the end for what were great movie theatres in Kansas City. The third article discusses the rebirth of another. Hopefully, the latter is the reversal of a sad trend, or at least a postponement of the extinction of these great showplaces.

It was a warm June evening in 1919 when the Newman theater at 1114 Main street opened its doors to the throngs of well-dressed Kansas Citians who had purchased tickets to see *The Roaring Road*, a silent motion picture starring Wallace Reid.

"There was such a crowd my wife and I sneaked down the back alley and went in the stage door," recalled Arthur H. Cole who was office manager of Paramount-Famous-Lasky corporation (now Paramount Film Distributing corporation) at the time.

SOLD OUT IN ADVANCE

"It was quite a night for Kansas City," he said. All of the seats had been sold in advance and some people had bought tickets who had never been in a motion picture house before."

But the Newman was a different kind of motion picture house— it was elegant. Writers at the time called it a "magnificent edifice." The decor and architecture were patterned after an Italian ducal palace."

* By permission from Rosalind K. Ellingsworth, "Defunct Theater Was Once Grand, *The Kansas City Times*, August 19, 1967. © 1967.

The Newman, later named the Paramount when that film company decided it needed a change in 1947, was beyond all dreams of local residents. It was compared to the Missouri in St. Louis, the Oriental in Chicago and the Metropolitan in Los Angeles.

Women attending performances at the old theater were awed by the beauty of the Italian tapestry wall hangings. The magnificence of the marble walls and flooring was overwhelming.

Never before had so many conveniences and luxuries been offered in a motion picture theater in Kansas City. There was a fully equipped nursery with a full-time maid. The gentlemen attending features could make use of a club room on the lower level equipped with massive lounging chairs.

PROMENADE BEHIND BALCONY

A salon promenade decorated with marble statues and elaborate stained glass windows was behind the balcony. On the floor were the men's restrooms and the ladies's "comfort room." It was a theater no one would be ashamed to attend.

"Oh, the Newman became quite the social meeting place," said Cole recently. "I tell you one thing, you never attended a feature there in your shirt sleeves."

In 1915 a 99-year lease was signed by the builder and operator, the Newman Theater company. Written into the lease were stipulations that the building must be designed so that it could easily be converted for mercantile uses. It seems one of the families leasing the land was afraid motion pictures wouldn't last.

The Newman, or the Paramount as it is now known, closed indefinitely August 1 with 47 years left on the lease.

During its life the old theater provided Kansas City with some of the finest filmed and live entertainment. The images of such well known personalities as Rudolph Valentino, Mary Pickford, John Barrymore, Jean Harlow, Fatty Arbuckle, Gloria Swanson, Charles Ray and Marguerite Clark appeared on the silent silver screen.

SOUND BROADENED SCOPE

Leo F. Forbstein, who later became musical director at Metro-Goldwyn-Mayer, conducted its symphonic orchestra from the 14 by 40-foot orchestra pit. Clara Bow, Bette Davis, Greta Garbo, Al Jolson, William Powell and Gary Cooper appeared after the theater was wired for sound.

"We always presented the best features available," said George Baker who was manager of the theater during the late Twenties and early Thirties. "A show never played at that theater for less than a week— live or filmed."

Lillian Roth sang some of her torch songs on stage at the Newman. Victor Herbert was a guest conductor in 1923. And there were always surprise appearances from celebrities stopping over for the night in the city.

"The Santa Fe Chief used to lay over here at night," explained Baker. "Once in a while Gary Cooper or Richard Arlen would stop in for a few minutes. They were impromptu things but they always thrilled the crowds and the Newman always had crowds."

While Baker was manager of the theater he remembers receiving calls every Saturday night from the city transit company.

"Twelfth and Main streets on Saturday night was the place to be then," said Baker. "It was a big night for us—we were always packed. So the transit company would call before the last show and see how large our crowd was so they could send the right number of street cars—sometimes the street cars would line up for two blocks."

The elegant Newman was a Kansas City showplace. Local residents would point out with pride the great chandelier suspended from the center dome—a chandelier 20 feet long, 12 feet wide and lighted by 220 candles. The hand painted murals decorating the center dome and the side walls of the auditorium were acclaimed as true works of art featuring cherubs and Grecian figures.

But now the Paramount theater looks as if the duke after whose palace it was decorated lost the motion picture palace to taxes. The murals, faded and soiled, are marked with patches of white plaster. The tapestries hang limp and, in places torn. The marble lacks luster and someone has made off with the large chandelier, leaving in its place only a large naked light bulb.

The Orpheum Goes — And Memories Hold the Light in Center Stage

Winifred Shields*

If the ghosts of old actors walk in abandoned theaters, a jaunty collection of sprites must be prowling the Orpheum in its final hours.

The old vaudeville house is coming down. Like some aged beauty who keeps her boudoir lamps turned low, the splendid derelict of Baltimore avenue awaits the wreckers in a merciful half-dark, friendly to shades.

What was that rattling sound? Only a French door in the upstairs salon banging in the wind. Someone must have left it open. Who?

Was that a face flickering for just a moment on the crackled touch-up mirror still hanging in the right wing?

The solitary figure standing in a penumbra of light on stage was substantial, though. It was Fred L. Spear, longtime theatrical press agent, and he was saying in a whispery voice suitable for valedictory occasions that it was a shame they were "tearing the place down."

A Muehlebach motor hotel will replace the elegant old theater, the architectural issue of a heady alliance between the Orpheum circuit and designer G. Albert Lansburgh.

No more gilt garlands of flowers and fruits. No more entablature, no more volutes and cartouches, no more grinning chimeras, no more helmeted heads rising from the polished railing of marble stairs.

Plenty of memories.

Admiral Dewey was celebrating his 77th birthday and the outer defenses of the fortress of Metz were under fire from French artillery on December 26, 1914. In Kansas City the opening of the $500,000 Orpheum theater caused more excitement.

You could buy a full set of false teeth, "perfect fit," with a 20-year

* By permission from Winifred Shields. "The Orpheum Goes—And Memories Hold the Light in Center Stage," *The Kansas City Star*, November 19, 1961. © 1961.

guarantee, at 1017 Walnut street for $5, silk mull bloomers with ruffled or gathered ankles at Bernheimer's Department store for 75 cents, or a genuine brass bed at North-Mehornay's for $9.95. But far and away the best buy in town was a 10-cent matinee seat in the top balcony of the Orpheum or a 75-cent box.

The opening-night audience heard child singer Little Cleo Gascoigne in arias from *Traviata, Faust* and *Tales of Hoffman,* applauded the juggling accomplishments of Morris Cronin and his Merry Men, and were suitably impressed by a posing act which had a blonde, a brunette and a redhead in "living representations of famous pictures."

Walter S. ("Rube") Dickinson, bumpkin comic, gave a monologue characterization of a smalltown justice of the peace. It was the last engagement of his career. Walking to the Orpheum for a matinee, he was struck and killed by an object falling from the Hotel Muehlebach, then in an early stage of construction.

The fortunes of the hotel and the theater have been ironically intertwined. Now the hotel is about to swallow the theater. Fifty years ago a proposal to erect the theater provoked the building of the hotel.

The Orpheum circuit which acquired its property on Baltimore in 1912 from A. C. Bilicke, a Los Angeles multi-millionaire who went down on the Titanic in the same year had an agreement with the Muehlebach estate, which owned the southwest corner on Baltimore. Each was to spend $500,000 for improvements within two years or forfeit, outright, $25,000 in cash.

Carl and George Muehlebach, brothers and brewers, were persuaded to put up a hotel. The Trianon Hotel corporation, which owns the Muehlebach, acquired the Orpheum in 1956.

Widowed by the end of vaudeville, the old girl had struggled through three decades as best she could, playing legitimate theater in the 1930s, motion pictures in the 1940s, and trying legitimate plays again in the 1950s, this time under the aegis of Fox Midwest Theaters, Inc.

The vaudeville era—those were her palmiest days.

They began in another century, in another house, in another section of town—in the old Orpheum theater which was opened in 1898 at Ninth and May streets by Martin Lehman, one of the founders of the fabulous Orpheum chain.

The old Orpheum enjoyed more than a decade of intoxicating success, offering as headliners such attractions as Will Rogers, who, at that time, had no monologue, simply rode on stage chewing gum and twirling a rope. The story goes that one day when Rogers told Mr. Lehman that his pony was sick and he'd have to skip his act, Lehman told him to go on without the pony, spin ropes, tell a few gags, and that everything would turn out all right. It did.

Sensing a shift of the town's business district to the south, the Orpheum began to look around for a new location "uptown" in 1911.

Mr. Lansburgh, a San Francisco architect who went on to design more Orpheum theaters across the country, drew the plans for the Baltimore vaudeville house, which was said at the time to resemble the Paris Opera house. It incorporated a startling new idea in theater building —a ventilation system providing "washed and cleansed air."

Martin Lehman's son, the late Lawrence Lehman, became manager of the Baltimore Orpheum, which subsisted happily on a kind of mousse au chocolate diet of rich and famous talent.

"Elsie Janis, Fanny Brice—she used to take a taxi up to Leavenworth penitentiary to visit her husband, Nicky Arnstein—Ethel Barrymore, Ted Lewis, Eddie Foy—he died at the old Baltimore hotel—Chic Sale, Nazimova, they were all here," said Mr. Spear, almost reverently, looking across the denuded theater from which all seats have long been removed.

"Frances White, who wore a size 3 shoe and sang 'Ohio.' One of her shoes was displayed in a jewelry shop window when she came here.

"Singer's Midgets. Always could sell out the balcony with them.

"Fred Allen, Emma Calve, Victor Moore, Billy Gaxton, Jack Benny," Mr. Spear went on. In 1923 he went to work for the Orpheum as its press agent and later became assistant manager.

"We had three-a-day instead of the usual two when Tom Mix played here," he recalled. "Long lines standing outside waited to get in and they never seemed to move," he went on.

"A lot of kids were staying for two shows hoping to get one of the blank cartridges Tom Mix fired in his act. Know what I did? I went to a Twelfth street shooting gallery and bought a bunch of cartridges and lured them out with these. Gave each child a Tom Mix bullet at the front door."

With something less than fondness, Mr. Spear recalls seals.

"Had to fumigate the dressing rooms every time they appeared," he said.

In its heyday, the Orpheum employed seven charwomen just to scrub marble every night after the show. Once a month an artist—Mr. Spear recalls that his name was Freyman—appeared with palette and a full set of paints to touch up the colors of terra cotta decorations in the lobby.

Composing a nightly telegram to the top Orpheum echelon was one of Mr. Spear's chores. He remembers that some of these communications were addressed to Joseph P. Kennedy, father of the President, then chairman of the board of the Keith-Albee-Orpheum Theaters corporation.

Stage plays flowered at the Orpheum in the 30s. There was *Dodsworth* with Walter Huston in 1935, and *First Lady* with Jane Cowl in 1936, followed by *The Night of January 16, Boy Meets Girl, Stella Dallas* and *Ghosts,* with Nazimova.

Speaking of ghosts, that door in the gallery began to bang again. We opened it and went out on the balcony, overlooking Baltimore. Three dead pigeons were at our feet. Inscribed over the door, a single word: Tragedy.

Reborn Midland Reflects
Many-Splendored Past

Dennis Stack*

The Midland Theater seems to have had as many ups and downs as its thousands of seats.

Born amid showmanship on an October night in 1927, the Midland has been host to generations of moviegoers, but has locked its doors twice. It has been jostled by the roar of bowling balls and a bomb, haggled over by opposing teams of lawyers and businessmen and, from time to time, visited by thieves. Again it is to dominate the movie world of downtown Kansas City, its original poshness and dignity intact.

The theater is widely considered to be a magnificent example of efforts to keep downtown as the entertainment center as well as the commercial and geographical heart of the city. More than a million dollars have been spent by Durwood Theaters to acquire and restore the Midland to its original elegance.

"The policy of the Midland—like that of other first-run Durwood houses—will be to play major motion pictures," an executive says.

Wednesday night the Midland will be reborn. To those who were not about in the 1920s, the era of its birth seems remote, hidden in shadows and dust. Those were the years when college girls were flappers and young men wore coon-skin coats and trained themselves to make a quick million. Rudolph Valentino died, Al Capone insisted he did not pull the St. Valentine's day massacre and, after a drizzly rain on a May morning in 1927, a tall, boyish-looking fellow flew nonstop to Paris.

* By permission from Dennis Stack. "Reborn Midland Reflects Many-Splendored Past," *The Kansas City Star*, July 11, 1965. © 1965.

401

Original first-nighters found the Midland not so much a movie house as a royal palace. Most of those who looked at the paintings, sat in the chairs and succumbed to the temptation to touch the draperies, had been eyeing the theater for months. They had looked at the tremendous excavation through gaps in the fence, watched the steel girders sweep skyward and had caught glimpses through the glass doors of walnut panels and gilt decorations.

The richness of the Midland's red damasks and gold polychrome was subdued when it became the background for a large audience. (It seated 4,000 persons). Vast chandeliers hung from the ceilings. Tables were decorated with cherub statues and roses. Walls were broken by towering mirrors and the grand staircase had posts of marble and ballustrades of bronze. Oil paintings created spots of color on the walls.

There was a round of applause when the big front curtain went up on opening night. There was a breath of astonishment as the orchestra, on its elevating platform, rose grandly into view. "Marche Slave," with David Rubinoff as guest conductor, was the overture. Behind the musicians, delicate lighting effects were thrown on a silver curtain.

Then came the show. Films, dancing girls and movie stars abounded. The stars were Ramon Navarro, Aileen Pringle and Buddy Rogers. Navarro, a young man who scored a wide success in *Ben Hur,* played the piano and made all feel that they were his personal friends.

Bill Wright, a theater man, once recalled the Midland's first days:

"At the time Loew's was nearly ready to open, I happened to be · playing the organ on M. B. Shanberg's circuit in Hutchinson, Kas. I was a member of Local 34 and Mr. Shanberg ordered me to report to the Midland.

"When I boarded the train at Hutchinson, I found that the stars were aboard. They were met by a big crowd at the Union Station. You can imagine what a thrill it was for a punk like me (20 years old) to be assistant organist to P. Hans Flath and to play the overture with the 32-piece Midland orchestra conducted by none other than Dave Rubinoff.

"The organ, grand piano and orchestra pit all were on electric elevators and it was fun riding them up to stage level from the basement. When the elevators were new, they stuck once in awhile and refused to go down after the overture. Dave would stand up there and swear in Polish until the electricians finally got us back down again."

In its third week the Midland booked John Philip Sousa's band—and reaped a $33,000 gross. Burns and Allen, Edgar Bergen, Fred Waring and Al Pearce and His Gang did a lot of business too.

Thieves have visited occasionally. About five years ago, Bobo, a bronze statue 17 inches high, disappeared. Bobo and a similar statue had occupied a table in the women's rest room since the theater was erected.

Her absence was quickly noticed and there was a great search for her—to no avail. Then, after a lapse of time, she reappeared—in a package in the mail. A letter of explanation accompanied her.

"My name is Bobo," the letter began, "and up until a few days ago I lived in the rest room of your theater. I was neglected and unloved. One day I was spotted by a sweet old lady who just loves old statues like myself. She loved me so much that she merely uprooted me and took me home.

"It wasn't hard to take me out of the theater because nobody is ever interested in little old ladies. All they ever watch is those dreadful young people, who, by the way, certainly do need watching, especially the boys.

"When my dear, sweet, little old lady got me home, she put me on the mantel and left me there. But when her grandchildren came to visit her, they did not approve of the statue and they were very unhappy that she had taken another one. You see, I am not the first statue the little old lady has taken. In fact, I am nearer the 20th. They have a joke in her family that the city had better hire a guard to keep her from getting the Pioneer Mother.

"Anyway, to make a long story short, the grandchildren made the little old lady send me back. I suppose I am glad to be home, but I am not sure. All I ask is, 'Isn't there some other place you can put me besides the women's rest room? It is so depressing living there.'

Affectionately yours,
Bobo"

Apparently Bobo became discontented. She and the other statue disappeared for good soon after she was returned.

The night of January 11, 1932, a bomb exploded in the lobby and killed a janitor, Frank Alexander, who lived at 1332 the Paseo. The bomb had been planted as the outgrowth of union troubles.

The janitor apparently had picked up the bomb, believing it was trash or a package lost by someone. It exploded as he reached the head of the main staircase at the north end of the lobby.

Three men pleaded guilty and were sentenced to life imprisonment.

In 1961, the Midland seemed doomed. Business was not good. The theater closed and was reopened as a bowling stadium.

Its role as a bowling area was short-lived. In 1962 the Durwood theater firm announced it had leased the theater on a long-term basis. The Midland opened. Then it closed—a result of "technical difficulties."

Now, through a combination of purchase and lease agreements, Durwood Theaters has acquired the theater property. The complications involved would baffle a genius with a degree in corporation law.

But the Midland is the Midland again. That's all thousands of hearts will ever wish her to be.

"The Graduate" Makes Out

Hollis Alpert

Hollis Alpert, in analyzing the effects of the stimulating film, The Graduate, *sees it as a very important breakthrough for the American motion picture industry in terms of both commerce and art. The success of* The Graduate, *more than any other individual film, provides a watershed in the recent history of the American motion picture.**

From a window of my apartment I have a view of a movie house on Manhattan's East Side, where, ever since last December, *The Graduate* has attracted long lines of patrons. During some of the coldest winter weekends, the lines extended around the corner all the way down the block, much like those at the Radio City Music Hall during holiday periods—except that the people waiting for the next showing were not family groups but mostly young people in their teens and early twenties. One night when it was eight degrees outside I passed the line and noticed how little they seemed to be bothered by the weather; they stomped their feet, they made cheerful chatter; it was as though they all knew they were going to see something good, something made for *them.* There were other cinemas nearby, but no one waited outside in the cold. *The Graduate* was the film to see.

It still is, although now, with the warm weather, I notice that older people have begun to intermix with the young crowd. Either *The Graduate* has begun to reach deep into that amorphous audience that makes the large hits, or the elders have become curious about the movie their offspring have been going to see again and again. For that is what has been happening. *The Graduate* is not merely a success; it has become a phenomenon of multiple attendance by young people.

* By permission from Hollis Alpert. " 'The Graduate' Makes Out," *Saturday Review,* July 6, 1968, pp. 14–15, New York. © 1968, The Saturday Review, Inc.

Letters from youthful admirers of the movie have been pouring in on Dustin Hoffman, the talented thirty-year-old actor who plays the unprepossessing twenty-one-year-old Benjamin Braddock. A strong theme of identification with Benjamin's particular parental and societal hang-ups runs through these letters, as it also does in the letters to Mike Nichols, the director with an uncanny knack for forging hits. They've even been writing to Joseph E. Levine, who backed and has been presenting the film. One boy from Dallas wrote Levine, bragging that he had seen *The Graduate* more than any of his friends, no less than fifteen times.

I have seen *The Graduate* three times—once at a preview, twice with audiences—thus satisfying, I hope, the Columbia graduate student who questioned my qualifications to assess the film after only one viewing. "But you must see it at *least* three times," she told me at a brunch given by her literature professor. "You see, it has meanings and nuances you don't get on just one viewing." She, and many others in her age group, cultishly attach all sorts of significance to the most minor of details. In the film's opening moments, for example, Benjamin is seen in the cabin of a huge jet, blank-faced among rows of blank faces. "Ladies and gentlemen," the captain's voice announces, "we are about to begin our descent into Los Angeles." My graduate student interpreted this as symbolic of Benjamin's arrival in his purgatory. Close to the end of the film, Benjamin is seen in an antiseptic church, outlined against a glass partition, his arms spread out. Many have interpreted this as suggesting a crucifixion theme, an interpretation, I have it on good authority, that was far from the minds of Mr. Nichols and Mr. Hoffman.

Viewers have made much of the symbolic use of glass and water in the film, signifying Benjamin's inability to get through, to communicate with the generation that has produced him. He peers through the glass of a tank at captive fish. At poolside, and in the pool, he looks out at his parents and their friends through the glass mask of a diving suit. At other times it is through sunglasses that he sees a home environment grown somewhat strange. Surely, Benjamin is alienated, but what is so odd here is that the generation-gappers who love the film regard this sense of estrangement as natural and normal, given the times and the middle-class values espoused by Benjamin's family and friends.

Hollywood has made strenuous attempts to appeal to the young film audiences in the past, from Andy Hardy to Elvis Presley. There have been bikini beach parties, rock'n'roll orgies, Annette Funicello, and Peter Fonda on LSD, but the coin taken in from these usually cheap and sleazy quickies has been but a pittance compared to the returns from *The Graduate*. I need cite only the fact that *The Graduate* has already taken in more than $35,000,000 at the box office, after playing in only 350 of this country's theaters. Marlon Brando, the revered James Dean, and Presley never came near doing that. But this film, without the so-called stars for security, has now done better, financially speaking, than all but a dozen films of the past, and it still has thousands of drive-ins to play throughout the summer; it has yet to open anywhere abroad; and there are still those lines in front of the theater I see through my window. It is quite possible that *The Graduate* will become one of the three or four most profitable pictures *ever* made, perhaps as profitable as *The Sound of Music,* which has done so sensationally well that some critics renamed it *The Sound of Money.*

But how can these two industry landmarks be equated? *The Graduate* would appear to be squarely attacking all that *The Sound of Music* affirms so prettily: sugary sentiment, the sanctity of vows, whether religious or marital, the righteous rearing of children, melody over the mountains. The one has the well-scrubbed Julie Andrews and a dozen or so cute kids, all of them singing the Rodgers and Hammerstein lush gush as thought it were the equal of Handel's *Messiah.* The other has the appealing but unhandsome Dustin Hoffman, Anne Bancroft playing a dissatisfied, alcoholic bitch of a wife, and a musical score by Paul Simon (performed by Simon and Garfunkel) that, contrasted with *The Sound of Music*'s sentimental reverence, chants: "And the people bowed and prayed/To the neon god they made . . ." Yet, a somewhat similar pattern of attendance has been noted about both films. The young audiences go to see *The Graduate* again and again. Housewives, matrons, women's clubbers went to see *The Sound of Music* again and again. We must hypothesize, then, that in this period of selective film-going there are at least two huge American audiences, there for the right picture, one made up of the seventeens to the twenty-fives, the other over thirty-five. The Motion Picture Association now advertises its more adult fare as "suggested for mature audiences," but one wonders which is the more mature.

I have encountered some members of my generation—let us loosely call it the over-forties—who haven't liked *The Graduate.* More than that, it made them angry. It was almost as though they felt themselves personally attacked, and it has occurred to me that their reaction is less objective and critical than emotional and, possibly, subliminal. These friends do worry about their children, they have brought them up well, given them opportunities of education and esthetic development, and they are quite certain they have managed to establish communication with their young. Their wives don't drink or seduce the neighbor's son. What's all this business about honesty and truth in *The Graduate?* The cards have been stacked against the middle-class parent and in favor of the rebellious "now" generation. They darkly hint at the commercial motives of Levine, Nichols, and company, who, it's true, hoped to come through at the box office, but had not the faintest notion they would come through so handsomely.

But *The Graduate* was not meant as an attack on a generation; it merely tells a *story*, as effectively as the makers knew how to do it. To understand the story it is necessary, however, to understand that Benjamin Braddock belongs to a milieu that has been termed the affluent society. He has never known financial insecurity—he has grown up among gadgets, among cars and swimming pools—and this he has taken so much for granted that it literally has no meaning for him. His parents, on the other hand, had presumably known hard times; they knew the value, for them, of money, of material success, of things. When Benjamin comes of age, literally and symbolically, he finds himself vaguely rejecting all that his parents hold so dear. He finds himself a kind of object, the proud result of proper rearing, a reward of his parents' struggle in his behalf. Somehow, he feels, this is wrong, but he doesn't yet know what is right. What guides and counselors does he have? "Ben, I want to say one word to you, just one word," a friend of the family breathes in his ear at a welcome-home party. Benjamin awaits the word, among clinking glasses holding machine-made ice and good bourbon and scotch. "Plastics," the fellow says, imparting the great secret of success in our time. "There is a great future in plastics." The young audiences howl, at least they did when I was there, and they're on the side of Benjamin and the movie, which pokes fun at the plastic society and those who believe in it.

It is also interesting that while Benjamin tunes out for a while, he doesn't turn on. He neither joins nor identifies with the hippies, the yippies, or the weirdies; he is still thoroughly middle class, affluent variety. As he lazes purposelessly in the California sun his thoughts turn heavily to those of sex with Mrs. Robinson, whose frustrating marriage has borne her only one good result, her lovely daughter, Elaine. Elaine will soon have the benefits of her young womanhood, while the mother will sink into her bitter middle age. Unconscious envy on Mrs. Robinson's part turns into willful determination, and she reveals herself in her nudity to Benjamin's unwilling gaze. He first runs from her as from the very devil; after all, there are the proprieties, not to mention the taboos.

But then, he backs into the affair with Mrs. Robinson, who uses him for the sex she doesn't get from Mr. Robinson. In only one moment does she allow Benjamin to reach her; their intimacy is, literally, skin deep. When Benjamin stupidly assumes that affection is necessary in a furtive affair, the surprised Mrs. Robinson expels cigarette smoke into his mouth. She, too, is aware of and insistent on the taboos; Benjamin is never, ever to take Elaine out, for she assumes that by her actions she has cheapened both Benjamin and herself.

And, of course, he does, forced into it by his unaware parents. Some critics have felt that the film breaks in two around this point, that the first half is a "seriocomedy" and the second a kind of campus romance with a chase finale. But this criticism seems to overlook the unifying fact of its all being viewed and experienced through Benjamin, who is in a process of muddle, change, and development. He is a truth-seeker, trying to cut through to some acceptable level of meaning. He even tells the truth to the outraged Mr. Robinson about the affair with Mrs. Robinson: "We got into bed with each other. But it was nothing. It was nothing at all. We might—we might just as well have been shaking hands."

One of the great appeals of the film to the young, and to the young in heart of all ages, is Benjamin's honesty. The most important thing in common between Elaine and Benjamin is that they share the urge to see honestly and clearly. But Elaine's emotions are still unstable. She allows herself to be rushed into a hasty, secret marriage with an available suitor, appropriately enough a medical student, a candidate for surgeondom.

It is the ending of the film that has annoyed some, and delighted many others. If it were not for the ending, I doubt that *The Graduate* would have aroused as much enthusiastic favor as it has among the somewhat inchoately rebellious young. The distraught Benjamin, madly seeking his lost Elaine—the pure, the good, the holy—manages to reach the church, but not (as is invariably the case in a Doris Day movie) in time, upon which his hoarse, despairing appeal cases Elaine to leave her newly wedded groom, the assembled relatives, and to take a bus to nowhere in particular with Benjamin. To hold off the outraged parents, the attendants, and the minister, Benjamin grabs a large, golden cross and swings it menacingly, then uses it as a makeshift padlock on the church doors.

Curiously enough, the writer of the novel on which the film is based, Charles Webb, who was not much more than Benjamin's age at the time of writing, had fashioned a different ending—not *very* different, but crucial nevertheless. Benjamin, in the book, did arrive at the church in time, and there was no further "moral transgression" on his part involved, except, perhaps, for that bit of cross-wielding. It turns out that Mr. Webb was disturbed by the changed ending. He wrote a letter to *The New Republic,* complaining about critic Stanley Kauffmann's laudatory interpretation of the film, and particularly by what Kauffman had approvingly termed the "film's moral stance." "As a moral person," Webb wrote, "he [Benjamin] does not disrespect the institution of marriage. In the book the strength of the climax is that his moral attitudes make it necessary for him to reach the girl before she becomes the wife of somebody else, which he does. In the film version it makes no difference whether he gets there in time or not. As such, there is little difference between his relationship to Mrs. Robinson and his relationship to Elaine, both of them being essentially immoral."

However, it *does* make a great deal of difference that in the film he does not get there in time, and the audiences have taken delight in just that fact. This film-bred, film-loving generation has seen that the ending is aimed, in a double-barreled kind of way, at what might be called general moral complacency in America, and also at Hollywood morality, which, from time immemorial, has felt it necessary to approve only the sexual love that occurs during the state of marriage, and that, up until only a decade ago, took place in twin beds, with at least one foot of the man on the floor.

Not only does Mr. Webb, in his letter, equate morality with marriage licenses, but he overlooks the fact that even in his novel Elaine would already have taken out a marriage license by the time Benjamin reached her. And there is a thing called consummation. The Nichols ending (relatively little story tampering was done otherwise) is a bold stroke that is not only effective but gives the story more meaning. We now see clearly Mrs. Robinson's tragedy, that she was unable to break out of the hollow formality, the prosperous smothering surface of her own marriage. "It's too late," she screams at her daughter, who is about to head for Benjamin. Upon which Elaine, seeing it all clearly for the first time, screams triumphantly back: "Not for *me*."

But, if that old Production Code has been forsaken, if Doris Day has at last been soundly spanked for her virginal sins, hasn't morality triumphed after all? Of course it has. Mike Nichols, perhaps without fully realizing it, has lined up old Hollywood with avant-garde Hollywood. He has contrived a truly moral ending, and a most positive one at that. Honesty wins the day. Sex without love has been put in its place. Ancient taboos have been struck down. Material values have been shown to be hollow. As uninhibited and refreshing as *The Graduate* is, we are still left in fantasy land. "Most of us," a friend of mine ruefully commented, "still miss the bus."

On the other hand, perhaps the reason this newly mature generation has taken so to *The Graduate* is that it thinks, assumes, imagines it can make the bus. Mike Nichols told of meeting, recently, one of the leaders of the Columbia University rebellion. The student had loved *The Graduate*, as had his associates in rebellion. "In a way," he told Nichols, "it was what the strike was all about. Those kids had the nerve, they felt the necessity, to break the rules."

The Graduate represents a break-through of sorts in the Hollywood scheme of things, aside from its fine acting, its technical accomplishment, its vastly entertaining qualities. For it has taken aim, satirically, at the very establishment that produces most of our movies, mocked the morals and values it has long lived by. It is a final irony that it has thereby gained the large young audience it has been seeking and has been rewarded by a shower of gold.

"Play it Again, Sam" — And Again

Wallace Markfield

*Wallace Markfield is a stout defender of the American movie and popular culture in general. The following article is written with a light touch, but it contains some very serious thoughts for students of the American movie.**

On that Sunday evening last September, when I went along with some 60 million other mass minds and picked *The Bridge on the River Kwai* over *Bonanza,* I was not immediately aware that I was helping (1) close off an era in cultural history; and (2) heap Job-like sorrows upon some of the wisest heads of our generation. But in the weeks and months that followed, as the networks hustled to buy up whatever canned goods Hollywood still had in stock, as trade-paper heads sang of FLIX CLIX and PIC PACTS, critics and commentators began to carry on like medieval chroniclers in a plague year.

Mostly they mourned and moaned over the passing of TV's Golden Age, when Paddy Chayefsky and Rod Serling and David Shaw presided over the midcult-and-suit industry, when week in and week out Ed Begley and Everett Sloane were telling us all there was to know about life in our time. Some, hoarse from crying bloody murder and stinking fish, began paying out muted tribute even to *The Beverly Hillbillies.* "For all its corniness and genuine narcissistic appeal," wrote one big brain, "the program reflects a genuine confrontation in American society. . . ." (Rough translation: At least it's not a movie.)

But matters got only worse (more new shows died in midseason) and worse (more networks scheduled more movie nights) for the high-minded, who mounted increasingly frenzied attacks on everything and

* Reprinted with permission of *The Saturday Evening Post.* © 1967. The Curtis Publishing Co. (*Saturday Evening Post,* April 22, 1967), pp. 72–79.

everyone in sight. They blamed Wall Street and Madison Avenue, teenagers and golden-agers, the debasement of public taste and the public taste for debasement, the human condition in general and the American character in particular—while Max Lerner hinted darkly that somehow we are all, all of us, responsible.

All of which shook me up and started me wondering and worrying over what I and the rest of the great audience were about to lose. I flashed back 10 or 15 years, cast a cold eye upon those thousands and thousands of hours of my television time and found myself in a state of near-total recoil. For no matter how I forced those calendar leaves to exfoliate, my remembrance of things past took in very little of what had once upon a time been hailed and hallowed. Thus, nothing, absolutely nothing, showed up from *Philco Playhouse* or *Playhouse 90;* and of the news and public-service stuff, the very best I could manage was a montage of Costello-Eisenhower-JFK-Oswald-Ruby, the clock and tick of computers on election eves, and one particularly cold "good night" from Huntley to Brinkley. Pressing, I came up with two Sid Caesar skits; five fast minutes by Jackie Mason; a nice routine by Susskind and Khrushchev; bits and pieces from *Naked City, Wanted—Dead or Alive* and *Gunsmoke;* an image of Gleason, in the old "Honeymooners," shuttling, with one long look, between aggravation and paranoia.

Yet—and I suspect I am no different from many Americans who first saw the light of the screen in the '30's—I have a movie memory as long as King Kong's arm. Under fire, I can repeat Paul Muni's first words in *Scarface,* his last ones in *I Am a Fugitive From a Chain Gang;* pick out, in the biggest crowd scenes, the faces of George E. Stone and Harold Huber and Warren Hymer and Nat Pendleton and Irving Pichel; distinguish between Colin Clive and Clive Brook, Phillips Montgomery and Douglass Montgomery, Frankie Darro and Frankie Thomas; tell you who slapped Bogart around in *The Big Sleep* and who got slapped around by Bogart in *The Big Shot.* Ask me about the last six specials on juvenile delinquency and urban development, and I'll most likely counter with a scene from *Dead End;* five minutes of Walter Cronkite on the Far Right are enough to start me thinking about *Meet John Doe;* let NBC analyze the state of our prisons, and I'll be assailed by wild longings for Alan Baxter and Barton MacLane.

To me, at least, television has all along existed for the sake of movies, and if its existence over the next decade or so will depend more and more on more and more movies, that suits me fine. Against the arguments of purists about heartless, mindless cuts and commercials, about what and how much a movie must suffer in transit from even the smallest screen to the biggest tube, I can muster only a mild "Uh-huh." For when the worst is said on the worst that's been done, television is still my personal, permanent film festival, my life-pass to the midway of mass culture, my museum without walls, my main currents of American thought, my journal of a misspent youth.

And in the dark night of the soul, when it's always time for the Late, Late Show, I can call back all my phantoms from dreamland: the jockies who talked to their mounts; the fighting priests; the wardens pleading into microphones ("Billy, it's your last chance, Billy"); the dancing co-eds; the mad doctors and their marvelous monster-making machines; the native chiefs who went, "Oomgahwah"; the ex-cons who couldn't go straight; the fight managers issuing their warnings ("Kid, you're not ready yet for the champ!"); the slum sisters ironing shirts for their wild, weak brothers; gypsy mothers wailing for their werewolf sons; honest cops who busted up crap games and told the young punks, "I'll be keepin' me eye on yez, Rocky, me lad"; the Negroes in Death Row singing *Swing Low, Sweet Chariot;* the princes who took jobs as butlers; dowagers with canes; the slim kid who wanted to be a diver, a lineman, an oil rigger; the city editors chomping cold cigars; tenement mothers hanging out of windows and calling their great ones ("Irving, Irving Berlin, you'll be late yet for the piano teacher!"); cabbies with cigarettes tucked behind their ears; coloraturas who belted out *Minnie The Moocher;* fresh-faced subalterns just up from Sandhurst ("Jolly good to be in your regiment, Father"); their seasoned sergeant majors ("Beggin' your pardon, sir, but you're playing into Mohammed Khan's hands!"); the earthbound angels hoping to earn their wings; all those Disraelis who counseled and cajoled all their Victorias; one-man dogs and one-dog men. . . .

The world they inhabited had its own loony laws and logic, and faulting these makes about as much sense as faulting the Keystone Kops for sloppy police work. What matter and what harm if nothing made by human stagehands could have held a Busby Berkeley production number? Is it crucial that no match ever was struck without lighting up whole rooms, no sweet young voice ever raised in the wilderness without benefit of the Hall Johnson Choir? Was the American Indian any worse off for talking like Akim Tamiroff or George Arliss? What would have been gained if the campus cuties had once in a while cracked their books, if newsboys had to dig up change for those five-dollar bills? Did the rich get richer because they never checked a restaurant tab? Or the poor poorer because they took only two bites of those lunch pail sandwiches?

Long, long after you have had your last laugh in the wrong place, you come to realize how much we still live with and by the images and ideas of the old movies. From them, we learned to smoke too much, to do without undershirts and pajama tops, to talk through our noses, or from the sides of our mouths, to get off a wisecrack and a left jab, to hold a glass or a girl, to make love and war, to enter the world like Mickey Rooney and leave it like Lewis Stone. They seemed to come at us from all sides and from under the woodwork, hitting us like flak, pumping us up and letting us down, promising everything and fulfilling next-to-nothing. They gave us, at most and at best, half-truths, but these, more than we probably are willing to admit, may be the only truths we care about.

For if those who made the old movies knew nothing else, they at least knew that the screen, as Robert Warshow has written, "will be filled at all costs." And they worked to fill it with the one thing that fills it better than any other thing: the City.

It comes to us again, this city, as it was for us then, an infernal metropolis steeped in dreadful night and racked by everlasting din, a study in terribly cruel contrasts. There was Easy Street or Dead End, the penthouse or the penitentiary, the royal suite or the railroad flat, the room that is lit by candlelight or by a flashing neon sign; let two kids start off together, and one must sit in the governor's chair, the other in the electric chair. It is a lonely place, but the city man must never be alone. For once the grocer pulls down his shade and opens his till, he is already dead for us, and so too, is the old, slow cop who hears the young punk's shot. Once the gangster steps inside a phone booth or lingers a few extra seconds in shower, in steam room, we will not see him again, except as a corpse flung from a limousine.

Much of the edge and energy of city cinema came from timeless small-timers who were impossible to miscast and were never less than almost perfect. They were matchless metropolitan types, so quietly pleasing and persuasive, so artlessly artful and anonymous that it is still hard to realize how powerfully they put themselves across. (To this day I have difficulty dealing with flesh-and-blood tailors who refuse to behave like George E. Stone.) Watching them from night to night, in movie after movie, will provide something like an absolute standard by which to measure what character acting should be, and a fair idea of how much it has deteriorated.

I have in mind the likes of Allen Jenkins and Frank McHugh, Everyman's Best Pals. And Glenda Farrell, who looked as if she had been born on a fire escape and in a housedress. And horsefaced Helen Donnolly, who could carry a scene as easily as that bowl of soup she was trying to force down Margaret Lindsay. And nervous little Edward Brophy, with his half-a-cigar and his Moon Mullins derby; the nicest thing that could happen to him was a smack on the head. And hugevoiced Stanley Ridges, who gave him that smack. And Patsy Kelly, broad of beam and low of brow; it was a black day for the black Irish when her patent lapsed on the half-sozzled housemaid part. And Joseph Sawyer, the dumbest of dumb cops; he looked capable of ticketing a hydrant for overtime parking.

Most of them started and stuck with Warner Brothers and provided the human backdrop against which that studio's top talents functioned. These were the stumpy, chesty, fisty bantams admirably suited for metropolitan melodrama, and for very little else. Each one had his own style, but each style was as broad and teeming with life as a boulevard. There was James Cagney, rocking and rocking his hands; there was Edward G. Robinson making sad-monkey faces; there was George Raft, the screen's best bad actor, stretching his syllables ("Awride, bay. . . . *bee!*"); there was Humphrey Bogart doing Humphrey Bogart things; and there was one who seemed born to play Hamlet—if only Hamlet had been born in the Bronx. So he did the next best thing and played John Garfield parts.

Of all the city men TV returns to us, Garfield gives the strongest sense of his time and of his place in that time: It is a rough time, and he is badly placed; everything is against him, but mostly he is against himself.

He entered movie history (*Four Daughters*) as easily as he might have entered a candy store. His step was tired, his voice strained, somewhat off pitch; droplets of sweat almost always hung over his brows, and anger and loss underscored every line in his face. When he opened his twisted mouth, he seemed to be speaking not for himself but for a generation—that generation which waited and waited for Lefty. It has been a long wait, and by now all those great expectations have dwindled to the size of a two-pump station. Maybe, maybe, as he wistfully muses in *Dust Be My Destiny*, "It'll have a coupla' rooms and a hunka' backyard. . . ." But in later movies the Garfield type is too far gone and too far away from the '30's for even such small joys; just about his happiest line in *Body and Soul* is, "Everybody dies." (On the same day I was watching *Body and Soul*, the same channel carried *A Walk in the Sun*, wherein John Ireland has this to say: "Nobody dies.")

Granted, Warners was not out to lose any money on Garfield, or Bogart, or Robinson, or Cagney or Raft. Compared, though, to the policies and products of other studios, Warners deserves not only honorable mention, but positive veneration. A case in point: M-G-M.

An M-G-M male of any period seems to have been made for long wear and hard use; he is as universal and as easy-to-take as gelatin. Who in his right mind could be offended by the voice, stance, face, or walk of a Robert Taylor? Who that is truly human would fail to wish long life and good years upon Robert Young, Tom Drake, John Hodiak, Don Taylor, Van Johnson, the early Robert Walker, the early-middle James Stewart? Who has not nursed the crazy hope that his father would one day bear himself a little more like Walter Pidgeon, or Spencer Tracy, that his grandfather would all of a sudden give out with Frank Morgan titters and Lionel Barrymore grunts?

It is mighty hard, though, to forgive M-G-M its women. Even after all these years, June Allyson, Laraine Day, Ruth Hussey, Esther Williams, Greer Garson, Cecelia Parker, Ann Rutherford, Vera-Ellen, Janet Leigh and Jennifer Jones still manage, singly or collectively, to work on my nerves like a nail on a slate. I don't mean to be vindictive; they did well enough at what they had to do, and looked, while doing it, in the pink of condition. And if they weren't spectacles in their own right, like Bette Davis, or Carole Lombard, or Rosalind Russell, or Barbara Stanwyck, they weren't supposed to be. Maybe it was simply their hard luck that history, as the Marxists used to say, was against them, that a lot of us have never forgiven them for being the good wives and girls named Jo who, simpering and whimpering, sent us— and Sonny Tufts—off to war.

All right, we went, and it was a long time ago. But now, suddenly, there is TV with those World War II movies to annoy and intrude and embarrass, to make noise and talk nonsense, like so many boozy old army buddies we never really cared for in the first place.

Most of them I caught 20-odd years ago, usually in some Times Square scratch house and in the company of one or two other wise guys. We sat up front, almost in the screen, and carried on like crazy, keeping score on the number of lines and bits of business we could anticipate. After a while it was no fun, no contest. The moment the top kick called for volunteers, we beat him to his, "Okay, Brown . . . Shannon . . . Donadio . . . Horwitz. . . ." Among that batch of hostages under SS guns was one who would sing out a litany to "ze liddle pee-pul," and we sang right along. We reminded the gum-chewing pilot to press his wad against the cockpit, to kiss his Betty Grable pinup, to find out over the intercom how things stood with the Dodgers. We had memory banks that could feed back the number of depth charges needed to make a sub's light flutter, the number of Japs who must get it from a grenade (never less than three, never more than five; and one must wear glasses) , even the number of times a Gestapo gorilla will slap a partisan (never less than three, never more than five) .

What did I expect the second time around? The worst, I guess, and I can't say I was exactly disappointed. God knows, there is enough and more than enough in most World War II movies that insults your intelligence and injures your stomach. And, doubtless, they are nearly everything James Agee once said they were: ". . . posterish, opportunistic, anti-human . . . one long orgy of meeching, sugaring and propitiation. . . ."

But all the same I felt none of these things; indeed, for once in my movie-life, I was feeling only the wrong things. Looking at *Air Force,* I found myself strangely untroubled by the fact that it was entirely lacking in what cinema enthusiasts call "values." The camera didn't move? So it didn't move. Wouldn't Eisenstein have massed those masses more massively, staged those deaths less stagily? Yes, on both counts, and he might have given us real corpses, too.

All I could watch were those wonderful Flying Fortresses; I hadn't realized I'd been missing them nearly as much as the rickety one- and two-wing jobs in *Hell's Angels* and *Ceiling Zero*. Likewise, that whole healthy crew, even the boy from Brooklyn, got to me. They struck me suddenly as altogether a decent, likable bunch, and I couldn't help thinking how much I'd rather serve with them than with, say, Belmondo. And when they fought the battle of the Coral Sea and flew off into a symbolic sunrise, and when the rays of that symbolic sunrise converged on an American flag, the pathetic artless- ness of it all seemed a positive virtue. Perhaps this equivalent of "Hoo- ray for our side!" expressed well enough what I felt, and was all the screen poetry I wanted. Or perhaps the accident of seeing, earlier that week, the exquisite effects Leni Riefenstahl, Hitler's favorite, once milked from a shot of Stukas over Rotterdam had soured me on all screen poetry.

Similar Philistine considerations intervened between me and my judgment of John Wayne in *Sands of Iwo Jima, The Fighting Seabees* and *Flying Leathernecks*. I had always liked him, but from a safe distance and in a very special way—the way, I suppose, one likes certain traffic cops or gym instructors. But this time he was no longer some unpolished instrument of democracy, he was no longer even John Wayne, and I hardly knew or cared whether he could act or not. I was too busy finding in his face qualities I'd never noticed be- fore ("Qualities!" I can hear my old cronies cry), qualities which are these days present in very few movie faces. It is a face which carries repose, completeness and utter clarity like the tool marks on Shaker furniture, the face of a man who knows what he is and why he is in the world. "How can you send those kids out to be killed?" Robert Ryan asks him, in *Flying Leathernecks*. "How can you live with your- self?" To which Wayne makes stonefaced reply: "Because I have to, because someone has to." He says it simply, softly, but with a certain resonance in his voice, as if with this cheerless platitude he has gone right to the heart of the matter.

And such is the cruel nature of television that the next voice I can remember hearing was Brando's; it was like the voice of a demented midget, and it yowled "Stella . . ." We didn't know it at the time, but it was telling us, among other things, that the war was over, that Louis B. Mayer was no longer the father of us all, that the escape valve was sealed off for good, that the end of the '40's was the end of innocence, that a movie wasn't just a 75-cent window on the world or 90 minutes of straight, scrappy narrative, that it was, really it was

. . . well, what was it, really? Maybe, as Manny Farber has been insisting these many, many years, it wasn't even a movie.

But whatever it was, it was certainly nervous. ("Hey, ya know," Judy Holliday whines in *The Marrying Kind*, "it's a nervous world.") Take, for instance, the small matter of titles. Back in the '30's, these were as innocuous and functional as bank statements: If you noticed them, fine; if you didn't, that was all right too.

Usually, you saw a set of quarto-sized vellum-bound books. A man's hand—Lewis Stone's, I once believed—moves out from the corner of the screen, makes love to each of the books, but settles, finally, on one, and that one is *A Tale of Two Cities*. Sometimes there was a trim British ship-of-the-line or a massive galleon whose sails, as they come into view, carry everything from stars to sound-mixer. Then, illuminated subtitles nail down place and time: *London, 1787,* or *Maracaibo, 1655, refuge of pirates, renegades and cutthroats.*

By the '50's, though, you needed titles for the titles. For what a far-out few—that is, Luis Buñuel, Man Ray, Hans Richter, Maya Deren, Jean Cocteau—had been doing a full generation back to light, sound, space and motion, was all of a sudden absorbed into Hollywood's visual vocabulary without a tremor in transition. Titles got longer and louder —three, four harrowing minutes of jazzed-up calligraphy and anxious objects that could evoke, within an eyeblink, anything from Krazy Kat to Kafka.

Old and arguable ideas suddenly hardened into doctrine. Hardest doctrine of all: the doctrine of the moving camera. And directors sweated to find new ways of moving it, new places to point it at, and new things to tell with it. Close-ups got closer . . . and Closer . . . and CLOSER, turning skin pores into something like a lunar surface. Enormous statements abounded, hidden meanings emerged and collided in the borders of the screen; sets verged on the abstract—or the "universal." (This "universality," by the way, seems to me characteristic of all kinds of movies in the '50's: *Picnic, On the Waterfront, The Rainmaker, Come Back, Little Sheba, The Man With the Golden Arm, Bus Stop, A Hatful of Rain,* even when shot on location, appear to be happening in a shadowy, timeless America that lies at dead midpoint between the Great Depression and the Great Society.)

Maybe the easiest way to understand where and how much movies have changed is to watch Westerns. Watch, first, the horses.

For they are not what they used to be. And what they used to be was something like Pegasus, but sweeter-tempered and happier to serve. All they wanted was the chance to use their teeth on a cowboy's bonds, to pull him out of quicksand, to come bucking and biting when he was cornered by a wild stallion, to kneel so he might mount when wounded, to carry him across a ravine with one long leap, to butt him, before the fadeout, into the arms of the schoolmarm.

They sought, in return, a pat on the muzzle, at most a couple of sugar cubes. But lately, it seems to me, they want a good deal more and will do much, much less. They falter, they fall, they lose their shoes and pick up stones, they shy at snakes; they seldom ride double, and water is almost always on their minds. Nowadays, the first sight we usually have of them is when they are being tied to a rail, or led, winded and sweaty, into a stable. In general they prefer being indoors.

And so, I notice, does everyone else. The town, once a mean way station on the road to an endless frontier, is increasingly called to our attention. We see how crowded it has gotten, how many more things are in it for the camera to fix and feed on: the ordinances outside the sheriff's office, the price list in a barbershop window, the steep stairs a Mexican woman must climb with her basket of wash, the sad face of a dancehall girl in a window above the saloon, the stupid, brutal face of the cowpoke who pulls the shade down, the flies attacking the poor old town drunk as he sprawls against the water trough.

Once it was only Saturday night in this town, but now it is always high noon of a working day. Here the Westerner seldom rides in to spend on his hot bath, his drink, his card game, and when he does, he spends less freely. Money is lately on his mind; we catch him picking up his change at the bar, pricing a saddle, a pair of boots, even a box of shells. He has, after all, good reason, for times are hard. "T'aint my fault," the storekeeper says, "if times are hard." (This storekeeper, who used to needle Gabby Hayes about his beard, has become as pompous as Polonius. We have had him with us since *High Noon,* and for the rest of our lives we will probably be putting up with his "The old West is dyin'." . . . "One of these days the railroad's comin' tuh Abilene." . . . "Got ourselves thirty new families last week.")

Hard times are a fixed condition for every adult Western: The more adult the Western, the harder the times. Wherever we look, work—bitter, brutal work—is being done, and this comes as a shock. For the Western was once all leisure and repose, the Westerner a man who shot a gun, rode a horse, fought with his fists, and did, finally, "what he had to do"—and what he had to do was shoot a gun, ride a horse, fight with his fists. To be sure, he once in a while helped a settler load up a wagon, though a sack of flour and a bolt of gingham was his usual limit. (If he did more, his guns would be in the way, and this must never happen.) As a rule, he couldn't make a decent cup of coffee, or mend a rip in his shirt, or wash out a pair of socks, or patch a harness, or grease an axle, or build a cabin, or raise a crop; when he turned marshal he was barely, barely able to nail up a

WANTED poster, and after it was up he complained about the paper-work. Who knew or wanted to know how he had freed himself from the strains and pains of making a dollar, how he had paid for his gun and horse, let alone that "little spread"? It was his West, his America, his culture, his civilization; he had no call to explain or justify him-self. "You belong here," the girl from the East tells the Virginian.

But when he appears before us now, his day is already over. ("Your day is over!" the storekeeper cries.) He is graver, more melancholy, worn down like the leather of his gun belt. Even the marshal's job is taken, and by an old friend who must order him out of town. ("It's not your fault, Ringo, only trouble just naturally follows you.") He has already been driven off the plains and out of history by the sod-buster, the cattle baron, the railroad, and in the next town he is most likely wanted. To add to his other troubles, his nerves are pretty well shot; he tends to talk more, and often says a little too much. When he doesn't come on with the self-pity of an Odets character ("All I ever got out of life," Gregory Peck broods, in *The Gunfighter*, "was this here watch"), he is addressing himself, Hamlet style, to a host of overwhelming questions: Am I slowing up? Who cares whether I live or die? How many more men must I kill? Why won't they let me alone?

No wonder, then, that he draws his gun less willingly and gets off fewer shots when he does draw. (I could be off by a couple, but it seems to me that I've never counted more than a dozen shots in any Western made after the '50's. The all-time low: three, in *The Gun-fighter*.) And after he has killed ("Don't make me do it," pleads Henry Fonda in *Warlock*, Joel McCrea in *Wichita*, Robert Ryan in *The Proud Ones*), he rides out dwindled and diminished, longer in tooth and shorter of breath. His horse steps slowly, for the street is crowded with buckboards; the homesteaders are stocking up on supplies, and the storekeeper is telling them, "The old West is dyin' " . . . "One of these days the railroad's comin' tuh Abilene" . . . "Got ourselves thirty new families last week." Stretching out before him is a Dust Bowl vista lifted straight out of *The Grapes of Wrath;* and the birds circling overhead look suspiciously like N.R.A. blue eagles.

How fast the time goes and how television marks and mocks its passage! Within a week you are watching the fawn-eyed, apple-cheeked William Holden in *Our Town* and *Meet the Stewarts* change into the *Stalag 17* hardcase. Or you can catch Gable and Lombard and Bogart and Cooper and Colman, and you're filled with an irrational anger against them; by what right, after all, do gods and goddesses die? Over-night, two decades' worth of judgments are thrown out. (The Marx Brothers don't hold up, yet Bob Hope does; Lionel Barrymore is a finer actor than John; Irene Dunne may have been only the most brilliant comedienne of them all; Frank Capra seems less sentimental, Preston Sturges more.)

So television makes us all film historians. And cultists. And titans of trivia. And sneaky weepers. It sends us to bed or Barcalounger drugged with memory and turned on like Proust. For in the world of the *Late Show* we have only time past, and we are helpless against it. We rise, open the refrigerator, try to fill our stomachs and close our minds. But nothing helps, nothing holds back the question that comes a moment before sleep—*What am I now that I was not then / Which I must act and suffer again?*

June Allyson Never
Kicked Anyone in the Shins

Bob Newhart

Here Bob Newhart, humorist and moviewatcher, looks at his folk heroes and their meaning to him. *

"He's groovy," the baby sitter said, interrupting my reverie. I call them reveries. Others might call them daydreams, others absent-mindedness and others galloping senility. "Who?" I inquired. "Bogey," she replied, never taking her eyes off the television screen. A perfect opportunity, I thought to myself, to bridge the so-called "conversation gap." (*Newsweek,* March 13, 1967, *Saturday Review,* March 18, 1967, *Christian Century,* March 8, 1967, *America,* March 11, 1967) .

I suppose there are some who will put me down as one of those who peruse magazines trying to find out what I should be alarmed about, but it does help to know what other people are alarmed about so that you won't independently alarm yourself over things about which nobody else is alarmed. It's important to be alarmed about the right things.

I took umbrage, and I am not one to take umbrage lightly, at a remark made by the same baby sitter a week before about one of the favorite movies of my childhood, the name of which escapes me at the moment. I do remember it was a war picture starring Helmut Dantine and Wayne Morris. Her remark at the time, which had brought me up short, was "Did you really go out and watch this kind of junk, Mr. Newhart?" The remark about Bogey, however, opened up a new area. How, I wondered, had the present generation, via the Late Show, accepted as its own some of my idols—Bogey and W. C. Fields—while

* By permission from Bob Newhart, "June Allyson Never Kicked Anyone in the Shins," *The New York Times,* July 23, 1967.

rejecting others—Wayne Morris and Helmut Dantine or George Brent and Carmen Miranda.

Elizabeth Taylor, oddly enough, occupies at the present time a sort of Limbo among the teen-agers. A sort of withholding of judgment. Elizabeth Taylor, to most of my generation, was the girl that every-one, with the exception of myself, wanted to marry. Actually a startling percentage of my generation did marry Elizabeth Taylor.

June Allyson was *my* ideal housewife. I mean, the way she coped with problems that would have floored any other female! She'd start to cry a little after running out of the living room, then compose her-self, set her jaw in that unmistakable way (*The Glenn Miller Story, The Stratton Story, Two Girls and A Sailor, Meet the People*) —walk back into the room, tell off Eugene Pallette, George Sanders or S. Z. (Cuddles) Sakall, at which point one of them would say, "I admire a girl with spunk," and Don Taylor or Ronald Reagan would get the job that he was most qualified for in the first place.

So maybe those old movies *didn't* prepare you for life or what a woman really is, her needs, sexual and otherwise. Maybe the New Wave people *are* preparing our teen-agers for life as it exists, the role of sex, the sordidness of life. I say take a couple of those New Wave filmmakers and wash their mouths out with soap and we'll see how many dirty pictures they'll make after *that*. I never thought of June Allyson and sex, and I am sure Don Taylor, Peter Lawford or Ronald Reagan never did either. I'm *sure* Ronald Reagan never did.

Maybe the teen-ager of today, with his TV heroes, is better pre-pared for life than I was with my movie heroes. I must admit I was a little taken aback when my wife didn't react to the first crisis in our marriage the way I thought June Allyson might have. My wife Ginnie kicked me in the shins and didn't speak to me for a month. I had never seen June Allyson do *that*.

The occasion of the first crisis in our marriage happened to be a scene from a June Allyson movie. Really. I was reading aloud some Balzac. Ginnie listened for about a half-hour and then said, "Do you get some perverted kick out of reading dirty books to a woman?" At that point she kicked me. In my defense, I must add that when Don Taylor read to June Allyson, he selected a clean passage, and I really didn't know the Balzac was naughty until I came upon the passage and it was already too late to stop. Our scene—the one between Ginnie and me—was supposed to end with my closing the book, a moment of silence and a shot of my hand turning out the living room lights. I know now what happened after the hand scene, but at the time I didn't.

I suppose June Allyson was one of the many fictions that Louis B. Mayer, Jack Warner and Harry Cohn perpetrated upon my generation, but there were other fictions. It didn't bother me when, in some musical opus, Judy Garland and Mickey Rooney, along with their pals Gloria Jean and Benny Baker, decided to put on a show in a barn in upstate Connecticut (no one apparently ever lives in downstate Connecticut) to help the kids at the camp. All on a very meager budget. Well, the stairway they came down for the finale had to cost a minimum of $22,000.

It didn't bother me that Tony Curtis couldn't have been a sheik's son, unless the sheik had sent his son to a school in Brooklyn. Or that Eleanor Powell or Parker, whichever one dances, played an entertainer aboard a German liner just prior to the start of World War II. Having overheard a conversation between the German spies, she tries to warn Bill Lundigan, the FBI agent, of the impending attack on Pearl Harbor. Instead of doing her regular dance number aboard the ship, she changes it to a dance using the Morse Code. Bill Lundigan, sitting in the audience, orders a friend, "Take this down." It didn't bother me, but her taps would have been translated as Gleff Nymasol Swswytor. These were their fictions, and I and millions of others were willing dupes.

I suppose that this is the way we wanted life to be. But it never really was and perhaps that explains why we can't give our children the answer they seek until they, too, marry and read a little Balzac and get kicked in the shins. So laugh, cool generation, at our folk heroes —June Allyson, Wayne Morris and Ronald Reagan—but don't borrow Bogey and W. C. Fields. They're *ours*. Find your own or you will have denied your children their inalienable American right to laugh at *your* folk heroes.

The Dream that Never Died

Olivia de Havilland

*Olivia de Havilland has received two Oscars for her excellent perform-
ances in* To Each His Own *and* The Heiress. *In the following article
she recalls her participation in the filming of* Gone With the Wind,
*and its special place in the history of American movies.**

Many, many little girls have been named Melanie since *Gone With
the Wind* was first premiered in Atlanta on a December night in 1939.
I know this because of the letters I have received through the marching
years, letters that came first from their young mothers, and then, as
they reached writing age, from the little girls themselves.

I think I know why those young women of 1939, 1940 and 1941
and the succeeding years when *Gone With the Wind* was released again
and again—why they dreamed of daughters and dreamed of naming
them Melanie. It has something to do with the young woman I was
when I dreamed of playing her, and then, when I received the role, lived
her life for the six happy months of filming *Gone With the Wind*.

For when the role of Melanie came to me, I was 22, and angry and
full of despair. Not only professional despair, because the creative
roles I wanted were seldom mine, but personal despair. Despair at
what seemed to be the reality of the life around me, the reality of the
powerful, brutal kingdom that was Hollywood, in which there was no
place for the values I had been brought up to believe in, values I
believed in, not only as a human being, but also as a woman.

Some of the men who dominated the kingdom were brilliant, imaginative, gifted, and some of them were not.

These others were the men who knew lust for power, for fame, for
money, for women. They had created in their own image and made
the sexual symbol of the day their female counterpart. She was bitchy,

---

* *Look Magazine*, December 12, 1967, pp. 113–114. By permission of the author.

she was destructive, and she saw men only in terms of use. She was capable of beating them at their own game, and like them, she was incapable of love. She was their ideal woman. She was their Eve.

I was not that woman. Nothing I wanted to be or believed I should be was that woman. How, then, in a world where the bad and the beautiful were the pearls of great price, and the good and the beautiful were somehow absurd, was I to survive? Survive and express those values about which I cared, in this very world that seemed to care about them not at all? The question not only made me angry and despairing but it sometimes made me frightened. Then came the way and the role, and the way was a film, and the role was Melanie.

It was through my sister Joan Fontaine that Melanie came. She had gone to see George Cukor, the director, to read for the part of Scarlett. When he asked her to read for Melanie instead, she declined and said, "If it is a Melanie you are looking for, why don't you try my sister?" And he did.

After I read for him the scene he had indicated, George asked me to commit it to memory and meet him at the house of the producer, David Selznick, at three o'clock the following Sunday afternoon. I did so, and dressed in a black-velvet afternoon dress with a round lace collar and short puffed sleeves, I was ushered into the great man's drawing room for one of the most richly significant moments of my life. But destiny has a piquant humor, and the scene that ensued was pure comedy; it was George's role to play opposite me. He was at that time portly, his hair was black, curly and closely cropped, his spectacles were large and thickly rimmed. To this day, I have claimed that it was his passionate portrayal of Scarlett O'Hara clutching the portieres that convinced David that afternoon he had finally found his Melanie.

The part, however, was not yet mine, for I was under contract to Warner Brother studios, renowned for keeping its players under discipline and on home ground. But during the suspenseful negotiations that followed, I found a friend and ally in Ann Warner, for it was Ann who persuaded her husband Jack to lend me to David. Then the afternoon came when I entered David's office to be photographed with a slight, beautiful, charming British actress as yet unknown to America, Vivien Leigh. An announcement went out to an expectant world and a bored and hostile Hollywood that a long search had ended, and here, at last, were Scarlett and Melanie.

In the days before David found Rhett in Clark Gable and Ashley in Leslie Howard, he scheduled the delicate physical transformation of Vivien into Scarlett and me into Melanie. I remember our hairdress tests and George's saying that there were coiffures and costumes true to the period and to the character that would make me look pretty, and others that would make me look plain. He told me that for a young actress, the choice could be dangerous and that the choice was mine. I chose plain. For I wanted to be true not only to Margaret Mitchell's clear physical description of Melanie but through that description, I wanted to say, in my young anger, that not only could the good and the beautiful be interesting, but also the good and the plain.

When the dove-dressed, smooth-haired Melanie looked back at me from my mirror, however, it was she who spoke to me and began to tell me many, many things about herself that I would not know in their entirety until the last day of filming and long, long after that.

We began shooting, and under George Cukor's sensitive direction, not only did Vivien and I grow sure in our characterizations but in my case, I discovered and felt the profound inner security that was one of Melanie's special qualities.

It was a security soon threatened. On the set of the bazaar sequence, Scarlett widowed, Melanie bereft of her brother, and both attired in black, Vivien and I learned that George would be leaving the picture, and another director, Victor Fleming, would be taking his place.

Of all the monumental tests of strength he met during the filming of *Gone With the Wind*, there was no greater test than David Selznick met that day. In our garb of deep mourning, Vivien and I stormed his office. For three solid hours we beseeched him not to let George go. As tears rained on David, he retreated to the haven of his window seat, and when we unfurled the forlorn banners of our black-bordered handkerchiefs, he nearly fled out the window.

At that point, however, he wavered not. Vanquished, tearstained and desolate, Vivien and I left the field convinced that with a change of directors, disaster lay ahead.

That night, unexpected encouragement came from the man with whom I dined and to whom I recounted the woeful events of the day. "Don't worry," said Howard Hughes, "everything is going to be all right—with George and Victor, it is the same talent, only Victor's is strained through a coarser sieve."

Those words were the armor of my reassurance when I worked with Fleming for the first time, and Victor proved them true. He said to me after the first rehearsal of the scene at Twelve Oaks where Scarlett and Melanie first meet, "Everything that Melanie says, she means, now rehearse the scene again, and really mean it." And through him, another of Melanie's qualities was affirmed, and that was: sincerity.

In spite of my confidence in the new director, however, there were moments in the months that followed when I felt the need of "the talent strained through the finer sieve." So I telephoned George Cukor and asked his help. Generously, at lunch in a restaurant or over a cup of tea in his house, George would give me black-market direction. I felt ever so slightly guilty toward Vivien about making these secret visits to George until, when the picture was finished, I learned that all during the filming, Vivien had been doing exactly the same thing.

I had not previously met Clark Gable. He seemed to me so awesome in his super-stardom that it was all I could do to say "Good-morning" and "Good-night." But the sequence came when I dared more. I began to realize how sensitive Clark was to the responsibility of personifying Rhett Butler, a character so clearly outlined in the imaginations of millions of Americans. This made him at once reticent and rebellious as we rehearsed the scene where Rhett Butler weeps with grief and despair at having provoked Scarlett's fall down the great flight of stairs, her subsequent miscarriage, delirium and, so he thinks, the irremediable rupture of their relationship.

If ever there was an actor who wished he had never taken up his profession, it was Gable the day we shot that scene. He was bothered, and he balked. He fumed, and he fussed. He threatened to leave for his farm and his tractor. For he was embarrassed. Embarrassed at the naked suffering of Rhett Butler. Embarrassed as a man, as an actor, and as Clark Gable. Victor tried to reassure him, and I shyly tried to do the same, for I knew so well how much encouragement could mean. Then the silent moment came, just before the final rehearsal, when we could feel that Gable had committed himself. And when the camera began to roll, we knew he had, for the tears came, and the humble grief and remorse and despair, and he was wonderful.

As time went on, and from all the scenes, I understood that the very core of Melanie's character and the source of her strength was love; and it was this love that directed her relationship with every person she encountered. And as I learned about her and lived her life, I began to feel her love, her trust, her faith, her value on the warm richness of physical union between man and woman, her happiness, for she was, together with so many other things, a perfectly happy woman.

The last day of filming came in early July, and although I had finished my own last scene four weeks before, I made a pilgrimage to the paradise we had all known together, working with so much affection and harmony under David's leadership, telling a story many of us felt would live forever. It was hard for all of us to leave Eden. Especially hard for me, for as the days passed, the special properties of Melanie slipped one by one from my grasp; her confidence, her insight, her faith, and her love, and the sum of all of them—her happiness. In the years since then, I have won them back from time to time, but have lost them again because my strength is not her strength, which in its quietness was so much greater than my own. Melanie was the woman I wanted to be, the woman I would like to be, the woman I was not, the woman I am not yet.

But in mid-December of 1939, I knew again the joy of being with our happy company, for we met once more in Atlanta. And there, with a million people from five states lining the streets to welcome us, David and Clark and Vivien and I and many of the others knew that David's extraordinary effort would soon be confirmed as an extraordinary achievement. We met and were photographed with Margaret Mitchell, the small and animated lady whose dream of a time gone by had given us so much fulfillment for so many months.

In 1961, David and Vivien and I kept a final rendezvous in the city where our story really began. It was the centennial of the commencement of the War Between the States, and all those years since 1939 and all the hopes and work and love had brought their proof that dreams live after one. Margaret Mitchell, Clark, Leslie Howard, Hattie McDaniel were gone, but *Gone With the Wind* was to be released again, and we were in Atlanta for the premiere. And there they were, the moment the film came on the screen, there they were, our dear companions, in all their vibrant life, there they were in joyful reunion.

I did not know that the next time I would return, in 1967, for yet another premiere of the film, I would do so without David, without Vivien. But that is the way it was. As I flew toward Atlanta, I thought of the film itself, and that I mustn't be sad, I must think only of the magical moment when I would see Margaret Mitchell's dream made visible, when David's dream would flash upon the screen, and I would be with all of them again. On an October night, this year of 1967, there we were once more, together.

And as Scarlett and Rhett and Ashley and Melanie and Mammy and Prissy and all the others told their story against the panorama of enormous struggle, defeat and renaissance, I looked at Scarlett, and knew she meant survival, the physical survival of a vanquished people; and I looked at Melanie, and knew she meant survival, too, the spiritual survival of the values and traditions of a lost civilization, and I understood why, for countries all over the world who have known conflict and defeat and survival, *Gone With the Wind* is their story, and Scarlett and Melanie are theirs too. And I thought of all the little girls named Melanie throughout the years, and all the little girls who *are* Melanie, who will have to survive not only their personal tribulations but also national cataclysm, for that is the lot of every generation, and I knew why their mothers named them so, and I wished them well.

The Eucalyptic Dream

Arthur Knight

Arthur Knight is a noted film critic, lecturer and writer. In the follow-ing critique he evaluates what he thinks that Hollywood is today and what are its limitations. Despite his objectivity, his fondness for the American movie shows through in this exceptional piece.*

Hollywood, it has often been said, is not really a place, but a state of mind; and for those who now work in the movie business, this has become particularly true. It is a state of mind that has spread west of Hollywood's original boundaries—west of Doheny and into the hills of Beverly and Bel-Air, and thence on to Malibu and the sea. It has spread north of the Hollywood Hills into the San Fernando Valley, where such communities as Studio City, Encino, and Tarzana provide the industry's upper brackets with ultramodern tract housing flanked by kidney-shaped pools and two-car garages. Indeed, geographically, Beverly Hills has supplanted the old Hollywood as the industry's heart-land. Not only do its broad, curving streets hold the highest concen-tration of filmland's talent (their houses cheek-by-jowl in the weirdest agglomeration of architectural styles assembled anywhere outside of a World's Fair), but physically it affords easy access to any studio in at most a twenty-minute run in the inevitable Porsche, Jaguar, or MG.

Despite this gain in square mileage, however, Hollywood remains a terrifyingly insular place. It is perhaps understandably difficult for men who work at make-believe to make believe that any world exists beyond their own. Or, if they are aware, intellectually, that not everyone dwells in a split-level, ranch-style home under eternally sunny skies (give a little, take a little smog now and then), and that some may even ride the bus or subway to work instead of tooling along in a sports con-

* By permission from Arthur Knight. "The Eucalyptic Dream." *Saturday Review,* September 23, 1967, pp. 70–71, 100. © 1967 the Saturday Review, Inc.

vertible, this information is filtered through their own rose-colored sunglasses. Not too atypical is the story—alas, not apocryphal—of a top producer in a major studio who protested to his costume designer about the elegance of his heroine's garment. "Remember, she's a school teacher," he admonished. "What can she make—maybe three or four hundred a week!"

The surface gloss that is the distinctive mark of the Hollywood film is not an additive, not an extra purchasable for a few dollars more. It is bound into the fabric of each production as inextricably as the stars themselves. It is part of the philosophy of film-making as an entertainment, part of Hollywood's state of mind. Nobody must go away mad, or even slightly riled up, because, after all, movies are made for fun—and for profit. Symptomatically, at the finale of one of this year's most somber and realistic dramas, a chain-gang story called *Cool Hand Luke*, Paul Newman as an escaped convict is savagely butchered in cold blood. But does the film end there? It does not. To mitigate this harsh conclusion, there follows a quick montage of still photos of Mr. Newman smiling his boyish, toothpaste grin. Mustn't send the customers home unhappy!

And is not this production philosophy precisely what gave the American film its economic, if not artistic, pre-eminence throughout the world? Audiences—particularly the vast, inarticulate, middle-class audiences that are the primary targets and supporters of the movie industry—have always shown a marked preference for, as a TV producer once phrased it to Herbert Gold, "happy stories about happy people with happy problems." This is something that Hollywood, by inclination as well as by orientation, has traditionally been turning out.

Originally New York-based, the American industry at first supplied moralistic little melodramas (interspersed with vaudeville-turn comedies and brief educational reels) to its preponderantly working-class audiences in slum nickelodeons. As early as 1909, however, film companies began to move into the Los Angeles area, attracted jointly by its unparalleled possibilities for year-round outdoor picture-making and its superb scenic variety. Almost simultaneously—although it would perhaps be unfair to suggest cause and effect—the pictures themselves began to change. They grew longer and more complex, borrowing their themes now from popular novels, theatrical successes, even grand opera (despite the fact that movies were still silent), thus deliberately switching their appeal to the middle-classes that had hitherto shunned the medium. They grew increasingly opulent in settings and costumes, affecting the tastes and styles of women all over the country. And, perhaps most far-reaching of all, American films introduced the glamour of the star system, and with it a whole firmament of archetypical figures to be emulated and adored. By the end of World War I, such stars as Charlie

Chaplin, Douglas Fairbanks, William S. Hart, and Mary Pickford had become household gods not only in the United States but, quite literally, throughout most of the civilized world.

Paradoxically, it was the stern reality of World War I that established Hollywood as the center of make-believe, the movie capital of the world. Coal and power shortages shuttered most of the small studios that dotted New York City, or that had sprung up in Fort Lee just across the Hudson. Their owners, after briefly casting eyes toward Miami and Chicago, hastened westward to join the pioneers, such as Cecil B. De Mille, D. W. Griffith, and Mack Sennett, who had already staked their claims in Los Angeles's enchanting environs. More important, the same shortages—plus the fact that celluloid, the film base, and high explosives both shared the same strategic chemicals—closed down completely most of the European studios. But people caught up in the throes of war desperately craved entertainment; and Hollywood rushed in to fill the vacuum. The American film at that crucial time gained a hold on the screens of the world that it has never since relinquished.

With money pouring in from Europe, and unchallenged in the rich domestic market, the Hollywood studios were enabled to enter upon a period of unparalleled expansion. In less than a decade, men like William Fox, Samuel Goldwyn, and Adolph Zukor had leaped from a marginal existence in a new and precarious field to positions of power in multimillion-dollar enterprises. Unlettered themselves, they were soon shaping the creative efforts of writers, directors, designers, and performers. Inevitably, the sybaritic luxury that their wealth permitted them to enjoy found its way onto the screen in the form of drunken orgies, petting parties, and overly acquiescent females. It should not be forgotten, however, that immediately after World War I, America itself was in transition from the stern Victorian morality that Griffith so primly depicted to the hedonistic pleasures heralded by Cecil B. De Mille and Elinor Glyn. De Mille swathed his ladies in satins and silks of the highest *couture,* dunked them in perfumed bathtubs, and beset them with problems of marital infidelity, incompatability, and divorce; Mme Glyn gave her esteemed approval to the frenzied escapades of the emerging flapper generation—and the word "It" to describe the flapper's special allure.

No sooner did these manifestations of the new morality appear on the screen than American housewives began to change not only their bathtubs, but their husbands as well; while their dancing daughters mastered the intricacies of the Charleston, bobbed their hair, and drank bathtub gin from the boyfriend's hip-pocket flask. And no sooner did *this* happen than the voice of the reformer was heard throughout the land, claiming that Hollywood was single-handedly paving the way to a twentieth-century Sodom and Gomorrah. Hollywood was, for the first time, caught up in a dilemma that has plagued it ever since. To be sure, the studios could amass ample evidence to demonstrate that everything they put into their pictures—and more—had its real-life counterpart, that their movies were merely reflecting the times. What they could *not* demonstrate—what perhaps defies definitive demonstration—was the extent to which their glamorized, fictionalized versions of life, plus the emphatic presence of their star personalities, gave the seal of approval to such behavior, and a green light to the Twenties' go-go generation.

Faced with the threat of a national censorship, the industry reluctantly backed down, agreeing, somewhat hypocritically, to a code for on-screen morality that has remained in effect, with strikingly few changes, right up until this past year. It was a morality created not to appeal, but to appease—an ad hoc morality, a codification of specific or hypothetical objections by state and municipal censors all over the country. This code gained its teeth when, in 1934, the Catholic Legion of Decency was formed to apply economic sanctions against any picture it found objectionable. For the next three decades, the industry's Production Code Administration worked hand-in-glove with the Legion to avert such a catastrophe. New fears beset the industry when, in 1948, the House Un-American Activities Committee began its investigations to ferret out subversives on the studios' payrolls. Again, the studios responded in characteristic fashion, withdrawing from production any script that smacked of progressive thinking, and forming an unofficial blacklist that everyone firmly denied, but knew existed.

Thus, Hollywood has had a long history of schizophrenia—a private face and a public face, a private morality and a public morality. And this dichotomy is evident in all of its films. Small wonder that the standard reaction to European pictures is that they seem "more honest" than the domestic product. They are so simply because their production is rarely surrounded by the special codes and compromises that guide the executives of Hollywood's major studios. And they are so because their budgets are rarely so astronomical that they have to be made wholly palatable to millions upon millions of people. It is safe to say that no film has ever gone before the cameras in Hollywood that has not been flawed by one or both of these considerations.

Despite these flaws, however, Hollywood's movies capture to an extraordinary degree the look of America, the feel of America. Behind Doris Day, that supermarket may be the one you went to this morning. Over Rock Hudson's shoulder, that service station might be the one on the next corner. Europeans who arrive here for the first time are rarely surprised by what anything looks like; they have seen it all before in the movies. In this area, at least, nobody tries to alter the truth—and probably couldn't, even if they wanted to. As critic Otis Ferguson once observed, "The men and women, from both sides of the camera, were in so many instances a part of common life just yesterday that they haven't had time to forget it, dress it up, and bury it." Indeed, the studios properly pride themselves on the verisimilitude of their back-lot New York streets, Western streets, and rural American towns—and studio executives audibly grumble when an independent producer today exercises his option to take his cameras off to an authentic locale.

But if an independent goes on location merely for the look of a place, he is wasting both his time and his studio's money. What needs to be found on location is the authenticity that exists outside of Hollywood's state of mind—the kind of authenticity, for example, that Arthur Penn was recently able to instill into his *Bonnie and Clyde.* It is less a matter of place than a manner of thinking, a scraping away at the barnacles that have gathered over the last half century upon the hulk of the Hollywood industry. Francis Ford Coppola managed it nicely recently in *You're a Big Boy Now;* Arthur Hiller tried it again, not quite so successfully, in his upcoming version of Murray Schisgal's *The Tiger,* retitled *The Tiger Makes Out.* Neither adheres to studio standards of morality, nor to conventional studio attitudes toward Mom and Dad, or husband and wife. As a result, whatever other deficiencies these films may have, they offer a freshness and originality that stamps them as almost anti-Hollywood.

Indeed, it might be stated almost categorically that any break in the conventions must come from outside of Hollywood itself, completely away from the inhibiting influence of the studio mentality. Stanley Kubrick is a good example of an American director who, while still working for Hollywood companies, found that he could function best 6,000 miles away from them, in England—with films like *Lolita* and *Dr. Strangelove* to prove his point. The studios themselves seem to undergo some kind of sea change once they leave Los Angeles; MGM could never have made *Blow-Up*—perhaps the most genuinely innovational film of the past decade—on its Culver City lot, any more than Universal could have approved the searing *Privilege* for production at its Universal City facility. These are not what used to be called "runaway productions." Although produced for Hollywood majors, both represent breakthroughs that Hollywood could neither countenance nor comprehend. Meanwhile, the home lots are being used increasingly as the base for TV's endless round of situation comedies and spy melodramas, and these represent no change whatsoever from the routine B and C pictures that studded the studios' production schedules in Hollywood's more halcyon days.

For Hollywood has learned to live quite comfortably within its limitations. It has mastered a form of doublethink that enables it to grind out, week after week, for theaters and for television, a glossy, highly commercial entertainment that is without counterpart anywhere else in the world, a kind of picture that is known and readily recognized as the Hollywood film. Unfortunately, the great majority of Hollywood's most successful film-makers, who are neither rogues nor clowns, are successful precisely because they have acquired its values as their values—and see nothing wrong with the process.

"I like to make beautiful pictures about beautiful people," producer Ross Hunter once said. "If audiences want to see realism, let them look at home movies." Not all movie people are quite so drastic, but it is part of Hollywood's self-imposed insularity that the home movies these beautiful people choose to look at themselves are all too often their own. In the warm glow of Southern California's golden sun, harsh truths tend to dissolve into fantasies of goodwill (*In the Heat of the Night*), and deeprooted social problems can still supposedly be solved by individual acts of heroism (*Up the Down Staircase*). If there is a war on poverty currently in progress, or a war in Vietnam, they have yet to appear in any of Hollywood's pictures—mainly because these cannot be "licked" by any of the studios' conventional formulae. Poverty and Vietnam just aren't commercial.

Hollywood, whatever its geographic boundaries, remains a state of mind whose principal export is a somewhat outmoded version of the American dream. Shaded from reality by eucalyptus and palm, caught up in a long tradition of compromised art and profitable fantasy, it has become a backward pocket in the swift current of the cultural revolution now sweeping through Southern California. One can only hope that, as the revolution is consolidated, Hollywood and its beautiful people will also be engulfed.